PARTNERS
IN
PLUNDER

J. B. MATTHEWS and R. E. SHALLCROSS

PARTNERS
IN
PLUNDER

The Cost of
Business Dictatorship

NEW YORK

COVICI · FRIEDE · Publishers

Contents

CONTENTS

PART TWO

OUTSIDE THE PARTNERSHIP

PART THREE

GOVERNMENT

INTRODUCTION

THERE has been much talk of late about the dangers of fascism in the United States. So far there has been a tendency to look for the manifestations of extreme political reaction and brutal indifference to the common weal in the *wrong,* or least significant, places. Many Americans would never recognize fascism in their midst unless it came in the garb of extreme anti-Semitism or Ku Kluxery and was outfitted with all the special terms and vague promises and scapegoats of the Hitler movement. The most serious and menacing manifestations of fascism are to be found in the intensification of the normal and accepted practices of conventional business, and in the sanctification of those practices by charlatans and more sober officials in government service. It has been our purpose to indicate the areas where business is at present clamping down upon consumers and workers to prevent them from striving for, or even being conscious of their rights to, higher standards of living in terms of both quantity and quality.

At the root of all the troubles which afflict the consumers of essential goods and services, lies the insistence of business that all goods and services must be subject to the chief and overriding consideration of profits. Adam Smith declared more than a hundred years ago that the only justifiable end of production is consumption. Business has made profit, not wages or salaries or consumption, the end of all production, and in so doing has grossly adulterated and catastrophically limited the supply of goods and services. The degree of political reaction, whether fascist or some other peculiarly American form which, when it comes, may employ the humanitarian language of Jeffersonian democracy just as Mr. Roosevelt speaks of a richer life while

effectuating a poorer one, is certain to depend upon what business men consider necessary to preserve their own control and
interests—and upon nothing else whatever.

It is not possible, as liberals are wont to do, to consider the
questions of fraudulent advertising, the misbranding of goods,
poisoned fruits and vegetables, poisonous and flagrantly mis-
represented medicines, worthless gadgets, high-pressure sales
tactics, the sabotage of inventions, the cheapening of products,
the acceleration of obsolescence in order to increase sales, and
many other common practices of business, in water-tight com-
partments. They all form essential parts and aspects of the entire
system. Much as some would like to do it, politics, the press,
the schools, etc., and the way in which they work as effective
arms of the business enterprise (and of chambers of commerce),
cannot be divorced from the fundamental questions of the
gravely inadequate quantity and ever-worsening quality of the
goods which Americans must consume.

In business, plunder is of the essence. The springs of thought
as well as the sources of physical life for the masses are poisoned
when poisoning is profitable, adulterated when adulteration is
profitable, and otherwise exploited in ways that blight and
despoil. Liberals will undoubtedly say that we have looked upon
the business enterprise with jaundiced eyes. Our rejoinder is
that true liberals, occupying by self-appointment the most unenvi-
able position of all in the social struggle, that is, of appearing to be
neutrals above the battle, *must* pronounce our findings a distortion, for only so is their bread buttered.

At every stage in the making and distributing of goods, there
is evident a clash of classes—on the one side those whose relationship to goods is primarily a function of use, and on the
other side those whose relationship to goods is primarily a function of exploitation. The establishment of an economy of *use*
is not furthered by slurring over the basic facts of the clash of
these irreconcilable interests. There is at the moment widespread
popular interest in the consumer, much of which is altogether

vitiated by a desire to find a method by which the liberals' eyes may be closed to the ugly facts of the predatory alliance of business and the state. Horace M. Kallen, of the New School for Social Research, believes that "classes, sects, castes and the like, will recede from his mind and cease to function as instruments for identifying individuals" when man attains the "primacy of consumption in his psychology." Our investigations of business enterprise have led us to the opposite conclusion, namely that the principle of the "primacy of consumption" makes the struggle of classes the more evident rather than to recede from the mind.

The present Administration at Washington, like its predecessors, is completely under the control of, and in another sense effectively a partner of, those who work for profits (not wages and salaries) against the interests of consumer-workers. Government more than ever is sensitive and responsive to the wishes of big business, and indeed promises to become even more so as the stresses and difficulties of business increase. In that direction lies the seed of the most dangerous reaction here, as has been the case in other countries, and it is the interest of all those who are really consumer-workers to know about this danger in order that they may combat it. We have again and again illustrated—primarily from business sources themselves—the inner character of the business enterprise, the prevailing practices of business, and the desperate grip which these business practitioners have on the whole of our social life, through government, newspapers and magazines, schools, and the radio. That grip must be broken before it becomes tighter, or nothing can spare us the gruesome excesses of an out-and-out fascist regime. The regime of Thyssen and Krupp will in America be the rule of du Ponts, Sloans, Morgans and Johnsons. The drift is all in the direction of a tighter grip of business on the whole of American life.

Fascism will be sold to the people by precisely the same methods by which they are now sold other worthless or dangerous things. In fact, a people susceptible to the multitude of tricks now employed by business is already half-sold into the slavery of fascism. There is no sharp line of distinction that can be drawn between the present conventional methods of exploiting consumer-workers and lowering their living standards, both in terms of quantity and quality, on the one hand, and the complete subjugation of their economic and social life which overwhelms them when fascism has been established. Ordinary business methods move naturally and ultimately, here as elsewhere if a halt is not called, into the excesses of black reaction.

Without access to the extensive files of Consumers' Research and without the most generous use of its facilities, the preparation of this volume would have been impossible. The responsibility for interpretation of the material is, of course, the authors'. To many members of the staff of Consumers' Research we are indebted for their helpfulness in many of the details involved in organizing the material and in the preparation of the manuscript. We are specially indebted to F. J. Schlink, the technical director of Consumers' Research, who has given unsparingly of his already crowded time for the reading and criticizing of the manuscript. Out of the wealth of his understanding and grasp of the myriad details of the business enterprise he has given numerous suggestions which we have incorporated in the final form of this volume.

J. B. M.
R. E. S.

January 1, 1935.

PART I
BUSINESS

CHAPTER I

Profit Is Pirate King

With the coming of the market—the social arrangements in which all things are the objects of barter and the pecuniary aim in life dominates all else—the use-motive in production fell upon evil days. Never having grown to full maturity, perhaps, in any economy, the use-motive was nevertheless once the recognized ideal that gave social significance to goods and services. Even the satisfactions of craftsmanship in production were subsidiary then to the idea of supplying a human need for food, clothing, shelter, and cultural enrichment. As soon as machine processes had begun to lift the limitations of scarcity from consumption, the thought of those who gained control over production by the new techniques turned more and more to the idea of goods as a means for their own private pecuniary enrichment and away from the idea of making goods as a way of life and as a response to the needs of consumers.

In 1776, a date usually associated with the death of an old tyranny and the coming of a new human emancipation, Adam Smith published his *Wealth of Nations* which was destined to become the classic formulation of the philosophy of the new, now moribund, limping and groaning, business enterprise. His work, therefore, marked the intellectual "coming of age" of a new human enslavement. Though Smith, nevertheless, voiced a wistful protest against the perversion of the new productive processes to non-consumption interests, the forces of industrial life swept forward with reckless indifference to his appeal. "Con-

9

sumption," he wrote, "is the sole end and purpose of all production; and the interest of the producer ought to be attended to only so far as it may be necessary for promoting that of the consumer. The maxim is so perfectly self-evident that it would be absurd to attempt to prove it. But in the mercantile system, the interest of the consumer is almost constantly sacrificed to that of the producer; and it seems to consider production, and not consumption, as the ultimate end and object of all industry and commerce." [1]

Smith's observation on the perverted motive of the mercantile system is true of the modern industrial system in a thousand new and developing ways of which he could never have dreamed. True, the logic of his own major premises and argument was *against* the priority of the interests of consumption over production, and it was inevitable that the later spokesmen for his school of economic thought should see this and correct Smith's inconsistency. Thus, 156 years later, the dean of American economists, an eminent expounder of *laissez-faire,* Professor E. R. A. Seligman, reversing Smith's principle, testified: "If there were no producers there would be no consumers; only stagnation and death. Therefore, as between the interests of consumer and producer, the producer should be, if need be, favored." [2] The function of consumers in the economic order, the Columbia University economist admitted, was reduced to one of providing for the "disposal of what producers must sell." This is what passes for economic learning in many an impressive, educational institution.

Adam Smith's insight failed him signally at the point of supposing that the consumer's interests could be served in a system which permitted the private ownership of the new instruments of production and their operation for private gain. It was the fallacy of the old theory that the best of all possible worlds is a resultant of every man's seeking his own interest, a theory which ultimately served to rationalize and perpetuate the grossest of social inequities and the most degrading poverty and squalor.

It took no account of the existence of conflicting social groups having irreconcilable interests, based upon their differently motivated relationships to production and consumption, and with enormously unequal power to protect those interests. The romantic theory of nineteenth-century liberalism which was a method of explaining away, as part of a Great Divine Plan, the terrible injustices which wrung the hearts of sentimental and kindly men, thus failed utterly to reckon with the cold facts of contemporary social organization, and even more obviously to reckon with the facts of the twentieth century in which these functional and social gaps have become still wider.

For liberalism to possess any degree of validity there would be required as complete a dispersion of ownership, and hence of the function of controlling production, as prevails in the case of the function of consuming. Without such a universal dispersion of ownership and control, it was inevitable that economic and social classes should arise corresponding to the unequal advantages in consuming power and prestige which stemmed from the unequal possession of wealth arising out of ownership and control.

Today, this system which Smith perceived to be dominated at the beginning with the service of indefensible ends, has run its course, and is at one and the same time in the throes of death and making desperate and frantic efforts to save itself from destruction. The last act of a consciously dying man is always an effort at recovery. With man it is a desperate straining after the familiar air which has hitherto sustained life; in a business society it is one or another aspect of fascism grasping for the once sustaining and power-giving income derived from ownership.

Recovery, it is alleged, waits upon official assurances from Washington that the profit system is not to be destroyed. So the proponents of business revival argue when attempting to account for the long delay in restoring the levels of economic activity to the plane which they occupied in 1926. There was no lack of official assurances on this point when the "Great Engineer" lived in the White House; but despite all the incantations addressed to the great god Private Enterprise in that period, dire calamity overtook his devotees and dragged millions, dependent upon their business operations, with them down to dire distress. If lip service to business aims were all that is needful for recovery, there should never have been a depression, for the active foes of the profit system have not at any time in recent American history numbered more than two and one-half per cent of the electorate.

If business men really fancy that there is an insidious plot within officialdom to destroy the profit system, they are poor judges of policies and personalities. In the very first speech which Franklin D. Roosevelt made, initiating his campaign for the Democratic nomination for the presidency, he declared that the "American system of economics and government is everlasting." [3] No reasonable interpretation of the words of this declaration can make it mean other than an express commitment, so far as the present incumbent of the presidency is concerned, to the system of business which is dependent for its operation upon the promise of profits. Furthermore, official deeds and many subsequent utterances of utmost definiteness and assurance have been suited to these words. There is, therefore, no reasonable doubt concerning the intentions of the Government of the United States, the coy flirtations of a few minor officials of the Government with non-profit conceptions of economic activity to the contrary notwithstanding.

Wonder grows when examination of the records reveals that the Roosevelt Administration has not been parsimonious with its assurances on the status of profits in its economic scheme. Business doubts have centered chiefly on the person of Rexford Guy Tugwell, but he was obligingly commissioned to Europe for the duration of the late Congressional campaign. To cabinet members the word was, apparently, passed along that their campaign speeches were to contain liberal doses of profit-blessing consolation administered to the doubt-prostrated Tories. Secretary Roper, without becoming articulate, himself constitutes an *assurance* in his own personality and business connections, having been, together with the National City Bank, the Chase National Bank, Charles Mitchell, and the late Percy Rockefeller,[4] a lifelong exploiter of Cuban sugar. The New York *Times* reported him as "scoffing at the prophets"[5] (not the profits) in a speech "timed to coincide," "considered by the administration as highly significant," etc. "To the business men of our country let me say that our government and the masses of the people resent unthinking statements or subtle suggestions that the profit motive in American life has been or is to be abolished," declared Secretary Roper. "It [the objective of the New Deal] contemplates entirely reasonable profits to industry,"[6] Secretary Hull assured a luncheon of the Associated Press. Secretary Perkins appeared before the annual convention of the American Federation of Labor in San Francisco, to deliver a speech [the manuscript for which, she said, had been "corrected in Washington"][7] in which she "made clear her belief that business has the right to a 'fair profit,' and that as profits increase 'employers are bound to recognize that workers must receive increased wages. . . .' "[8]

Throughout the summer and fall of 1934, nevertheless, business men everywhere were asking for official assurances concerning the profit system. The Liberty League was launched for the express purpose of bringing pressure to bear on an Administration which was alleged to be shaking the faith of the people in the everlasting validity of the profit motive, the one and only indispensable sanction for business activity. "Back of much of the agitation for liberty and constitutional rights," said a New York *Times* columnist, "there is no doubt the prime desire to protect property and profits, as though the New Deal were destroying both."[9] *Advertising & Selling,* influential mouthpiece of advertising men who do much of the economic thinking for business concerns, was noting the speeches in which the President omitted direct mention of profit and capital.[10] "Sacred pre-election promises" were held to be violated by these omissions. It was pointed out that when the President was campaigning in Oregon in the fall of 1932, he declared that "private capital should be given the first opportunity to transmit and distribute electricity on the basis of the best service and the lowest rates to give a reasonable profit"; whereas, in the summer of 1934, "he made no reference to private capital" [11] in the course of a speech delivered in the State of Oregon.

"Proper profit must be actively encouraged—not merely tolerated," declared another prominent spokesman of business. Shedding crocodile tears over the plight of the unemployed, the writer continued: "The revival of the sick industries, the re-employment of the unemployed, depend on the reappearance of generous profits. Only so can those unfortunate workers who are dependent on the capital and durable goods industries, on the luxury and service occupations, hope to regain a foothold in our industrial society." [12] "Proper profit" is here defined as "generous profits," and this provides a clue, perhaps, to current business discontent, since the word "generous" is of unlimited elasticity.

The National City Bank of New York in its October letter expressed its belief "that the chief lack in the business situation is the lack of confidence in the ability to carry on trade and industry at a profit." [13] *Editor & Publisher,* surveying the temper of the classes, wrote: "Perhaps the most embittered people of the day are those who are trying to stretch severely limited incomes from bonds, stock and realty holdings over a cost of living that continues on a boom basis. The place to listen in on that acid discontent is the fashionable club or snobbish summer hotel. It's heartbreaking to hear the wails about how tough it is to get along these days on $50,000 a year, when family expenses are geared to $100,000 income. Such folks seem to favor Fascism as the way out." [14]

Why was there acid discontent at a time when the index of corporation profits had risen from —6.9 of March, 1933, to + 33.2

for the second quarter of 1934, and at a time when *Standard Statistics* could report, in the case of 506 companies, a rise in profits from $157,579,000 for the first half of 1933 to $408,572,000 for the first half of 1934? [15] Surely the days of profits, generous profits, "proper profit," had not gone forever when the United States Steel Corporation could turn a deficit of $8,627,367 for the second quarter of 1933 into a profit of $5,350,241 for the second quarter of 1934, the highest in three years. General Motors Corporation reported a profit of $69,586,613 for the first six months of 1934, and du Pont de Nemours & Company netted $23,553,598 for the same period, hardly evidence of bankruptcy. Both of these corporations declared extra dividends at the mid-year of 1934. On the basis of these and other returns, *Business Week* predicted that managements would be able "to make the most of conditions" and "turn even a small improvement into a large increase in profits," [16] thus rejecting the view that the profit system is dead. The populace was still composed chiefly of beardless, bourgeois conservatives, as demonstrated by Gillette's $1,063,876 profit for the quarter; while unwashed radicals did not appear to be on the increase when Colgate-Palmolive-Peet trebled its profits to reach the mark of $2,416,887, and Procter & Gamble cashed in on its slogan (*not,* please note, a guarantee) of "99-44/100 per cent pure" with a profit well above $3,000,000. From this impressive showing for profits at a time when at least ten million industrially disfranchised workers were still unemployed, and living upon the charity of friends, relatives, and the State, it should have been clear even to Alfred E. Smith, John W. Davis, Irénée du Pont, Jouett Shouse, and Herbert Hoover that "liberty" is still firmly entrenched hereabouts.

The persistent demand for assurances on the subject of the profit system is, it would appear from the evidence, simply a business alibi for its own incompetence and lack of social plan and purpose in fulfilling a rational place and meaning in human society. The "New Deal" is, on the whole, invulnerable to the shafts of criticism that come from profiteers and their defenders.

However, one of the items in the "New Deal" which has been most distasteful to a limited section of the business world is the Tennessee Valley Authority (TVA).[17] This governmental agency started out with a program that insisted upon the merchandising of an electric refrigerator at a price substantially lower than the prices which had been prevalent, and then set up the Electric Home and Farm Authority (EHFA) for the purpose of helping buyers (and sellers) to finance these marked-down boxes. This plan had some real marks of social consciousness. Immediately there were protests, lacking nothing in vehemence, that dealers were being robbed of their margins of profit by this governmental pressure to market a refrigerator at $77.50. One simple-hearted but businesslike dealer exclaimed that the Government had so far forgotten its true function that it was "looking after the masses, not the dealers."[18] *Electric Refrigeration News* declared, editorially, "that the well-meaning TVA officials, in their zeal for the public weal, [had] upset the balance of one of the most finely adjusted distribution mechanisms in the country."[19] On second thought, therefore, the governmental agency became characteristically attentive to these plaintive outcries of the trade, and made a ruling that any firm which had an approved TVA model in the electric refrigeration field could have the benefits of EHFA financing on all of its higher-priced models. The dealers forthwith announced their intentions regarding the TVA "chest refrigerators." Said one: "We will probably use chests altogether as *leaders*."[20] [Italics ours.] Said another: "It will surely be a good teaser." "Leaders" and "teasers" are but merchandising decoys which lure the prospective consumer within the range of the salesman who thereupon exerts all possible pressure to sell a higher-priced and more profitable piece of merchandise, usually with success. The editor of *Electric Refrigeration News* puts the matter graphically when he says that lukewarm dealers "intend to use the chest model as a 'nailed-to-the-floor' refrigerator, employing its low price as a bait to draw store traffic."[21] Other business concerns are behaving with more discrimination in the use of the chest model. In certain instances they will permit the chest to be pried loose from its moorings on their sales floors. "An example of the effective use of the chest models to pry open low-income markets is afforded by the Ohio Public Service Co., which offers its salesmen 20 per cent on the sale of every chest model to homes on its minimum account list (users of very little electricity), but which will give the salesman *nothing* if he sells one to a home (not now an electric refrigeration user) in the higher income brackets." [22]

In short, the only spot in the "New Deal" which had any apparent vulnerability to the criticism of the profit-seekers turns out to be a project which the otherwise atrophied imagination of business men turned into the customary opportunity for private gain. What was first hailed by some as a threatening socialistic enterprise is, as it comes out under "New Deal" leadership, characteristically adaptable to the requirements of business interests.

The demand for profit at any time is a demand of something for nothing. Given the *status quo* in profits, any acid discontent with the functioning of the system is a demand of more and more of income for less and less of service and function. This is the spirit which, as *Editor & Publisher* correctly pointed out, breeds fascism.

It is hardly necessary to argue the point that business is run for profit, and that where generous returns are not in prospect, business ceases. This is not less true with respect to the absolutely vital necessity of food than it is with respect to radios and automobiles. "The whole idea," says the vice-president of General Foods Corporation as reported in *Advertising Age,* "is to make . . . profits in a large way." [23] In case anyone naïvely supposes that the candy business or any other exists to promote general happiness, there is enlightenment in the frank statement in the *Confectioners' Journal* that "the whole business system in the United States is based on the competitive principle, with adequate profit as the sole goal of those who are engaged in it." [24] "In the last analysis, men are in business for profit, not to exploit their ideas," [25] says Claude C. Hopkins who knows the business world from the inside if anyone knows it; for when he says, "I made for myself a million dollars on Pepsodent," [26] he is alluding to only one of his many very remunerative business enterprises and connections.

No matter from what department of the business enterprise he comes, the testimony of the acknowledged spokesman for the business world points to profit as the be-all and end-all of the system. "We are entitled to feel confidence in our own power of recovery," [27] writes Walter Lippmann, ex-socialist, ex-liberal, and ex-editor of the *New Republic,* "if only the Administration will proceed resolutely with its financial policy and allow that policy to revivify private industry." The way to revivify private industry, according to Mr. Lippmann, is to raise "prices above costs and thus restore profits." "For in the American economy [note the manner in which the distinguished columnist of the *Herald Tribune* identifies "American" indissolubly with "profit"] it is under the stimulus of profit that enterprise brings idle men and idle money together, permits them to create wealth and improve the national income." The reference to "idle men" is not too clear, but it was probably intended to designate the unemployed workers and not the yachting and coupon-clipping rich. "The present social order," says Willford I. King, a distinguished academic spokesman of the system, "rests upon such pillars as the right of private property, the sacredness of agreements and freedom of contract . . . with the right to make and keep profits." [28]

Thus the supplying of goods and services in a business society is dependent, at all times and in all circumstances, upon whether the processes are profitable or not. If found to be, or believed to be, unprofitable, goods and services are withdrawn, except as an indecent minimum is provided in the form of relief and then, regardless of the suffering occasioned by the stoppage, only as insurance against the hazards of revolution. Furthermore, there is no compulsion exercised by the business state which requires that necessary honest goods and services be supplied in any emergency without regard for private gain. A society which makes the bread supply of the masses dependent upon whether its provision is *profitable* or not to a certain handful of owners of mills and factories stands condemned without argument. Furthermore, a society which permits the adulteration of its bread supply, without regard to the detriment to health involved, is one in which the provision of goods is obviously oriented to interests which would be wholly extraneous and indeed pernicious in a consumers' economy.

When natural calamity stops the flow of goods and services to a community, the event arouses a keen sympathy for the victims of such a stoppage and there is some well-modulated lamentation over man's "helplessness" in the presence of Nature's uncontrollable and brute force. It has been estimated by entomologists that insects and their near relatives (no reference here to human parasites) inflict an economic loss of not less than $2,500,000,000 annually in North America.[29] This enormous loss occasioned by the devastating arthropod enemies of production is trivial when compared with the losses occasioned by the anthropoid enemies of consumption. Yet government and private agencies wage a desperate chemical warfare against the arthropods, and then unblushingly serve as the instruments to further the purposes of the far less explicable anthropoid parasites. Dr. F. C. Bishopp, entomologist in the United States Department of Agriculture, says that "the adult tick is very sly" for it "has learned to crawl from a person's feet to the hair at the back of his head, a favorite feeding place, without being felt."[30] In the field of advertising and salesmanship, adroit maneuvers of this sort are called scientific marketing, but these types of behavior escape the notice of the government scientists and popularizers.

When human cupidity stops the flow of goods and services or adulterates the stream, we are in the presence of wholly and simply controllable forces but we refuse or fear to apply the obvious solution to the problem at its source. Men today are relatively free from the destructive caprices of Nature, but the brute force of man, made adamant by the demands of the few for profit, at any cost to the social order, continues periodically and disastrously to interfere with the always inadequate provision of necessary and useful goods and services.

In terms of simple human relationships, *profit* is a divorcement between productive *effort* and *income*. Profit is a claim-check upon production, the possession of which requires no personal attendance upon any of the processes of production or risk of injury, or sweat or grime associated with them. Managerial pay, for example, is not profit, although such pay may be and more often is in excess of all useful service. Neither is profit to be confused with every difference between buying and selling prices in the transactions of the distributor. In so far as the distributor performs a useful social service by the distribution of goods, he may be said to create the utilities of time or space (delivery at the time and place where needed or wanted) or both. Income for this service he usually calls "overhead" and not profit. Profit in its strict sense is income from the legal convention of ownership. This legal convention is in force whether its holder is in the neighborhood of the physical process of production and distribution or whether he is on the other side of the globe climbing Mt. Everest, an Alpine peak, or hunting big game in Africa or India. J. P. Morgan,[31] for example, may spend as many months as he chooses away from his tulips and his counting house, cruising in the waters of Palestine with the Archbishop of Canterbury in the palatial Morgan ocean-going yacht, the *Corsair IV,* without any interruption of income occasioned by his absence, or without the annoyance of tax collectors, thanks to the operation of a well-ordered legal pattern that exempts such incomes as his from government levies.

Profit opens up the possibility (and in many cases achieves the actuality) of an income considerably in excess of consumption requirements for the recipient. With the surplus remaining over and above all possible needs for consumption, the holder is vested with a form of power which may be exercised in various ways, such as enlarging his control over production, influencing by purely monetary pressure the thinking of the community, being elected to the Senate from Delaware or Pennsylvania, being appointed Ambassador to Turkey or Great Britain, and determining the cultural patterns dominant in business civilization. In sharp contrast with these extensive powers (in government and in management of production and consumption) of income from profit *unresponsive to and free from any form of democratic control*—or, practically speaking, any social control whatever—stands income derived from work which as a rule and for the masses permits of no excess over and above the requirements for subsistence. It is, therefore, hollow pretense to speak of democracy in a profit economy—*any* profit economy. Wage or salaried workers do not purchase yachts, endow cathedrals and universities, establish research foundations and fellowships, contribute substantially to political campaigns, elect senators and give them orders respecting legislation, subsidize directly or indirectly newspapers and magazines (of influential circulation and business power), or launch industrial enterprises. That their collective power, if assembled, would enable them to do all of these things is obvious, since their aggregate resources in any field exceed those of the class which lives by profit. But herein lies the precise reason why the latter oppose with all the forces at their command any type of collectivism over which the essential consumers (wage workers and the salaried) exercise control.

Whatever disagreement there may be on the meaning of the word profit, there is complete accord among the friends and the foes of business society that it is the central consideration in all conventional or approved business practices. It is the motive power without which the machinery stops dead, and mill and mine and shop fall into dust, rust, and disuse. Not only is profit the indispensable condition of business enterprise, but it determines the standards of value which are applied to all social institutions under its sway. When profits are plentiful for the few, there is said to be "prosperity," even though more than seventy per cent of the entire population may be living below a safe standard for health, to say nothing of comfort, or culture. When mass *profits* are declining, there is said to be a "depression." When the entire population, profit-making and wage-earning alike, is called upon to boost for "recovery," again the significance of the term lies in its orientation to a freer flow of *profits*. Shrinking profits, and shrinking incomes for those who live by them, constitute or occasion a "crisis"; and out of the crisis-psychology generated thereby comes fascism. *But fascism, it must be emphasized, is simply the projection into conditions of crisis of the normal methods and purposes of a business society.* It is the attempt, by overt force to stabilize consumption at levels which are physically and culturally devastating to the masses of consumers. In the shift from the pseudo-democratic state to the frankly coercive state of fascism, the abiding principle is profit-protection. Fascism is unthinkable without the familiar system of private enterprise and its profits. The ultimate alternative to fascism is, therefore, the elimination of all principles and institutions that are in conflict with an economy oriented to and driven by and for consumers' needs and wants.

Fascism has been usually defined and described with reference to its "dramatic" techniques and its characteristic repressiveness in racial and political matters. Far more rarely has it been viewed in the light of its principal effects upon the living standards of the vast majority. Yet its chief objective result is the beating down of these living standards in the course of its desperate defense of profit. Any assault upon the living standards of the many, in the interest of maintaining the investment "earnings" of the few, is infused with the spirit of fascism. This is an age-old practice of the plutocracy of wealth and it may be objected, therefore, that it is insufficiently differentiating to give us a clear distinction between modern fascism and its political predecessors. On the other hand, it is in precisely this essential spirit and drive and distortion of government by the profit motive that we find the important continuity between fascism and its precursors. This continuity of form and policy outweighs in importance the dramatic break involved in a change of the political forms of capitalism from "democracy" to "dictatorship." We must not underestimate the crucial differences between political instruments, but we must emphasize the fact that the dominant purpose of an economic system for those few who are its major and traditional beneficiaries may be served by radically differing political institutions.

From a business-controlled civilization, fascism stems as naturally as does war, and represents no serious rupture in the continuity of social development in such a civilization. It is not in any sense of the word "revolutionary." It is a stage, perhaps the last and highest (or lowest), of business society, to which the rulers of that society are brought by the same motives which impel them in pre-fascist stages of social organization. The menace of fascism in the United States today is not from those who have already put on this or that "shirt," but comes from that motley assortment, politically disunited at the moment, who on the one side are crying "liberty," "the Constitution," "assurances to business," and those who, on the other, are with heart and soul serving business after the manner of the "New Deal."

There has been a widespread tendency to look upon fascism, war, and economic depression as lapses from the normalcy of the system. Normalcy, however, cannot be judged by a single mode of social behavior, where a variety of behavior expresses the innermost impulses of a society. Fascism, war, and depression are as normal, under given exigencies of capitalism as are those periods of expanding production, security speculation, and sales success, which are usually styled "prosperity." It is not permissible, though it is natural for business men and economists to do so, to view one segment of the "cycle" as normal, another as abnormal. The "cycle" itself is the working of the system under varying conditions of production. The whole "cycle," not merely one part of it, belongs to the system. It is as normal in a profit-oriented economy to arm an American schoolboy to kill German schoolboys as it is to sell him lead-poisoned candy and apples. Both are done in obedience to the interests of those who have investments to protect and to make and keep profitable. In this economy, it is as normal to shiver in a breadline as it is to pace feverishly back and forth before a forest of cotton spindles. The interests of profit-seekers demand the first, under one set of conditions, and the second, under another set of conditions. It is as normal to recruit millions of the credulous in uniformed fascist bands and throw the dissidents into concentration camps as it is to sell them *Pepsodent* tooth paste with cheap and false Amos 'n' Andy caricatures of Negro mind and life. All these are among the infinite manifestations possible for the working out of a single motive— the desire for monetary gain regardless of human welfare.

Given the characteristic impulses and motives that dominate a business-banking civilization, as expressed, among other ways, in the familiar frauds of distribution and salesmanship, it follows that economic classes stand forth, most easily distinguishable in terms of their relationships to goods and services, whether by their consumption in the one case, or by their exploitation of them for profit in the other. This gross inequality of access to goods and services which sets the receivers of profit off in a class from those who live by their work, when indeed they are able to find employment, is not simply a matter of privilege on the one side and underprivilege on the other; it is a matter of comfort or misery, health or illness, life or death for the underlying community of the underprivileged. Lack of proper diet, housing, medical care, and sanitation means that "unskilled laborers die off twice as fast as the higher-paid business and professional men," according to a 1934 survey of the Public Health Service made in ten states. This report characterized "the excess [of deaths] in the lower economic levels" as "a challenge of the first order to health authorities." [32] It would have been infinitely more to the point to characterize it for what it is, a challenge of

the first order to the whole scheme of a society which permits
the distribution of all its goods and services on the basis of the
principle of "all that the traffic will bear."

To many business men, indeed, there are essentially two classes
in society: the competent and the incompetent. Arrogating to
themselves the first of these classifications, they hold that those
whose incomes are disastrously curtailed or wiped out by depressions of business, or who find themselves in unemployment, belong
among the mentally or physically incompetent. This simple interpretation of the inequalities of consuming power in business
society does no credit to the intellectual competence of those who
offer it. After five years of enormous mass unemployment, this
explanation is still put forward by business Bourbons who have
learned nothing from their observations of social phenomena but
convenient rationalizations of their own self-interest. The editor
of *Nation's Business* lists the following among the unfortunate,
impecunious, and indigent members of society: (1) "an organized
group of hoboes, who refuse to do a stroke of work, and glory
in their position"; (2) "the physically and mentally incapacitated"
who belong in institutions; (3) those "who lack the will to produce more than barely enough to sustain life"; (4) "the inefficient
. . . who need minute supervision of the most humble task"; (5)
"the shiftless"; (6) "the thriftless"; and (7) "the economic moron
who wastes because it is his nature to waste." Over against these
seven types of unfortunates, the editor sets "those who have the
mind and the spirit to make their way and pay their way in the
world." [33] Not one ray of light has penetrated to the darkness
of this business mind, nor does such a mind so much as raise
the question whether the "economic morons" are all among the
impecunious. The quest for profit obviously does more than
effect gross inequalities in the distribution of income; it appears
from the intellectual level of this editor's analysis, and thousands
of others just like it from business sources, to effect an even
greater disparity in the distribution of social sympathy and understanding and even of ordinary intelligence or "common sense."

Delusions of grandeur are well-known psychic phenomena in madhouses; delusions of intelligence in the madhouse of business are, in their social consequences, far more serious derangements.

The grossly unequal sharing by these classes, the propertied and the propertyless, in the function and advantages of consumption leads to the basic, not the sham, political conflicts that characterize such a society, and determines the general political and cultural organization of that society. In times of "crisis," the strains due to unequal power and ability to command goods and services are accentuated; and if the "crisis" reaches a certain stage of severity, those who are shut out of privileges, while others retain their command over necessities and luxuries, express their protest in ways which impel the dominant political and economic interests to set up a more rigid and repressive political organization of society—an overt business dictatorship! Thus, fascism has its roots deep in the everyday life and exploitative relationships of owners, and their salesman Janizaries, to consumers; and business society and its governmental adjuncts and aids in the exploitation of the underlying population are racketeering in a very literal sense.

A speaker at the annual convention of the Advertising Federation of America last year dropped a confidential hint on how a little suppression may help to keep the general public from having too clear a picture of business. "While there may be reasons for keeping certain reports and discussions about business racketeering out of the public press," he said, "there is no valid reason for keeping the battle against rackets out of the business press." [34] Obviously the speaker was not supporting our contention that profit and racketeering are inseparable, but even a small admission from such quarters is instructive. There is a fine, and usually wholly arbitrary, line between what is considered legitimate business and illegitimate racketeering. The difference is, as a rule, more important to the inner relationships of business than it is to consumers. "A criminal in prison," says a frank writer in the *Manufacturing Chemist,* "is only an ordinary person who has had the misfortune to have been detected." [35] To adopt the viewpoint of this business commentator, it is the undetected "criminal," the *legitimate* racketeer, who menaces the well-being of consumers. The social consequences of an act do not flow from its *legal* quality. All the highwaymen of history have done less violence to the social values of property, or indeed to the "rights" of private property, than have the legalized acts of the private expropriators of property; of firms like Standard Oil, the Mellon and du Pont interests, and the United States Steel Corporation.

The Assistant Attorney General of the United States, Joseph B. Keenan, expressed pained astonishment at a popular attitude toward the late John Dillinger. "It is beyond comprehension," said Keenan in pleading for a new attitude toward lawlessness, "that when Dillinger's picture was thrown upon the screen in Washington the audience broke into applause." [36] But how is the "public" to follow with fine discrimination all the legal and technical intricacies of law and lawlessness? When thousands of Negroes have been lynched over the past two generations, officials have in one way or another connived at these murders. Washington Administrations, Republican and Democratic, have been indifferent to enactment of federal legislation that would place a curb upon the bloodthirstiness of sadistic mobs or have been altogether dilatory in the application of existing laws which could have been enforced for the punishment of easily detected and often well-known members of torture and murder carnivals. When arch-racketeers, whom the "public" was taught to applaud to the echo, led the United States into the World War and ran up their profits to unprecedented billions of blood-money (absolutely legitimate business), it was Mr. Keenan's own department of federal government that acted as the "strong arm squad" *for* (not against) the arch-racketeers, and for years conducted illegal raids upon those who exposed, not those who applauded, the racketeering. The days of A. Mitchell Palmer and Harry Daugherty and all their illegal and legal brutality are fresh in the memory of many still living. But if it be alleged that times have changed, then it may be asked what the Department of Justice has done to combat arrant and brutal and defiant lawlessness in California in 1934. When the police departments of the state, including the police department of Los Angeles, were conducting typical "Mitchell Palmer" raids, Mr. John Edgar Hoover, a respected and powerful functionary of the United States Department of Justice, answered an inquiry concerning the attitude of his Department toward Captain W. F. Hynes, head of the Los Angeles Red Squad, in the following words: "It is not the policy of this Division to express commendation either verbally or in writing for individual members of various police departments. I desire, however, to state that the relationships existing between this Division and the Los Angeles Police Department collectively and individually have been most cordial and friendly at all times. The Los Angeles Police Department has always cooperated fully with this Division in all matters of mutual interest." [37]

The history of illegal violence in the strike-breaking activities of the largest and most "respectable" corporations, carried out with the well-paid assistance of gunmen (often euphemistically called "detectives"), does not indicate that the Department of Justice has been unusually diligent in suppressing this type of big corporation gangsterism. While the practice is a matter of common knowledge, full information concerning this phase of corporation activity rarely, if ever, gets into newspapers. Now and then it appears as an "aside" and long after the event, as, for example, in the case of one Peter De Vito who was "news" when injured in an explosion in a Brooklyn brewing plant. Further to identify the injured man, the New York *Times* stated: "De Vito was well known to the police as a strike-breaker who broke strikes in Brooklyn for the Standard Oil Company and the American Can Company several years ago. *His earnings from these two jobs* provoked an indictment on charges of evading income tax payment, on which *he was acquitted*." [38] [Italics ours.]

The fineness of the line between what are commonly called

business and racketeering will be evident if we sketch the main steps in the careers of America's most successful business man and America's most successful racketeer. The following biographical outline will serve the biographer of either man as a framework upon which to build the story of his hero's accomplishments: (1) He traded upon a common article for which there was an effective demand. (2) From small beginnings, his business grew to immense proportions with corresponding increase in its financial returns. (3) In the course of the development of his business, workers in his employ were subjected to gross exploitation. (4) Gunmen were his reply to their grievances. (5) Business competitors were driven from the field by methods that lacked nothing in fierceness. (6) With monopolistic conditions established, consumers were gouged for *all the traffic would bear*. (7) When he had grown fat upon profits, he lavished funds upon careful publicity calculated to lionize him in the public esteem. (8) Biographies appeared in which his brave struggles and rise to success were depicted. (9) He purchased a Florida estate on which to bask in the sunlight of America's sub-tropics. (10) His name was on many lips, and to this very day its most trivial mention is "news." ... Thus runs the story of John D. Rockefeller, Sr., or of Al Capone, as you will. True, legality and illegality have made a difference in the manner in which these two men employ their present leisure.

The ease with which practices are legalized or outlawed, and the controlling motives behind these changes make it clear that law as an instrument of government is in fact and of necessity a tool of the ruling interests in society. It is one of the illusions of a now thoroughly discredited social philosophy that the law is an impartial arbiter between all conflicting interests in society. There is no magic which sanctifies a statute—any statute—without respect to the interests, motives, and processes which lay behind its enactment. Since this is a business and not a consumers' society, it follows that the legal and the illegal are defined with reference to the fixed or changing interests of the former and not, in any substantial way or with any significant frequency, with reference to the interests of consumers. Those who adopt the philosophy of a consumers' society in anticipation of its eventual establishment must evaluate existing institutions and their economic and social performance by the standards of their adopted philosophy, and not by any narrow legalistic conceptions of the *status quo*. In general, when we use the words "pirates," "racketeers," and "plunderers," we are not speaking of the Capones, the Insulls, the Foshays, and the Harrimans, who have run afoul of existing laws, but rather of that eminently respectable and numerous group that, by its day-to-day contacts and drives, dominates business and government and the schools, colleges, and universities, and all other major social institutions today, and whose chief enterprise, the quest for profit, will be declared the major crime in the consumer-workers' society of tomorrow.

Until such time as society is completely reorganized in the interests of a new ruling class—the consumer-workers—a change in the law here or a change there may close one door of opportunity to the racketeer, but his ingenuity and his resources of money and the legal and technical advice which "his" money buys for him, will find another portal of unearned gain wide open. Time and again, the passage of a new protective law for the consumer-worker (like the famous section 7A of the National Industrial Recovery Act) has simply provided employment for a host of legal sharks and trade advisers who devote tremendous energies, with effective help from the government itself, to finding a way around provisions which at worst turn out to be only a temporary embarrassment.

Belief in the actuality of a democratic society in the United States—"our country has such a long and so deep-rooted a democratic tradition"—and skepticism on the possibility of fascism here (the corollary of such a belief), are consonant only with the grossest failure to recognize the true nature of business society— its aim and methods. Knowledge of *what is* leaves no room for doubt about *what may yet come*. Where a fundamental perversion of economic activity to anti-consumer purposes is whole-heartedly approved or cynically tolerated, and is connived at and fostered by government as we shall later show, there are no limits set upon the extremes of perversion to which the system may lead except the limits of inner necessities determined by the "crisis" itself, and by the mentality and conditioning of the business men who operate the system.

Fascism cannot be understood as a simple or mysterious manifestation of anti-Semitism or anti-whatever-the-American-form-will-take, or the unaccountable behavior of a social order under the control of a mad leader or neurotic; it is rather the final repressive organization of society as a "whole," with conformity and circumspection demanded of the "parts," *in the interests of businesslike and parasitic racketeers of government, manufacture, finance, and trade.*

Business, under a profit-dominated system, has been perverted into a variety of techniques which operate against the interests and welfare of the ultimate consumers of goods and services. Lacking all rationality of social purpose, and being quite devoid of concern for or interest in such purpose, and driven by the necessities of keener and keener competition for the profits to be derived from man's consuming activities, all the veins which the business body has, run with the poison of racketeering. The cynics of the age have accepted these rackets, little and big, as the inevitable expressions of imperfect human nature, and refuse to contemplate the possibility of a basic re-orientation of all economic activity to the purposes and needs of consumer-workers. The rackets, born of this business society, have arrayed men against men as swindlers versus swindlers, and swindlers versus suckers, with the goods and services essential to human happiness and welfare debased to the level of mere implements in the swindlers' struggle for control and profit. No amount of grandiloquent phrasing by the cheaters can dignify a society in which its preponderant element—the great mass of consumer-workers—has been precipitated to the low levels of those who are the perennially and ubiquitously robbed and cheated. On the aim and methods of business society, we accept the burden of proof, and our proof shall be developed from this point forward.

From among the great variety of techniques employed by the business racketeers of society against their victims, the consumer-workers, we have chosen the following for the purposes of illustrating the essential methods and motives which prevail in seller-buyer relationships: trade puffery; high-pressure sales tactics; the testimonial racket; the cloaking of meretricious claims with scientific respectability; gadgetry with its spurious evidence of progress; meaningless and confusing changes of merchandise; acceleration of the rate of obsolescence; the wilful deterioration of quality; adulteration; the vending of toxic and shoddy substances as wholesome and sound; trade-marking and brands to conceal price relationships and frauds; and the profiteering on consumers' ignorance by the absence (and suppression or distortion) of standards, or the use of misleading names for grades and qualities.

CHAPTER II

The Rococo Front of Business*

Few things impinge more continuously upon the consciousness of ordinary mortals than advertising. There is scarcely any escape from it within the routines of present-day living except being blind and deaf. The highways of travel, the channels of news, the "ether lanes," and the centers of amusement are cluttered up with the seller's appeals. Man has become preëminently a buyer—only derivatively a consumer. The next telephone call may be the appeal of an oil-burner or vacuum-cleaner salesman; the next telegram may be one urging you to try Slitto bran flakes. There is no social intercourse which is above being utilized as a seller-buyer relationship. "Wherever possible it is to your own 'self interest' to boost your industry,"[1] is the counsel of the Pacific Coast Electric Bureau to utility employes. The bridge table is an appropriate place to broach the subject of "electric water heaters or ANY product that uses electricity," if you are in any wise connected with the power companies, for "it is the rate of increased use of electricity that establishes the rate of our growth, *your* growth and the growth of the industry."[2] Advertising itself has become a primary datum in human experience.

Man as a buyer—his responses to sales stimuli—has been observed and analyzed with a care and an expense rarely if ever before bestowed upon him in any other capacity. "I get the same feeling as I watch a sales curve as I used to get watching a rat in

* *rococo*: "florid; fantastic; feebly pretentious"—*Webster's New International Dictionary.*

a maze," [3] says the greatest behaviorist of them all, Dr. John B. Watson, former scientist and now vice-president of the J. Walter Thompson Advertising Agency. It is time to turn the tables and do a little rat-watching of our own, and take a look at the advertisers themselves, their professional confidences, their motives and their techniques, what they reveal in their own behavior concerning the system which has produced them and the social institutions which give them perspective—or to reverse the figure, to take a "rat's" eye view of the builder of the maze.

"In fishing for buyers, as in fishing for bass, one should not reveal the hook. . . . From start to finish offer service." [4] These are the words of one of America's most successful advertising experts. The frankness with which advertising men often speak to each other, and sometimes within the hearing of their "fish," is one of the best sources for an understanding of a business-controlled society. Advertising trade journals which constitute their regular media of intra-fraternal communication are better, albeit unwitting, expositions of prevailing economic theory and practice than any of the literary output of academic theoreticians in the departments of economics and political science and, particularly, that bastard science of them all, the economics of marketing. The academic economist or research expert is all too likely to employ a crustaceous objectivity which conceals the homely facts that are the working and driving part of the intellectual equipment of the men engaged in the business enterprise, or else to become engrossed in large abstractions that miss the minutiæ of ordinary living—and money-grubbing. In his lapses from professional contemplation, the academician probably knows that business treats consumers as so many fish or other sub-human and easily managed species such as sheep ("People are like sheep," says Claude C. Hopkins, who declared that "the trend of the crowd" was the most "effective thing" he had ever found in advertising),[5] but he deals professionally as a rule with such majestic abstractions as the law of supply and demand.

Such abstractions have a degree of interest as pleasant simplifi-
cations, at a certain stage of investigation or formula-making,
but they are not always instructive, and are frequently misleading.

The rough and ready advertising man, particularly of the old
school, looks with disdain upon the learning of the schools. "I
know nothing of value," says Mr. Hopkins, "which an advertising
man can be taught in college." [6] Lest the reader miss his point,
Mr. Hopkins proceeds to reinforce it: "Some of the greatest
successes I have ever known in advertising were ignorant men.
Two are now heads of agencies." [7]

Today, advertising is on the defensive, especially when its
practitioners are speaking "not for publication." Advertising has
been thoroughly frightened by the movement for legislative
curbs upon its freedom. "Honest business must resell itself to
the public," [8] declares Allyn B. McIntire, president of the
Association of National Advertisers. His halting reply to the
aroused critics of his profession is that the critics "should realize
that advertising and salesmanship, the educational methods and
devices of business, are no better or no worse than the educational
methods of other institutions of society such as the university,
the church and the government." [9] The truth of this defense
is evident, but it has the effect of a sweeping indictment of the
major social institutions of a business and advertising-dominated
society rather than an exculpation of advertising and salesmanship. Advertising, according to this same distinguished spokesman, can rehabilitate itself in the popular esteem by making it,
among other things, "vibrant with believability" [10]—the latter
word being one of the contemporary verbal stereotypes in the
professional jargon, and carefully to be distinguished by prac-
titioner and laity alike from the more familiar and ethical concept
of "truth" or "accuracy."

Another authority from the inner sanctum of the profession
concedes that the "urge to overtop, overleap, outshout and out-
shine competition leads to excess, extravagance, brag and vul-

garity." [11] He calls upon the advertisers themselves to clean house and thereby circumvent the outspoken Chases, Schlinks, and Rortys.

Few men in the advertising profession itself have ever come closer to the point, without cant or ambiguity, in describing the nature and purpose of advertising than has J. P. Derum, the substance of whose essay on "Must Advertising Wear a Halo?" [12] we quote herewith:

"True, advertising is an art. But it is not a noble art.

"It is an extremely mercenary art, whose chief business is the extraction of money from the pockets of those who have money. . . .

"The Barnums of advertising—I think 'racketeers' is too unjust—know their psychology. Their contempt for the human race is kindly because it is informed and educated.

"They are quite inclined to agree with Lincoln. They know they can't fool all of the people all of the time.

"But they are not trying to fool all of the people. Their aim is to fool some of the people. . . .

"Advertising has only one mission, and that is, profit to the business which pays for advertising space or time."

A national advertiser, writing anonymously, is convinced that no profession or business can purge *itself;* and he proposes, therefore, that a "czar" be set over advertising for the purpose of correcting its evils by Cæsarian edict. Due care must be taken, according to the author of this plan, to encourage the "czar" to be "untouchable." "He must be paid well enough to render him untouchable no matter what his reputation for integrity—and that means $50,000 or so a year." [13] The significant item about this proposal is the advertising man's conception of the size of the financial consideration placed upon untouchability. Quite clearly a newspaper or magazine advertising manager at $6,000 to $10,000 a year is held to be a person easily to be corrupted or bought.

Edgar Kobak, president of the American Federation of Adver-

tisers, issues a blazing counter-charge against the critics of advertising. "Advertising," he avers, "is only one of the important
elements of modern American life which has been heaped with
invective by persons who are either too ignorant to understand
its functions or who suffer from an emotional grudge which
has been nursed into full-fledged intellectual spite." [14] Modestly,
if not unselfishly, he estimates that "not more than 5 per cent
of all types of present-day advertising seems to be objection-
able in any way and merits the criticism which now is being
directed indiscriminately at all advertising." This mild admission
of culpability is evidence of no little callousness toward prevailing practices, in the light of some of the estimates of his
colleagues. "We draw all sorts of codes of fair conduct," says
Kenneth Collins, formerly of R. H. Macy & Co., now of Gimbels,
"but the indisputable fact remains that lies continue to be very
prevalent." [15] Nor is Roy Durstine (prominent advertiser, recently a visitor in Russia) prepared to subscribe to a belief in a
95 per cent purity of the current brands of advertising. "Early
in 1933," he maintains, "advertising was at its lowest ebb in
recent times. It wasn't merely lowest in volume; it was lowest
in tone. The columns of our publications seemed to contain
nothing but charts of our innards, photographs of frightened
women and agonized men. . . . Fear, shame, ostracism, snobbery,
disgrace—these were the appeals which advertisers in great numbers nailed to their mastheads." [16]

Mr. W. C. D'Arcy, president of the D'Arcy Advertising Company, delivered a stinging attack upon present-day advertising
in his speech before the American Association of Advertising
Agencies. "The tide, gentlemen," said Mr. D'Arcy, "has turned
against us. The signals show red. . . . Something has got to be
done. . . . I feel it when I thumb through a magazine, periodical
or newspaper and notice the blatant bad taste that is laid there
on the advertising pages for fools like me. And when I say fools
I mean it—because the men who prepared it give me, and millions
like me, to understand without a shadow of a doubt that that is

largely what they think of the vast market of American citizenry. Just a nation of morons, morbid in tastes, perverted in desires, and unclean in lives and persons." [17]

But an exactly opposite view is supported by Anna Steese Richardson, of the *Woman's Home Companion,* who says: "Women like advertising that thinks for them, does all the thinking for them." [18] She certainly has a high regard for the critical intelligence of women.

Mr. A. M. Miller, director of advertising of the Chrysler Corporation of Canada, Ltd., interprets the revolt of consumers against present-day advertising as a wave of "puritanism." Always practical, as good advertising men are, he asks his colleagues: "Would it not be better for you to find some way of climbing on to the puritan band-wagon and thus avoid the very real danger of ruinous legislation or a destructive wave of public opinion?" [19]

It must not be assumed, however, that all the affected interests are mildly repentant or cautious. Some are boldly defiant of criticism and have, apparently, taken their stylistic cue from General Hugh Johnson. According to Harper Leech, long and favorably known in utility circles, the critics of advertising are simply those malcontents who seek to build "a world regimented to conform to their complexes and psycho-pathological hatreds." [20] Professional resentment against criticism overrides much of the confession from the "inside." "I am tired of seeing women who never earned a dollar in their lives assail the honesty and the sincerity of business men," [21] shouted Anna Steese Richardson, as she warmed to her subject of women and advertising at the convention of the American Federation of Advertising last year. Her spirited reference was to the women who, living protected lives as bourgeois liberals, have grown critically indignant at the frauds of advertising, since they are not required *directly* to participate in them. Mr. Kobak unwittingly gave away a little secret, not knowing that he was speaking for publication, by disclosing the intention of manufacturers to "heap ridicule" upon the heads of consumers' organizations and particularly upon the technical director of Consumers' Research, F. J. Schlink. "We were just waiting for Schlink to stick his head out before we hit him . . . and to put this over right, we are getting the backing of the American Legion." [22] Having fought one war for Morgan and "democracy," are the Legionnaires now prepared to follow General Kobak as he leads his hosts to battle in defense of those sacred American institutions of sales ballyhoo and "believability"?

The issue which has been joined in recent discussions of advertising is certain to become more, rather than less, acute. Advertising and business generally are anticipating a determined effort on the part of consumers to secure more effective measures of protection against the prevalent frauds in advertising and salesmanship. "Now is the time," writes the editor of a trade journal, "for people engaged in the manufacture of drugs and cosmetics to present their case to the members of Congress. . . . Senators and Representatives are now at their homes and they have much more time to spare than during the rush of the sessions of Congress." [23] Some of the members of the advertising profession now see that an excellent opportunity for serving their own interests was lost by their not pressing for the enactment of the comparatively innocuous Copeland-Tugwell bill, strongly supported by the bourgeois liberals already referred to, in the form in which it stood at the close of the Seventy-third Congress.

On the whole, advertisers think rather highly of themselves, as their financial and social prestige perhaps makes natural. J. D. Adams, of the advertising firm of Batten, Barton, Durstine & Osborn, regards the situation of the profession cheerfully. "Advertising," he says, "is full of quaint, delightful illusion and dramatization. The public loves it, and is not deceived." [24] We shall have more to say presently of this "quaint, delightful illusion" which is the principal technique by which goods are moved in this sucker-swindler economy.

It may surprise some to hear that advertising is regarded anywhere, even by its beneficiaries, as the bulwark of industrial democracy. But the editor of *Advertising Age* has the following to say on the subject: "As long as the small business has access to the ear of the public, and as long as any entrepreneur with courage, a good product and a little money, is free to advertise his wares to millions of eager consumers at small cost, there is no reason to fear that the American industrial democracy is in danger. Only the fetters of a bureaucratic regime of advertising regulation would make it really difficult for the little fellow." [25] In the very same issue of *Advertising Age* there were two brief news items: one reporting that "51,354 grocers went out of business in 1933," [26] and the other announcing a "phenomenal increase" of more than $83,000,000 in the 1933 earnings of General Motors.[27] Such are the fortunes of the "little fellow" in an industrial democracy kept functioning by advertising! Where are the successful *little* men in the automobile business, or in the ice cream or breakfast food business? "Only the fetters of a bureaucratic regime of advertising regulation would make it really difficult for the little fellow."

Mr. Kobak says that it is only the marginal 5 per cent of advertising that justifiably comes under the reproach of the critics. If that were true, there would indeed be a strong case for dismissing, as of no great importance, the general indictment against the ballyhoo artists. The contention requires examination, however, before any clean bill of health is issued. What are the characteristic methods of the "best" advertising? What is the remaining 95 per cent, given such sweeping approval by Mr. Kobak, doing toward the modification of the habits of consumers, and how are they doing it?

Nothing is more common than the use, directly or by implication, of odious comparisons by the writer of advertising copy. Claims for superiority of the product which he is at the moment selling constitute the very essence of the copy. Does it matter to advertisers that there are no grounds for the asserted superiority? Frank E. Fehlman, writing on the subject of "Advertising During a Depression" in *Advertising & Selling,* says: "There is not much difference in products of competitive companies in the same field; but advertising can and does lift many a product above that common level and give it real distinction and character." [28] Claude C. Hopkins, who rose to fame writing copy and conducting selling campaigns for *Pepsodent* tooth paste, *Van Camp's* pork and beans, the *Overland* automobile, *Puffed Wheat, Palmolive* soap and many other nationally distributed products, makes a very significant admission in connection with *Van Camp's* evaporated milk which he was called upon to boost. "Evaporated milk," he says, "is a standard product. It must be made to certain standards to meet governmental requirements. *One cannot establish or claim an advantage on natural or standard products.*" [29] [Italics ours.] There is the answer to our question in a nutshell. Where consumer standards have been set up, and intelligible specifications have been stated, the ground is removed from under the whole advertising structure, and the whole affair is reduced to one incredible and fantastic edifice of verbal rococo. There is no wonder that advertisers are vehemently opposed to the setting up of consumer standards. "One cannot . . . claim an advantage . . . on . . . standard products." The making of wholly fictitious claims for their clients is the essence of advertising after it is stripped of all its magniloquence of "service" and cant about "the American spirit." Undermine the foundation for these fictitious claims of superiority by establishing *standards*—something to *test* them by—and a mortal blow is struck at the whole extravagance of waste.

Mr. Hopkins' major exploits in the field of advertising were carried out while he was in the employ of Lord & Thomas, of whose board Albert D. Lasker is chairman. Few have been more bold in sounding the merits of advertising than Mr. Lasker, who was, for a brief interlude in his advertising career, the chairman of the United States Shipping Board. In a widely publicized address, delivered under the auspices of the Boston Chamber of Commerce and in coöperation with Harvard University School of Business Administration, Boston University College of Business

Administration, and Massachusetts Institute of Technology (a superb business combination to give appropriate auspices to such an address), Mr. Lasker correctly assessed the significance of setting up standards and gradings for the guidance of consumers. It will mean, he said, that "the private competitive system, at least so far as trade-marked articles go, will have been, by and large, made impossible . . . and advertising, as we know it, will for the most part have ceased to exist . . . because in its final working out it would be almost impossible for the advertiser to make the slightest emotional appeal." [30]

Mr. Hopkins, who was so steeped in his craft as to be frequently off guard in his autobiography, gives an illustration of the "quaint, delightful illusion," of which Mr. Adams says advertising is so full. Mr. Hopkins was assigned to the work of selling *Van Camp's* pork and beans. When the campaign was moving a bit slowly, Mr. Hopkins hit upon the idea of challenging comparison with competing brands of pork and beans. "Try Our Rivals, Too," was the copy that went forth with a show of supreme confidence to a gullible consuming public. "But," confesses Mr. Hopkins in his autobiography, "we could not bake better beans than our rivals." [31] This was established by an actual test in the Van Camp factory itself. "When we met in the factory and served a half dozen brands," says Mr. Hopkins, *"not a man present could decide which was Van Camp's."* [32] [Italics ours.] This reduces Mr. Hopkins' copy to bombastic trade puffery without a scintilla of foundation in experience and *actually known to him by testing to be without foundation.* This may not be technical perjury, as the copy did not say in so many words: *Van Camp's is superior to all rivals;* but it is, as all disinterested minds will discern at once, plain unvarnished prevarication. "Believability," you will note, is not offended or endangered. Nobody in the trade ever charged Mr. Hopkins with belonging to Kobak's villainous 5 per cent; he is one of the most honored and emulated practitioners of advertising in this generation. His book indeed is universally recommended to tyros of the business, as a basic and important text-book and mentor.

Mr. Hopkins' own story of how he advertised the automobiles of R. E. Olds is equally instructive.[33] He advised Mr. Olds to adopt the copy "My Farewell Car" for a forthcoming model. "But," protested Mr. Olds, "I don't intend to retire." Whereupon Mr. Hopkins explained to the guileless manufacturer that "Sarah Bernhardt made seven farewell tours" and "every farewell is subject to reconsideration." "So we came out with ads, headed 'My Farewell Car' and signed 'R. E. Olds, Designer,'" writes the winner of the argument over the use and meaning of the word "farewell." "The ads were written to typify the man," observes Mr. Hopkins concluding the narrative, "the man of rugged honesty [sic] . . . who put his reputation far ahead of profit." Another "quaint, delightful illusion" of the copy writers.

The Quaker Oats Company has decided recently to revive the advertising copy, written for it ten years ago by Mr. Hopkins, about *Puffed Rice* and *Puffed Wheat* being "the food that's shot from guns." Some of the experts have demurred at this revival. "Others feel," says *Advertising Age,*[34] "that the increasing competition for the favor of the consumer of breakfast foods means that new and more powerful appeals [than guns and explosions!] should be developed." "Mr. Hopkins frequently built advertising campaigns around spectacular features in production," *Advertising Age* continues, "feeling that the average consumer, unfamiliar with industrial methods, would be keenly interested in a story of this kind."[35] The fact that the particular production feature emphasized in this advertising copy is trivial and wholly irrelevant to the quality and utility (and, of course, economy) of the product, is of less importance to the advertiser than the fact that the consumer is assumed to be something of an infant not long out of his mother's arms whose fancy is caught by a story of shooting his breakfast food out of guns. The more powerful appeals that are needed today, in the opinion of those who disagreed with the plan of the Quaker Oats Company in resurrecting the old gag, would probably utilize "science" with its hocus-pocus about "precious mineral substances," "extra digestibility," and vitamins A to Z.

While we are on the subject of the Quaker Oats Company, it is appropriate to ask who pays the costs of these powerful appeals that are employed in advertising campaigns. The answer is, of course, that the entire cost is passed on to the consumer who pays it as a sort of exorbitant correspondence-school tuition fee for his miseducation. When Mr. Hopkins undertook to tickle the fancy of the American people with breakfast food "shot from guns," his first act was to ask for a 50 per cent increase in price of *Puffed Rice* in order to raise his advertising budget.[36] This is by no means an unusual mark-up for the purposes of *consumer miseducation.* A professor of marketing of the School of Business at the University of Chicago says that "industry spends billions annually to educate the consumer." [37] This is another "quaint, delightful illusion" of the advertising end of business. The dullest scholar in the Business School of the University of Chicago should know that industry does not spend a cent to educate the consumer, but that consumers, in the final reckoning, spend these billions for *their own miseducation.*

In advertising circles, such stories as that of the breakfast food "shot from guns" are called *subjective values added to the wares.* The theory of the subjective values is that consumers enjoy spending 50 per cent more for puffed rice when they can eat it with the knowledge of its *unique* manufacture. "If a consumer derives three thousand dollars' worth of satisfaction out of the purchase and use of a two-thousand-dollar automobile, I can see no ground upon which to criticize the business concern whose imaginativeness has been such as to add a subjective value of one thousand dollars to a mere mechanical contrivance," [38] says the professor of marketing at the University of Chicago.

The author of this brilliant piece of business logic is James L. Palmer, who not only holds a professor's chair at the University of Chicago, but who is also the *"Administration* member of four code authorities"!

The cost of these advertising schemes to the consumer sometimes runs far above 50 per cent. We are let in on the secret, for example,[39] of "how General Mills used advertising to maintain earnings last year [1933] despite a sharp drop in physical volume. The company transformed ordinary flour into three specialty products—*Bisquick, Wheaties,* and *Softasilk,* gave advertising a chance to prove its power, and *realized $50 per barrel instead of $7."* [Italics ours.]

One advertiser has doubts about the effectiveness of all this costly miseducation of the consumer. His confession, if not his misapprehension concerning the consumer's skepticism, is factually founded. "But superlatives, generalities, baloney testimonials and pseudo-science, while legal in the name of puffery," he says, "are transforming Barnum's proverb so that what is born every minute is not a sucker but a skeptic, like Skippy's pal, always belittling. Soon advertisers may have to start hawking elephants to make people believe they have a mouse to offer." [40]

Not long since, organized advertisers, whose economic sensibilities had not been dulled to the point of failing altogether to register any of the swelling volume of protest over the mendacity of advertising, adopted the slogan "Truth in Advertising." It is axiomatic in the history of social discontent that the offenders against human welfare offer a phantom palliative when protest can no longer be ignored, instead of really coming to terms with the rebellion. "Truth in Advertising" as understood by the authors of the slogan does not outlaw the obnoxious and misleading puffery, the meaningless testimonials, the pseudo-science, and the appeals to irrelevant emotions; or raise factual questions of utility. And most pertinent of all, it does not begin to comprehend the importance of the question of *relevant* truth as a competent guide to *use.* It may be perfectly true that a certain actress uses a certain soap, but there is no relevancy in the statement of that fact; and what is more, there could be no such thing as relevant consumer's truth concerning a *useless* article (the category in which many of the most widely advertised articles demonstrably belong) except to state the fact of its uselessness. When the day of relevant truth in advertising arrives, almost all of what we now know as advertising will pass with many other present institutions and habits into the limbo of pre-civilized living. Needless to say, those who live by virtue of advertising are not, as a group at least, advocating principles that are self-destructive. It must not be forgotten that advertising is a billion-dollar adjunct to the business system. Its beneficiaries may try to toss a slogan or two as a sop to consumers who demand to know relevant facts about what they use, but they will not meekly surrender to curbs upon their freedom to serve business and themselves according to prevailing standards. Thus, Gertrude B. Lane, editor of *Woman's Home Companion,* professed model of journalistic guides for consumers, said in a press release attacking the Tugwell bill: "I admit quite frankly that my selfish interests are involved. *I have spent thirty years of my life* in building up a magazine which I have tried to make of real service to the women of America, and *I have invested all of my savings* in the company which publishes this magazine." [Italics ours.] Miss Lane's personal interest in preserving her investments of years and savings does not move us—Czar Nicholas II ruled Russia twenty-three years before he was deposed, and he had enormous "investments"—but it is indicative of the nature of the forces that fight against any change in behalf of consumers.

James Mangan, advertising manager of the Mills Novelty Company, comes along with the declaration that *truth* is not the issue in advertising. Advertising cannot be true, he argues, setting up the metaphysical and wholly irrelevant speculation that "no such thing as perfect truth in anything is possible." [41] In his eulogy of advertising, he digresses with some observations on the American spirit. "Of all the great forces that have served to build this country," he says, *"advertising is perhaps the nearest to the real American spirit.* [Italics ours.] It is a speculative enterprise, it guarantees its buyer nothing in advance, it's as wide open and free as the eagle in the air. Its mettle is American, the spirit which takes a chance, assumes a risk, is willing to pay if mistaken, is ready to collect if right. This is the spirit that built America. This is really the whole underlying spirit of American business! There's nothing exact, or definite, or tangible about it. It's business. Most of it is wasted. *Fine, I say!* What we need is still more private waste, and economy in government; instead of what we are getting now, namely, private economy, and waste in government." [42] Here are suggestions for at least two new orders of "hoopla": the Daughters of the Advertising Builders of America (DABA) and the Mystic Fraternity of Private Wasters in the Public Interest (PWPI).

Mr. Mangan's formula, "no such thing as perfect truth," is a convenient sophistry. In a little circular seal on its advertisements, Gimbels, one of the largest department stores in this country, says: "Gimbels tells the *truth*." In a recent advertisement of the company, $5 *Conklin* fountain pens were announced for sale at $1.98. "Then why the drastic cut in price?" queries the advertisement. "All these pens," replies the advertisement, "are in marine green, a color that is being discontinued for 1934." [43] (Are we to understand that we paid $3.02 for the "marine green" in 1933?) On turning to the advertisements of the Conklin Pen Company itself, we are led to ask: *does Gimbels tell the whole truth,* or in the case of its advertisement of *"obsolete" Conklin* pens such a wee little bit of the truth that a whole host of such small angels of veracity could easily dance on the point of the pen? According to the advertisement, the 1934 model *Conklin* is an "ultra-new sacless pen" (streamlined for speed writing, it appears from the picture) and, *mirabile dictu,* there is a *word-o-meter* on the transparent ink chamber which "tells you at a glance" whether you have gone 1793 "words" or 6041. [44] After every 7034 words (so the ad says) you must stop at an ink-filling station. . . . Now it is plain that this ultra-new 1934 sensation of a fountain pen has brought about $3.02 depreciation of the 1933 model, and that the "marine green" had nothing to do with it except as it is a symbol of the pre-progressive era in *Conklin* pens. . . . The attention of those who are interested in verbal long distances is directed to the *Parker Vacumatic* pen which claims a performance of 12,000 words on one filling.[45] The *Chilton Lox-top Pen* claims, in its own descriptive leaflet, to give "twice the writing *mileage* [italics ours] as any other sac pen of like size." What most writers would now appreciate from all these distance-minded pen makers is an AUTOMATIC NON-STOP WONDER PEN.

For years the managers of selling campaigns have used the sampling technique with success. Samples of the articles are given away in order to build up a market. This is a relatively expensive method, and it is now proposed that it be abandoned in favor of "sampling with words." In an article first published in *Printers' Ink* and then reproduced in part in the *Ice Cream Trade Journal,* T. Harry Thompson, copy supervisor of N. W. Ayer & Son, wrote: [46] "Obviously, you cannot sample such things as taste and aroma through the medium of printers' ink. Therefore, the next best thing to sampling (aside from photographs and drawings, which are really marvelous today) is descriptive writing that stirs the imagination, and, in the case of a food or a beverage or a cigarette, sets the taste-buds of the tongue to palpitating in eager anticipation." This is the way in which Mr. Thompson proposes to sample with words: " 'Imagine red-ripe strawberries, bursting with juice!' The reader has seen—has eaten—such strawberries, plump and tender and bulging with sun-ripened nectar. It sets his mouth to watering. 'Picture them tossed into a swirling sea of golden cream,' the copy continues. Here is the ice cream freezer, turning, turning, with its precious cargo of farm-sweet cream, reflecting the pale gold of a winter's sun. . . . As the paddles flail it to whipped cream consistency, the taste-buds of tongue and uvula literally hunger to surround this cooling morsel of nourishment." Mr. Thompson knows, all advertisers know, and the ice cream makers know better than anyone else, that this word picture is purely imaginary. What really goes into commercial ice cream is dried skim milk, dried egg white, artificial flavor, artificial color, corn sugar, a gelatine or gum thickener, and a large percentage (as high as 50 per cent) of air to increase bulk (i.e., profit). Indeed, "it can be assumed in these days," says a manufacturer of food dyes, "that the average person is well aware . . . that strawberry ice cream is not likely to have interviewed the luscious fruit. . . ." [47] But this knowledge does not deter the advertisers, the ice cream makers, or *Printers' Ink* from their approval of such copy. To give an illustration of the frightful conditions that really obtain in the ice cream industry, we quote from the *Monthly Bulletin* of the Indiana Division of Public Health, reporting its July (1934) inspections: "About 40 per cent of the ice cream samples examined chemically were illegal." [48]

Mr. Thompson could not resist his vocabularian proclivity, and proceeded to offer the following suggestion to perfume makers:

"Rain, sudden and slanting and silver, enters the garden— brushes the honeysuckle, fingers the roses, lingers by the jasmine— and, passing, as swiftly leaves, souvenir to the sun, a more enchanting fragrance than before. There is a perfume made to recreate those lovely moments of the garden; to number, like the sun-dial, only shining hours. Orchis is the blending of a hundred fragrant blossoms, tuberoses and lilies, violets and acacia. Orchis is a melody, woven of rare sweet scents." [49]

Standard Brands, Inc. (Chase & Sanborn) is now engaged in a tea advertising campaign, the copy for which is physiologically unfounded. "It [*Tender Leaf* tea] pleasantly stimulates the flow of thought, and sharpens the perceptions," [50] says the advertisement which has appeared in the leading women's magazines. "Most highly cultivated people the world over have long appreciated these facts," runs the appeal of *Tender Leaf* distributors to those who would dread being left out of the category of the "highly cultivated."

For the New York *Times'* sake we are asked to believe the

impossible. "When a dish after being cooked is lacking in flavor, simply add a few dashes of *Maggi's Seasoning*." [51] When you have done this, the advertisers declare that you have multiplied "the delicious *natural* flavor of the food itself, without substituting any taste" of *Maggi's Seasoning*. "Believability" collapses under the weight of this palpably indefensible claim.

First prize for new kinds of advertising *rococo* probably should be awarded to the Campbell Soup Company. In a full page advertisement in *Time*[52] there appears the statement that Campbell's supplies "21 kinds to choose from"; whereupon there is a list of 22. What is the key to this arithmetical mystery? The editor of *Time* supplies it: "Every year, since 1931, from 400 to 700 alert advertisement-readers . . . write to Campbell Soup Company calling attention to the discrepancy, *which pleases the company immensely* [italics ours]. The error is deliberately written into the advertising copy to make people talk about it. . . ." [53] How distressing it must be to 700 alert (alert, did they say?) advertisement-readers to find that they have spent $21 on postage alone to inform the Campbell Soup Company of an error that turns out to be no error at all but a not-too-honestly conceived piece of moronic advertising.

The "illusions" of advertising are not limited to the use of words; the graphic arts also have their uses in exaggeration and misrepresentation. "Don't go in for artists' exaggeration of certain features *except where trade practice absolutely demands it (e.g., autombile tires, women's wear, etc.)*," [54] [italics ours] counsels a leading journal of advertising. The next time you thumb through a mail order catalog or study the pictures done in four colors in the advertisements of the high class women's magazines, you are entitled, on the basis of this "inside" evidence, to ignore the artists' beautiful illustrations as just so much more "quaint, delightful illusion," unless, of course, you know precisely where "trade practice absolutely demands" a misrepresentation and where trade practice permits an artist's honest reproduction.

The four-point philosophy upon which the advertising profession builds, and which all but completely explains the character and content of advertisements, has been set forth by a member of the profession, as follows:

"But after all, this is a *very vulgar* world.

"It is an *extremely credulous* world.

"It is an *exceedingly sex-conscious* world.

"And the Lions and Rotarians and other such delightful associations given to luncheons, song and service notwithstanding, business does not exist primarily for service but for *making money*." [55] [All italics ours.]

The author of this advertising philosophy might have added that it is also an extremely health-conscious world highly susceptible to all the disease-phobias, real or imaginary, which advertising health-quacks can din into its consciousness; or perhaps this is covered by his observation that this is an "extremely credulous world."

While there is no defense for a mid-Victorian, or mid-anything-else, foppery that shunned the mention of many of the well-known facts of life, there is no sign of social health in the vulgarization of these facts to sales' purposes. If this is a "very vulgar world" it has been made so by no other influence so much as by advertising. In the advertising columns of the most "respectable" journals, beautiful ladies now carry on animated conversation on the subject of toilet tissue. To us it seems that the nethermost depth of vulgarity on the subject of toilet tissue, however, was reached by *Good Housekeeping*[56] and the advertisers of *Northern Tissue*.

In the craze over "vitamin D" in which a procession of *foods* has been irradiated for the addition of this queen of the vitamins, *toilet tissue has also been irradiated.*[57] *Tide* reports that "hot dogs blessed with Vitamin D appeared in the Midwest" last year, and that "in Chicago the Orbit Gum Co. achieved a Vitamin D chewing gum."[58]

The food faddists stand near the top of achievement in appealing to the world's credulity. Once it was calories, now it is vitamins, laxative qualities, bulk, and what have you; tomorrow and tomorrow there will be other bait for the credulous as surely as advertising men have access to the dictionaries and close business relationships with scientists. Not that calories, vitamins, laxative foods, and balanced diets are unimportant, but our education in these matters which should have proceeded on a strictly scientific basis with sole consideration for consumers' welfare has, like every other necessity for healthful living, fallen into the hands of salesmen. "The exploitation of some of our prepared foods has degenerated into a regular racket," warns the *Journal* of the American Dental Association, "and it is costing the consumer a vast amount of money and serving a much less beneficial purpose in the human economy than the simpler and more nearly native foods."[59] The dietetic experts in food-corporation-subsidized universities are underwriting the fanciful claims of the advertisers. The "scientists" have lately revealed the beneficial laxative qualities of bran and, *au contraire,* the dietary uselessness of bread crust as mere indigestible roughage! This is buttering the dietetic expert's economic bread on *both* sides.

The historical and dietary truth about bran has been set forth by Dr. J. F. Montague, as follows:[60]

"With the threatened passing of the horse, the flour manufacturer saw the possibility of a vanishing market, so he shrewdly contrived to 'educate' the public to the advisability of eating bran to keep 'regular.' He, therefore, devised tasty breakfast foods and formulated recipes for muffins, bread and such—all containing the horse-food bran. *Anything and everything to put back in our diet the very thing he first extracts as unfit for human use.* Now, however, he calls it a health food."

"Say what you will, bran can and does irritate; indeed, there is excellent reason to believe it acts mainly *because it is irritant* to the soft lining of the colon. Imagine, if you will, rubbing a piece of sandpaper over the red part of your lips (this, too, is a mucous membrane) and you will understand what I mean when I say that the roughness of bran is unacceptable to the mucous membrane of the colon." [61]

While a Columbia University dietetic expert[62] pronounces bran a useful article for human ingestion, a University of California expert[63] carries on research which produces findings against bread crust. This pronouncement against bread crust (a human food since the days when man turned from his nomadic and pastoral ways to till the soil) is in line with what we may expect as the next general "revolutionary" development in the tactics of the bread salesman—the sliced crustless loaf packaged in Cellophane. An enterprising Brooklyn baker has already started the "revolution"; and pictures of his product have appeared in the *Northwestern Miller*.[64] There will be financial returns six ways if our prediction concerning the crustless bread packaged in Cellophane is fulfilled: (1) The baker will sell more bread by eliminating the crust; (2) The dietetic expert will have justified her researches and will win new clients; (3) The "roughage" campaign of the bran sellers will have the impetus of a new appeal when the bread crusts, a safe and normal roughage, disappear from the diet; (4) The smart engineer who makes the crust-removing machinery will grow rich on patent royalties; (5) The machine manufacturer will profit out of the production of a new gadget; and (6) du Pont will have a new Cellophane market until the next war opens up opportunities for more of those billion-dollar profits. And, lo! the poor consumer will get, and pay, the bill. It has remained for a state official to think up a new way for increasing bread *sales,* not, necessarily, bread consumption. The state director of agriculture in Oregon, Max Gehlhar,[65] has hit upon the artful device of cutting the loaf into *fewer* (therefore larger) slices, on the theory that bread is eaten by the slice, and not by weight. The unconsumed portion, if any, of the larger slice stands a good chance of being tossed into the garbage can, and thus the bread sales' curve will show, it is hoped, an upward tendency—and the sales of some other product of agriculture in Oregon will tend downward.

Business society has accomplished wonders in the mass production of phobias as well as of automobiles. The ills that flesh is heir to, real and imaginary, have been exploited to the utmost limit of their profit-yielding capacity. The following list of phobias and their guardians makes, of course, no pretensions to completeness:

> *Halitosis:* Listerine.
> *B.O.:* Lifebuoy Soap.
> *Office hips:* H. & W. (Corsets) Co.
> *Asthenia:* Pluto Water.
> *Athlete's foot:* Absorbine Jr.
> *Sulphide breath:* Haley's M-O.
> *Domestic hands:* Hind's Honey & Almond Cream.
> *Pink toothbrush:* Ipana Toothpaste.
> *Coffee nerves:* Postum.
> *Nerves:* Camel Cigarettes.
> *Cosmetic skin:* Lux Toilet Soap.
> *7 stains:* Colgate's Ribbon Dental Cream.
> *Film:* Pepsodent Toothpaste.
> *Gingivitis:* Ipana Toothpaste.
> *IF:* Walker-Gordon Acidophilus Milk.
> *Pyorrhea:* Forhan's Toothpaste.
> *Psoriasis:* Siroil.
> *Morning mouth:* Astringosol.
> *Scurf:* Pinaud Eau de Quinine.

Walker-Gordon's "IF" should not be confused with Kipling's well-known poem; it is simply the initials of the words "intestinal flora." In addition to these and many other carefully cultivated phobias that have to do with bodily welfare, there are also the equally powerful phobias of unconventionality. "Humiliphobia" (a newcomer) is designed to lure college boys to the correct clothes of Rogers Peet.[66] A social error, to be avoided by all correct hostesses, is committed when plain tomato juice is served as a cocktail, or when the guests were expecting a cocktail, according to the makers of *College Inn* products.[67]

The essence of racketeering is to "sell protection" against dangers which are either wholly fictitious or the creation of the racketeers themselves. The gangs which prey upon the fish market in New York City, for example, by "selling protection" against their own depredations, lay a far lighter financial toll upon society than do the creators of imaginary or exaggerated phobias against which millions are wheedled into buying protection.

From a study of advertisements, it would be easy to gain the impression that at least half the human race is devoid of all interests except that of its personal appearance as a means of attracting some member or members of the opposite sex.* If, as the advertiser quoted above stated, this is an "exceedingly sex-conscious world," what other influence is comparable to that of advertising in making it so? The ecclesiastical moralists all but completely miss the point in their agitation for "cleanness" in films. It has never, apparently, occurred to them to center their fire upon the economic system whose many perversions include this special one of falsifying and exaggerating the function of sex in human society. There are, of course, good reasons why ecclesiastical moralists avoid the fundamental insights that would lead to such a course of action. Furthermore, a sense of being highly moral (obviously necessary to the ecclesiastical mind) is preserved by concentrating fire upon the little marginal and irrelevant matters of prolonged and sensuous osculation or the highly attenuated clothes of actresses, which are to be seen in the movies. Certain ways of commercializing sex have been known from time immemorial as *prostitution,* but far be it from us to suggest that the "street women" of any land or age have been comparable, in their techniques or ability to turn sex into cash, to modern manufacturers, advertisers, and magazines that have made sex appeal the prime foundation of profitable salesmanship.

* For a full discussion of cosmetics, see *Skin Deep* by M. C. Phillips (New York, Vanguard Press, 1934, $2.00).

An authority in the advertising field, addressing the inner circle of business, declares that "judicious flattery, in combination with its sisters, sex appeal and snobbery appeal, is certainly one of the prime foundations of modern, or indeed of any, advertising." [68] It is small wonder that the business enterprise has produced in a particular stratum of society a full quota of sex-conscious snobs. (We cannot forbear at this point calling attention to the powerful element of sex-conscious snobbery which has been present as an unprecedented and particularly brutal sadism in the Nazi movement of Germany, but a discussion of this phenomenon and its intimate relationship to the business enterprise must be deferred to a later section.) The following examples of the advertisers' copy, taken from recent numbers of *McCall's, Ladies' Home Journal, Good Housekeeping, Delineator,* and *Woman's Home Companion,* are a few illustrations of the familiar use of sex appeal: (Initials indicate the magazines in which the advertisement was found.)

"A man just isn't human, if he doesn't respond to a lovely smile."—COLGATE'S RIBBON DENTAL CREAM (LHJ—McC—GH)

"Awaken romance with the charm of beauty."—MAX FACTOR (GH—McC)

"Don't let roughened fingers cheat you of romance."—JERGENS LOTION (GH—LHJ—WHC—McC)

"Every man adores it!—now every girl can have it!"—WOODBURY'S FACIAL SOAP (LHJ—McC)

"Indeed, there's almost nothing that money can buy which equals the power of a few drops of a delightful Coty *Perfume* to give one that joyous consciousness of being a lovely, desirable—and *desired*—woman!" (GH)

"Let him look at you with ardent eyes."—RICHARD HUDNUT (LHJ—McC)

"Look what I found when I lost the 7 stains." [an engagement ring]—COLGATE'S RIBBON DENTAL CREAM (GH)

"Make up your lips for kisses."—TANGEE (in all five magazines)

"Men stay in love with the blonde who makes the most of
her hair."—BLONDEX (WHC—McC)

"Our marriage was about 2 inches from the rocks."—CHASE
& SANBORN'S COFFEE (GH)

"Why doesn't young Hustler dash to the 7:45 any more without kissing his wife goodbye?"—PILLSBURY'S PANCAKE
FLOUR (WHC—McC)

"Within 30 days—you, too, can be ready for Romance!"—
WOODBURY'S FACIAL SOAP (McC)

A people as susceptible as Americans have shown themselves to
be, to the regimentations of purposeless or harmful consumption,
will easily be prevailed upon by the identical techniques to submit
to the regimentations, when occasion and need arise, that have
set the masses of Germany goose-stepping behind a patently psychopathic house-painter. In a society where commercial leaders
have habituated the populace to a system of promising-everything-
and-delivering-nothing, there is no tradition powerful enough to
immunize it to fascism. Fascism is the art of mendacity raised to
its highest effectiveness by mass appeal to phobias that have been
assiduously cultivated and elaborated for ulterior purposes. Where
a people can be regimented by this process to fight off with a
given soap the dread menace of "B.O.," it requires no stretch of
the imagination to see it successfully regimented by the purveyors
of a fraudulent political nostrum to fight off the "menace of
Bolshevism."

Advertising, in its spirit and purpose, is germinal fascism.
Hitler was the first European politician who saw the significance
of the techniques of commercial advertising for politics. In *Mein
Kampf* he used the distinctly commercial word *Reklame*, advertising, to describe his political method.[69] Advertising is more than
sales ballyhoo; it is a form of social organization which utilizes
the most modern mechanical contrivances for a regimentation
that is both commercial and political.

CHAPTER III

High Pressure—Low Resistance

IN THE PREVIOUS CHAPTER we have examined the bombastic, fantastic, and pretentious manner in which business makes its impact upon the consuming public through the use of printed matter, especially in magazine and newspaper advertising.

Advertising is by no means the full extent of the techniques employed by business in its ceaseless sleuthing to track down consumers' purchasing power. In a very real sense, every unspent consumer's dollar is marked for arrest on sight for vagrancy, unless it has a stalwart bodyguard who has learned the art of sales' resistance. Few escape being taken into custody; but resistance *is* still legal even if unconventional. Nevertheless, few consumers of the total population are any match for the ubiquitous salesman set upon their trails.

The principle of the collective bargaining of labor for the purpose of equalizing the power of the parties to a labor contract was a long time receiving any recognition. It still, of course, lacks recognition by the great business enterprises, such as the chain stores, power stations, and the telephone monopoly. Even now the principle of collective bargaining is more often honored in the breach than in the fulfillment, but the principle (by which business men and governments often mean something which is accepted in theory only to be ignored in practice) of the collective bargaining of labor is "established." The idea of the right to equalization of bargaining power in the transactions between salesmen and consumers would, if ever widely mentioned, excite only stupefied wonder at the fantastic character of such a conception. In many quarters it is assumed that one of the oldest of human privileges, fully consistent with all moral and ethical standards, is that of the seller's right to drive a hard bargain, the hardness to be limited only by the shrewdness of the buyer. *Caveat emptor* (let the buyer beware!) is alleged to be an ancient principle in seller-buyer relationships, whereas, as a matter of fact, the ancients would scorn to admit the parentage of this particular "deformity." [1] *Caveat emptor,* as a matter of historical fact, is a rationalization of modern business!

"The consumer . . . enters the market place ill-equipped and unprepared to predict or diagnose the tactics of the salesman or merchant. He is an easy victim, not necessarily for the charlatan, but equally for the merchant bent upon taking from the consumer a greater value than he receives." [2] This is the observation of the professor of marketing, already quoted, who quite consistently found it justifiable for the automobile salesman to add $1,000 to the price of a car if the buyer could be persuaded to purchase that much "subjective value" in addition to $2,000 paid for the motor vehicle itself. In spite of the authorship of the statement, however, there is unquestioned accuracy in the observation that the "consumer enters the market place ill-equipped and unprepared" for the tactics of the salesman or merchant.

Merchants generally look upon a consumer as already half-snared if he enters the market place at all. It is, therefore, elementary in the tactics of selling that merchants strive to build up "store traffic." Dollars, it is assumed, have an almost irresistible affinity for the merchants' cash drawers if only their unsuspecting and gullible owners can be lured within sight of goods.

We have already seen how the "chest" model refrigerators of the TVA are being used as "teasers," "leaders," or "nailed-to-the-floor" merchandise. Low-priced dishwashing machines are now being developed for the same purposes—not to be sold, but to be utilized as decoys or bait to lure store traffic. "E. H. Campbell, manager of the sales promotion department of Rex Cole, Inc., distributor for General Electric refrigerators and other major appliances, said yesterday," according to a New York *Times* story, "that the General Electric Company, along with a number of other producers, is concentrating research activity on a low-price dishwashing machine."[3] This method has, according to Mr. Campbell, been proved a remarkable success for the merchants and manufacturers. "Consumers, attracted to showrooms by the low-price refrigerator, it was explained, have become interested [under sales pressure] in the better grade equipment and, in at least 50 per cent of the cases, have ordered the higher price units."[4]

Installment sales are often desired by merchants for the reason that they increase store traffic. Says a writer in *Electrical Merchandising*: "The third result is somewhat related to the credit situation, inasmuch as, since the customer must come into the store four times a month to make payments, other merchandise in the store has four times more influence upon his desire to possess it, than it does when the customer comes in once a month. Perhaps he will see something he wants and will buy it, even though he hasn't completed his first contract."[5]

The bread-makers are now suggesting this tactic of *store traffic* as an important factor in grocers' cultivating regular bread consumers. "Get them to buy your bread," says a tactician of the baking industry, "and they will come into your store every day. And once they are in, you have a chance to sell them all their grocery needs."[6]

The Norge Corporation, makers of electric refrigerators, brought out during the summer of 1934 "a Norge 'Mystery' model, in an exclusive spectacular new finish"—"a marble finish of gray pearl tone, designed to appeal to women." If you were one of the thousands who passed the Norge display rooms and went inside to investigate this "spectacular" refrigerator, you were simply one more "store traffic" sucker fulfilling the shrewd and calculating purposes of the Norge Corporation which were, in the words of John H. Knapp, vice-president of the concern, "to pull greater crowds into the store." "Only 6,000 such units have been produced," says *Electric Refrigeration News* of this *Norge Mystery* model, "the intention being to provide one to each dealer for promotion purposes *rather than for sale.*"[7] [Italics ours.]

One dealer has gone to the length of penalizing his salesmen who fail to make the most of the store traffic which has been built up by "teasers." " 'Sock Salesmen for Selling' is the slogan of a middle west furniture house," reports *Electrical Merchandising.* "It advertises a pretty good washer at a price that's a chiseler's dream and the suckers come a-running hot foot. Once inside, the salesman's job is to trade 'em up or else take a nick of 15 dollars off his next commission check. That's what it costs him as penalty for selling the loss-leader."[8] This is a new kind of incentive for the salesman. "We've all tried the stimulating effect of larger commissions, bonuses, prizes and pats on the back as reward to the salesmen for selling what we *want* sold. This scheme of plastering a stiff fine on the order-getter when he sells what we *don't want sold* has its possibilities."[9]

Another instance of instilling powerful incentives in the salesman is furnished by the columnist of *Electrical Merchandising,* Frank B. Rae, Jr. "Store advertises 'No Carrying Charge' on time payment sales but has one price for cash and another for credit. It is up to the salesman to find out how the customer intends to pay before quoting the price. If he guesses wrong and quotes the cash price to the time payment customer, it costs him ten [$10]."[10] It should be remembered that the trade journal which carries the accounts of these selling tactics goes to thousands of merchants and provides them with a supply of hints on effective methods of moving goods at a maximum profit, and maximum hardship, distress, and loss to their customers.

With what results the "domestic science class" method of salesmanship is frequently employed, the "Margaret Nevins' domestic science club" of the Syracuse (N. Y.) Lighting Company amply illustrates. In a single year a store traffic of 72,000 Syracuse women was drawn to the sales rooms of this public utility concern. These women were "flattered" into a sense of having been invited to "join" something by filling out a registration card. "The little card works," says *Electrical Merchandising* in reporting Miss Nevins' phenomenal success in adding to the company's yearly receipts not less than $70,000—the estimated retail value of almost 4,000 electrical appliances sold as a result of this "clubby" affair in which, it is reported, the women were soon calling Miss Nevins by name. With what thinly veiled contempt the women of Syracuse who fell for this sales device are viewed by the trade, these residents of a great university city should see. "The fundamentals of the demonstration," says the reporter in *Electrical Merchandising,* "are the usual hokus-pokus of all home service operations." [11]

The manner in which the sales of electrical appliances are closed is illustrated by the following advice entitled "Sales Wisdom" in the trade magazine, *Light:*

"When your front [office] door opens you should be instantly on your toes. Here is your opportunity—if you meet it—good. It may pay your rent for a month. . . . Say to your assistant or someone in your establishment, 'See that I am not disturbed for a time. I will be helping this lady to select her fixtures,' or 'I don't want to be interrupted until we have selected the fixtures for this gentleman.' Either remark lends an importance to the customer and her mission which is flattery to her and good business for you. It drives away the idea of 'just looking around.' Remember, you are out for an order—not for a tour of your fixture department, or even an estimate. . . . If your prospects are seated while you remain standing your statements have a psychological air of authority that cannot be obtained if both of you are standing and shuffling about. . . ." [12]

Space does not permit further quotation from this most instructive manual on the numerous psychological tricks employed by the salesmen of electrical appliances.

Salesmen are by no means dependent entirely upon the building up of store traffic in order to bring their goods and appeals to the attention of prospective buyers. They have carried their campaigns, with unusual aggressiveness, into the homes of prospects. The salesman engaged in the house-to-house campaign works under careful and elaborate printed instructions provided for him in a sales manual. The *Realsilk* salesman, for example, has read the following instructions in his guide book on tactics:

"*Getting into the Home*

"Positive action. Step back, smile, step forward.

"Pick up case and enter.

"Have prospect at ease (seated).

"Demonstrate door opener. [A souvenir or gift to the housewife to induce her to listen further to the salesman.] . . .

"Get out order book with presentation book. . . .

"Where prospect does not order, or hesitates, shows little interest or is non-committal, go right along with your demonstration. Do not hesitate, go right along." [13]

The ubiquitous *Fuller Brush* salesman likewise acts the part of a carefully instructed robot. In his manual, he finds the following inviolable instructions:

"If possible carry old wooden-back bath brush.

"Look disgusted.

"Draw a picture so realistic of germs, etc., that she will throw away her old brush." [14]

There is a belief current among salesmen that where more than one of the senses of the prospective buyer can be brought into play, the chances of closing a sale are greatly increased. The principle of the "store traffic" is that the prospective buyer's sense of sight is utilized for effective sales purposes. If, in addition to sight, the sense of smell is also brought into play, it is the theory of salesmanship that the article is practically sold. Thus, in the selling of *Ever-Dry* (a preparation for ending *under-arm odor*—or should we say *odeur?*), "the manufacturers have prepared an ingenious counter display card holding one bottle," and the card "is so worded as to get the customer to pick up the bottle and examine it, drawing attention to the *delicate fresh fragrance* of the product." [15] [Italics ours.] The prospect's sight, touch, and smell having been stimulated, there is created an opportunity for some seemingly natural, but irresistible little sales comment or question which sends the leisurely store visitor out in possession of a bottle of *Ever-Dry*. In addition to these sales tactics, there is also a little gadget in the form of an *applicator* which goes with each bottle of *Ever-Dry*—and the gadget is the final perfection of sales pressure! The buyer of this outfit, having been unequal to the resistance requirements of the occasion, is now prepared to enter polite society where, according to the advertising stereotypes, his casual friends discuss toilet tissue with him, but even his closest friends won't (as the ads imply) tell him if he has B.O., halitosis, and under-arm odor.

In cosmetics merchandising, the *American Druggist,* representative of a business which was once primarily engaged in the preparation and distribution of medicine, advises druggists[16] to use "demonstration display and sales talk [which will] appeal to *all five senses*." [Italics ours.] Presumably, the "cream rouge," recommended by the author of this advice in the *American Druggist* for use on the lips, is to be *tasted* by the prospective buyer if all five senses are to be stimulated. For *hearing* there should be a musical lipstick holder.

In an article on "The Surest Closing Method is Demonstration," published in *Electrical Merchandising,* Gerald E. Stedman, vice-president of The Cramer-Krasselt Company, places the *five-sense stimulation* method first on the list of successful sales pressure tactics. *"Demonstration in which the prospect participates,"* writes Stedman, "is a much better method in that the prospect is compelled to touch, taste, smell, hear, see, or manipulate the product. It builds greater appreciation because the prospect is acting as well as observing. It kindles greater realization of value as a home comfort because the prospect is using it as she would in household use. It eliminates interruptions and objections because the prospect is so busy doing things that her attention is not apt to wander from the track of the presentation." [17]

Many years ago Europeans attempted, without success, to compete with the Indian makers of camel's hair shawls. The shawls from India had a *certifying* odor which enabled those who knew nothing of textile manufacture to distinguish them from the European-made shawls. European shawl-makers then set to work to identify the distinguishing odor of the shawls from the East. They found it to be largely oil of patchouli.[18] When this was added to their product, their shawl market picked up immediately and thereafter thrived on the deception. But no one was deemed guilty of unethical conduct, and no court would have held the odor-applier culpable.

Deceptions of smell are well-established in the tactics of the salesmen. "In the opinion of the manufacturers," says Dr. M. T. Bogert, eminent Columbia University odor-chemist and expert in sales appeal, "the judicious use of appropriate and delicate perfumes and the air of luxury thus created have often determined the sale of their high-priced automobiles quite as much as the persuasive eloquence of the salesman."[19] Perhaps it is the delicate perfume which creates the "subjective value" for which the buyer is pleased to shell out an extra $1,000. At that rate the smell adds a sizable amount to what the traffic will bear, and Columbia University smell-chemists should be in increasing demand. "High-grade silk stockings are often faintly perfumed to increase their appeal to the prospective customer," says the same expert. But the luxury lines have no special monopoly on sales' appeals to *olfaction*. Smelling tricks are used in selling bacon, too. "A Middle West meat packer has the Cellophane wrappers for his prize bacon packages printed with *inks* which themselves *possess a bacon aroma*."[20] [Italics ours.] We have seen a waxed paper wrapper for bacon which has *lean meat* pictured on it in such a clever and ingenious fashion as easily to create the illusion that the purchaser is looking upon lean strips inside the wrapper rather than a camouflaged picture of just the right tint and arrangement printed on the outside. With bacon smell and looks both transferred to the wrapper, we are led to wonder how long it will be before the contents of the package will be dispensed with altogether and consumers sold only the "subjective values" of bacon created by the chemical and graphic arts without the aid of farmers and meat packers.

Changes of merchandise (sometimes in the name of "style" and at other times in the name of "progress") are one of the commonest devices for increasing business turnover. *Advertising Age* reports a "trade promotion campaign being pushed by the millinery code authority, with NRA approval," the object of which "is to make the woman shopper think in terms of four rather than two hat seasons a year." [21]

The Colgate-Palmolive-Peet Company provides an instructive example of the so-called "change in merchandise" as a sales tactic. For many years this company has sold a shaving stick, of medium size, which retails at 10 cents. Now it has placed on the market a larger stick which retails for 35 cents. The costs of the respective containers are negligible in comparing the prices of the two sticks. *But the new and larger size has a "Handy Grip" feature* which represents the company's "change in merchandise." Weighing of the two sticks on laboratory scales revealed that the older 10-cent stick sells at the rate of 40 cents per 100 grams of soap, while the newer stick (with the "Handy Grip" feature) sells at the rate of 63.6 cents per 100 grams of soap. This difference represents an increase of 59 per cent in the cost of the merchandise to the consumer, when the "Handy Grip" feature, the consumer-confusing addition, is left out of the calculation.

What is man, that the salesmen are mindful of him? He is a congeries of emotional responses that the god of all good salesmen collected and deposited in bipedal organisms in order that this might be a salesman's paradise. "The head of a large department store once remarked to me," writes Professor Walton H. Hamilton[22] of Yale Law School and member of this week's NRA governing board: "'God created the masses of mankind to be exploited. I exploit them; I do His will.'" In some of these bipedal organisms, it will be admitted by marketing-survey makers, the mixtures of emotional responses have been more perfectly blended than in others. The ideal combination would seem to be about equal portions of fear, shame, egoism, religiosity, gregariousness, rugged individualism, optimism, cupidity, ignorance, acquisitiveness, conformity, and docility—God's perfect set-up, according to the "head of the large department store," to enable that enterprising merchant to do the divine bidding, and play his assigned role in the Great Plan.

There may be more reverent ways of phrasing the salesman's philosophy, but hardly more accurate ways; for the social proprieties are often nothing more than formulas for slurring over and making more palatable and less coarse and crass the manifestations of the basic facts and attitudes of human relationships. In the *Harvard Business Review*, for example, we read that "man is *not* a volume consumer first and foremost, but rather a sleeper, a singer, a lover, a dancer, an adventurer, a reader, a chatterbox, and a hundred other things at heart." The inference which we are evidently supposed to draw from this conception of *man* is that it does somehow admit that business men should have some regard for the "masses of mankind" in respect to their freedom to sleep, to sing, to love, to dance, to adventure, to read, and to chatter. In the quotation which we have cited, the writer in the *Harvard Busines Review* is paraphrasing Walter B. Pitkin in the latter's book, "The Consumer—His Nature and His Changing Habits," and his own opinion is that Pitkin's "analysis shows that the consumer is a complex person, whose habits the business man may view profitably through the eyes of the psychologist and the philosopher." [23] As long as the masses of mankind continue to be viewed by business men through the eyes of psychologists like John B. Watson and "philosophers" like Walter B. Pitkin, there will be need for man, the consumer, to fight collectively, desperately even, for honest goods and services against the system of salesmanship which approaches *man* as something less than a high-grade moron to be regarded as a source of income and the occasion for the merry sound of cash register bells.

Have you ever given attention to the formulation of the questions which are asked you at the filling station or at the soda fountain of the drug store? These questions are not the casual and improvised-on-the-spur-of-the-moment inquiries that many may think them to be. They are the result of careful experimentation and planning by the boards of strategy in the sales departments. "Shall I fill her up?" was once the accepted way of putting the question to the owner of a car at the filling station.[24] Statistical estimates showed that the question increased sales by 20 to 40 per cent. Embarrassment, it was presumed, would make it difficult to answer "no" to the question. Merely to buy two or three gallons became preposterous, and a social blunder! The boards of selling strategy then went into another conference and came out with the question, "How much will she hold?" This, they figured, would stir the pride of the automobile owner in the capacity of his tank. Sure enough the new formulation added another 10 per cent to the sales.

"Will you have your dessert now or later?" is the advertiser's recommended form of putting the question to a customer who is about to finish a sandwich at the soda fountain.[25] While there may have been no intention of ordering dessert at all, this particular form of the question is believed by the experts in salesmanship to induce a sudden and overpowering dread in the customer's mind of appearing to be so irregular as not to finish his lunch with a sweet. It is claimed, on the basis of statistical tabulation, that few customers hold out against the appeal and stubbornly shatter the high faith of the well-instructed soda clerk in their dietary regularity and, from his boss's point of view, their profitableness. The appeal is said to be almost 100 per cent effective when the customer is accompanied by a guest and has to preserve not only his imputed regularity in the eyes of the salesman but also in the esteem of his guest as well. To the class-conscious consumer, there is another and equally important point in the situation, and that is the long chance that when the dessert comes it will not be fit for human consumption. At a soda fountain almost all of the ingredients, from fruit ice cream to "strawberry" syrup, are likely to be the products of a scientific age which has perfected the art of culinary deception by the use of chemical preservatives, synthetic flavors, and artificial coloring.

A. Stein & Co., maker of *Paris* garters for men, is in a panic over the pronounced tendency of men to dispense with its particular kind of merchandise. The company recently issued a blast, in pamphlet form, to 35,000 executives in the men's clothing and furnishing industry throughout the United States. Is Stein's concerned lest a garterless generation regard not the Constitution with due fetishistic loyalty? Its fears go far deeper than even our divinely inspired Constitution, for the company finds that nudism is a "challenge which barbarism has hurled at civilization." Nudism is a "destructive force—morally, socially, and certainly economically." When the male sex leaves off wearing garters there is evidence that "people's minds have been fertilized with 'Nudist' ideas to such a degree that unconsciously they are ready to yield to the slightest suggestion that one item after another be discarded." [26] What is to be done to save "civilization" from perishing for want of garters? Stein's answer, aside from the pamphlet to the men's clothing merchants, is a full-page advertisement in the *Saturday Evening Post*[27] offering two million able-bodied defenders of civilization their money back if after buying a pair of *Paris* garters they are not altogether pleased with "this sensational new development—Miracle Elastic Paris Garters"—which "will stretch around the waist." Stein's sales appeal to religiosity and the age-old sanctions of a design of garter that may be all of twenty years old is not novel, but it is hardly paralleled in the weird annals of selling for its ludicrously unconcealed economic motive.

Rarely do salesmen miss an opportunity to turn any significant event into a sales appeal, especially if it is conducive to a development of the fear-motive. The general strike in San Francisco has provided the electric refrigeration business with a sales talk on "Preparedness Against the Strike Hazard." "When the ice wagon doesn't come around for days and days," writes the editor of

Electric Refrigeration News, "housewives who still have ice refrigerators are bound to get exasperated." On the other hand,
families "which possess larger-sized electric refrigerators got along
quite comfortably during the strike." Therefore, "the next time
an electric refrigerator salesman comes to one of these [ice refrig-
erator] homes, he will probably find the housewife ready to listen
to his story." [28] But will he tell her of the problems of the electrified home faced by a strike in the electrical power plant?

The "gift" method of selling is an old one. It lures the consumer
into the salesman's snare by creating the illusion of giving something for nothing. In Grand Rapids, Michigan, last year, an electric refrigerator dealer gave a resort lot free with each refrigerator
purchased.[29] Land values in the immediate neighborhood had
dropped to such an extent that the dealer was able to purchase the
lots at a cost of only $3.00 each, but the same size plots at a popu-
lar resort not far away were selling for $150 each. Under the
illusion, which any one or all of the purchasers might have dispelled with some simple inquiries, the public of Grand Rapids
responded in large numbers to the dealer's trick. Soap companies
were reported last year to be "offering everything from baby grand
pianos to life insurance annuities in their sales campaigns." [30]
This was probably an exaggeration, but since the report came from
the trade journal *Soap,* it was indicative of the sort of sales pressure
used to dispose of large stocks "probably made," according to *Soap,*
"in the big rush back in February, March and April to beat the
excise tax." *Westinghouse* and *General Electric* have been trying
out a new method of selling, known as "provocative gifts." [31]
General Electric gave brooms away in the metropolitan area of
New York with the idea of developing new sales contacts from
the blanks filled out by applicants for a free broom, and of exerting
new sales pressures upon the recipients by impressing them with
the drudgery of using the old-fashioned broom in contrast with the
superior performance of a "G-E Three-Feature Vacuum Cleaner."
Westinghouse, in an attitude of pity and condescension toward the
backward users of ice boxes, offered to give away 5,000 *Nuchar*

food savers to women who were still " 'getting along' with an old-fashioned ice box."

Milk *months,* doughnut *weeks,* and hat *days* are a few of the endless procession of special periods set aside as occasions on which to boost special merchandise. The old religious calendars are nothing in the frequency of their special festivals (which also had an economic aspect or sales motive which is usually over-looked by church and laity) compared with the concentrated drives of the sellers of goods to fix public attention upon some item in the diet or wearing apparel of the people. The sanctuaries of the religion of business are the stores, and their high priests are the sellers of gastronomic or other brands of temporal salvation. Under the aegis of the business priesthood, even a creed for the faithful is in process of final formulation. It runs somewhat as follows:

I believe in Business Almighty, author and perfector of Progress;

I believe in General Motors, General Electric, General Foods, and General Johnson;

I believe in Vitamin D, the blessed mother of all irradiated foods and face creams;

I believe in the Sanctity of Patents and pledge my household in everlasting fealty to Super Suds in its fight against the alleged impostor Rinso;

In my rising up I drink one quart of Borden's milk, for this is the will of Governor Lehman, of New York, and in my lying down I eat a dish of Corn Flakes for it induces, says Dr. Laird, of Colgate University, 6 per cent more sleep;

I believe in *Paris* garters and wear them 365 days in the year and 366 days in leap years;

I count my gadgets over, every one apart, keep them burnished and beautiful, and faithfully replenish my supply of them in season and out of season, for only so can goods be moved;

I purify myself for the coming of the autumnal equinox by celebrating September 15th as National Felt Hat Day;

I change my habitat only on May 1st or October 1st for this is profitable to the moving vans and realtors;

I believe that halitosis is better than no breath at all, but when Listerine and Lifebuoy have served their ends and putrefaction overtakes me, I shall confidently entrust my remains to the sanctifying containers of the National Casket Company.

The newest thing in selling tactics is represented by the firm of W. Howard Downey & Associates (Chicago, New York, Atlanta, and Toronto), who provide "Trained Propagandists for Every Purpose." The method of this firm, as described on its form of contract, is to send out propagandists "to perform their duties in units of two (2)," who "shall give out said information to the general public at places designated on the copy, in this or other localities, such as riding in SUBWAY, ELEVATED and RAILROAD TRAINS, STREET CARS, STEAMBOATS, OFFICE or DEPARTMENT STORE BUILDING ELEVATORS, and also attend THEATRES, CONCERTS, PICNICS, FAIRS, BASEBALL and FOOTBALL GAMES and other events and other places of public assemblage." The Downey firm, so far as has been ascertained, operates chiefly in labor disputes in the employ of industrialists who wish to discredit unionism by whispering campaigns among working men and their families. In the nature of the case, it is difficult to track down espionage organizations of this character. It is known, however, that the whispering method in sales campaigns is now taking on unprecedented importance all over the United States. "A Detroit department store used an organization to boost its sales of women's dresses," writes Lionel Houser in the New York *World-Telegram*.[32] "The organization sent out groups of young women in pairs. They rode in elevators in office buildings at rush hours, in street cars, and strolled in theatre lobbies, while one told the other of the bargains at 'X's' store. The store is said to have sold 3,000 dresses the next day." Mr. Houser also declares that "One major advertising agency in New York said frankly that it is carrying out a campaign of verbal propaganda at the present time for one of the largest corporations, makers of a product sold to millions annually." This is a reversion to the primitive way of spreading "news" before the era of printing presses. The paid public conversationalists may not only discuss the bargains to be found at a given store, but may also circulate rumors which are damaging to the competitors of their employer. These campaigns have been much talked about, and noted in trade journals with much fear and mystery, and in most guarded terms, in recent months.

The "whispering propagandists" and their contemptible techniques would suggest, if the business order were already completely dead and not just in a state of accelerated decadence, the maggot-infestation of a corpse. They properly excite grave apprehension, not so much because they represent the depths of scurrility and cowardice to which competition drives the business enterprisers in their "fratricidal" struggles within the capitalistic order, but rather because they may be employed against the forces of intelligent social change whose resources will be seriously taxed in an effort to combat the poisonous campaigns of unseen cowards.

"From various straws in the wind and good hunches," says *Tide*, "department store merchandisers are taking seriously the talk to the effect that there is a huge expansion in the installment business in prospect, and in the not too far distant future." [33] This prospect means the instigation of new social and advertising and governmental pressures upon consumers, with the train of individual and social consequences that inevitably follow a spree of installment and other high pressure selling.

Causes of Bankruptcies Among Consumers is the title of a pamphlet issued by the U. S. Department of Commerce. It is "A Study made in Boston with the cooperation of the Institute of Human Relations and the Law School of Yale University." [34] While calling attention in less prominent portions of the pamphlet's text to the "persuasive methods of high-pressure salesmen" as a factor in the bankruptcies of consumers, the investigators, whitewashing business, as is the standard government practice, place the responsibility wholly upon consumers, in their chart of the major causes of consumer bankruptcies, by designating "extravagance" of consumers as the prime factor in the financial delinquency of consumers. The government and university investigators are clearly guilty of perpetrating a purely subjective accusation against consumers in the name of objective science. In their detailed tables, only "managers and officials" are made to appear relatively free from extravagance; while four categories of "employees" and "laborers" are presented as guilty of extravagance as the first, or a major, cause of their financial delinquency. Another piece of monstrous subjectivism and whitewashing of the really predatory trends in business practice parading under the name of academic scientific investigation! Boys of grammar school intelligence and information know that installment buying under high-pressure tactics ($200 radios and $1,000 cars sold to apartment house janitors!) is what the Institute of Human Relations at Yale gratuitously calls "consumer extravagance."

While the Yale Institute of Human Relations charges consumers with extravagance, salesmen are busy persuading consumers that it is "saving" to buy and "extravagant" to refrain from buying. Thus Mr. Stedman, who has already been quoted as an authority on selling tactics, says: "It is important to capitalize all savings to be gained from product [i.e. refrigerators] use *in a manner that will convince the prospect that she is throwing money away unless she buys.* [Italics ours.] Use a mimeographed form itemizing the types of savings, the national average savings on each and provide a column where the particular prospect's savings can be estimated after talking her individual situation over. Thus you can compare the savings expected with the monthly payments required and can also capitalize the return on the investment over a term of years. This is vital to closing the sale—you must justify the purchase." [35] Mr. Stedman would have salesmen go "armed" with $100 bills to illustrate the housewife's reprehensible waste in *not* buying: "By this type of demonstration you show the prospect what all members of her family are actually losing in convenience, pleasure, and saving. You use a blackboard to compute the prospect's daily, monthly, or yearly loss. This form of demonstration can be made more dramatic if you actually use money (for example, a $100 bill) to dramatize the extended loss, or by dropping change into a can repeatedly to illustrate the constant daily loss." [36]

The importance of correct voice manipulation is stressed in the advice which Gerald E. Stedman offers to ambitious sellers of merchandise. In a passage which deserves to be placed among the archives of business classics, Mr. Stedman says: "Watch the inflection, speed, pronunciation and enunciation of your words. Enrich your expression with a sincerity of tone. Modulate your voice from low to high as you work up to the climax of registering each selling point. If your prospect starts to argue in a high voice, always drop back to a low pitch. An argument is impossible with a soft-spoken opponent. Vary the speed with which you talk from low to rapid as you work up to each climax. Be sure to pronounce your words correctly. Nothing is so aggravating as continual mispronunciation. But if you find the prospect doing so, wilfully follow suit rather than damage her ego by revealing that she has mispronounced a word." [37]

Manufacturers, whose imagery stops at nothing where profits are in sight, are going in for anthropomorphic conceptions of their products. One manufacturer thinks of himself as the proud sire of a new razor blade. When, therefore, Gillette announced "Probak, Jr." in the fall of 1934, hundreds of Western Union boys who delivered packages of the blades to distributors throughout the United States "wore a large lapel badge depicting a stork making delivery of a 'new arrival.' "

Another manufacturer thinks of himself as a parent presenting a daughter débutante to society. Let us take a look at one of those gay occasions when a new refrigerator is introduced to business society. A writer in *Business Week* gives the following account: [38] "A concern has an improved household appliance which must make its début under promising auspices. No fond mother prepares a social send-off more anxiously than do the sales executives of this company. They take a swanky hotel suite in one of the big centers. Engraved invitations go to the trade press, to agents, to distributors, to retailers. On the appointed day, the

new model is the center of interest. No crude, direct selling is
indulged in. The sales force would book an insistent order, but
the real jobs on this occasion are to beam, to answer questions, to
distribute publicity handout and other descriptive literature. Guests
are gently stoked into a state of affection for 'the product' with
food and highballs. Often the scene is beautified by the presence
of girls, symbolizing (dimly) the housewives who must later
decide the fate of débutante."

The advantages which today belong to the seller or salesman in
transactions with consumers constitute the weight of the profit-
making power of business. It is clear, therefore, why business will
not graciously surrender these advantages, and clear also why
any attempt to increase the sales resistance and bargaining power
of consumers sends business into tantrums about the danger of
radicalism undermining "our cherished institutions"; and accounts
for such threats as Mr. Kobak's (see Chapter II) to bring the
American Legion's artillery into the field to suppress an agency
such as Consumers' Research for jeopardizing the ease with which
business takes away consumers' money and bargaining power and
deprives consumers of their critical judgment. It is always the
normal function of the business-state to protect these advantages
against encroachments by consumers. Politics is an equilibrium of
pressures. Where high pressures exist on the business side and low
resistance on the consumers' side, there is a political structure involving the existence of opposing and uneasy classes. The class
which is in possession of the highest pressures is, by virtue of this
political and economic power, the ruling class. The class which is
characterized by low resistance and easy exploitability is the vic-
timizable and the victimized class. Those who stand today in a
consumer's relationship to the supply of goods and services lack
the essentials of political power: information, communication, and
organization. It is the aim of all business methods to preserve the
existing equilibrium of advantage on the seller's side and disad-
vantage on the consumer's. Conversely, it is the aim of the builders of a consumers' society to reverse the existing equilibrium and

weight all advantages heavily on the side of the users of goods and services. A mathematical equalization of bargaining power would result in an impasse and would be pragmatically impossible for more than a passing moment. Both the quantitative and the qualitative improvement of the supply of goods and services wait upon the readjustment of fundamental political power in this manner. Further accentuation of the existing equilibrium of business society already heavily loaded for producers and sellers means political reaction and eventually fascism; readjustment means revolution in purpose, form, relationships, and quality of the entire social structure. *Only when all men stand primarily in the position of consumers with reference to the available goods and services of a society* will it be possible to eliminate class differentiations and advantages, and thereby establish a classless community.

CHAPTER IV

Gadgetry: A Century of Mechanical Comedy

THE TERRIFIC DRIVE FOR SALES—and profits—necessary under competitive distribution has given rise to *gadgetry*. There is no sales talking point like a gadget, and the greater the number of gadgets attached to an article of some rational utility, the greater the number of its sales features. The gadget race has been carried to the most ridiculous extremes, and the end is not yet in sight. The next "century of progress," if there is one, promises to reveal a world under the complete governance of the gadget mind, if indeed this mechanized civilization has not been crowded off the habitable area of the earth by the expanding graveyard of discarded gadgets and Gillette razor blades.

Now and then some member of the business world pauses to bewail the multiplication of these jiggers that are spawned with such amazing fecundity by technology wedded to sales necessity. "A birth control movement should be started," says the editor of *Electrical Merchandising*, "in the electrical appliance industry." [1] "Not that we talk against improvement and development," he observes, "but it occurs to us that when 47 per cent of all advertising in a recent issue of *Electrical Merchandising* is based upon the single word 'new,' we must all be thinking a little too much about gadgetry and a little too little about service." The editor forgets, for the moment, that, in a profit-dominated system, "service" itself is only one more of the *talking points* of the salesman—the bait which conceals the hook, according to one of advertising's most eminent authorities, Claude C. Hopkins, but

78

not an effective contraceptive to reduce the birthrate of gadgets. Mechanical progress has unquestionably taken place under the impulse to outdo sales competitors, but such progress is entirely too helter-skelter to be called rational. Gadgetry nonsense and waste are disproportionately large in the mechanical output of the production and distribution system.

Among the articles advertised in his journal, about which the editor of *Electrical Merchandising* may have been speaking in his citation of the 47 per cent of advertisements based upon the word "new," is the *Lovell Pressure Cleanser*. In the old-fashioned parlance of domestic affairs, this device would have been known as a clothes wringer, and it would never have occurred to the housewife of yesteryear, who had a homely regard for the meaning of words, to attribute to it a "cleansing" function. The author of the advertising copy of the *Lovell* product emphasizes the idea of *newness* (we are not claiming that a wringer is a gadget) as the major element in successful business. "Articles that yesterday were the pride of the home," he says, "are today only sentimental curiosities . . . so rapidly do the needs and preferences of humanity change. Therefore, only through unceasing effort to keep products in step with the times can a successful business be perpetuated." [2]

In the *Thor Electric Servant,* gadgetry approaches the climax of this button, knob, and doo-dad age. "It has so many sparkling, patented and exclusive sales features," says the *Thor* advertisement[3] addressing the distributors, "that you'll go home nights thinking about all the things this table-top washer can do! Think of all the exclusive *sales features* in this one machine!" What are these exclusive sales features? A *Monel* metal top that serves as a buffet— "a place to mix drinks where the varnish won't come off." A utility outlet for the attachment of small kitchen appliances— and, as an overpowering appeal to sweep the most stubborn of domestic sales resisters off her feet, the *Thor Electric Servant* is wired for radio! The thing, we should add, is basically a washing machine. If the manufacturers are contemplating expansion into the Oriental market, we suggest that the *Thor Electric Servant* be equipped with a prayer wheel with induction-motor drive, with a view to civilizing the Tibetans, and translating them more certainly to a mechanical salvation.

One by one the familiar landmarks of living pass into history. The bathroom is undergoing a metamorphosis, that is if General Electric has its way, and is emerging as "the health room." In the All-electric Home maintained by the General Electric Institute at Nela Park in Cleveland, this glorified bathroom (or health room if you will) "provides ultra-violet and infra-red radiation" and "a versatile [sic] lighting system for shaving and the application of cosmetics" among other overpowering sales features.[4] Along this line of the march of progress comes also the "absolutely new" *Neo-Angle* bath tub exhibited by the Standard Sanitary Manufacturing Company at Chicago's recent wonderland of a century of gadgetry.[5]

The *Thor Electric Servant* is not far ahead of the *Estate Electric Range* whose advertisement in an electrical trade journal says: "you can put your finger on fifteen features . . . and sell!" Feature number eight is a "Built-in Radio."[6] Now you can get the World Series on the washing machine, if you own a *Thor Electric Servant;* or hot tips on the stock market will come to you right off your own cooking stove if you have purchased it from the *Estate*.

The number of contraptions that have been thought up by bright technicians is so large that many volumes would be required for their listing with the briefest possible descriptions. We venture to name a few of the very latest.

"Family peace is promoted by a new bed lamp which has two bulbs," we read in *Nation's Business* for September, "so divided under the shade that they give light to both bed occupants, or light to one and darkness to the other."[7] So far, so good, but what about the mental concentration of the studious half of the family, if the other half on the darkened side of the bed snores? Is there no Snore Extinguisher with Duochrome Sea Shell Inlay?

Again quoting from *Nation's Business:* "Those who don't like to come home to a dark house are offered a new floor lamp having a timing device which turns the light on (or off) automatically at any desired time. It's so built that it can be connected to actuate the radio." [8] We can think of a wholly untapped market for a gadget that would turn the radio off after the first word of every piece of trade puffery that advertisers send across the ether. The possibilities here are commercially and culturally intriguing, and may be the saving of a civilization, if it is yet salvable.

A literal minded inventor of gadgets has just patented a "sucker" (the gadget, not the user) which may be jammed into citrus fruits without bothering to peel them and through which the juice of the fruit may be drained with the combined pressure of massaging and sucking. This treasure is described and pictured in the *Food Field Reporter*.[9]

There is simply no end, except the limit of the wildest imagination's reach, to the things that the gadget makers will promise. Imagine for a moment a homely girl (and it can be safely assumed that there are plenty of them in the vicinity of SAKS at 34th and Broadway) haunted with the idea of her homeliness after having spent a large part of her life listening to the advertising beautifiers point the way to romance with this soap or that lipstick or the other tooth paste. She has used *Camay, Tangee,* and *Colgate's Ribbon Dental Cream,* and yet romance has tarried in spite of all their not too subtle hints that it could be found by applying something to the skin, the lips, or the teeth. Discouraged, perhaps, but with hope springing anew at every piece of advertising ballyhoo, she picks up a copy of the New York *Times* ("All the news that's fit to print"—nothing said about the advertisements) and there before her wistful eyes is the picture of something new in beauty promises. It is the *Youth-O-lator* sold by *the New SAKS* for $7.00 —one day only at this price and then this *"beauty wand creating beauty from within by means of invisible rays . . . complete with irradiated oil"* will cost her $10.00. [Italics ours.] The *Youth-O-lator,* she is told, "has virtually swept the country by storm" and "has been acclaimed by famous beauty authorities everywhere." [10]

The New SAKS is one of the largest and most reliable department stores, she may reason to herself, and the New York *Times*
is impeccably discriminating in its news and advertisements. She
buys the *Youth-O-lator* at a considerable sacrifice and . . . but
there is no need to labor the obvious. There are some gadgets that
only amuse; others arouse a fleeting curiosity; this beauty gadget
should beget some old-fashioned indignation at its palpably misleading claims. If there were justice in the world of business, it
would bring a squad of police.

The memory of this generation runs back to the days when
there was employed, with good effect, the political slogan, "two
cars in every garage." Today, the drive is for *a radio in every
room!* The slogan originates in the sales departments of the power
companies and the radio monopoly. The Pacific Coast Electric
Bureau offers the following counsel for the solution of the terrific
cultural conflict allegedly found in every home: "This demand
for different types of radio entertainment exists right within a
single household. The answer is: *'personal' sets*—in the nursery,
kitchen, bedroom, den—each room in the house. . . ." A leaflet
sent to the members of the industry "suggests that you talk about
'a set for every room.' " [11]

At least one house in America has almost, though not quite,
attained the suggested standard in the number of radios. Not only
that, but it has pushed far out in the true American pioneering
spirit with the installation of an average of seven electric gadgets
per room.[12] Oddly enough, this house is in Schenectady, New
York, and the appliances are mostly G-E. The bathroom has an
electric "vaporizer for inhaling medicated vapor." The dining
room is equipped, among other things, with an electric "egg
scrambler." The garden, which was not forgotten, has an "electrostatic bug killer" threatening intruding insects, an "electric lawn
mower" and an "electric hedge trimmer." For some reason, not
stated, the bathroom and the basement are not furnished with
radios. The circular which describes this amazing collection of
gadgets is introduced with the caption, "Modernization Promotes

Beauty and Order." Believe it or not, the owner of this house is one Ripley, not the cartoonist, but certainly the ranking G-E caricaturist. A not impertinent question is: Who paid for the 80-odd electric contraptions in this caricature of a residence?

Mr. Ripley's "electrostatic bug killer" has nothing on the "Electric Worm Getter"! The *worm-getter,* or *charmer* as it is also called, is described and pictured in *The Electric Home*—a volume by E. S. Lincoln. The *getter* or *charmer* consists of two metal rods (electrodes) with attachments for current. These are stuck in the ground a few feet apart, and electric current is then turned on. An electrified zone is created in the ground between the electrodes; and any worms that may be in that area get a shock which sends them hurrying for the surface. Fishermen and poultrymen, it is believed, will be in the market for these *worm-getters.*[13]

The "Century of Progress" at Chicago, aptly described as "a veritable Roman Holiday of salesmanship,"[14] had among its exhibits a Frigidaire air-conditioned house equipped with a "multitude of devices."[15] Windows were opened by the pressing of buttons. Other buttons raised or lowered the bed to give sleeping, reading, or eating positions; turned the "cold" on or off, and opened or closed the doors, to mention only a few of the things which buttons promise to do for future man. The device which carries all of these push buttons is appropriately named the "Lazy Bug." It rests on a night table alongside the bed. This is the kind of domicile that hard-pressed salesmen lie awake nights thinking up with the hope of making "our groggy capitalistic system" steady on its feet once more.

There is, in fact, arising a school of recovery preaching the gospel of economic salvation by gadgetry. According to the editor of *Electric Refrigeration News,*[16] the nation is now faced with a choice between (1) Fascism, (2) Communism, (3) the New Deal, and (4) Air-Conditioning; and he, of course, favors the adoption of the last-named road to salvation. Quoting Professor Walter J. Shepherd, of Ohio State University, to the effect that we wait for a miracle in the form of a "sudden revival of industry through the invention of some machine which will become an immediate necessity in every American home," the alert editor offers "air-conditioning" as fulfilling the specifications for the miracle. "Air-conditioning," he says, "may well be the shot-in-the-arm which our groggy capitalistic system needs." Such a miracle would perform the double function of (1) "enabling a manufacturer to obtain his share of a magnificent waiting market," and (2) "of preserving the guarantees of freedom and liberty contained in our now apparently *passé* Constitution"—that is, of protecting us against the perils of fascism, communism, and the New Deal. "Without any doubt," says R. E. Hellmund, chief engineer of the Westinghouse Electric & Manufacturing Company, itself no mean maker of gadgets, "air-conditioning has *unlimited* possibilities both as a potential business for the manufacturers and as a load builder for the utilities." [17]

Among the potential markets for air-conditioning mentioned by Mr. Hellmund, there are, of course, not only the 20,000,000 homes of the land, but also "restaurants, barber shops, stores, mortuaries and many others." Why omit to mention specifically, Mr. Hellmund, the jails and penitentiaries—home of at least one of the utilities magnates today? As for the mortuaries, there is sure to be a protest from the Society for the Prevention of Premature Burials, in London, which not long since proposed steam-heated morgues for the allegedly deceased until all doubt was removed as to the possibility of their resuscitation.

Electric Refrigeration News hails Alfred P. Sloan, Jr., president of General Motors, as a convert to the theory of recovery through air-conditioning.[18] Writing in the *Atlantic Monthly* of September, 1934, Mr. Sloan declared that the home of tomorrow "will have all modern conveniences for reducing housework, on a scale and of a variety not surpassed in the costliest mansions of the day." Furthermore, "its equipment," Mr. Sloan predicts, "will include special devices for bringing instruction and recreation into the home—the teletype for news dispatches, television apparatus to portray the world's great events as they occur, and radio sets embodying visual projection, so that motion pictures and operas can be brought directly to the view of the home circle." [19] There is at least one thing wrong with Mr. Sloan's picture of this paradisiacal domestic gadgetry, and that is the lack of assurance that the air-filtering system of the air-conditioning plant will keep out the putrid, toxic, and rancid sales stuff that now enters in culturally lethal quantities.

For the moment at least there is the little matter of inadequate purchasing power that deters a gadget-minded people from installing the air-conditioning apparatus and the multitude of devices that are promised to perfect our comfort and culture. The young men on duty at the "Air-Conditioned House" at the Century of Progress informed inquirers that the cost of installation of airconditioning alone is approximately $400 a room, and that operation costs for the entire house are about $15 a month.[20] This sounds like the heaven-sent answer to the power companies' prayer for an ideal "load builder"! Of course, there is always the possibility of bringing back the good old days of installment (a kind of financial slot machine) prosperity by furnishing homes with the apparatus "free of charge" and attaching a slot machine for "pay-as-you-cool" purposes. David Lawrence's *United States News,* speaking of slot machines, announces that the "latest of the coin devices is the home air-conditioner, which either warms or chills the house for the small sum of one dime or maybe a quarter." [21] The banks should be glad to finance outright purchase by home owners at 9.72 per cent interest rates which they are now obtaining on loans under the home improvements scheme of the New Deal.

The YMCA Schools of New York have already demonstrated their faith in the bright future of this plan of terrestrial salvation by "starting a new course in Air-Conditioning, which will cover the technical principles, approached from the physiological point of view of how to make human beings more comfortable." [22]

The Young Men's Comfortable Association can be counted on to do its part in hastening recovery for the utilities and the gadget makers.

A recent discovery related to air-conditioning holds out a bright future for the food industries in discouraging a heat-stricken populace from sketchy lunches and small meal checks. *Business Week* reports "a radical change in eating habits of passengers riding on air-conditioned trains of the Pennsylvania during the unusual heat this past summer. . . . Sketchy lunches of salads, sandwiches, and iced drinks were crowded out by steak dinners, full course meals, pastries, hot soups, tea, and coffee. The average meal check jumped well ahead of previous summer levels." [23]

Gadgetry is admittedly a device of the private profit-makers. There is at least one man *on record* in the United States who objects strenuously to the fact that he has not been set upon by sales-eager gadget vendors. He lives in a town with a municipally owned light-plant, and under all such socialistic monstrosities business falls into stagnation; wherefore let all who lay up hope for recovery born of gadgetry "give thanks . . . that *95 per cent of the electric industry in this country is privately owned.*" [24] This exhortation is directed to the readers of *Public Utilities Fortnightly* (an Owen D. Young publication) by Neil M. Clark, the aforesaid denizen of the town from which private ownership of the light-plant has been banished. "For in the sixteen years I have lived here," says Mr. Clark, "neither I nor any member of my family has been approached a single time, as far as we can recall, with any suggestion on the part of the village light-plant management that we ought to have an electric refrigerator, or an electric range, or a few more electric clocks, or any other electric gadgets whatsoever. The village sells such equipment. Come and get it if you want it. But the only intensive selling campaigns we have experienced have been those aimed at us by outsiders. Perhaps we would be using half again as much electricity if we had been urged." [25]

Mr. Clark's testimony (given unwittingly, perhaps) is important confirmation of the view that *greater* individualism in consumers' choices is to be expected under a system from which private profit has been banished. Under the terrific economic pressure of the pursuit of private profit, consumers are wheedled into the use of twice as much electric current as they consider necessary when left to their own individual choices, not to mention the purchase of the "multitude of devices" that consume it. If this is so in the case of a man like Mr. Clark, it must be emphatically true for millions of less sophisticated buyers. Compulsion and regimentation in the most important function of consumption are, on the testimony of Mr. Clark, found *only* under a system of privately owned industry.

Predictions of recovery based on a sudden revival through the mass production and distribution of a new gadget are predicated upon the national economic experiences which followed upon the automobile and radio booms. One half of all household electrical appliances are customarily sold on the installment plan, the installment sales of radio sets running as high as 75 per cent of the total. In 1929, retail installment sales rose to a grand total of $7,000,000,000, one-half of which amount was used to purchase automobiles.[26] It is not impossible perhaps for high-pressure salesmanship to market a few billion dollars' worth of air-conditioning equipment on the installment plan in the next year or two. If it turns this trick by the fall of 1936, or is well on the way to turning it by that time, it will guarantee the reëlection of Franklin D. Roosevelt. But by now it should be manifest to everyone that a gadgetry boom is a spurious prosperity from which the bottom must inevitably fall out with a bang. With the prevailing character of economic intelligence guiding national affairs in industry, finance, and politics, even such manifest bastardy in prosperity is no deterrent from deliberately pursuing the course. Its beneficiaries are willing now, as they have always been, to risk a future crash of any proportions. To accomplish with accelerated speed another dizzying swing of the economic cycle, a nation of bigger and better gadgeteers and button-pushers is ideally suited. After that, a cycle-weary people may decide to order its economic progress without benefit of gadgetry and its promoters of wonder-houses and "health rooms."

CHAPTER V

Confederates of Screen, Stadium, and Salon

At first glance testimonial advertising may be a puzzling phenomenon. What possible relevancy can there be in the fact that Mrs. James Russell Lowell and Mr. Ellsworth Vines smoke *Camel* cigarettes? [1] Why should anyone care to know that Carole Lombard uses Max Factor's *Super-Indelible Vermilion Lipstick*, [2] or that Loretta Young and Ginger Rogers lave themselves in the suds of *Lux* toilet soap? [3] Claudette Colbert eats bread three times a day. [4] Really? The depression must be over. Is there any useful information in knowing that Lady Cecil Douglas, from the land of lords and ladies, took part in *Woodbury's* Beauty Test? [5] What does it matter to millions of American women that Mrs. Victor du Pont III applies *Pond's Vanishing Cream* to her face regularly, [6] or that Mrs. Reginald Vanderbilt uses *Pond's Cold Cream* on her "lovely magnolia skin"? [7] Is it worth any stranger's while to learn that Ethel Barrymore and Mrs. Howard Chandler Christy use *Cutex* on their finger nails? [8] What earthly connection is there between Admiral Byrd, at either pole, and *Grape-Nuts?* [9] If Mrs. Franklin D. Roosevelt likes *Berkey & Gay* furniture [10] should all the world know it? Why shout from the housetop that Yale's All-Eastern tackle, Pierre Bouscareu, has an *Elgin* watch and an *Elgin* tradition in his family? [11] Or broadcast that West Point's star halfback, Cadet Cagle, owned, back in the days of his fleeting fame, a *Royal Portable* typewriter? [12] Has it anything to do with refrigeration that Verna Hillie of Hollywood can pose, gracefully clad in negligee, inside a *Norge* refrigerator? [13] These and a thousand other such questions pose the problem of the relevancy in ascribing the uses of these articles of trade to such a galaxy of the great and near-great.

The most unsophisticated reader of the ads knows that the purpose of all testimonializing is to increase sales. If he has gone a little further in his economic education, he may appreciate some of the increasing difficulties in moving goods, where their distribution is plainly obstructed by growing competition on the one hand and the decreasing buying power of users on the other hand. New strategies are constantly necessary in order to outdo sales competitors in bidding for a deliberately restricted market of consumers. Every known social force is sooner or later drafted to do its bit to keep goods from remaining on store shelves or in manufacturers' warehouses. Testimonial advertising of the kind we have indicated is the utilization of one such social force: the power of social prestige to stimulate imitation and emulation.

Testimonial advertisers have hit, quite by accident, upon some profound psycho-cultural secrets of which they probably know nothing in the historical sense. They are the secrets of magic and idolatry which have been utilized by the shamans and witch-doctors of all primitive societies. Men and women, so long as they remain at the primitive levels of idolatry, *strive incessantly to re-create themselves in the image of their idols.* Find an idolater's true idol, and you can measure his aspirations by reference to the qualities of his idol, qualities which may be either real or putative.

Your idol smokes *Camel* cigarettes; you must smoke them, too, and thereby enjoy the similitude of social station. Your idol uses *Lux* toilet soap in her bath; you must also use it, for it helps you to reject the testimony of the mirror to your homeliness (the advertiser says "your loveliness"). Your idol applies *Pond's Vanishing Cream* to her face; you must use *Pond's,* for it is the badge of the social registerites and places you on an equal social footing in this respect at least. Your idol writes his sermons with a *Waterman* fountain pen; you must have a *Waterman* and thereby simulate his verbal wizardry. Thus by the myriad imitations of consumption you will eventually and magically re-create yourself in the image of your idols. Identified at a hundred little points with the consuming habits of the socially select, you, though perhaps a tenement dweller, may even in your fancy be mistaken for a resident of some highly exclusive neighborhood.

Idol-making has always been a profitable enterprise, whether in the early stage of the cruder arts or in the later periods of refinement of form and color. Idol-making was once a handicraft enterprise in which the more grotesque the idol the more excellently it served as an object of veneration, as a visit to any museum will readily disclose. In the Age of Halitosis, idol-making has become a fine art and a major industry employing all the latest in technology and terminology. No more of the grotesque in modern idolatry; the gargoyle features have been removed from the exteriors at least. Far be it from us to enter into a discussion of the inner spiritual meanings of the newest creations of idolatry.

Every civilization throws up its own peculiar objects of authoritarian veneration. In England the standard testimonial is to say: "Caterers by Appointment to their Majesties the King and Queen." That "the king can do no wrong" is an ancient maxim; and, by deduction, he is the symbol of all that is correct in consumption. If he were to go in for garlic, garlic would in a twinkling become reputable.

America has no king, not at least of the crowned variety, but it has a ruling class which demands flattery; and the supreme flattery has always been that of imitation by commoners. The imitation, however, must not extend to all subjects, but must be confined to the little marginal trivialities where imitation is good for business, and proper social distinctions are held to without encroachments upon class prerogatives and power.

The prime requisite for an American idol is that of "success." Since the American economy is one of business pure and simple without any vestigial relics of royalty from the days of feudalism, "success" is entirely a matter of acquiring great sums of money;

or, at least, those who are most acquisitive are adjudged pre-
eminently "successful." It follows naturally that the highest-priced
idols are made of the plutocracy of wealth, and the cash value
of testimonials is determined by ranking in this plutocracy. Thus
a Vanderbilt testimonial commands $2,000, while a Mrs. Franklin
Roosevelt testimonial has brought only half as much. No Holly·
wood testimonial ever brought $2,000, but a Hollywood star in
addition to being successful in terms of money-accumulation is
also invested with the illusory glamor of synthetic, exhibition-
istic romance. The impulse for romance is deep-seated, in spite
of its tawdry counterfeits in filmdom, and that impulse can be
made to yield its business profit value in a system of "idolatrous"
consumption. The film star represents in his fashion (like
Cynara's lover) the almost universal dream of romance. Ancient
cultures depicted love in terms of great loyalties like that which
was alleged to exist between Ruth and Naomi. In the Era of
Filmdom, Rudolph Valentino becomes the Great Lover. Screen
lovers, therefore, stand next to the authentic rich in their testimonial value, having a combination of large income and exhibi-
tionary romance. Football heroes, transatlantic aviators and
channel swimmers, and Arctic explorers all but complete the
galaxy of the great ones whose little idiosyncrasies of the boudoir
are as private as the lives of goldfish, and are to be imitated by
all who aspire to social importance. In sharing these details of
the private lives of the great, immense satisfactions are to be
derived for the idolaters, and much profit accrues to the caterers
to vicarious greatness. "Now you may share the luxury of the
personal make-up for Carole Lombard and the host of other
Hollywood stars," is the adroit way in which an advertisement
puts the matter in a half dozen of the leading women's
magazines.[14]

The shamans of Polynesia had a theory of magic that "like
begets like," as Jevons and others have pointed out. Their pre-
scientific minds grasped the connection between the rains and the

winds. When, therefore, a heat-prostrated people desired rain, it was the practice of the shamans to simulate wind by the waving of a pitiful little rag on the end of a stick. Rain always came— eventually; and magic had its pragmatic justification. Many a department store girl working for $14 a week is today simulating the Park Avenue heiress, the Broadway actress, or the Hollywood star by using the toilet soap, the face cream, or the lipstick specified by the witchdoctors of American business, in the hope that like will beget like; but the pragmatic justification will be a long time coming, and mostly, it will never come.

Little the admiring crowds care for the utter irrelevancy involved in the star's endorsement of a certain brand of toilet soap or the social registerite's commendation of so-and-so's furniture. To be in the limelight is to possess an authority which extends to fields far beyond the range of any performance or behavior which may have placed the hero and the heroine high in the popular esteem. This authority has its cash value and business men came finally to see it. Consummate ignorance in the testimonializer of the recommended article is no disqualifying circumstance. In some cases the testimonializer may never have seen or used the commended object. All this is beside the point and of no consequence to those who must, whatever the facts may be, adapt words and pictures to the disposal of goods in this highly competitive market.

Camel cigarettes recently pictured in its advertisements the tennis celebrity, Ellsworth Vines, holding a *Camel* in his hand. But, in an interview published in *The Open Road for Boys,* Vines said: "I don't smoke except, perhaps, that once in four or five months I may have a pipe of tobacco, or a cigar at some dinner. . . ." The son of one of the managers of the Packard Motor Car Company discovered this discrepancy in Vines' "Boy Scout" and business testimonials.[15] It must have been as shocking to the lad as learning that there is no Santa Claus. It must not be expected, however, that the advertisers, who do not stop at far more serious breaches of consumer confidence, will have a mind for such inconsequential details as the evidence that Vines did not smoke cigarettes at all. Vines is a star on the tennis court and in these days when athletic prowess may or may not be highly publicized by the owners of the publicity-techniques, according as the successful athlete is amenable to business wishes, he easily becomes a businesslike force for increasing the sales of cigarettes, no matter what his private habits may be in such matters. If he doesn't get one kind of "lift" with a *Camel,* he may avail himself of another—a real one.

An athlete of other years bemoans the fact that he clipped the quarter-mile dash in 53 seconds before the days of the *Camel* "lift." "Why, oh why, didn't I live in this enlightened age," is the wail of C. E. T. Scharps, "when I was trying to be a quarter-miler? I never smoked or drank, and all I had to quit to go in training was apple pie. If I only had known what the Camel people know! *We* thought, ninnies that we were, that smoking was bad for the wind. How dull." [16]

Testimonial advertising is not old, but its origins are nevertheless difficult to trace with certainty. It appears to be a post-War business idea originally conceived by the makers of *Corona* typewriters who used the testimonials of war correspondents. Shortly after this practice of obtaining recommendations of war writers, the *Corona* firm turned to sports writers for their copy, and secured the endorsement of Jack Lawrence, into whose *Corona* typewriter the giant Firpo sent Jack Dempsey, himself of no mean stature, sprawling from the ring. Lawrence declared that his machine ran better than ever after he disentangled Dempsey from the keyboard. [17]

Royal Portable immediately picked up the endorsement of an allegedly stellar student at West Point who had gained fame as halfback on the Cadets' football team. "I wouldn't be without my *Royal Portable,*" averred Cadet Cagle. "It's the greatest aid in keeping up my grades—and you know army grades." Unfortunately, the grades of West Pointers are published, and some malicious busybody (it is not of record that an Annapolis Middy found sweet revenge in this exposure) looked up Cadet Cagle's grades just to see how well *Royal Portable* helped him to keep up. Page 49 of the Official Register of Officers and Cadets told a shocking story. In a class of 266 men, Cadet Cagle, with the aid of his *Royal Portable,* held doggedly to position number 207 in scholastic attainments, with the following record: 232nd in Mathematics; 207th in English; 237th in French; 239th in History; 211th in Drawing; 212th in Tactics; 122nd in Conduct.[18] But for his unusually good standing in Conduct and the aid of his *Royal Portable,* Cadet Cagle might have occupied the unique position of 266th man in his class.

Biographers and testimonial-solicitors failed grievously to get together in the case of Cadet Cagle, but after all there are relativities in scholarship, as we have tried to point out in the case of West Point's star halfback. In the case of *Old Gold* cigarettes and James Cagney, screen star, no slight degree of reconciliation between biographer and testimonial-solicitor is possible. Biography and testimonial are in absolute and irreconcilable contradiction. *Advertising & Selling* cites the following unfortunate disparity between them:

"One of the New York newspapers afforded a distressing incident lately. In one issue was the Old Gold ad in which the tough Mr. James Cagney winked at the universe and said there was nothing tough about his throat, and that's why he smoked O. G.'s. And next day in the Hollywood correspondence was an innocent little piece about Mister Cagney, which said he wasn't tough at all, and among other things, didn't smoke! You just can't avoid these typographical errors!"[19]

Alva Johnston has recorded the epic of the testimonial industry in the story of Constance Talmadge who posed for 400 testimonial photographs in one day. "Where many advertised articles were engaged in cut-throat competition with one another,

she endorsed the whole field," Johnston states in his very revealing narrative; "she posed, for instance, showing a set of fine
white teeth due to the exclusive use of Pepsodent, Iodent, Koly-
nos, Dentyne, Ipana, Squibb's, Lyon's, Colgate's or Pebeco, according to business arrangements to be worked out later; she
faced the camera drinking a cup of coffee which was Maxwell
House, Hotel Astor, Yuban, Alice Foote McDougall, Kaffee
Hag, Sanka or whatever brand might come to terms with her
manager, Emil Jensen." As Miss Talmadge embarked for
Europe immediately after the gruelling ordeal of 400 poses,
Jensen busied himself selling her photographic testimonials to
the advertising agencies of as many products. The results, Mr.
Johnston writes, were as follows: "In *Liberty* of October 29,
1927, the star appeared being roused from sleep by an Ansonia
alarm clock, wearing a Benrus wrist watch, demonstrating a
Thorens Sure-Fire cigarette lighter, flashing Dentyne whitened
teeth, using Gold Seal tubes in her radio and Air Container
inner tubes on her car, keeping slim by Marmola and displaying
a Juliet Wedding Ring." [20]

Soap, a trade journal of the industry, announces a coming
campaign of *Colgate's Ribbon Dental Cream.* " 'Brighter smiles'
is to be the keynote of the campaign which will spotlight the
testimony of Hollywood directors, beauty experts, psychologists
and chemists to demonstrate that white teeth are the first essential of beauty. Colgate's 'Seven Stain' story will be stressed." [21]

Boston, New York, Philadelphia, Chicago and Richmond
social circles are giving *Camels* a "lift" at present. The Lowells,
the Coolidges (there are Coolidges and Coolidges, remember),
and the Cabots, cream of the oldest New England tradition,
express their emphatic and distinguished preference for the
"costlier tobaccos" of *Camels.* The Cabots, who, according to a
legend once current, were on speaking terms with God only (or
was it the Lowells?), have now included the sales department
of R. J. Reynolds Tobacco Company in their privileged circle
of conversationalists.[22]

For testimonializing in behalf of *Berkey & Gay,* makers of exclusive furniture, in 1930, Mrs. Graham Fair Vanderbilt received $2,000, Mrs. J. Borden Harriman $1,000, Mrs. Franklin D. Roosevelt $1,000, and Mrs. A. J. Drexel Biddle $750. The amounts of these testimonial retainers were disclosed in 1933 when the Federal Trade Commission had *Berkey & Gay* on the carpet for unfair practices.[23]

When these distinguished ladies are a bit reticent in meeting the representatives of advertising agencies who are soliciting their testimonials, it is sometimes necessary to make indirect approaches through their social secretaries or less exclusive friends, in which case the ad-men have been compelled to pay two ways. In the hearings of the Federal Trade Commission against *Cutex* (made by the Northam Warren Corporation and advertised by the J. Walter Thompson Company), it was disclosed that Mrs. Howard Chandler Christy received $500 for the following bit: "My hands can meet even my husband's critical artist's eyes." But there went also to Miss Lassie Honeyman "a personal friend of Mrs. Christy for services in helping to secure the said testimonial from Mrs. Christy, the sum of $150." Ethel Barrymore and Anna Pavlowa were recipients of $1,000 and $500 respectively for attributing some of their stage impressiveness to the use of *Cutex.*[24]

In 1933, *Liberty* magazine obtained statements from a host of distinguished liberals, intellectuals and near-intellectuals (a class whom Heywood Broun recently described as willing to sell out *their* side for nothing) which formed the basis of an extensive advertising campaign in other periodicals. Thus in *Time,* in a *Liberty* advertisement, Professor Ellsworth Faris, of the University of Chicago, was quoted as saying in response to the solicitation of the editors of *Liberty:* "There is no question of the influence and importance to be exerted by an aggressive liberal magazine that can be widely read." [25] The innocent professor, while not directly endorsing this most reactionary weekly of the day, nevertheless permitted *Liberty* to quote his remarks in such a manner as to convey the magazine's desired impression. Professor Woodbridge Riley, of Vassar College, similarly appeared in one of *Liberty's* advertisements declaring that "a liberal periodical with a forward looking program is much needed in this country." [26] At the very time these professors and other liberals were walking into *Liberty's* trap, the notorious weekly of Bernarr MacFadden was running some of the red-baiting stuff of George Sylvester Viereck who, as was later disclosed, was in the pay of Hitler's Nazis for just such propagandistic anti-liberal purposes in this country. [27]

A testimonial by a distinguished clergyman had telling repercussions according to reports of the recent biennial gathering of the Congregational Church. S. Parkes Cadman was slated to become the moderator of this distinguished body of ecclesiastical liberals when someone unearthed and circulated in the convention a picture of this eloquent divine attributing, with his customary profuseness of language, special thought-stimulating qualities to the *Waterman* fountain pen, of which he had six before him on his desk and one in his hand. The clergymen had the grace to put Dr. Cadman aside and elect another to the post of moderator. There was still open, however, the position of honorary moderator, occupied since its creation only by Calvin Coolidge, and to this Dr. Cadman was elevated where he could "be seen but not heard." [28]

General Mills, Inc., is now engaged in a nation-wide campaign to encourage bread-eating under the direction of Betty Crocker. In an elaborately made-up booklet entitled "109 Smart New Ways to Serve Bread," Miss Crocker sets out to smash the "Hollywood libel," which had it that bread did not make for slender figures. You should hear the Hollywood stars rave about bread! "I always eat some bread at every meal," says Mary Astor. "No meal is ever complete without bread. I eat plenty of it," declares Ann Dvorak. "I enjoy all kinds of bread," writes Sylvia Sidney to Miss Crocker. "I love bread—always eat it in some form, three times a day," vows Claudette Colbert. There! the libel is smashed, pulverized, "shot from guns" if you please, never to be reinstated where veracity is honored, and General Mills, Inc., is now prepared to introduce you to 109 ways of serving bread—*smart* ways, too.[29]

In a proposed NRA Code for Advertising (which was, significantly enough, never adopted) there was a provision which expressly forbade the use of testimonials "which do not reflect the real choice of a competent witness."[30] Advertisers have been shrewd to observe that, even if serious restrictions are embodied in codes, the NRA is a "lenient taskmaster."[31]

Not all testimonializers are paid in cash for their services. But there are more ways of paying for what the advertisers want than by the use of the currency. Actresses, athletes, and social registerites are not averse to the advertising which they themselves receive by means of the unpaid-for testimonial ad in which they are pictured in all their coiffured loveliness or muscular prowess or Grover Whalen mustache, where millions may look upon them and remember their names. Box-office receipts, among other considerations, are not to be forgotten in this best of all vulgarized worlds. Drawing power and salary are sustained by frequent mention of the actor's name, even if only in a testimonial ad for a cigarette which the actor does *not* smoke. Or what if the social registerite, more delicate than a mere actress, must forego the conscience-elevating practice of turning over to charity a check for $1,000—or whatever amount the name and fame and photo of the social luminary is reckoned to be worth in the currency? It has been a common practice for the socially élite testimonializers to present the advertiser's check to the Salvation Army or some other benefactor of the poor—a form of ostentatious alms-giving which in itself yielded satisfactions that were beyond reckoning in terms of the coin of the Republic.

So, testimonials continue.

Goods are moved.

The idolatrous multitudes are fashioned by their consuming habits and, above all, by their spendings into tawdry little resemblances to the idols of their choosing.

Science, stern iconoclast (when not bought and paid for), waits to guide the consuming habits of a people that learns to look with scorn upon the imbecilic irrelevancies of *who-uses-what*. The answer of science, translated out of its polite reserve, reads very much like: Who the hell cares?

CHAPTER VI

Science Lends a Hand

"SCIENCE" is the most awe-inspiring and latterly the most profitable superstition of capitalist society. It possesses a potency in the folk-ways such as was never known in the horse shoe or the rabbit's foot. On its say-so millions will cheerfully swallow useless, deleterious, or toxic substances with a faith as serene as that of any Hindu who ever walked on beds of burning coals. If only the "scientist" directs it, they will cover themselves from scalp to between-the-toes with secret and quite likely dangerous compounds of drugs and chemicals. A more fearsome authority issues from a modern "scientist's" laboratory than ever came out of the Council of Trent. The theocratic sanctions of Jonathan Edwards never made sinners tremble and desire to flee the "wrath to come" with anything like the corresponding effectiveness that accompanies the "scientist's" offer of chemical salvation from "crepy skin," "paralyzed pores," "bromidosis," "gingivitis," "seven stains," "pyorrhea," "psoriasis," and "halitosis"—for being guilty of any one of which modern man is made to fear excommunication from the community of his friends and relatives.

The new superstition of "science" makes for happier, more unrepressed personalities. It is emphatically not the kill-joy of the old theocratic superstition that spread gloom and produced unadjusted and unhappy saints. The new ideal, than which aspiration can reach no higher, is to be the "life of the party." To this end "science" works endlessly in providing all the necessary *aids to dissipation*. The whole complexion of life, accordingly, has changed, thanks to "science."

The new situation is nowhere so well illustrated as in the use of cigarettes. The social proprieties (or the moral codes as they are sometimes called) have established speed records that make the 400-mile-an-hour achievements of the airplane look like mere loitering in space. Less than ten years ago, the "smoking woman" belonged in one or another of the categories outside the pale of respectability. If our researches are correct, no advertisement would have dared to fly in the face of the accepted mores in the far-off early twenties, by picturing a woman smoking a cigarette. All that is changed, utterly changed. Eminent scientists and college professors have been at work. When cigarettes first became popular in this country, they were commonly referred to as "coffin nails"—ignorant savages we were, that knew nothing of the power of nicotine to stimulate the adrenal glands and release fresh supplies of sugar into the blood where it is burned in the form of energy, all-night energy that will keep the smoker "lifted" through a twelve-hour round of what was once called "dissipation." Right here before us in the *New Yorker*[1] (it might be in any one of dozens of other magazines) is a full length picture of Miss Mimi Richardson "who was voted the most popular débutante of the season." In a Bergdorf-Goodman gown of golden beige satin and a full-length quilted wrap, Miss Richardson holds a *Camel* cigarette, holds it "scientifically," too, and says: "Keeping on the go is easy now. I can *dance all night long* and never feel tired if I smoke a Camel now and then." [Italics ours.] Débutanting, it is declared, is one continual round of luncheons, teas, dinners, dances—through which a débutante must be gay, vivacious, at her best at all times.

Some of the other aids to dissipation which "science" has helpfully brought to the assistance of those who would otherwise pay in headaches and depressed vitality for their strenuous efforts at sociability or "charm" are: (1) "Bromo-Seltzer has been a standby for over forty years, for 'morning-after' loginess."[2] (The acetanilid in Bromo-Seltzer is a habit-forming drug[3] and the product is a dangerous one, the advertisements to the contrary notwithstanding.) (2) Alka-Seltzer makes possible not only "over-indulgence in alcoholic beverages" but also claims to neutralize *nicodosis* or "over-indulgence in tobacco." [4] (3) *Lith-A-Limes,* carrying the seal of *Good Housekeeping* magazine, presents the picture of an anonymous girl who looks the perfection of demureness and propriety but who declares: "I was indiscreet last night. The party was so gay. I was carried away by its lively spirit. But this morning I felt fine." The secret was that a thoughtful hostess "mixed the drinks with Lith-A-Limes exclusively." [5] (4) Or if you only wish to gorge your stomach with food, the secret of no-after-effects is disclosed in an advertisement in *Delineator.* "Once a party like that—with a big meal," says the dissipator, "would have given me heartburn, probably lasting for hours, spoiling my whole day. But not now! For I am one of the millions who have learned about Tums." [6] (5) "This is a hurly burly world—rushing around—gulping down food—staying up late—no time for exercise." Ex-Lax offers to fit you for life in such a world. [7]

Two Swedish scientists started the revolutionary change in the smoking mores by research which disclosed that diabetics might smoke. They were members of the Royal Caroline Medico-Surgical Institute in Stockholm. The advertising copy writer for *Camels* found the Swedish scientists' paper which had been published in *Acta Medica Scandinavica.* [8] The new era dawned; no more about "coffin nails" but much about the "lift" of *Camels.*

Meanwhile another scientist, Dr. Bogen, was at work making investigations out of which came a booklet, entitled "Theory and Facts of Cigarette Smoking," published by the Axton-Fisher Tobacco Company, Inc., makers of *Spuds.* Dr. Bogen, of the University of Cincinnati, found that "in order to avoid the irritation from hot smoke and the increase in the toxic agents which such smoke may carry, it is advisable never to smoke a cigarette down much beyond half its length." Other marvelous things are explained in "Theory and Facts of Cigarette Smoking." [9] There is the question of the *temperature* of the burning tobacco. By "static lighting" instead of the old crude method of "dynamic lighting," it has been shown that a cigarette may be smoked at a temperature of 1200 deg. F. instead of 2000 deg. F., with the result that a much smaller portion of high-temperature tars is produced. "Dynamic lighting," still practiced by the vast majority of ignorant, pre-scientific smokers, is that of applying the flame *with* suction; while "static lighting" is effected by holding a cigarette in the hand and applying the flame *without* suction, carefully rolling the cigarette around until the end is glowing. When one cigarette manufacturer begins to invoke "science" in its sales campaigns, others must invoke "science" or lose caste. So we read in the current *Chesterfield* advertisements: "Everything actually known to Science, that will make a good cigarette, is used in making Chesterfields. An eminent scientist [name and institution not stated] wrote, a short time ago: *'Chesterfields are just as pure as the water you drink.'*" [10]

The people of the United States smoke over a hundred billion cigarettes a year, an increase of more than ten-fold during the past twenty-five years. The steady pushing of the cigarette-sales curve upward now requires the aid of the "scientists." The two outstanding contributions of university laboratories to this end have been: (1) the discovery of the energy-producing effects of nicotine on the adrenal glands, and (2) the discovery that only half of a cigarette should be smoked instead of two-thirds or three-fourths of it as pre-scientific smokers are in the habit of doing. The Axton-Fisher Tobacco Company found a way of making the public pay for the "scientific" information which it makes available for cigarette smokers. The impressive thing to do was, of course, to set up a "Research Institute"—there is nothing comparable in its impressiveness to a "Research Institute." The Axton-Fisher Tobacco Company placed a half-page advertisement in the *Saturday Evening Post* announcing *for sale* its "Theory and Facts of Cigarette Smoking," and the advertisement was signed by the "Cigarette Research Institute." The name of the author, Otis Allen Kenyon, which appears on the title page of the pamphlet did *not* indicate that Mr. Kenyon is the treasurer of the advertising agency which handles the advertising of *Spuds*.

A *directory* of the research institutes and laboratories would be a bulky volume. Few of the research laboratories have at their heads men who are so skilled in advertising copy writing as does the Pacini Laboratories, Inc., of Chicago. Dr. Pacini, hailed by one writer as a "brilliant scientist," is also a notably practical man and an effective writer of good advertising copy. In the *National and American Miller*[11] there appeared the following copy of the Pacini Laboratories:

"Let's explore the realm of bigger profits. That world exists for you: where ordinary profits leave off and bountiful returns begin. Commonplace products earn commonplace profits. *My business is deep research into the unknowns.* [Italics ours.] Fortunes hide behind the ordinary. It is our work to tear these masks aside and reveal the magic 'something the public wants'—new products that lure the consumers' dollars." [12]

A more succinct and straightforward statement concerning the aim of much scientific research under capitalism could hardly be written. Dr. Pacini is prepared to make scientific explorations into the stratosphere of profits for any and all enterprising manufacturers. He promises to come back to earth with "new products that lure the consumers' dollars." Bill Mayor, writing in *National and American Miller,* quotes Dr. Pacini on one of his pieces of research, as follows:

"Taste is the dominant factor in foods. Our work begins with the national palate. . . . Most people like the flavor of meat, so that's a good taste to work with. . . . Extract glutanic acid from wheat and you have a powder that tastes more like meat than wheat. Dissolve it in water and *you have beef tea.*" [Italics ours.] Oh, no, you don't; you have glutanic acid and water!

The Truesdail Laboratories, Inc., in Los Angeles, is another of the scientific institutions providing advertising men with helpful sales pointers. Dr. Truesdail is, apparently, one of the experts in vitamins. In an article, entitled "Looking Forward in Food Advertising," published in *Western Advertising,* we encounter some of his helpful advertising pointers. Among the suggestions waiting to be *"exploited by advertising carrying the conviction of scientific knowledge,"* [13] [italics ours] we read:

"For western foods and food manufacturers the increasing knowledge of food values has special significance. . . . For example, the amount of sunshine received by growing fruits and vegetables is known to be a factor affecting the quantitative aspect of their vitamin values. There may be in this fact an unexploited advantage for many foods produced on the Pacific Coast."

Out in Dr. Truesdail's sun-kissed West "the cow may also be bathed in sunlight of a higher ultra-violet value." The mountain forage which the "irradiated" cow eats may also be "receiving more of the sun's ultra-violet rays." Hence, sun-drenched cows eating sun-drenched forage give Vitamin D milk!

Dr. Truesdail tells of a garlic flavor or extract which eliminates "G.O." (garlic odor). "It seems," says Dr. Truesdail, "that the aromatic and flavoring constituents of the garlic, as removed by this process, are held in an inactive state" and, when eaten, "the flavor is released, but no 'G.O.' is left on the breath." [14] The punning distributor who sells his garlic under the brand name "Eureka" (there really is garlic sold under this name) would better have a care for his business! This new extract of garlic may well merit a patented brand name like "Eu-don't-reek-a."

We also learn from Dr. Truesdail's writings of a new *embalming* method used in the curing of hams. "The iliac artery is exposed and the curing pickle is injected through a nipple from a hypodermic needle." [15] The ham may thus be cured in a few days instead of the weeks required by the old method.

The research institutes and laboratories, in the nature of the case under a capitalistic system, are wedded (if so respectable

a relationship is the appropriate way of describing the connection) to commercial institutions and are identified with them
in purpose. Health Products Corporation, makers of "Clo-Dee,"
give the secret of all this hullabaloo about Vitamin D away in
their advertisement in *Food Field Reporter*.[16] "Are you looking
for a new sales appeal for your product?" queries the advertisement. "Perhaps Vitamin D is the answer." It is "a builder of
sales," and "a sound merchandising appeal for greater volume
and profits." There may be new and better ways of preparing
food for human ingestion than the ancient customs of natural,
traditional foods, but when and if they are discovered, they will
be found by research that is freed from the anti-consumer motives
of sales building, merchandising appeals, and profits. Until then,
there can be no reasonable assurance that the interests of physical
well-being are duly protected. As a matter of self-protection, it
will probably be wise to *avoid* all foods for which special health
claims are made. Neither the maker nor his advertising writer
will know, or care, or trouble to investigate what are the real
facts about the product and its safety to consumers.

The milk trust, like the tobacco trust, is under the pressure of
yielding dividends to the limit of all the traffic will bear. Sales
must be boosted. To this end the New York State Legislature was
prevailed upon to appropriate $500,000 of *state* funds for a milk-
advertising campaign. Newspaper advertising accounted for the
bulk of this expenditure. The copy urged greater use of milk for
children because it is "as necessary as sunshine and almost as
cheap." [17] The first part of the copy is a gross exaggeration
as respects cows' milk, and the second part, referring to the cheap-
ness of milk, is blatant falsehood—an immorality of which any
milder characterization would itself be guilty.

While irradiating milk by direct exposure to ultra-violet rays
and feeding yeast to cows in order to increase the Vitamin D
content of the milk involve what Dr. Pacini calls "deep research
into the unknown," there is no sort of justification for the misleading advertisement of milk which Borden's perpetrated in

the name of and on the authority of its own hired scientist, Dr. James A. Tobey[18] (B.S., Dr.P.H., LL.B., M.S.). The advertisement, well worded to avoid out-and-out falsehood, unmistakably conveyed the impression that a scientific authority had underwritten, on the basis of experiments, the novel theory that drinking milk would prevent baldness. Skirting the edges of truth has become one of the fine arts of wording advertisements. Worse yet, the Borden Company did not state that Dr. Tobey was an employee of the firm; certainly an important bit of information for the consumer who needs all such facts when reading an advertisement.

Dr. Donald Laird, of the psychology department at Colgate University, provides the distributors of sundry foods and bedroom articles with scientific authority for their sleep-inducing qualities. *Restaurant Management,* for example, is pleased to announce that "Dr. Donald Laird, of Colgate University, has made tests which show sleep is improved 6 per cent by eating a bowl of cornflakes and cream before retiring." [19] Dr. Laird's 6 per cent sleep-gain is insignificant when compared with the money-gain to the restaurant when you eat a dish of some of these *beginfast* foods (it was an advertising error ever to have associated them especially with *breakfast,* and the magical power of "science" is required to correct the error). In a later issue of *Restaurant Management,*[20] *Kellogg's PEP* shows the restaurant trade, by impressive diagram, how 81 per cent of the price paid by a customer for a dish of the cereal is clear profit for the restaurants. Dr. Laird should now tell us how much better (in precise percentages) the *restaurant owners* sleep when they sell a lot of *Kellogg's PEP.* With 81 per cent clear profit in their gross receipts from "breakfast" foods, they should not need to rub *Absorbine Jr.* on *their* necks to prevent torturing sleeplessness.

Cosmetic makers are among the chief dependents upon the superstitious regard which a miseducated public holds for "science." The anonymous dermatologists, in particular, ascribe the most magical qualities to the most ordinary mixtures. *Pepsodent,* fresh from its stupendous sales triumph with toothpaste, branched out into the facial cream line. "At first but an idea in the mind of a scientist," says the *Pepsodent* ad for *Junis.*[21] "Then a glorious new adventure in loveliness for women." We have been around some recently, with both eyes open, but we missed evidences of this marvelous "new adventure in loveliness for women" which *Junis* created for a waiting world. The *Junis* advertisement, while intended to sell only a *facial* cream, uses the picture of a girl who apparently belongs to a nudist club, her bare toes alone being modestly screened from view by a tube of *Junis. Junis* isn't going to make the mistake of the "breakfast" food advertisers by a too exclusive association of the cream with the *face,* just in case they decide later, after the market for the face has reached a saturation point, to advise its application to wider anatomical areas.

"In collaboration with a university scientist," *Barbara Gould* developed "a skin food irradiated with just enough ultra-violet rays to *benefit* the skin without tanning it!"[22] *Barbara Gould's* advertisement pictures the "scientist" in laboratory garb and one of his sleeping beneficiaries exposed to the rays of "this marvelous new Irradiated Skin Food." But alas and alack, there is no such thing as "skin food," apart from food which is eaten and so nourishes the entire body.

Pond's Vanishing Cream likewise invokes the authority of a "noted dermatologist" who explains "keratolytic" properties of the cream which "melt dead surface skin."[23] What could be more impressive, especially when the face of Mrs. Victor du Pont III is used to illustrate the principles of the dermatologist and "keratolytic" wonders?

Pond's Cold Cream not only won the testimonial of a Roumanian queen (Queen Marie said that testimonializing was a mere routine for Roumanian royalty), it actually gets authentic Vanderbilts for its laboratory work! "Beautiful Vanderbilts examined by Dermatologist for Skin Age . . . both get 20-year-old rating," says the advertisement of *Pond's*.[24] There they are, Miss Frederica Vanderbilt Webb and Mrs. Reginald Vanderbilt, "seven years apart" according to the old reckoning of ages, but in the new "scientific" skin-age both still below the voting limit.

P. W. Fattig, professor of Biology at Emory University, deserves to be ranked as one of the most useful scientists in America to his business patrons. Parenthetically, it should be recalled that Emory University has had as its principal benefactor the Coca Cola family of Candlers. Professor Fattig has conducted research over a period of years with a view to determining what effects, if any, result when persons drink carbonated beverages that contain "foreign substances."[25] His tests have consisted of placing the "most poisonous insects and small animals" obtainable in bottles of soft drinks and then persuading human guinea pigs to drink the polluted concoction to determine whether or not poisoning or illness of any kind occurs as a result of drinking the potion. Four hundred thirty-three individuals, including the professor, have submitted to the tests. The following are some of the "foreign substances" which have been thoroughly soaked in the beverages: black widow spider, Central American scorpion, poisoned cockroaches, grasshoppers, snails, frogs, caterpillars, nine varieties of flies, beetles, stink bugs, bees, millipeds, and centipedes. The *National Carbonator and Bottler* declares that it is "proud to publish such an article" as Professor Fattig's account of his experiments. This trade journal reminds the bottlers of the country that the Coca Cola biologist has furnished them with the necessary defense in any litigation based on "alleged 'foreign substances'" in the bottled beverages. The professor concedes that the psychological effects of seeing the "foreign substance" in the drink may in some cases cause vomiting. (Our own stomachs not being psychologically reinforced by an Emory University salary have scarcely withstood the nauseating impact of the *reports* of Professor Fattig's experiments.) But, he maintains, no *illness* has followed upon the imbibing of these polluted drinks. In a healthier moment, with a flash of courage, we may drink a toast, for which Coca Cola alone would be fitting, to Emory University and its entomological scientist, Professor Fattig.

The nation's bottlers held a convention in Buffalo in November, 1934, and had as their "outstanding scientist" none other than Dr. Walter H. Eddy, Columbia University professor, Director of the Bureau of Foods, Sanitation, and Health for *Good House-keeping* magazine and chairman of the food and nutrition section of the American Public Health Association. In announcing the appearance of Dr. Eddy, *National Carbonator and Bottler* said: "He will explain the role of carbonated beverages in reducing diets and calcium utilization, also reviewing valuable experimental work. *Bottlers attending should glean some valuable promotional ideas here.*" [26] [Italics ours.] With Professor Fattig furnishing the bottlers with material for legal defense, and Professor Eddy supplying them with promotional ideas, the sweetened water business should prosper. It is no small business; and it is amply able to engage the services of eminent scientists. Down the gullets of the American people flow annually the contents of thirteen billion bottles of soft drinks for a total retail value of $650,000,000.[27] Something like 80 per cent of this sum is *profit* to the bottlers and retailers, mostly to the bottlers. Here, for example, is a typical analysis[28] of the costs to bottlers of all this sweetened water:

Water (carbonated), 1 cent a case (24 bottles)=	$0.00041
Sugar, $20 for 8,040 bottles =	0.00248
Citric acid solution, $2 for 8,040 bottles =	0.00024
Patented syrup, including artificial coloring =	0.00248
Cost to bottler per bottle	$0.00561
Cost to bottler of 335 cases (8,040 bottles) =	$45.10
Sold to retailer at 80 cents a case =	$268.00
Sold to consumers at 5 cents a bottle =	$402.00

The bottlers are fortunate in having the eminent scientist of *Good Housekeeping* magazine and Columbia University explain to them the great boon to the nation in its consuming 600,000,000 gallons of water and 600,000,000 pounds of sugar (with a little flavoring and coloring added).

Dr. John A. Killian, of the New York Post-Graduate Medical School and Hospital, provided the makers of *Scot Tissue* with the material for a sales campaign which reeked of Science. The J. Walter Thompson Advertising Agency handled the account for the Scott Paper Company and placed its advertisements in such leading journals as *Woman's Home Companion,*[29] *Ladies' Home Journal,*[30] and the *Saturday Evening Post.*[31] This brazen piece of pseudo-science was debunked in the *Journal* of the American Medical Association, which declared that those responsible for the *Scot Tissue* stuff had butchered science to make an advertising holiday.[32] According to the findings of Dr. Killian, 455 out of 660 brands of toilet tissue tested contained harmful acids, or mercury, or arsenic. When asked how the mercury was determined in these "dangerous" tissues, Dr. Killian clearly inferred that the paper was first ashed and the mercury determined in the ash! Any student in elementary quantitative analysis knows that *mercury is one of the volatile elements.* When confronted with the pseudo-scientific statements in their copy, a representative of the J. Walter Thompson Advertising Agency "admitted frankly that the advertising was exaggerated; and opined that if advertising was 70 per cent accurate, it was considered quite honest copy—otherwise, it would lack the necessary emotional appeal." Mr. Kobak says advertising is 95 per cent above reproach.

Future historians may well describe ours as the Age of Chemical Man. From cosmetics to international conflicts, we are under the sway of the chemical scientists. Whether it is the beauty of women or colonial empire that we seek, our history is "a tale of the scientist's refusal to fail and of the industrialist's willingness to allocate vast sums to scientific research."[33] Julian Huxley says that "science is for the most part either an intellectual luxury or the paid servant of capitalist industry or the nationalist state." [34]

Back in the early days of NRA, the following indictment was drawn for inclusion in a proposed "code of fair competition for advertising agencies": "Pseudo-scientific advertising, including claims insufficiently supported by accepted authority, or that distort the true meaning or application of a statement made by professional or scientific authority, constitutes an unfair practice." [35] But the indictment never got beyond the stage of a press release. It was quashed; the agencies had too much power from the alliance of "science" and "industry" which has been more strongly cemented than ever before.

Not long since, a group of really eminent scientists issued a manifesto warning against the prostitution of science to the purposes of fascism. "Through misuse of and contempt for free research there is imminent danger that the whole structure of scientific knowledge will be destroyed and from the fragments a new series of enslaved pseudo-sciences will be erected, which will be harmful for the progress of mankind." [36] To these rare, courageous friends of the scientific mind, the answer is that the damage has already been done. They are describing not an "imminent danger" but a *fait accompli*. They speak of Germany as a land where "quacks" are elevated to positions of equality with acknowledged scientists and where "colleges are forced to establish chairs" for them. In Germany, they observe, "the gates are open to superstition and deceit." All of this is unquestionably true, but what the signers of the manifesto fail to comprehend in its menacing significance is that Germany is no exception and that the science of all capitalist lands is almost completely subordinated to the economic and political interests of the ruling class, and reduced, therefore, to a mere handmaiden to the works and aspirations of banking and commerce, a drab for patent medicine and cosmetic trades and the magnates of milk and telephone.

Truly, "science" has labored and brought forth a sales talking point.

CHAPTER VII

Counterfeiters of What Our Money Buys

THE DEGREE OF DILIGENCE with which the United States Government proceeds against counterfeiters of the currency is matched only by the degree of its carelessness and indifference towards those who counterfeit what the currency *buys*. On first thought this seems passing strange; and it appears to be a glaring inconsistency in the Government's vigilance for the preservation of honest exchange. On second thought, it appears to be no inconsistency at all but a striking example of the consistency with which the Government serves the interests of that class which has the greater stake in the currency as wealth-in-itself. One and the same class profits by an *un*counterfeited currency *and* the counterfeiting of the goods which the currency buys. Whether it is better to exercise the greater vigilance in the protection of an honest currency or the protection of honest goods depends entirely upon the standpoint from which the matter is judged. Probably no better example could be furnished of the identification of government with the interests of the moneyed and money-making class than is supplied by its attitude on this question. A system operated in the interests of those whose chief concern with goods and services is their consumption could tolerate a great deal of counterfeiting of the currency, but it could not tolerate counterfeiting of goods. A system operated in the interests of those who profit by manipulations of the currency finds its financial mechanisms and adding machine calculations gravely upset by lack of standards or stability in money, but it thrives upon shoddiness and adulteration of goods; the greater the adulteration and cheapening of the articles of common consumption, the greater the money profit to be derived for those who live by control of financial devices and operations.

It has been claimed that adulteration is as old as civilization itself. Even if true, this is no vindication of the practice; and an economy which bends its chief efforts to the supplying of honest goods will outlaw adulteration with a vigilance like that with which the federal government implacably runs down counter-feiters of the currency and throws them into federal prisons for long terms. The prisons, if emptied of lesser offenders, would not begin to hold those who are now committing the crime of adulterating the supply of goods. It makes no difference how old the practice may be. What if Pliny the Elder did complain that the wines from Gaul were artificially colored and flavored? Or that in the modern era as long ago as 1820 Dr. Frederick Accum exposed food and beverage adulterations of a most per-nicious character and thereby earned the nickname of "Death in the Pot," along with an enforced exile from England?

The sanction of age will one day not stand up as a defense of a practice that injures the masses of consumer-workers, albeit current protests against counterfeit goods are beyond the com-prehension of those who have identified themselves with the preservation of a system that is nowhere more indefensible than at this point. Not long ago the Soviet Government of Russia placed a pair of galoshes on trial and in a public hearing, at which technical experts and users testified, found them "guilty." [1] It proposes to continue this practice in public prosecutions of all consumer goods. The world of capitalist-adulteration greeted the news of this unique trial of the galoshes with merriment or derision. It was, to them, the sort of thing that only the strange communist outlanders could take seriously. The All-Union Council of Scientific Societies is acting as public prosecutor of shoddy and adulterated goods in the Soviet Union. How different from a civilization in which technicians and engineers aid and abet the superstitions of "science" by testimonializing for, and not against, the frauds that are perpetrated by the makers of goods in the interest of profits, and not only give their insincere bought-and-paid-for testimonials, but also prostitute their chemical and other scientific knowledge to the purposes of concealing from the users of goods the frauds that are so profitable to their masters, the makers and advertisers of those goods.

The next trial in the Soviet Union will be held in the Moscow Radio Theatre and will place Soviet-made phonographs, needles, and records before the bar of consumers' justice. Later trials will conduct prosecutions of electric irons, bicycles, and household utensils. They will not be, in any sense of the word, mock trials either. One Ralph Borsodi, who maintains a "School of Living" at Suffern, N. Y., and who has gained something of a reputation as a writer on distribution problems and the restoration of handicraft work in the home, appears to be even less able than the hide-bound bourbons of the profit-system to comprehend the epochal significance for consumer-workers of what the Russians are driving at in their trials of consumers' goods. "This news has distressed us terribly about the prospective world communist revolution," says Mr. Borsodi, quite off the point. "What's the use," he asks, "of escaping the devil of commercialism only to jump in the deep sea of galoshes that won't keep out water, non-adhering house-paint, heatless stoves, etc., etc.?" [2]

Science has performed some of its modern marvels in the technique of concealing the inferiority of products and of setting up meretricious claims for goods in the profitable business of duping and bilking the consumer. Synthetic flavoring, artificial coloring, photographic imitation of Nature's realities are among the manufacturers' clever processes for simulating Nature. These are only gestures of obeisance toward Nature—as empty as Mussolini's homage to Victor Emmanuel III—reminiscent of a distant past when men relished the golden glow of fruit which had not been "ripened" by ethylene gas, and were festive with liquor that had not been "aged" by sulphuric acid and potassium permanganate.

Not all of these processes are always technically or legally deceptive. Due notice of the simulation may be given occasionally in an advertisement, sometimes in a brand name, or when required by law in a label description of ingredients. More often there is no such notice or any other warning whatever, in which case the maker claims in self-defense, if found out, that consumer morons, lawyers, and professors alike, are uniformly sophisticated in such matters. Thus, for example, a food color manufacturer says that it "can be assumed in these days that the average person is well aware that gelatin is not 'born' with all the pleasing shades of jelly powders." The same manufacturer looks upon himself as a great benefactor of humanity, especially in time of depression, when the use of his food colors *is warranted to brighten the task of eating.*[3] [Italics ours.] Having read this, we are prepared to read of some casket maker who offers to brighten the task of suicide for an unemployed cabinet maker in time of depression. (The suicide rate has risen considerably in this period of economic crisis.) Eating is a problem, not a task, for the masses, but it will become a "task" if adulteration goes much farther. In all cases of simulation there is a hope in the maker's mind that his product will make an impression of genuineness as an aid to vendibility, and vendibility at the highest possible price.

The chemical industries are finding new and highly profitable markets as the practice of adulteration, use of artificial preservatives, addition of "pleasing" colors, flavors, and smells, grows under the stern compulsions of mass production and competitive marketing for profit. Consider, for example, the market for glycerin:

"Many uses are found for pure glycerin in the food industry. Due to its hygroscopic, antiseptic and saccharic properties, it is used as an ingredient of child and invalid foods. Glycerin increases the water absorptive properties of gluten in bread without fermentation. It is a preservative and keeps standard the moisture content of foods, such as grains. It retards drying and mold formation in cake making and improves the finished appearance of cake. Glycerin is used as a sweetening and moistening agent in making chocolate, sweetmeats, aerated waters, for sterilizing shelled eggs (see British Patent No. 325,045 for further details), mustard preparation and meat foods, in confectionery, jellies, chewing gum, cordials, liqueurs, wines, beers, for artificial ageing of new whiskey. It improves the palatability of rough, sour-tasting wines. Glycerin solutions are claimed to be superior to borates, salicylates and benzoates for preserving meats, fish, etc." [4]

It will be noted that among the uses for glycerin there is found that of making stale bread appear fresh. Long ago, the making of bread ceased to be a home industry and became one of the major factory industries, on about the ethical level of the manufacture of Grand Rapids furniture, or penny candies for school children. This change introduced the problem of freshness. Where large factories are located at a central point from which an area reaching out to many miles is served, the minimum time required for distribution often involves several days. Chemistry was the answer to the problem.

We have it on the authority of *Food Manufacture* that arsenic "is not an uncommon impurity" which enters into bread through baking powders. Consumers' Research has found arsenic in a number of well-known brands of baking powder. The same trade journal informs us that plaster of Paris has been the occasion of prosecutions for bread adulterations and that its presence arises "from the use of low-grade calcium phosphates." [5]

In Italy the masses are made to endure the lowest living standards of the western world—compelled at the gun's point to take up the slack in their belts—but "democratic" America in one respect is behind fascist Italy. On this point at least the United States will have to make progress to catch up with a system of stark reaction! In the *Siebel Technical Review* we read that "Italy is one of the European countries in which all chemical flour treatment is prohibited," and that this fact is "deemed to be of interest to the American miller and baker as demonstrating some of the difficulties of these vocations in foreign countries." [6] The American millers and bakers are not subject to such restrictions. "The most widely used improvers at present are ammonium persulphate, potassium bromate (one part in 100,000), chlorine and nitrogen trichloride (one part in 200,000)," we read in an article on "Improvers" in the same journal.[7] We are assured that the object of the use of these chemical improvers is not adulteration or the substitution of a cheaper ingredient, and that the treatment definitely improves the baking properties of the flour. It is not the object of the use of chemicals in bread which interests us or the alleged improvement of the baking properties of the flour. It is rather the effect of the use of chemicals upon the physical well-being of those who eat it. It should be noted that the trade journals in such cases are interested in the baking properties of the flour (usually this means the extra amount of water that can be introduced into the mix and sold at bread prices) rather than in the question of edibility and nutritional value for its consumers.

In order that bakers' cakes sold at the grocery store may look fresh long after they have ceased, in fact, to be fresh, it is necessary to resort to these "very special chemical formulas, high in starch, sugar, and vegetable shortening of high melting point and dangerously low digestibility." [8] It has been estimated *by the baking trade* that the wholesale bakers' cake is usually four days old before it reaches the consumer and five and a half days old before he has eaten it. "Among the hydrophyllic [water-holding] colloids which are most successful [in preserving cake from staleness] are gum tragacanth, gum acacia, citrous pectin . . ." [9]

Counterfeiting of goods is not limited to deceptive appearances produced by chemicals, but also extends to devices which manipulate prices and quantity in such a way as to hoodwink the consumer. A report from Oklahoma City states that the bakery industry in that region hit upon the device of making two sizes for their loaves; one for the hotels and restaurants which was the "normal" size, with an increase of two cents in the price per loaf; and another for consumers which was kept at the "normal" price, *with the size of the loaf reduced two ounces*.[10] This is a good example of the "changes in merchandise" for "holding quotations down." There was no trickery by which the rise in price could be kept concealed from the hotels and restaurants; they belong in the category of "rational" buyers who purchase, to one degree or another, on specifications. But for the ordinary consumer, the price-increase was easily concealed and profits enhanced by a decrease in the size of loaf. Such consumers are buyers who are subject to "temperament, whims, and caprices" in their purchases. It is only by reason of the general ignorance of consumers that the device of product-deterioration is made to conceal a *real* rise in prices and a *real* drop in "utility income."

It is now common practice among the manufacturers of ice cream to make a quart out of what was once a pint, by the magic of an air-inflating process. This enables the manufacturer to double the "real price" by the inexpensive method of adding a "pint" of air. A new ice cream disher is now on the market, for the use of soda fountains, which prevents the packing of the cream in the disher when it is filled. This is accomplished by a good sized hole in the bottom of the disher which allows the ice cream to escape back into the soda fountain can as soon as the disher is full *but not packed*.[11]

Diacetyl is used to give margarine the flavor and aroma of butter, and poor or stale butter the apparent qualities of the finest sorts.[12] Homogenisers, available at moderate prices to delicatessen stores and restaurants, are now coming into use to put margarine or other fats into skimmed milk and give it "rich cream content." Inasmuch as homogenised products will shortly be the subject of extensive advertising campaigns, it is well for us to understand the nature of the homogenising process. *The*

Manufacturing Chemist gives us the following description: "Homogenisers have a well-established position, and are being employed in increasing numbers in those industries whose products involve the preparation of uniform and stable emulsions. [Mayonnaise and cream are examples of common emulsions.] In many processes the economy effected in the use of emulsifying agents justifies the employment of mechanical emulsifiers, apart from the improved quality of the emulsified product. In other processes homogenising provides a means of producing emulsions of stability unobtainable by the use of emulsifying agents alone." [13]

A chemical treatment, ethylene, "unmasks," according to a Department of Agriculture protocol, the rich, ripe color which Nature, if given time, would have put upon our oranges.[14] Having got a jump on Nature by the use of ethylene gas treatment of the oranges, the fruit may be further prepared for "eye appeal" by polishing with rosin or paraffin. An antiseptic wash with a solution of borax is recommended by the chemists as a preservative against decay.[15] In connection with this permission of the Department of Agriculture for orange growers to unmask the hidden colors of the orange, it is interesting to read in the *Food Field Reporter* that such processes have been forbidden in the State of California in meat and meat products.[16] The color of frankfurters was the great issue at stake. There is no color suggestive of Nature's processes which may be unmasked in a "hot dog." Nor is the "hot dog" such a distinguished mainstay of the peculiar California culture as is citrus fruit.

The layman will be surprised to read in the trade journal, *Soap,* that "the word 'olive' in the name of this soap is not *always* [italics ours] a misnomer, for various of the lower grades of olive oil and foots find their way into the kettle, depending upon prevailing prices," and further that the "green color in this soap, of course, is derived from the dye, which can be either an oil or a water-soluble one."

In contrast to the unmasking effects of ethylene on oranges, we have the masking effects of pine oil disinfectants on natural stenches. "The pine oil increases this detergent effect through its solvent power," says S. J. Miller, in *Soap*, "and creates very strongly the *impression* [italics ours] of cleanliness because it is able to destroy or to mask the malodorous conditions in washrooms, corridors and similar much used, but little respected, places." [17] *Impressions* of cleanliness constitute the essence of vendibility under the profit system of production.

A new problem in creating the impression of freshness and cleanliness has been introduced by the widespread use of Du Pont's *Cellophane* in packaging. *Cellophane*, itself no mean monopoly, has accentuated the visual selling appeals, and brought with it new necessities for chemical treatment to produce the *appearance* of freshness in goods. In addition to this, the *Cellophane* wrapper gives a sparkle to the package which is pleasing to the uninitiated consumer—and to Du Pont stockholders.

From the September (1934) issue of *The Manufacturing Confectioner* we cite a sufficient number of illustrations to establish the truth of these statements. [18] The magazine, intended for the trade primarily, if not exclusively, conducts a monthly *clinic* in which it examines confectionery products. In the issue before us, 53 candy products are given ratings (with brand names and the names of manufacturers omitted). Twenty-five of these are wrapped in *Cellophane*, thirteen in glassine. In *appearance*, all of the samples are rated *good*. The manufacturers have taken no chances on appearance or visual appeal! In *quality*, however, it is a very different story. Even from the standpoint of the trade, almost half of them are rated as seriously deficient in quality. The following are some of the comments of the clinic:

"Peanuts tasted old. . . . Coating had a very cheap taste."

"It needed considerable more molasses to make it taste like a molasses bar."

"Peanut butter was not good; jacket had a bad tasting flavor."

"This candy is not up to the standard this company was putting out a year ago."

"No honey could be tasted." (A Honey Bar.)

"The coating is of the cheapest kind."

"It had an off-taste."

"Very cheap tasting."

"The coating had a bad taste. Cream hard and tasteless."

"Lemon flavor is of the cheapest kind."

"Bar looked like chocolate but did not taste like chocolate."

"It was not fit to eat."

The editor of the department says: "Some of the bars that were very fine eating a year or so ago are now made of cheap raw materials." If submitted to the exacting tests of a public trial in Moscow, it is extremely doubtful if any of the 53 samples would have been "acquitted." It is noteworthy that the editor of the department declares that quality is steadily and rapidly deteriorating. With the coming of *Cellophane* manufacturers are putting everything into appearance, and are, it would seem, convinced that quality is not an aid to vendibility, whereas "flash" is such an aid. All is not fresh that sparkles in *Cellophane!* Scarcely any commercially produced confection is fit for consumption in this age of chemistry. Chemical analyses of candy have recently revealed the presence of 0.7 per cent of some color "having the characteristics of indigo," and 0.2 per cent of talc, the presence of the latter probably due to the use, by some manufacturers, of talc for lining the moulds in which the candy is allowed to set.[19] Shellac varnish containing arsenic is a classic coating to give candies an alluring sheen.

Glass packing has long been common for liquids; it is now becoming popular with merchandisers of bulk goods, such as ground coffee. "With the introduction of glass-walled packages, improvements in processing and packing became necessary to secure fine appearance from the top of the container to the bottom," says a writer in *The Glass Packer*. Hence, "methods were developed which . . . conceal chaff more completely . . . and effectually hide the dust." [20]

In Canada where standards are often higher than in the United States, we learn that "cheap jams demanded by chain and department stores led to the growth in the use of pulps [fruit pulps chemically preserved and shipped in barrels] grown in other countries." The Toronto *Daily Star* says, "it is no idle statement to say there is no fresh fruit going into Canadian jam today." [21] Practices of this sort cannot be confined in their efforts to the health-considerations of consumers. They have wide ramifications throughout the whole social structure. "The frozen pulp racket," reports the *Daily Star*, "has further reduced the price of fruit." Farm products, counterfeited at a hundred points by stealthy profit-seekers, are no longer required in the former proportions as ingredients for the marketed products of industrial adulterators. Furthermore, "farm labor has been forced down to a dollar a day and even less" because of these methods. Labor and agricultural producers have everywhere ignored these questions of adulterating the supply of goods, but they do so at their own increasing peril. There is no way by which the social effects of the counterfeiters can be localized. Honest material and honest labor are displaced in favor of adulterated products and short-cut methods of machine production.

We are now experiencing a deluge of propaganda which is intended to lure consumers away from home canning to the use of commercially canned goods. Is it not fitting that the Continental Can Company should be in the forefront of this movement to "protect" the public against the hazards of fresh and home-canned foods? "Health and Freshness come in cans," says the advertisement of the Continental Can Company.[22] Is it not natural that *Good Housekeeping* magazine (large advertising beneficiaries of canned foods at $5,600 a page) would be on the side of canned foods, too? In its September (1934) issue, the magazine featured an article by Miss Elizabeth Frazer, entitled "Hold That Can, Please!" in which the superiority of commercially canned foods was duly touted. The *Canning Trade* acknowledged with due gratitude this boost from *Good House-keeping:* "As the mouthpiece of this great industry we wish to publicly thank the publishers of *Good Housekeeping* and Miss Elizabeth Frazer, for the most excellent article in the September number of that famous journal. . . . It ought to be used as advertising material by every canner in the business. . . ." [23] In spite of all this puffery by the Continental Can Company, *Good Housekeeping* magazine, and the *Canning Trade,* we read an advertisement of a packing company last summer which was seeking one thousand tons of *field corn* in canning condition. A million cases of horse corn were packed during the 1934 season. "If it ever gets abroad in the land that canners use horse corn," says the *Canning Trade,* "prices will sink to far below cost figures, and the consumption of corn will soon drop below five million cases." [24]

Turning to "Technical Food News" in the *Food Field Reporter,* we read that a caustic solution softens corn. "If sodium hydroxide solution is used as the caustic ingredient," says the technical expert on food, "subsequent treatment with dilute hydrochloric acid neutralizes the caustic residue." [25] How can you tell whether the can of tender corn you buy is Nature's product or a chemical counterfeit which has suffered a dousing with a powerful alkali and a corroding and poisonous acid? Or it may be chemically treated horse corn, in which case do not noise it abroad and ruin the trade in canned corn, i.e., if you are connected with the industry, directly or via magazine advertising, or a "housekeeping institute."

Imperial Chemical Industries, Ltd., a British concern, has discovered that Lissamine Green V is useful for "giving foods a more attractive appearance," [26] canned peas in particular, which require a green dye to create the illusion of freshness.

Magnus, Mabee & Reynard, Inc., is a company which claims that "more and more are manufacturers in the Food Field turning to us and our efficient research department in solving their manufacturing problems" and "more and more are manufacturers in the Food Field depending upon our organization as their chief source of supply for the raw materials we furnish." Follows a list of the raw materials, which this firm sells to food industries under the recommendation of "purity," which includes: "Imitation Liqueur and Cordial Flavors, Imitation Flavors (All Kinds), Imitation Fruit Elements, Imitation Fortifiers, Aromatic Chemicals." This company offers "Special Flavors for Bakers, Confectioners, Extract Makers, Grocery Specialties, Ice Cream, Meat and Condiment Manufacturers." [27]

Meat preservatives are in common use, but in addition to preservation against decomposition, uniform coloring with a view to sales appeal is also sought by the packers with due use of chemicals. In *Food Field Reporter* we read that one of the largest packers in the country has taken out a patent for this purpose. "A uniform red color is imparted to the lean portion of meat by using a solution of sodium nitrate in water in which to soak the meat. Patent covering this has been issued to Swift & Company of Chicago, Illinois." [28]

Wherever benzoate of soda is used as a preservative, the law specifies it must be mentioned on the label. But an ingenious way of avoiding mentioning the presence of benzoate of soda on the label has been found in the use of natural cranberry juice which contains it. "The use of natural cranberry juice as a preservative in the commercial bottling of beverages of low alcoholic content is said to make it unnecessary to use benzoate of soda which must be mentioned on the label." This artifice is explained in the *Food Field Reporter* under the heading, "Scientific Flashes." [29]

The Florida Cane Products Corporation reports a method of artificial ageing of liquor by which "four years' time is saved." The chemical agents employed for this purpose are sulphuric acid and potassium permanganate, both of which are highly poisonous. It would never occur to the Corporation to inquire how many years may be lost to the consumer of his chemically aged liquor.[30]

A new trick in food counterfeits is reported in *Food Industries* in an item headed, "Baby or Babied?":

"Baby carrots can be made out of large ones by cutting off the tips of the roots. Then the tips are put into a vegetable peeler and given a few whirls to round off the ends and edges of the cut surfaces.

"Since the physiological age of the tips and of young carrots of the same size is approximately the same, there is no appreciable difference between them." [31]

This trick may have been suggested by the old practice, of makers of preparations for infants' use, of photographing midgets who were well above the voting age, and then presenting the pictures to fond parents as examples of what this talcum powder or that pap would do for their infant prodigy. Thus the millions who have looked upon the chubby features of a talcum powder "baby" were, in fact, looking at the likeness of a matured midget, Franz Ebert.[32]

Have you ever wondered about the photographs of fine up-standing looking Americans that you see in testimonial advertisements where only the occupation of the testimonializer, not his name and address, is given? Or have you naïvely thought these photographs were of persons who in real life engage in the designated occupations beneath their likenesses? One of the leading concerns that make a specialty of photographing models for advertisements is John Robert Powers Publication of 247 Park Avenue, New York City. On page 466 of their 1932 volume of portraits, we find the picture of one John Martin Brennan. Now if you will turn to the advertisement of *Goodrich Safety Silvertowns* tires in *Business Week* for November 9, 1932, you will find the portrait of John Martin Brennan, not named but described as a "cleaner," giving a testimonial for *Goodrich* tires. Does this conform to Mr. Kobak's conception of "truth in advertising" or is it just plain fraud and counterfeit? The reader may recall Edgar Kobak's assertion that not more than 5 per cent of all advertising is reprehensible in any way. Mr. Kobak was vice-president of McGraw-Hill, publishers of *Business Week,* when this advertisement appeared in that journal! Perhaps Mr. Kobak would say that John Martin Brennan is 95 per cent "cleaner" and 5 per cent professional advertising model, and that we should not be fussy about such small margins of error!

The commonly held theory that the "best stores" are not guilty of selling counterfeit and adulterated goods, fails to stand up under investigation. Tests of silk sold in the leading shops of New York (and elsewhere), made for Consumers' Research by a qualified chemist who is specially skilled in this field, give the lie to claims for the special integrity of the "best stores." * A full report of these tests will be given elsewhere by Consumers' Research, but we cite a few of the more glaring examples here:

Subway Silk Shop; kind of fabric purchased and tested: *Faille;* the manager and the clerk insisted that it was "pure dye silk." The test showed 62.2 per cent of material other than silk. Price: $1.17 per yard.

W and R Silk Shop; kind of fabric purchased and tested: *Faille;* said to be all silk and wool. The test showed 56 per cent cotton. Price: $1.50 per yard.

Lord & Taylor; kind of fabric purchased and tested: *Imported French Taffeta;* said to be pure silk taffeta, not weighted. The test showed 23.2 per cent of material other than silk. Price $5.20 per yard.

John Wanamaker; kind of fabric purchased and tested: *Flat Crepe—Printed;* said to be pure silk, weighted medium. The test showed 53 per cent of material other than silk. (This apparently gives a new meaning to the word "medium"!) Price: $1.97 reduced to 94 cents per yard for special sale.

Gimbel Brothers; kind of fabric purchased and tested: *Faille;* said to have *some* weighting. Test showed 64 per cent of material

---

* These purchases and analyses were made by Pauline Beery Mack, textile chemist, and her assistant, Mary Elizabeth Deck, as a part of a long-time study on what the consumer of silks gets for her money.

other than silk. (Does Gimbel Brothers have a new meaning for the word "some"?) Price: $1.84 per yard.

Paris Silk Shop; kind of fabric purchased and tested: *Flat Crepe;* placard said "All Silk Printed Crepe." Test showed 54.8 per cent of material other than silk. Price: 59 cents per yard.

The Federal Trade Commission has set the legal definition of "pure silk" as a fabric having not more than 10 per cent of material other than silk in its finished weight (in the case of black silk, 15 per cent). It will be apparent from the existing state of silk manufacture and selling how effectively the legal definitions of the Federal Trade Commission are applied!

A writer, reporting the frightful conditions now prevailing in Fascist Germany, makes the following statement on adulteration of goods under the Nazi regime: "Already, food adulteration is going on, under force of necessity, on a grand scale. Even bread is adulterated. By government order, all flour must be one-third potato starch, or 'shorts.' Clothing, too, is being reduced in quality. All wool cloth must contain shoddy." [33] The most casual survey of the practices of adulteration in the United States will lead anyone to wonder that the writer on Nazi Germany thought there was anything worthy of special comment in the adulterations which he reports. American manufacturers have no reason to fear that Hitler is about to outmode their policies in respect to the various and sundry chemical chicaneries by which goods are counterfeited.

It is, in fact, one of the proud boasts of American business that it is in the vanguard of progress in this age of imitation. The editor of the *Dyer,* an English trade journal, thus extols the age of counterfeiting: *"One of the blessings of modern industrialism is that it has conferred on the masses of the people highly successful imitations of things that were formerly enjoyed only by the wealthy few."* [34] [Italics ours.]

CHAPTER VIII

AAA-I Extra Fancy

Lᴇᴛ ᴜs ɪᴍᴀɢɪɴᴇ ᴛʜᴇ ᴘᴜʀᴄʜᴀsɪɴɢ ᴅᴇᴘᴀʀᴛᴍᴇɴᴛ of a great railway writing a steel manufacturer regarding a shipment of rails. With dispatch and courtesy the reply comes back that the steel concern will be all too happy to "serve" the railway. Furthermore, a work of graphic art in four colors carries, over the signature of Dolores Joy, famed screen beauty who makes numerous trips from Hollyway to Broadwood, this declaration: "ɴᴇᴠᴇʀ ᴍɪssᴇᴅ ᴍʏ ʙᴇᴀᴜᴛʏ sʟᴇᴇᴘ ᴡʜᴇɴ ᴛʀᴀᴠᴇʟʟɪɴɢ ᴏᴠᴇʀ ᴘᴜʀᴏʀᴇ sʟᴜᴍʙᴇʀ ʀᴀɪʟs." Then follow a few touches such as "You can go *far,* but not *wrong,* on Purore Slumber Rails, 'Superfine AAA-1'—mined from mountains that are the Symbol of Endurance." "Beware of *imitations;* demand the 'Seal of Good Car Keeping Institute.'" . . . Preposterous? Indeed; but it is preposterous because business is only partially moronic and otherwise rational.

Let an eminent authority describe for us the distinctions which prevail in these matters, rational and moronic: "The 'Industrial Market' is quite different from the market for consumers' goods. . . . Industrial marketing is conducted largely on a rational basis, quality, utility, and price being the most important factors. Industrial goods are bought for a specific and rational purpose. . . . In the case of many types of consumers' goods the motive back of purchases is not always clear. . . . It may be, and frequently is, that the purchase of over-the-counter goods by the public is not a rational process, but a highly emotional one. The temperament, whims, and caprices, to say nothing of the pecuniary status of the purchaser, enter into a very large part of all retail transactions." [1]

Such is the contrast, mildly stated, between the rationality of purchasers in the market for "industrial goods" and the irrationality of buyers in the market for "consumers' goods," as set forth in a report by the United States Chamber of Commerce. It means simply that when a manufacturer buys for industrial use, he goes about the business equipped with the highest possible degree of technically competent assistance as well as a clearly defined purpose; whereas consumers almost uniformly approach their purchasing with a maximum of ignorance and caprice, and a minimum of knowledge, either practical or technical. A railway buys on specifications; consumers buy, or are expected to buy, on ballyhoo pitched at the intellectual level of low-grade morons or movie fans. The difference between these two types of buyers is admirably set forth in a brief characterization of the purchasing and advertising departments of a large corporation. "By definition," says Kenneth Laird, vice-president of The Western Company, "the purchasing department is cynical, hardboiled, disillusioned, insistent upon brass tacks information. The advertising department is or should be creative, dreamy, somewhat ingenuous in its point of view toward the world." [2] Whenever consumers become "cynical, hardboiled, disillusioned, insistent upon brass tacks information," a cry goes up from full-throated manufacturers that constitutional guarantees and ancient liberties are in jeopardy, and that all believers in the established verities and sanctities should rally to repel the wicked menacers of civilization. The psychology of advertising is calculated to make its appeal to the most trivial and irrelevant of consumers' considerations. The consumer's ignorance is the salesman's bliss, profit, and promotion. As such it constitutes one of the most profitable of the vested interests of those who make and distribute goods in an economy that is organized around essentially non-consumer and anti-consumer purposes.

It has not always been so with consumers. In the days of a simpler economy, purchasers of consumers' goods possessed a practical knowledge of the quality and utility of the things they bought that would, if it were widespread today, wreck the business and goodwill of many an industrial concern making consumers' goods. But chemical and physical scientists have pushed the arts of simulation to a level of achievement where only those who are equally scientific, or who have the disinterested services of equally trained scientists at their disposal, can avoid being duped into accepting specious appearances for solid reality.

The determined hostility of advertisers and manufacturers to the fixing of "quality standards" is due entirely to the fact that prices to consumers are, and must remain, deceptive or meaningless in the absence of known quantities and qualities that are considered absolutely indispensable data to the purchaser in the market for industrial goods. The industrial purchaser, if he buys according to modern standards and without too much pressure from interlocking directors, buys only on specifications. As long as prices are kept unrelated to quality (as in the case of *ultimate* consumers), the potential profit to the seller is greater, and the opportunities for advertising to do its work with consumers are unobstructed except by competitive goods, likewise of unknown quality. In a recent issue of the Bulletin of the United States Department of Commerce we read that a group of consumers made a survey of price and quality based on an examination of some hundred and fifty cans of vegetables which were purchased at different stores in the regular manner, and that the survey revealed "that there was no discoverable relation between price and quality."[3] As a matter of fact, *high* price is often nothing more than a deceptive device designed to suggest *high* quality where it does not exist. In the absence of quality standards, the helplessness of consumers is well illustrated by the fact that the experts themselves are not able to estimate quality with any degree of accuracy until they have performed tests under laboratory conditions. Dr. Robert A. Brady reports that "an expert shoe manufacturer confessed to being unable to tell the difference within $2.00, between a $4.00 and an $8.00 pair of shoes *without tearing them to pieces."* [4] [Italics ours.] The case of the shoes is only one among many. "The catalogue of a large Mail Order House," according to Dr. Brady, "lists over 40,000 different commodities. Most of these go through complicated processes and methods. Quality differentials can only be told by the expert in each particular line. And then only after laboratory tests."

There are many systems of grading employed in the field of consumers' goods, most of them being established by private agencies. They constitute simply one more deceptive device, as the following examples[5] indicate, in the persistent hoodwinking of consumers. "U. S. No. 1" signifies second grade in California oranges, while its use in grading cheese means third grade. In butter, "Firsts" means third. "Best Extra" describes the *lowest* quality of raw silk, or sixth grade. "A-1" stands for fifth place in asbestos yarn, while it falls to sixth position as a classification of silverware. Thus the English language in the hands of advertisers and merchandisers means almost anything but the obvious and natural thing, and is wholly undecipherable, without a key (which consumers do not possess and are not freely given, even by government), in terms of the language of quality.

The United States Department of Agriculture has approved or established grading terminology which is quite as misleading to the uninitiated as the examples given of grading by private agencies. The Department, for example, uses "U. S. Standard" for third-grade eggs. The various states have their own systems of grading. Thus, a first-grade egg in Illinois is labeled "A"; in Iowa it is "Special"; and in New York it is called "Fancy." "Fresh" eggs may not be older than fourteen days in some states, while other states extend the period of "freshness" to thirty days. The obvious course, from the standpoint of consumers, would be to date the eggs with a stamp; but it has always been maintained by sellers that this is mechanically impracticable. On the other hand, a very complicated and very expensive mechanism was devised for use in stamping walnuts—because to do that, with a brand name, gave an advantage to the larger distributors. A

German scientist has proposed that cold-storage eggs be treated before storage with a one per cent "alcoholic solution of a chemical indicator, phenolphthalein." [6] The housewife could then readily determine whether or not she was purchasing "tired" eggs by the application of moist baking or washing soda crystal to the shell, which, if the eggs were cold-storage, would show a pink coloration. This, it must be admitted, is the kind of information and technique which will be generally available to consumers only after a wholly new kind of society has been created with new orientations in its dominant motives.

The vested interest which manufacturers possess in the form of profound and widespread consumers' ignorance receives not only the positive support of "scientists"; it also claims the passive support of governmental agencies in the form of official insouciance toward essential consumer-interests. The Bureau of Standards at Washington, D.C., could with its present organization supply 125 million consumers in the United States with invaluable information on the quality and utility of the things they require for efficient living standards. All efforts to utilize this governmental agency in the interests of those who buy in the market for consumers' goods have been frustrated. Government officials seem quite unable to focus their minds clearly on the question. The argument is allegedly to the effect that since consumers do not buy rationally, they should be left in their present state of irrationality, while purchasers in the industrial market, even those who have been in the habit of purchasing unscientifically, like consumers, should receive all the benefits of the testing which is done in the Bureau of Standards. Up to the present time, under the Old Deal and the New, this has been the winning argument!

While 125 million American consumers have been denied the services of the Bureau of Standards which could have been made available to them in the testing of consumers' goods and the publishing of reports of such testing in a usable form, *foreign industrialists* have found the work of the Bureau extremely useful to them. The Bureau of Standards is as proud of its service to foreign industrialists as it is resentful of all efforts to utilize the Bureau on a large scale and in a significant way for the benefit of American consumers. The French Society of Photography and Cinematography, at its meeting held on January 26, 1934, "unanimously voted to award the silver medal of the Society" to two members of the staff of the Bureau of Standards at Washington, with the statement that "the work of these two men . . . has been of great benefit to French investigators and industrialists." The *Technical News Bulletin* of the Bureau of Standards states that "the Bureau greatly appreciates the action taken by the French Society in thus honoring two members of its staff. . . ." [7]

We have no concern to make a point of the fact that the industrialists served by the Bureau of Standards were *French*. The issue is not one of nationalism, but one of serving exclusively the interests of industrialists, of whatever nationality. A discussion of why government agencies thus serve industrialists, with indifference or detriment to the interests of consumers, must be postponed to a later treatment of the basic nature and function of the State. Meanwhile, it is pertinent to point out that there are scarcely any limits to which government will not go in providing information of the most detailed or elaborate sort to those interests which stand on the production side of economic activity. We have before us, for example, three pamphlets issued by the United States Department of Agriculture, and prepared by capable men paid to serve the insect-trapping and smiting industries, which list patents on devices for killing or catching flies.[8] One of them has the following introductory paragraph: "This list of 86 patents includes all those relating to devices for killing flies by hitting them with rubber, paper, wire screen or other flexible material attached to a handle, which devices are commonly called fly swatters." Another of the pamphlets lists 52 devices which fix a one-way traffic (exit only) for flies through screens.

Many writers have presented irrefutable arguments for correcting the present "producer-consumer unbalance" by giving consumer-workers an aggregate purchasing power which matches the enormously expanded productivity of the factory and the farm. The problem of the distribution of purchasing power is only one aspect, admittedly of crucial importance, of the whole question of reorienting production to consumers' interests. The essence of a planned economy is the deliberate organization and correlation of the grand aggregate of economic resources and *of all its parts* with a view to the improvement both in quantity and quality of the general living standard. Distribution of purchasing power in such a way as to create an effective consumer demand for the goods of the system operating at capacity production is the quantitative side of the purpose in planning. But income in strictly quantitative terms is not more important than income in terms of the quality of what one can buy with it. Absolute income was long ago seen to be meaningless as an index of living standards. A more expressive index was needed and this was achieved by relating absolute income to the shifting price structure by a system of indexes in order to arrive at *real* income or wages. A still more expressive index is required to indicate the movement of living standards. For it is possible by deteriorating or debasing the quality of goods to lower the level of mass living standards at the very time that so-called *real* wages are rising. The *utility wage* is therefore an important concept, to be added to the concept of the *real wage,* even though the new term may not yet be susceptible of exact statistical determination. In the present economic situation in the United States, the qualitative considerations in income, inseparable from standards, are of first-rate significance, and a subject which, needless to say, statistical and technical experts in the government service are *not* working at.

Here, for example, is a report in the April number of the magazine, *Tide:*

"Results that have already appeared and are to be expected from all the price manipulations currently jogging the nation's economy are myriad. An outstanding one has, until recently, received little attention; namely, the effect on the quality of merchandise. Retailers and manufacturers are well aware that consumers are in the habit of buying according to certain fairly rigid price levels, and to meet these prices at a time when the materials of production are mounting skyward seems to call for one procedure—debasement of quality." [9]

The *Journal of Commerce* gives a similar picture of the widespread tendency at present to drive qualitative standards down as other factors, including governmental policies, are forcing income levels measured by the quantity of supplies, down:

"Substitution of lower quality for standard products continues on a substantial scale and prevents consumers from realizing the full import of price increases that have taken place.

"Retail prices in many lines have been arrived at after study and experience with mass buying habits. Merchants conclude, therefore, that they must preserve these established price levels even at the cost of sacrificing quality, to maintain their physical volume of sales.

"This reasoning has been found so practical and effective in many instances that manufacturers of branded and trade-marked merchandise have been adopting the same policy in increasing numbers, it is reported. In some cases, manufacture of the previous standard quality is being given up altogether." [10]

The grave hazards to life which may be involved in the debasement of quality standards were illustrated in the disaster of the Long Beach, California, earthquake last year. Paul H. Nystrom, writing in *Advertising & Selling* on the subject of "The Disintegration of Quality Standards in Consumer Goods," set forth the "criminal neglect" involved in the practice of deterioration of goods in the following language:

"Almost every fire and building accident reveals skimping of proper materials, inadequate provision for stress and strain, criminal neglect of minimum fire and safety regulations, to say nothing of slipshod, hasty, half-baked workmanship. Recent reports indicate that the destruction of life and property in the earthquake in Southern California early this year [1933] was due to the crumbling of improperly and dishonestly built houses and business buildings. Well-built structures did not crash and people who occupied them were not even injured." [11]

Much of the quality to which the consumer is entitled is eaten up by advertising costs. "It is my impression that if we took half the money spent for advertising and put it into the product, we wouldn't need so much advertising," said a sage observer at the International Automotive Engineering Congress. [12]

Common practice of manufacturers has established what is known to them as "the point of required utility" for a consumer's product. With the low levels prevailing in consumers' demands for quality, it is considered bad business to go above this point of required utility. In a recent A.M.A. [American Management Association] *News Letter*, Mr. Boulware is quoted as saying:

"We must face the fact that a passably and satisfactorily good product will go much further when the designer and maker have stopped at the point of its required utility and have given over the rest of the available margin for the promotion of the product with consumers than is secured with a product twice as good but with no margin left in it to have people know that it is even good at all." [13]

The margin left over for promotion is the amount which consumers are charged for their general incompetence. This margin, which under a scientific system of distribution would be applied to improvement of quality, is channeled into promotion expenditures (advertising) with a view generally to creating the myth that the superior quality actually resides in the product. Actual quality may be placed just as low as the ignorance of the consumer permits, thus enlarging the margin for promotional purposes until it far exceeds the cost of production which goes into the commodity itself. The possession of scientific standards of testing by consumers would place a rigid limit upon promotional possibilities of this character.

The opposition to the fixing of quality standards for consumers' goods is taking the line of ridicule. Thus the editor of *Food Field Reporter* pays his respects to the romantic disposition of the consumer: "If she prefers not to turn the retail store into a reading room for perusing the engineering measurements printed on cans, she will simply grab a can with a label she respects and read her daily newspaper or a book of poetry instead." [14] (The newspapers and poetry have been a good escape for consumers from the realities of their ignorance and lack of skill.) Albert D. Lasker says that "the average consumer would not understand a government standard if he bumped into it in broad daylight." [15] *Food Industries* (a McGraw-Hill publication) is inclined to think that pride more than ignorance would prevent the consumer's making an intelligent use of accurately and intelligibly graded goods: "There are definite disadvantages to such a series of designation as 1, 2, 3, 4 or A, B, C, D. The housewife is a bit too proud to ask the store for Grade C peas or third-grade peaches." [16] Evidently, the idea is she'd prefer to ask for U. S. No. 1 and *get* third grade, and so come to associate her government and her grocer in one common cause to cheat her of her rights in the market place.

The editor of *Electrical World* (another McGraw-Hill publication) is apparently a deeply religious man for he believes that "people have a God-given right to decide what they like and what they do not want." [17] Therefore, away with all irreligious proposals to substitute for this God-given right a system of scientifically measured standards! "Through experience," declares editor Morrow of the *Electrical World,* "men and women learn to judge quality in silk and wool, in hardware and groceries." Professor Walton H. Hamilton, of Yale University, has blasted this myth about the sufficiency of "experience" in judging the quality of goods [italics ours]:

"In the purchase of soaps, drugs, canned fruits, bric-a-brac, vacuum cleaners, dictionaries, radios, motor cars, and many another article, the buyer's inability to judge the quality of the ware is in striking contrast to the general *legal* presumption of his competence. . . . *Only if his personality is corporate, or he associates himself with like buyers,* is he able to oppose science with science, match technique with technique, and share in the terms of the bargain." [18]

CHAPTER IX

What's in a Name?

PROBABLY THE MOST APPROPRIATE TRADE-MARK ever registered in the Patent Office of the United States is the newly chosen brand name of a candy manufactured by the Williamson Candy Company of Chicago. That company has selected the name "GUESS WHAT?" for its newest confection.[1] It correctly suggests that the layman will be at a total loss to identify the ingredients, and it might therefore admirably serve as the family name for the whole assortment of trade-marked articles registered in the Patent Office. The disability of the layman in guessing the ingredients of trade-marked articles does not apply, however, to the skilled chemist; and when the latter has completed his analysis, we are forced to the conclusion that there is plenty of profit "in a name," but little else to warrant the veil of secrecy which brand names throw about very simple, sometimes harmful, and always inexpensive concoctions.

The *Journal* of the American Medical Association puts the matter accurately when it says: "When one buys a 'patent medicine' one buys a name and not a thing."[2] This is essentially true of all other articles sold under brand names, including the heavily advertised medical specialties out of whose advertising the American Medical Association earns a large share of its income. It is the brand name upon which the property value is erected. The *thing* may undergo a complete change of ingredients while the name remains the same, and for that reason the property value is unimpaired. *Jad Salts* was first a "kidney remedy," and

141

as such it was three times declared fraudulent by the Food and Drug Administration. With the removal of two of its eight ingredients, *Jad Salts* became the "new hope" of the obese. The formula was further drastically altered and the name was only slightly changed to that of *Condensed Jad Salts*.

What an enormous property value has been erected upon sheer chemical *secrecy,* is evident from the fact that there are over 300,000 trade-marks registered in the United States Patent Office. But this is only the beginning of the system of keeping ingredients dark secrets, for it has been estimated that only one in five of the trade-marks in actual use in the United States is registered in the Patent Office. We have, then, something approaching 1,500,000 trade-marks in use, or approximately three times as many names for goods as there are words in the English language.[3]

The utter meaninglessness of these names, and also the increasing difficulty in finding new ones, are suggested by a new device for coining them. "A set of four discs carrying suitable letters and combinations of letters is provided, and by revolving the discs a set of names, every one of which would appear to be suitable for some particular product, appears."[4] How to operate the discs is set forth in a book with which they are sold. The reviewer of the volume, writing in the *Manufacturing Chemist,* says that he is "convinced that anyone trying to find a trade name could not possibly do it so well without these discs as with them." There may be some who believe that Gertrude Stein employs some such system of whirling discs in composing her books, but it must be admitted that the eccentric, adjective-less, and comma-less author is a model of profundity and lucidity by comparison with the system under which articles are vended in this ultra-idiotic fashion.

The trade-marking of articles may be ultra-idiotic, as we have said, but it is also highly profitable. By it, manufacturers are enabled to sell what is called their "good will" (certainly a high-priced form of incorporeality) at fancy prices. Even the *material* base for this "good will" is often composed of more than half water, or air, or sand, the three cheapest ingredients known to business enterprises.

There is, for example, a product which bears the trade-mark *Mirax,* recommended by its makers as an "instant glass cleaner." The labeling says, among other things: "World's fastest cleaner for glass. No water. No muss." Chemical analysis has revealed 77.4 per cent water in this "fastest cleaner." The remainder of this substance (22.6 per cent) is denatured alcohol colored with a trace of green dyestuff and perfumed with a small amount of essential oil.

One of the more exclusive tooth powders sold in drug stores at $1.00 has been analyzed by the Council on Dental Therapeutics.[5] The analysis yielded up the following secrets:

Sodium chloride (salt)	59.5 per cent
Sodium bicarbonate (baking soda)	19.8 " "
Sodium perborate	14.9 " "
Magnesium carbonate	4.9 " "
Methyl salicylate	0.6 " "
Oil of cloves	0.3 " "
	100.0 per cent

The total value of the ingredients of this $1.00 tooth powder (excepting the flavoring) is approximately 4 cents. Any ten or twelve individuals using this tooth powder could well afford to engage the services of a chemist to make such an analysis as this. The results would contribute something to their understanding of the nature and workings of the profit system. The analysis which we have given here is the "inside" story of *Pycopé*—a trade-mark which looks as though it might have been arrived at by whirling discs. If any reader should assume that *Pycopé* has been cited because it is unique in the nature of its ingredients or the enormous spread between cost of raw materials and retail price, we would have done an injustice to the makers of *Pycopé* so far as that reader is concerned. The fact is that *all* tooth pastes and tooth powders have something like the same "inside" story.

Mouth washes and gargles, profitable specialties of drug stores, have even larger proportions of trade-marked "good will" and water in them than have the tooth pastes. The *Journal* of the American Dental Association gives the following report on *Alkalol:* "From the present examination, it may be concluded that Alkalol is essentially a flavored aqueous [i.e., water] solution containing sodium bicarbonate, 1.0 gm.; salt, 0.5 gm.; and potassium chlorate, 0.5 gm. per one hundred cubic centimeters. These conclusions in general confirm the earlier findings. It is apparent that Alkalol is another example of the usual mouth wash. Placing a dash of this and a dash of that in these mouth washes and gargles is simply playing to the gallery."[6] According to the estimates of the *Journal* of the American Dental Association, the total cost of the ingredients of one pint bottle of *Alkalol,* which sells for 85 cents, is less than one cent! Water is costly when purchased under a brand name.

The distinguished Doctor-Senator Testimonializer Royal S. Copeland is against requiring a "label declaration of name and quantity or proportion of all active ingredients of drugs other than those recognized in the Pharmacopoeia and Formulary," on the ground that "so sweeping a requirement would not operate fully in the public interest, because to the lay public *the names of many drugs are more impressive* than their actual therapeutic worth."[7] [Italics ours.] The Doctor-Senator Testimonializer has had much unmerited criticism heaped upon his head by the makers of foods, drugs, and cosmetics; for the history of recent attempts at food and drug legislation reveal the Senior Senator from New York as one of business' warmest and most effective friends.

Billions of dollars have been spent in recent years to make American consumers *brand conscious*. The efforts have been highly successful from the standpoint of business. A recent survey showed that 91 per cent of New York buyers ask for branded goods. Of 2,394 articles purchased, 51 per cent were national brands, 40 per cent were private brands, and 9 per cent were in bulk.[8] It is increasingly difficult to obtain some of the most commonplace articles of consumption in *bulk*. The striking growth of brand consciousness among consumers in recent years indicates a great increase in the degree of exploitability which the makers of goods are effecting. Goods purchased in bulk have a relatively low degree of exploitability; those purchased under the "impressive" trade-marks, have a very high degree of exploitability, like the biblical grain, some yielding a forty-fold and some a hundred-fold increase. Whenever the exploitability of labor *in the process* of production becomes more and more difficult because of effective labor organization, or more and more antiquated because of technological displacement of labor, the ruling class of the American economy finds new sources of enrichment by the exploitation of consumer-workers *in the product*. Exploitation in the existing system is a double barreled proposition: in one instance it is ruthless exploitation in the process (that is, on the job), and in the other instance, it is exploitation through the product. *The brand consciousness of consumers is the antithesis of the class consciousness of consumer-workers;* the former is a surrender to the ballyhoo of the most adroit exploitation ever devised by a ruling class, the latter is the absolutely prerequisite state of mind for any successful opposition to the exploiters.

CHAPTER X

The Junk Heap's the Thing

THE MOST OBSOLETE THING in American society is the set of principles by which it is run. The retention of these principles, in spite of their obsolescence, is attributable to the fact that they are profitable to the class that rules America. *Progress* has not been incorporated in the principles of the system as an objective that is worth while in itself. The American rulers are neither *for* nor *against* obsolescence; they are neither *for* nor *against* progress. They are for *either,* if and when profitable, and for *neither,* if and when unprofitable.

Progress is held in check by the patent system, and is not in the least accelerated by it, as some commonly suppose, and as patent lawyers persuasively argue, after the fashion of lawyers, on the basis of scientific ideas and practices out of date seventy-five years ago. Long ago it became customary for corporations which had a vested interest in outmoded machines to buy up *all* new inventions in their particular fields in order to prevent new enterprises from utilizing them and thereby rendering outmoded machines and methods unprofitable. Progress must be held in leash by the purchase of patent rights. Such rights are bought for suppression, and not for use until their owners find their introduction necessary for profits. Walter S. Gifford, for example, testified as follows before the Senate Interstate Commerce Committee: "The Bell system now has patents and rights in its field to the number of 15,000 and 1,300 applications for patents pending. *These patents and rights are not obtained for purposes of*

146

exploitation, but in order to give us a clear field." [1] [Italics ours.]

The "patent racket," as the anonymous authors of *High Low Washington* have shown with great thoroughness, is operated in a way not entirely to be differentiated from that in which Al Capone worked. The Radio Corporation of America under the leadership of Owen D. Young held, within eleven years of its birth in 1919, four thousand patents or alleged patents on radio apparatus. In the course of a few years it had brought into existence a six billion dollar combination which dominated the field of broadcasting, electrical appliances, communications, motors, and amusement. Beginning with General Electric, it eventually included the American Telephone and Telegraph Company, Western Electric, the United Fruit Company, Westinghouse Electric and Manufacturing Company, and General Motors. [2] Through its enormous financial and political power, and particularly through the control of four thousand patents, it easily destroyed competitors or brought them to its terms. In this way, patents became the neck of the bottle through which progress was rigidly controlled in the interest of profits.

In many instances it is necessary to own only the sustaining patents upon which all later inventions are based, in order to prevent other interests from entering the field with new and better methods. *Laissez-faire* was dead and decomposing long before Franklin D. Roosevelt supplanted Herbert Hoover in the White House. In fact, in the history of modern times, *laissez-faire* never got beyond a theoretical still birth.

Progress, if defined in terms of the universal and secure consumption of improved goods, is also held rigorously in check by what business describes as "skimming the cream of the class market." "Altogether about 5,000,000 electric refrigerators have been sold and the cream of the class market probably lifted," says an advertising journal. [3] When the "class market" has been thoroughly exploited at a price level which is congenial to it, it is then the practice of business to lower the price level to tap the lower gradations of income. But, as long as the serving of the class market is satisfactorily profitable, there is a pronounced aversion among manufacturers to bringing their goods within the price range of the masses of consumers, even though mass production makes this entirely consonant with substantial returns. C. F. Hughes, who contributes a regular column to the New York *Times,* under the heading of "The Merchant's Point of View," describes this practice as follows: "The object in too many cases has been to obtain very nearly as much as the public would pay and get high profit out of a limited market. It will be recalled, perhaps, that an electric range manufactured to sell well under the $100 mark several years ago was quickly scotched by one large company." [4]

Another rigid check which is applied to progress by the rulers of business society is the practice of holding goods and services only at the point of "required utility." As long as the mass of buyers do not demand the better goods and services which are well within the possibility of technological knowledge and skill, there is no sort of compulsion within the system which demands the improvement of goods for the sake of providing a rising standard of living. Dr. E. E. Free, a well-known physicist consultant to big business, and editor of scientific articles and publicity for newspapers and magazines, has conducted experiments on the musical ear and mentality of Americans, and has concluded that "after a certain point in the approach to perfection, efforts spent for closer perfection will not be worth while, because the customers cannot distinguish any difference." [5] Dr. Free, therefore, nominates "as the most profitable single activity which the radio industry could undertake" a series of psychological experiments "to decide just what is the point of musical quality, beyond which average American ears and mentalities make it unnecessary to go. . . ." Nothing could demonstrate more conclusively the cultural barbarity of business, and of science in the service of business enterprise. Cultural advancement under a business system is not a worth while end in itself, but is to be served only as the considerations of profit require it. Dr. Free disregards the obvious technical fact that reproduction of music by radio and phonographs is at a level that can only be described as atrocious, and the psychological fact that the education of "American ears and mentalities" will not and cannot be advanced until a basis for such progress has been laid *in experience*. Discrimination in the fine arts is not a part of man's instinctive equipment but is entirely a matter of education which results only when the *best* provides opportunity for discrimination out of the entire field of that which is available.

Progress is on the other hand permitted, in a business society, when three conditions exist: (1) when a class market has been saturated and new markets in the lower income brackets offer the only opportunity for new profits in satisfactory amount; (2) when lowering the costs of production by the substitution of machines for labor offers an opportunity for maintaining profits; (3) and when a rapid turnover of goods, through the stressing of *obsolescence,* and the selling of replacements, promises the most profitable results.

We have already seen how progress is consciously retarded or accelerated with reference to the class market. In recent years there has been an ever increasing emphasis upon the lowering of the labor content in the product as a means of reducing the costs of production. In addition to the lowered production cost which results from a substitution of machines for men, the makers of goods also avoid the uncertainties which are attendant upon labor's demands, discontent, and organization. The period of the current economic crisis has witnessed a rapid acceleration of technological advance in production for the sole purpose of eliminating the higher costs and potential obstruction of labor to profits and freedom of management. But with the problem of unemployment in the foreground of social consciousness, business men have sensed the impropriety of continuing to call their new equipment "labor-saving machinery." For the purpose of softening the hard facts of unemployment and thereby detracting something from the salutary bluntness of commercial realism, manufacturers have begun to substitute the phrase "cost-reducing equipment" for the older phrase "labor-saving machinery." [6]

There has likewise been in recent years a new emphasis upon the specter of obsolescence as a spur to moving goods. Manufacturers have begun to take into their vocabularies such phrases as "controllable wear" and "limited life." A speaker at recent sessions of the Society of Automotive Engineers stressed "the desirability of building automobiles with a limited life." [7] Just how to make automobiles that will, like the famous one-horse shay, suddenly fall apart at a predetermined time is a problem which engineering skill has not yet solved, although engineering minds desire it and are planning towards it. Another speaker at the 1934 summer meeting of the Society of Automotive Engineers suggested that all of the parts of trucks "might be designed for 'controllable wear' as well as imperceptible wear." [8] Imperceptible wear was the old standard of workmanship in engineering design to which the technicians were once trained in college and drafting room! Colleges and college teachers, especially in economics and the mechanic arts, may always be relied upon to fall in line with business necessities and provide the intellectual sanctions for them. Thus we read in the *Kansas State College Bulletin: "We need a new viewpoint.* The average person should not consider a home as an absolutely permanent investment. . . . The home should be considered in much the same light as the automobile. . . . Automobiles wear out; houses wear out. Automobiles become obsolete; houses become obsolete." [9] [Italics ours.] We expect any day now to see that the building trades have adopted as their slogan, "Two houses for every family!"

Social habits which are age-old must be broken down to make way for business necessities. There is, for example, a well-established habit, which now begins to appear to be sheer obstinacy, of hanging on to contraptions for the simple reason that they still serve their intended purpose. This is most reprehensible in a capitalist economy for it retards the movement of goods which is the mainspring of American civilization and business profit. Not until the American consumer learns that these things were not intended to be used as long as they are found serviceable, but only long enough to enable the manufacturers of the goods to line him up for a new model, will the basis be laid for a "sound" businesslike consumption!

Just before the historic crash of 1929, one business leader set forth the principle of "progressive obsolescence" as the requirement for continued "prosperity," in prophetic and stirring words. Writing in *Advertising & Selling,* J. George Frederick said: "If we are to have increasingly large-scale production there must likewise be increasingly large-scale consumption. . . . *To get more money into the consumers' hands with which to buy* . . . is a mere *minor stopgap.* There is, however, a far greater and more powerful lever available. I refer to a principle which for want of a simpler term, I name *progressive obsolescence.* This means simply the more intensive spreading—*among those people who now have buying surplus*—of the belief in and practice of buying more goods on the basis of obsolescence in efficiency, economy, style or taste. *We must induce people who can afford it to buy a greater variety of goods* on the same principle that they now buy automobiles, radios and clothes, namely, *buying goods not to wear out, but to trade in or discard after a short time when new or more attractive goods or models come out.* The one salvation of American industry, which has a capacity for producing 80% or 100% more goods than are now consumed, is to foster the progressive obsolescence principle, which means buying for up-to-dateness, efficiency and style, buying for *change, whim, fancy.* . . . We must either use the fruits of our marvelous factories in this highly efficient 'power' age, or slow them down or shut them down." [10] [Italics ours.]

In spite of Mr. Frederick's admonition and against the trend of the best sales-manager doctrine in all successful enterprises, goods were not moved with sufficient rapidity and the crash came, but his principle survived and is now being employed in a strenuous effort for recovery. Louis E. Kirstein, former member of the

NRA Industrial Advisory Board, vice-president of William Filene's Sons, Co., Boston, and among the New Deal Administration's advisers on economic theory and recovery, addressed a luncheon meeting of the Fashion Group at the Ritz-Carlton Hotel as follows: "The creating of obsolescence is a prime necessity if we are to avoid stagnation in depression like that through which we are passing. To take up the slack we must create obsolescence." [11]

The General Electric Company utilized the space at the bottom of the April page of its gift calendar to remind obsolescent-minded housekeepers that "house cleaning time is a good time to replace all lamps." More than one user of *G-E* bulbs has been lax in discarding them, and has thoughtlessly continued to leave them in their sockets beyond the season of house cleaning merely because they were, carelessly enough, so well made as to continue to give light efficiently.

Then there is the thoughtless radio fan who keeps serviceable tubes in his set greatly to the annoyance of the manufacturers who have estimated that American radio owners *should* (just for RCA's health and happiness and a richer life for Gerard Swope and Owen D. Young) purchase at least 100,000,000 tubes a year, whereas "sales of tubes to the public for replacing defective tubes in their receivers [have only] increased somewhat to about 30,-000,000 tubes a year." [12] The radio fan is slow to understand that he is retarding recovery by not calling in the radio service man to advise him to junk his tubes at once. The service man educated in the RCA school of tube-junking will do just that, given the slightest opportunity to examine an ailing set.

Many motorists have been known to use their spark plugs with satisfactory service for 30,000 miles or more, but the continuance of this practice is in bold defiance of the advice of plug salesmen. "*Change* all your spark plugs every 8,000 to 10,000 miles!" [13] is the advice given in Sears, Roebuck's catalogue in its advertisement of *New* Champion or AC Plugs. The motorist is told in the mail order catalogue that the automotive engineers of one of the outstanding spark plug manufacturers found out that great economy in gasoline is effected by this frequent change of spark plugs. Technically, of course, such advice is nonsense. Economically, it isn't, but ought to be, designated a crime.

"*Radio Retailing,* omniscient organ of that industry, has coined a phrase: 'If it's not All-Wave, it's obsolete.' There you have the rallying cry that has given a lot of radio dealers a new lease on life." [14] It would be tragic and ill-advised to the nth degree, for the radio trust to adopt for its slogan, in selling the new All-Wave sets, "Ask the man who owns one."

Beginning in September, 1934, the American Stove Company launched a selling campaign based upon obsolescence. "Such curiosities as the old coffee grinder, wooden washtub, hitching post and hansom cab [were] pictured in an effort to make the women of the country realize that the gas range which is a few years old, is almost equally ineffective." [15]

The capital goods industry has made some feeble efforts to gain a new lease on life by emphasizing obsolescence. The National Printing Equipment Clearing Association, an agency set up under the NRA for the purpose of taking "obsolete" machinery out of use ("clearing" is a nice word for junking), adopted as its slogan "Scrap the old and outworn." Hugh S. Johnson, crackdown economist, in approving the graphic arts code, commented as follows: "Schedule A of this code, for the disposition of used and obsolete printing machinery which has been obstructing the market for new modern machinery, is an attempt to solve a situation which had a depressing effect on all capital goods industry." [16] Style-mindedness is, however, an attitude which can be successfully developed only in gullible ultimate consumers. Business men are far too rational where their own interests are at stake to accept the ballyhoo of obsolescence in capital goods where those goods still meet the requirements of profitable enterprise. One has but to examine the ancient and well-worn machinery still doing steady service in the largest manufacturing plants of the country; radio factories, for example, making sets which are to make your old set of last September seem a hopeless and shameless hangover from a pre-scientific age.

Irving Caesar, a New York song writer, whose economic ideas have a common origin with General Johnson's, but go further and are more obviously nonsense, has the distinction of having thought up the idea of how radio is "distorting American social life." He is greatly perturbed because he finds that "for two and a half hours each day 40,000,000 people are busy at their dials, and while thus engaged they cannot walk down the shop-lined streets, wear out their shoes or their wearing apparel; nor can they ride the highways in their automobiles, with the attendant consumption of gasoline, tires and wear on engine." [17]

Again we assert that the most obsolete thing in American life is the set of principles by which all its economic enterprise is directed. A set of principles so against all logical consistency and ordinary common sense and consideration for human welfare is the one thing that needs preëminently to be thrown on the junk heap before ordered and rational progress can be set in motion.

CHAPTER XI

A Brisk Trade in Poisons

IT IS IMPOSSIBLE TO ASCERTAIN the exact number of the victims of industrially indifferent and commercially callous sellers of poisonous commodities. It is considered journalistic bad taste, and it *is* distinctly journalistic bad business, to give full and specific details concerning the serious injuries and deaths that result from the use of goods in whose manufacture or preparation the science of human toxicology has either played no appreciable part or received no attention whatsoever. In a system whose primary orientation is to the manufacture and distribution of goods for profit, this would, on purely *a priori* grounds, be expected. This *a priori* judgment of the economic-minded man is fully justified by the fragmentary records which have been gathered from incidental references in newspapers and medical sources. These records dispel any doubts regarding the character of a profit-making society. The position of the press, with its alleged "freedom," is of central importance in this matter. In publicizing a salacious sex scandal touching the private lives of ordinary, unbusinesslike individuals, there are hardly any limits to the publicity and exposure of private and personal matters which the journalistic caterers to sex sensationalism provide. This is, it must be admitted, good for circulation in a society whose basic attitudes on most important matters have been grossly perverted by the emulation of those whose every activity and attitude are determined by pursuit of profit; and, furthermore, it rarely, if ever, damages any business whose advertising accounts are the mainstay of journalism

—the way, as Mr. Hoover once put it, we get so much fine reading matter so cheaply. In the light of its most "tender" regard for business and its reserved mien in the matter of the peccadillos of sellers (especially when they are large corporations) of goods which maim and kill their users, the customary defense of the journalistic practice of providing sex sensations is shown to be nothing more than a wholly specious and dishonest rationalization of profits to be derived from circulation. In the matter of reporting injuries and deaths from harmful and poisonous goods, the press may possess a theoretical freedom, but it rarely chooses to exercise its constitutional privilege, so bravely and blusteringly defended by Elisha Hanson in a manner reminiscent of "Crack-Down" Johnson himself. Where large financial interests are at stake, it is often the *disposition* to be critical rather than the right which is suppressed.

From the front page of a recent issue of the Chicago *Daily News* we take the following story: "Suffering from strychnine poisoning after eating some of her mother's reducing pills, a 2-year-old baby girl is in a critical condition at the Children's Memorial Hospital. . . . Her father, Benjamin Lasavage, told Shakespeare Avenue police the pills were purchased from a drug store which advertised them over the radio."[1] It will be noted that this story does not include the brand name of the reducing pills or the drug store which sold them, or the name of the radio station or of the broadcasting chain or newspaper of which it formed a part.

In Tulsa, Oklahoma, a high school boy died after eating a hamburger "said to contain meat to which a chemical had been added as a preservative."[2] A press item reporting that 200 pounds of hamburger meat had been seized following the death of the 17-year-old boy states that the name of the owner of the chemically treated meat "was withheld." Names of truck drivers who run over 17-year-old boys are *not* withheld. The use of sodium sulphite for preserving spoiled hamburger is a common practice.

There is grim irony in the fact that the father of Tulsa's hamburger victim is a feed and grain inspector for the State Board of Agriculture, and now has his own special interest in prevention of harmful adulterations. In the State of Illinois, where 21,100 samples of meat were examined between February 1, 1933, and July 1, 1933, 47 per cent of them contained sodium sulphite.[3]

In the Troy (N. Y.) *Times* we read an account of how "husband and wife narrowly escaped death from effects of leaking gases" from their electric refrigerator.[4] The refrigerator had been "recently purchased," but the name of the maker of the nearly fatal box was not mentioned, nor, of course, the name of the dealer who in selling it acted as the "skilled purchasing agent" of the consumer.

New ways of being poisoned are added to the old ones as industry and commerce pursue their course of so-called progress. Dr. J. A. Campbell, writing in the *British Medical Journal,* holds that cancer of the lungs is definitely on the increase due, among other things, to the exhaust fumes from motor engines.[5] There is no doubt whatever about the technical possibility of eliminating absolutely from the risks to which consumers and workers are exposed the hazards of motor exhaust fumes, if engineering and chemical skills were applied as energetically in the interests of human life as they are in the interests of commercial profits.

Automobile drivers and taxicab operators, college and high school teachers of chemistry, and automobile engineers who have been impressed by the great advertising campaigns for lead-impregnated gasoline may be interested in the following story from the New York *Herald Tribune:* "The victims' brains contained gasoline and lead, lead being a constituent of some much used modern brands of gasoline. The conclusion was that the men found dead had entered the house to set it afire, taking with them some of this lead-impregnated gasoline as tinder. For some reason the firing of the premises was delayed. Much of the leaded gasoline was breathed."[6] It may be assumed that relatively few individuals who read this account contemplate arson, but many of them may have noticed a tendency to drowsiness and a metallic taste in their mouths when driving their automobiles.

Research carried out by the National Council for Safety indicates that a very high percentage of automobile accidents which resulted in a new casualty record in 1934 are due to drowsiness induced by carbon monoxide. To the carbon monoxide hazard is now added, but *not* mentioned in newspapers which print a very large amount of advertising for ethyl gasoline of a score of brands, that of gasoline impregnated with a peculiarly dangerous and subtle poison, a *volatile,* inhalable form of lead, most poisonous of metals.

In a summary of a United States Public Health Report on "Fumigation Deaths as Compared With Deaths from Other Poisonous Gases" given in the *Journal of Industrial Hygiene* we read: "Statistics gathered from news clippings are presented showing that deaths from fumigants are slight compared with those from automobile exhaust gases although the actual rates are high. The author recommends legislation controlling fumigation but *cautions against emergency or ill-considered action.*" [7] [Italics ours.] Deaths are no cause for emergency action where human life is pitted against commercial interests! Any summary action in favor of consumers would, we are certain, be held by Dr. Williams and his bureau to be ill-considered action. This, it will be noted, is the view plainly implied in this government, not private, document, a view consistent with the standard attitude of government officials nowadays, whenever a question is involved where the safety of consumers is required to be balanced against money to be saved or dividends to be "earned" by business.

The Chicago Department of Health recently reported ten deaths as a result of the leaking of refrigerant gases from electric refrigerators.[8] One of the most highly poisonous of refrigerant gases, methyl chloride, contains no "warning" property, so that the victims of the leaking gas from refrigerators perish the more easily.

A subsidiary of one of the most powerful chemical concerns in the United States, the Carbide and Carbon Chemicals Corporation, lists sixty-one chemical products in its catalogue. Many of these products are of high toxicity, enough to involve real hazards to their users, but scarcely a word of caution on this point appears in their description. In respect to these products, detailed technical information of the type most useful to manufacturers purchasing the products is given—including acidity, odor, color, specific gravity, freezing point, boiling range, and so on—but toxicity, which is most important of all, and especially to the worker in the plant and the consumer who purchases the automobile radiator fluid, the enamel or varnish or paint remover or hair tonic, is not discussed. Such callous indifference to simple safeguards is characteristic of the dealers in poisonous products. Page after page of the kind of information dear to commercial chemists, and the usual commercial puffery, is offered, while the doctrine of *caveat emptor* is supposed to take care of the supremely important question of toxicity, the one factor about many of these products which should be studied, known, and reported in detail above all else. Among the common perils of these commercial chemicals is poisoning from their use as fumigants, as refrigerant gases, as anti-freeze mixtures, as germicidal agents, and in lacquer and other finishes. Among the products of the Carbide and Carbon Chemicals Corporation which are of known distinct toxicity are Methanol (about which a mild word of caution against "over-exposure to its vapors" is given); Isopropanol (described as having a "pleasant characteristic odor" but no hint of its toxicity); Butyl Alcohol; Isobutyl Alcohol; Acetic Anhydride; Ethylene Dichloride (described as having "no deleterious action upon the other constituents of lacquers"); Trichlorethylene. In the one case only, which we have noted, is there any suggestion that dangers to users are involved. At least twenty more of the products of the Carbide and Carbon Chemicals Corporation listed in this pamphlet are of known minor toxicity.[9]

In a previous chapter we have shown how common it is for

the "best stores" to sell "pure silk" with very high percentages of impurity. Much of this silk is lead-weighted. In the trade journal, *Textile World,* we find the admission that the "irritating effect of the silk has been definitely established." [10] This is indeed a mild way of putting the matter inasmuch as non-commercial investigations have indicated the presence of the serious hazard in lead-weighted silk, a hazard second in its imminence and diffusion only to that of ethyl gasoline already mentioned. When these investigations of leaded silk, showing its hazard, were brought to the attention of the National Federation of Textiles, the matter was cavalierly dismissed with an ironic little poem about rats and the silk pants they wore in the tests conducted by an expert textile chemist.

At the Skin Clinic of Cologne University a recent study of bakers suffering from eczema reached the following conclusion: "Ammonium persulphate, which is largely used as an improver, is regarded as an injurious substance and it is recommended that it be excluded from improvers." [11] Ammonium persulphate is commonly used in this country as an "improver" for flour. The bakers only handle the flour. The rest of us eat it. Our stomachs and intestines are bathed in the products of its digestion!

"Arsenical cancer is found . . . among furriers, tanners, taxidermists and farmers using arsenic sprays." [12] With the increasing production of commercial fruit and vegetable crops, there has come a great increase in the hazards of poisoning from the spray residues used to attack the commercially hostile arthropod parasites. In some quarters, it is now common to denounce Consumers' Research for its work in bringing the hazards of spray residues forcefully to the attention of many thousands of consumers. The dangers involved can be considered of an "alarmist" character only from the standpoint of a commercial callousness which disregards every consideration except that of its own profitableness. The most recent of the several deaths attributable to the spray residues which has come to the attention of Consumers' Research was that of Mrs. Ersa Kinsman of Seattle who died on August 28, 1934, after eating arsenic sprayed pears without peeling them.[13] (They had been intended for canning, and her mistake in judgment cost her her life.) A civilization in which life depends upon pears being correctly labeled with skull and cross bones to avoid injury and death is the final *reductio ad absurdum* of a commercial culture.

According to W. B. White, of the United States Food and Drug Administration, "the residue control problem is immeasurably more serious in this region [State of Washington] than in any other section of the country."[14] The problem is, however, by no means confined to the fruits and vegetables of the Northwest; it is merely worse there, because farming is on a more aggressively businesslike, factory-operation basis on the West Coast than in any other part of the country (as California farm laborers know to their sorrow).

The attitude of producers is well illustrated in one of their New Jersey publications. Attacking the Food and Drug Administration for clamping down on growers if their fruit carries more than the prescribed tolerance of arsenical residue, the editor of the *New Jersey Farm & Garden* writes: "Other departments have learned how to cooperate in meeting serious problems. But the attitude of the Food and Drug Division is not only inconsistent with the policy of helping the producer, but it offers no middle road. It continues its arrogant and non-cooperative idea that fruit is either clean or unclean, and it does not recognize the necessity of meeting the growers on a more friendly basis."[15] If the Food and Drug Administration were far less lenient in the matter of arsenical spray residues, as friends of consumers have urged in many writings over the past three or four years, the belligerent attitudes of the New Jersey farm journal toward it would evidently amount to open insurrection. Attempts at control of tolerances for spray residue have "on more than one occasion" almost incited the recalcitrant growers to mob violence, according to W. B. White of the United States Food and Drug Administration.[16] What the growers really desire is absolute non-interference with their freedom to sell poisoned fruits and vegetables at tolerances which are convenient to themselves. According to business, the Government must be openly and consistently, not covertly or merely predominantly, the ally and sword-arm of business. It should be pointed out that the powers of the Food and Drug Administration extend only to fruits and vegetables which enter into interstate commerce. There are no controls over spray residues on produce which is raised *and* consumed in the same state, except such limits as the growers themselves are pleased to permit local officials to set. On this point R. L. Webster, of the Washington State Experiment Station, testifies as follows: "Where washing equipment is not available, the grower either will have to install such equipment or be forced to dispose of his apples *within the boundaries of his own state.*" [17] [Italics ours.] E. J. Newcomer, of the United States Bureau of Entomology, states that the fruits which do not come under the legal lead tolerance are sometimes "disposed of to by-products plants." [18] The by-products plants referred to include those where jams and jellies, and pectin and cider vinegar are made. Whether it is better to suffer lead poisoning from eating apples or from eating apple sauce and apple jelly is a fine point for metaphysicians.

Grapes often involve exceptionally dangerous consequences when sprayed. J. M. Lutz and G. A. Runner, of the United States Department of Agriculture, indicate the hazards in the following words: "Grapes may carry as much as five times the arsenical tolerance when sprayed only twice, the last application being applied shortly after blossoming, three months before harvesting. A third arsenical application a month after blossoming may result in an arsenical load of ten times the tolerance." [19]

When the embattled growers are hard pressed by governmental control over the use of one kind of spray, they often employ others, equally poisonous, knowing full well from a long series of fortunate experiences with governmental control, that a considerable lag occurs between the introduction of a commercial poison and its effective regulation or suppression. W. B. White points out that fluorine compounds are being substituted for lead compounds as insecticides: "As lead has grown in disrepute, fluorine compounds have come to the fore. I regret to say that enthusiastic high pressure salesmen have grossly belittled the human health hazard of this type of insecticide. We have consistently maintained the position that the latest knowledge indicates that fluorine compounds may be every bit as dangerous from the standpoint of chronic poisoning as are arsenic compounds." [20] It has been ascertained that fluorine compounds are highly destructive of the enamel on the teeth, one part in ten million being sufficient to deteriorate the enamel of the teeth. "There are definite indications that, contrary to early predictions, fluorine compounds, when used with the same type of oil sprays," says Mr. White, "are much more difficult to remove from apples than arsenate of lead." [21] Two other deadly poisonous metals, selenium and manganese, are of late coming into use in the endless and uncontrolled attempt to control the insect damage by chemical rather than rational means considerate of consumers' safety.

On the ghastly effects of mercuric compounds also being resorted to, Mr. White speaks as follows: "Mercury, in various organic combinations, has been recommended for certain leafy vegetables and as an emulsifying agent for citrus sprays. The exceedingly deadly nature of mercuric compounds causes us the gravest apprehension even though it is asserted that no poison can possibly contaminate the edible portion of the food. This has too often been assumed in the past to the sorrow of regulatory officials. I cite cauliflower and peas as examples. The form in which selenium is used as an insecticide is probably of relatively low toxicity. The menace here is the tendency for selenium compounds to enter the plant metabolism and to replace sulphur in the harvested crop. In this form selenium produces effects upon higher animals which can only be characterized by the term 'ghastly.' " [22]

The reason why growers object so emphatically to any publicity attending illness and death as the result of poisoning from spray residues, or even publicity concerning government seizures, is well illustrated by the fact that "in one city the price of loose-leafed cabbage dropped fifty per cent overnight due to seizures occasioned by the wanton and reckless use of lead arsenate by ignorant growers." [23] In a California city after a mass poisoning from eating broccoli at a country club dinner, the sales of this vegetable dropped from a carload daily to a single case, and the lax California authorities were put under sufficient pressure from consumers that eighteen inspectors were put to work in the city market to control and prosecute offending wholesalers.

While it may be relatively rare that immediate death results from poisoning, the main issue is not one of sudden lethal consequences for the victims of commercial fruit growers, but rather of slow, cumulative poisoning, without any warning signals, over a period of years. Mr. White's warning on this subject is sufficient to give pause to any who consume commercial fruits and vegetables where the most rigid enforcement of legal tolerances is known to be lacking, and this is in the present state of control, practically anywhere in the United States. He says: "I think we can take it as pretty definite that there isn't any doubt about the danger of lead as a cumulative poison and about the mysterious way lead breaks out for no apparent cause at all when you have had a slight intake, for five, six or seven years. All at once, in painter's colic you get an outbreak, out of the bone marrow. It goes into the circulation. I don't know whether anybody knows why, but it is a dangerous sort of thing to be administering lead in small doses over a long period of time." [24]

Mr. White's view is fully corroborated by numerous studies in the field of cumulative poisoning. Dr. W. C. Hueper, of the University of Pennsylvania, indicates as a possible cancer-producing condition "the prolonged ingestion of small amounts of arsenic found on vegetables and fruits . . . in recent years since the introduction of arsenic-containing sprays as insecticides." [25]

Dr. Hueper's study on another important family of commercial poisons, reported in "Aniline Cancer of the Bladder," concludes that "a characteristic of aniline tumors of medical and social importance is represented by the fact that these neoplasms may develop many years after the contact with the carcinogenic substances has ceased." [26]

There is no comfort to be derived from the hope of being among the lucky ones to escape serious injuries and ultimate death from the effects of these new commercial methods. Dr. Hueper points out that the substantial increase in bladder tumors during the last thirty or forty years coincides "with the constantly extended use of synthetic chemical products with which the majority of the population has come in constant and close contact during this period." [27]

In respect to another kind of insect sprays, the amazing ingenuity of salesmen is observed. We learn that a movement is now afoot to mask "the nauseating odors which characterized the insecticides of the past." [28] The "smell" chemists have been called in "to provide suitable odors which would blend" with the natural odors of the product to be sprayed "whether that product be Kentucky Tobacco, apple pie, or strawberry shortcake."

Workers in these industries, like the consumers of their products, are victims of a laxity which has its source solely in the rapacity of commercialism. Protection for workers and consumers against the extreme hazards involved in these products is both complicated and expensive and, therefore, it is stated, "often omitted for economical and competitive reasons." [29]

Young Vest C. Terry, Jr., of Tulsa, Oklahoma, was only one of the innumerable victims of poisoning from the eating of decomposed meat which has been chemically treated. If full knowledge of the situation with regard to putrid and decomposed foods now on the market were suddenly brought to the attention of consumers, many would doubtless be moved to go on a hunger strike, or to go back to the land and raise their own foodstuffs under conditions in which the process could be observed from beginning to end, and the addition of poisonous adulterants of a surety avoided.

The offenders in this regard are by no means limited to the small and ignorant enterprisers in the food industries. Names of the largest firms are often found among those against whom judgments are issued. Dr. Albert C. Hunter, in charge of the Bacteriological Laboratory, Food and Drug Administration, testified in the case of UNITED STATES V. 1,443 CASES, MORE OR LESS, CANNED SALMON, etc. (LIBBY, MC NEILL & LIBBY, Claimant) that the claimant had a record of more than eight seizures of adulterated or decomposed fish during the past fifteen years. In spite of this somewhat unsavory record which the Food and Drug Administration claimed sufficient ground for the court to deny the claimant's petition for the return to his custody of the 1,443 cases of salmon, the court ruled as follows: "Order to destroy decomposed portion and sell wholesome part of canned salmon, sought to be condemned as adulterated, *held* unwarranted, in view of evidence that each can must be punctured or opened to determine whether contents are wholesome and wholesome portions resealed and recooked to preserve them. . . ." And further: "Claimant of canned salmon, sought to be condemned as adulterated, *held* entitled to decree for delivery thereof on payment of costs and giving statutory bond not to dispose of it contrary to federal or laws of any state, territory, district or insular possession. . . ." The question of actual adulteration (decomposition) was not a point at issue. The witnesses of Libby, McNeill & Libby testified to an "adulteration of approximately 5 per cent." The testimony introduced by the Food and Drug Administration indicated an adulteration of 11 per cent, while pre-seizure samples showed 25 per cent of the samples adulterated.[30]

In a recent case in which adulterated canned salmon was involved, where the court's decision went against the government in favor of the canner, the presiding judge remarked: "We must admit people may be expected to eat some putrid food." [31]

Who can estimate the millions of protesting infants who have had cod-liver oil forced down their throats by innocent parents who took at face value the claims of the cod-liver oil advertisers? (Cod-liver oil and related medicinal substances provide, by the way, one of the largest classes of advertising accounts in the *Journal* of the American Medical Association.) The following report on cod-liver oil by Madsen, McCay and Maynard, of Cornell University, as summarized in *Chemical Abstracts,* may well give pause: "Goats, rabbits and guinea pigs were fed synthetic diets consisting of cellulose, starch, casein, sucrose, yeast, lard, inorganic salts, cod-liver oil and orange or tomato juice. Goats grew normally upon such diets for 2 or 3 months, after which they dropped dead suddenly. Post-mortem examination of these goats showed severe heart lesions and frequently lesions in the muscles of the legs. Guinea pigs and rabbits tended to develop lesions of the leg muscles in the course of a month when fed such diets. Many of the rabbits' hearts had also undergone pathological changes. The cod-liver oil of the diet was partly responsible for producing these muscle lesions. Rabbits fed 2 to 3% of cod-liver oil in a synthetic diet died sooner than those fed only lard with no supplement of fat-soluble vitamins. . . . *In all cases cod-liver oil was fed at levels frequently recommended for human consumption.*"[32] [Italics ours.] Lafayette Mendel points out in the *Yale Journal of Biology and Medicine* for July, 1934, that many commercial brands of cod-liver oil contain from 1 to 5 parts per million of arsenic.

It is no idle conjecture to connect a recent report on the number of school children suffering from heart trouble in New York City with the enormous ingestion of cod-liver oil to which they have been subjected by well-intentioned parents and physicians who get their information more from attractive and persuasive medical journal advertising than from reports of dry and intricate papers by chemists, pathologists, and toxicologists. Sixty thousand pupils in the public schools of New York City are found to be suffering from heart trouble, according to investigations made by the Department of Health of the Board of Education.[33]

A sizable volume could be written on the single topic of the toxic hazards in that octopus-like racket of the patent and proprietary remedies which were far from banished by the crusade against them a generation ago. In a recent number of the *Rocky Mountain Druggist* we read the following: "The 'reducing racket' has a group of new and dangerous drugs, dinitrophenol and related compounds. Racketeers are selling these drugs in fat reducers in spite of reports of deaths caused by their compounds, says W. G. Campbell, Chief of the Food and Drug Administration. 'Reducing agents containing these drugs,' says Mr. Campbell, 'have sprung up like mushrooms all over the country, and are endangering the lives of patrons. The Federal Food and Drugs Act has no jurisdiction over products of this type, dangerous though they may be. All that the Food and Drug Administration can do is to warn the public that these compounds are dangerous.' " [34] This is exactly as though the Department of Justice should say: "All we can do is to warn the rich that kidnappers are dangerous; we have no jurisdiction over them, dangerous though they may be." Where, however, the financial interests of the wealthy are involved, you may be sure that one or more departments of government have jurisdiction to give protection.

The awesome properties of radium have made it a profitable substance for misrepresentation and exploitation. Hair tonics, bath compounds, tissue creams, tonic tablets, face powders, mouth washes, and radioactive waters are among the products which exploit the magical reputation of radium to the grave peril of those who are ignorant enough to take the greatest risks. Radium is a carcinogenic agent when improperly used even though it is used in the treatment of cancer. At least thirty horrible deaths are on actual record of workers employed in the painting of the luminous figures on watch dials. While this industrial hazard has probably been ended (it would never have existed if due concern for the health of workers were a part of industrial practice in the initiation of all industrial methods), there is at present no curb upon the vendors of nostrums which contain sufficient quantities of radium to cause death. Dr. Leonard B. Loeb, of the University of California, in reporting one of these nostrums says that two glasses of the water, taken daily as recommended, would over a period of one year contain "at least ten times the lethal amount if stored." Dr. Loeb says in conclusion: "That the vending of such dangerous or fraudulent preparations, with the misinformation accompanying their advertising, should be permitted in such an enlightened country as the United States is almost unbelievable." [35] It is *unbelievable* only from the standpoint of those who assume that the health and life of workers and consumers is a genuine concern of the makers and sellers of goods.

Space forbids our going into further details concerning the poison hazards involved in the consumption of goods which are produced in an economy whose primary purpose is swelling the bank accounts of an investing class. Clearly, these conditions permit of rectification only by the adoption of entirely new and opposite motives and controls in the production of goods and services.

Ralph E. Flanders, president of the American Society of Mechanical Engineers, says that "the term 'business' is an honorable word," and proceeding with suspicious re-iteration, he declares that "'profit' should be so defined that it becomes an honorable term." [36] So are they all, all honorable terms! A well-rounded education including Shakespeare would have saved any protagonist of business and profits the mistake of thus paraphrasing Marc Antony's description of Brutus and his fellow-assassins. Nevertheless, in spite of Mr. Flanders' slip, we are disposed to let the characterization stand under the circumstances. Business is an "honorable" term! Profit is an "honorable" term! So are they all, all honorable terms.

CHAPTER XII

Druggéd Individualism

THE PROFIT MOTIVE WAS A CONTAGIOUS MALADY which spread rapidly throughout the entire social organism. The assumption, which is quite common, that while the business enterprise (that is, the transfer of goods to ultimate consumers) is, by some decree of Nature, conducted on the basis of profit-making, the essential social services are free from that virus, is without substantial foundation; and those who reason from that premise will fail to understand many of the most important phenomena of a business civilization. The "traffic in health" could not, in the nature of the system, escape the impulses and motives that dominate all the other major activities of a business society. This is not to say that there are *no* socially minded physicians who conceive of the medical profession primarily in terms of serving the health requirements of the population, and who are on call twenty-four hours in the day for the relief of physical suffering.

On the other hand, the medical profession in a profit-oriented system has perforce come under the sway of motives of private gain. The proposal to socialize medical service has met its most determined opposition from the medical profession itself. Resentment at every encroachment by measures of socialization upon the privately controlled territory of the medical profession resembles in every way the resentment of traditional business toward the socialization of the means of production and distribution. Any move to make available the largest possible degree of health services to the masses who cannot, under the prevailing conditions of income-distribution, purchase them in the "health market" of medical and surgical services and hospitals and nursing care is regarded as a form of muscling-in where private interests have established a professional monopoly for the ends of private gain. There is, of course, no transcendently greater condemnation implied in this observation than is involved in the similar observation on the traffic in goods. Health considerations begin with the general conditions under which goods are distributed, and if those conditions are rightly left to the control of the principles and exigencies of private profit, there is no good reason why all other considerations of health should not be similarly controlled. It is no more, nor less, reprehensible to limit the opportunity for medical attention to the *economic status* of the sick than it is to limit the opportunity for general consumption of goods to the *economic status* of the healthy individual who needs and wants them. It would be a wholly anomalous situation in which the *terminus a quo* and the *terminus ad quem* of life, a man's birth and death, could be sanctified by either religious or medical rites of unselfishness when all the privileges of consumption between the *termini* are available to him only under the severely limiting conditions of their being profitable to some one else and available at that some one's pleasure, and a group's pleasure if it be a monopolistic group as is the case with medical services.

If any proof is required to establish the dominant attitudes of the medical profession on these questions, it is available in abundance in the literature of the health-business. *Hygeia,* a monthly publication of the American Medical Association, in presenting reasons *for* and *against* entering the medical profession, cites as one of the *disadvantages* to which the present-day physician is subjected, "the competition offered by public and semi-public health organizations and the meddlesome interference of numerous lay bodies." The "competition" and the "interference" to which reference is made are those of groups that endeavor to make medical services available on the basis of *need* rather than on the basis of providing some physician with large fees. "For some reason," says the writer in *Hygeia,* "various philanthropists have become intensely interested in providing medical attendance for the middle class, and the private physician in the larger cities has much really unjust competition to meet." [1] The words "unjust" and "just" are, like all conceptions of "justice," strictly relative terms. In the quotation which we have cited, "unjust competition" is that which curtails the money-income of private physicians, albeit a curtailment resulting from a positive and socially necessary provision of medical services for the impecunious and needy sick, and for helpless children and indigent old people.

In order to reach a full understanding of the nature of a society that is built around the profit-motive, we must destroy the illusion that the professions are free from the toxins of income-mindedness, the illusion that a great gap in motives divides medicine from high finance. How so eminently desirable a health program as preventive medicine may be brought under the dominance of profitableness is shown in the words of a speech delivered by Dr. C. C. Bass, of the School of Medicine of Tulane University, before the American Medical Association's Congress on Medical Education, Medical Licensure and Hospitals, which assured physicians that *"a person prevented from dying unnecessarily in early life lives longer to have other diseases for which medical service is required."* [2] [Italics ours.] If preventive medicine succeeds in keeping millions alive a while longer, the increased longevity will supply the makers of misbranded, adulterated, deleterious, and toxic foods and nostrums, from arsenic-bearing cabbages and apples to *Ex-Lax,* with an increased opportunity of damaging their health, which in its turn will call for the repeated attendance of physicians. The manufacturers are doing their part in this scheme most admirably, and are thereby placing money-minded physicians greatly in their debt. What a boon it is to mankind for "preventive medicine" to add ten years to man's life and particularly those last ten years in which the cumulative poisonings of forty years previous register their effects in organic disturbances.

"All ultimately die," observed Dr. Bass (and the truth of the observation is axiomatic), "but the longer they live the more medical service they require" (also a truth which is not debatable under the profit-system). Dr. Bass's conclusion is, therefore, that "preventive medicine actually increases instead of decreases the total income ultimately received by the medical profession." That even one physician of standing could, under the highest professional auspices, give expression to so crass a view of the income-producing values of human ailments, is evidence that the very main-springs of life are poisoned in a system which suffers the exploitation of *any* compelling and undeniable human need, whether for health, medicine, food, or clothing, for the purposes of profit.

Intimate business relations between medicine and manufactures spring up as a matter of course. The manufacture of nostrums is a highly profitable business; the physicians organize professionally and publish magazines which in turn are most easily financed and made profitable by advertising the products of the manufacturers. Mutual favors are given and expected. The sick pay the bills (if they are able, or if unable, they experience a mortality rate which is directly determined by their financial incapacity and the social disorganization of medicine). The *Journal* of the Michigan State Medical Society shows how far this intimacy of medicine and manufacture has gone. The item reads: "By the way, the Petrolagar man was in this afternoon and I told him I could not use his products unless his company advertised in the Michigan State *Journal*. He said that they had spent so much money on the Exhibit at the World's Fair they had no money for state journals. I told him that was no way to help the doctors who recommended their products. I told him, also, to write his company that a doctor in the Whitney Building would not use his product unless they advertised in our *Journal*. So that's that—to help the Business Manager." [3]

The editor of the *Journal* of the American Medical Association claims to represent "the medical point of view" on broad social questions, even those which lie entirely outside of the field of medicine. He registers emphatic protest against the naming of Edgar Sydenstricker to the President's Committee on Economic Security on the ground that "Sydenstricker indicated his opposition to our entire economic system." [4] He bases this allegation concerning Mr. Sydenstricker's social views on the following statement which the latter is reported to have made before the Academy of Political and Social Science: "Any program of action to be given serious consideration at present must assume the continuance of the economic system under which we now live—a system that is characterized by a grossly unequal distribution of wealth and an inability to pay for the essentials or luxuries of life." This, apparently, not only puts Mr. Sydenstricker on record against the present social system, but in the opinion of the *Journal's* editor it likewise places Mr. Sydenstricker on record as "completely antagonistic to the medical point of view." Physicians, including the editor of the leading professional journal, are entitled under a profit-motivated system of medical organization to their own political and economic views, but it will strike the uninitiated as strange that the spokesman for the profession so completely aligns the "medical point of view" with that of the bourbon reactionaries of privilege and profit-first.

A writer in the *American Medical Association Bulletin*[5] abandons the medical point of view in favor of that of economic poetry, with the surmise that "it may be that the genial flower of medicine blooms with difficulty in the stark and rigorous atmosphere of Communism." This protagonist of the "genial flower of medicine" (or should it be classified among the odorous *fauna* rather than the *flora?*) is in entire agreement with the position of the American Medical Association which has launched repeated and vicious attacks upon the proposal to socialize medicine. Doctors, though mainly an irreverent lot, like politicians and industrialists, are ready to invoke the sanctions of religion when in desperate need to prevent any threatening encroachments upon the domain of private profit. Thus the British medical reviewer, quoted in the *Bulletin* of the American Medical Association, wonders "whether a polity under which there is nothing for a man to worship but the material things his own hands have made, does or does not carry within it some inevitable seeds of decay." Begrudgingly, he concedes that "the Soviet Government in the meantime has achieved much in health organization, and may be expected to achieve more, even to the extent of establishing throughout a great part of its territory medical services which, though ranking below Western standards, will be competently mass-productive of physical efficiency." This is the strangest plea, by indirection, we have ever read on behalf of druggéd individualism! This defender of "the genial flower of medicine" and druggéd individualism sees in the Soviet health organization "the plan of the despotic Communist Party, which is to provide for labor and defense." How many bodies, one may well ask, did British and American doctors patch up for the purpose of sending them back into the hell-holes of Northern France to make the world safe for the Morgan and du Pont and Citroen millions and the Bank of England? If provision for *"labor* and defense" is an unworthy medical objective, does the American Medical Association aim to provide for the physical comfort of idle parasites at one end of the social and economic scale, and for the physical hardihood of those who fight the wars of the parasites, at the other end?

The following story divided into three parts (certainly nothing but pure gall in this instance)—"What Happened," "The Problem," and "The Solution"—should generate more than a little skepticism regarding doctors and druggists:

"WHAT HAPPENED

"A local doctor was in the habit of prescribing magnesium sulphate, intending same to be used in solution as a compress. We had filled many prescriptions calling for this particular salt until we ran up a snag.

"A customer, who apparently had a smattering of high school learning, brought in a recipe for magnesium sulphate. When we told him that the charge for six ounces was fifty cents, he wanted to know why we asked fifty cents for an item, a pound of which he could purchase over the counter for fifteen cents.

"Secondly, he felt that we were putting something over on him (and for that matter, so was the doctor) for not telling him that all the physician wanted was Epsom Salt.

"THE PROBLEM

"We could not satisfactorily reply to his first query except to tell him that our minimum charge on prescriptions was fifty cents.

"However, on his second question, we told him that we were not allowed to inform the patient what the doctor had ordered and if the doctor cared to tell him, that was his option.

"All in all the situation was somewhat embarrassing and provocative both to us as well as the customer. Needless to say, we lost the customer and the doctor suffered the loss of his patient. But, how could we prevent a recurrence?

"THE SOLUTION

"I approached the doctor and told him what happened. He naïvely asked me how he could avoid such pitfalls. I suggested to him that the next time he has occasion to prescribe magnesium sulphate or any other chemical or drug known to the layman, to incorporate another ingredient that will preclude detection. In this instance, I hinted that a little potassium permanganate [which would give a strong color and disguise the simplicity of the prescription] could be used with satisfaction. He took our advice, as a result of which we never had trouble of that nature." [6]

The foregoing narrative is taken from the department of "Perplexing Problems and Their Solutions," in the *Practical Druggist and Spatula Consolidated*. It constitutes an appropriate introduction to the methods and motives that characterize the druggist's end of the "traffic in health." There was a time, long since, when the drug store was primarily an institution for the compounding of prescriptions issued by physicians. Much of the public confidence in the druggist is a vestigial relic of that period. This confidence, it is suggested by the pharmacists' trade journal, should be utilized for merchandising purposes which, since the metamorphosis of the drug store into an odd combination of soda fountain, lunch counter, all night grocery store, reduced-price book store, cosmetic supply house, and curling-iron and electric lamp emporium, dominate the profession. The following is found in the same very businesslike journal of pharmacy under "Hints on Advertising":

"By the very nature of his business he [the druggist] normally enjoys the confidence of the public to a remarkable degree. If a finger is cut, or a slight burn or bruise is sustained, or a cold or sore throat contracted, the victim nearly always goes first to the druggist for help. When, therefore, the druggist advertises, he is already assured of the confidence of his readers." [7]

How the druggist should proceed to advertise to these confident readers with assurance of success is set forth in the following advice from this same trade journal:

"When the advertiser can say 'Well-known doctor recommends so-and-so,' that is a good advertisement, and if able to mention the doctor's name it is a better one. But if one wishes to link the advice of the medical profession on general health with a proprietary medicine it is as well to keep the inference general. 'Doctors recommend so-and-so' is a useful type of slogan, so long as it has some basis of truth, but better still is to give a general health rule and link it up with the thing advertised. For example, a headline such as 'A large percentage of ailments originate in the nose and mouth' is a safe statement, and it can be qualified and justified with 'Your doctor will tell you that,' or 'Statistics prove that to be a fact,' then you can go on to build up a sound argument in favor of using a certain commodity as a mouth wash or gargle. In this way public confidence is secured, a good sales reason is presented for the article, and no offense is given to anyone." [8]

With merchandising aims in the ascendancy in drug stores, it is not surprising to find that the state boards of pharmacy include in their examinations questions on elementary business arithmetic. In the list of questions asked by the Missouri Board of Pharmacy (not, please note, of Arithmetic, or Merchandising, or Accountancy) last year, under the head of "Pharmaceutical and Chemical Problems," we read:

"3. A pharmacist bought a kip of Chamois skins (30 skins) for $26.39, with 3 skins free, and sold the lot for $1.50 a piece. (a) What was his gross ¡rofit? (b) What was his percentage of profit on the cost? (c) What was his percentage of profit on the selling price?"

"8. A pharmacist bought 5 gallons of cough syrup for $20, which was 33 1/3 per cent off the list. (a) He sold four gallons to a physician at 25 per cent off the list. What was the price paid by the physician for the 4 gallons? (b) The pharmacist then sold the remaining one gallon of cough syrup at 15 per cent above the list price. What was his gross profit on the transaction?" [9]

In a letter to a druggists' trade journal, Joseph Jay Gold, Ph.G., of Brooklyn, N. Y., writes: "Primarily, we pharmacists are interested in devices which will help turn over merchandise more rapidly . . . what really counts is results . . . 'the main idea is to move goods.'" [10]

When "life and death" may be so easily balanced in the pharmacist's scales, it is alarming to find that pharmacists are so completely absorbed in the purely business concern of "moving goods." *A careful investigation of filling prescriptions in Chicago's drug stores recently revealed that 300 out of 400 prescriptions were incorrectly compounded.*[11] An exactly similar situation was reported by government authorities in the District of Columbia, but of course no action was taken or seriously considered in either place to end the hazard to the drug stores' customers. It is a gullible and indifferent people that permits ignorant salesmen of chamois skins to put bichloride of mercury, as actually was done, in a prescription that called for calomel powder. "A grave error in filling a prescription calling for calomel powder to be used externally was evidently made recently," reports the *Monthly Bulletin* of the Indiana Division of Public Health. "The powder upon analysis," says the report, "was found to contain the poisonous bichloride of mercury." [12] But when pharmacists must concentrate their attention on selling 98 cent books (originally priced at $3.50), worthless mouth washes, and gadget burdened electric appliances which serve the "load building" ambitions of the public utilities, there is no wonder that such mistakes occur, or that 75 per cent of prescriptions filled in Chicago's drug stores were incorrectly made up.

The danger of having inexperienced and ignorant men dispensing drugs which are, in a large measure, poisons, is no trifling matter. Remember, when you take your next prescription into one of these general merchandising stores with a pharmacist's shelf attached, that you are also taking your life in your hands. Consumers' Research files give ample evidence of the unreliability, and unscientific and often dangerous quality of druggists' work in devising proprietary remedies and compounding prescriptions. There are a few members of the profession who are cognizant of the existing conditions. The *American Druggist,* for example, declares that the situation persists "because the public does not realize, as yet, the full danger." [13]

The arms makers' "traffic in death" has aroused keen indignation among sentimental and unrealistic pacifists, but it should be borne in mind that the makers of death-dealing war appliances are no more subject to the dictates of the profit-motive than is all the rest of the business world, and that probably far more deaths occur annually in the United States as the result of permitting the "traffic in health" to remain under the control of profit considerations than resulted from the participation of this country in the World War. When a leading druggists' trade journal says: "Boost Citrate of Magnesia; it means the largest profit for a single dose" [14]; and when a supporter of a medical journal will agree to recommend Petrolagar only on condition that the manufacturers buy advertising space in the journal, there should be no further doubt that all the veins which the social organism of capitalism possesses run with the poison of profit, and that the basic condition of human existence in such a social organism is that you submit your body to its rulers as a mere convenience for the louder and more frequent jangling of their cash registers and the busier grinding of their adding machines.

CHAPTER XIII

Cycle or Whirlpool?

"THE BUSINESS CYCLE WILL CONTINUE," [1] declares Ralph E. Flanders, newly chosen head of the American Society of Mechanical Engineers. "The rhythms of industry are as inevitable, and may be as invigorating, as the rise and fall of ocean tides," says this distinguished engineer, long groomed by the mechanical engineers' society to provide a liberal "front" for its aggregation of steel and textile and paper mill and utility operators, in a highly poetic mood. This should bring three rousing cheers for the depression from millions of husky throated workers, now that they have America's foremost engineer to interpret for them the broad and invigorating social significance of weary hours' standing in bread lines or before employment agencies, or waiting at home for the letter that never comes. Mr. Flanders not only finds the alternating tides of swollen profits for the owners of industry and mass destitution for the workers and consumers invigorating, but he believes a national plan should be adopted for the refreshing return of mass unemployment. "We must therefore plan for repeated periods in which unemployment increases somewhat above the normal resulting from the preceding causes," says this sage of bolts, gears, and high-speed steel. On December 5, 1934, Mr. Flanders received the Worcester Reed Warner Medal "for his contributions to a better understanding of the relationship of the engineer to economic problems and social trends." [2]

The editors of the *Magazine of Wall Street* take very much the same view of the matter; they see the world from much the same vantage point as the employing engineers (the kind who become presidents of national engineering societies). They find in current protests against the idiocies of capitalism only the recurring plaint of distress which lifts its voice with a repetitive rhythm, which so far from disturbing their complacency only gives them added assurance of the endless and salutary alternation of protest and approbation in this best of all possible business worlds. "Criticism is rampant, uncertainty persists and the daily news would give the impression that the difficulties of modern times are without parallel," say the editorial spokesmen of the money-changers and money-gatherers. "Yet," they add in supreme confidence, "Daniel Webster's description of conditions almost a century ago, is as apt today as it was in 1838." [3] Here is the 100-year-old opiate of Daniel Webster which the editors find so soothing:

"There are persons who constantly clamor. . . . In a country of unbounded liberty, they clamor against oppression. In a country of perfect equality, they would move heaven and earth against privilege and monopoly. In a country where property is more evenly divided than anywhere else, they rend the air shouting agrarian doctrines. In a country where wages of labor are high beyond parallel, they would teach the laborer he is but an oppressed slave. . . . They can mean nothing but disturbance and disorder, the diffusion of corrupt principles and the destruction of the moral sentiments and moral habits of society."

Therefore, reason the "dough" boys, unrest and protest are just old American customs which are periodically revived, but which also subside before invulnerable American institutions with the same periodicity, as soon as the uncouth and ill-mannered masses have wearied of their yammering.

Joseph A. Schumpeter, Harvard economist, speaking of the current crisis, says cheerfully that "there is no reason to despair—this is the first lesson to be derived from our story." Why? For the simple reason that "fundamentally the same thing has happened in the past, and it has—in the only two cases which are comparable with the present one—lasted just as long" and "in *all* cases, not only in the two which we have analyzed, *recovery came of itself.*" [4] [Italics ours.] Schumpeter's analysis is characteristic of the academic writing world.

Another business contribution to the explanations of the current crisis is found in a volume entitled *We Have Recovered Before!* The author, Walter W. Price, offers the typical evidence of the cycles as proof of his central thesis. Avoiding all conclusions that would seriously indict business for its economic defects, the recurrence of crises is assigned a cause in deep psychological mysteries. "Perhaps," says Mr. Price, "the high, dizzy peaks of booms and the deep, dark valleys of depression are but a reflection of a peculiar cycle of mass psychology." The thought gains weight with Mr. Price and, dropping all claims of mere probability, he proceeds immediately to *assert* that "these swings from periods of extreme prostration to periods of excessive prosperity . . . always reflect a certain psychological direction in the changing temper of the mind and attitude of men." [5] Thus a mystical mass psychology is saddled with the responsibility for the mass misery attending depressions when, through a convenient ignorance of economics, the author is incapable of assigning intelligible causes. His triumphant peroration offers the "faith of the cycles" to any would-be doubters in the business world. "There has come," he maintains, "after each successive trough of economic collapse, a return to levels of prosperity not previously attained." [6]

We may as well follow the "faith" of the French astronomer, Abbé Th. Moreux, who assigns supra-mundane rather than psychological causes to earthly sorrows. To M. Moreux solar activity is the key to social upheavals on earth. "In the periods of minimum activity," says the French astronomer (or should it be astrologer?), "it is notable that the world has usually been at peace, while those of maximum activity seem to create a nervous tension that causes peoples to fall upon one another in mad and savage struggles." M. Moreux predicts that 1936 and 1937 will be years of great solar activity! And therefore of wars!

But the imperialists and the munitions merchants are not to blame. Future scientists, no doubt, will spend *all* of their time finding celestial and sociological scapegoats for the guilt of the iron masters and other masters of men.

It is noteworthy that the cyclical theory of business is held most firmly in periods of "depression." In periods of boom, there is a pronounced tendency among the "leaders of thought" to declare that the cycles have ceased. At least so far as the American system was concerned, this was declared to be the case in the late boom. "With impressive proof on all sides of magnificent progress no one can rightly deny the fundamental correctness of our economic system," [7] said Herbert Hoover in his acceptance speech in 1928. Growing even more effusive in his optimism, Hoover declared in his inaugural address: "Ours is a land rich in resources; stimulating in its glorious beauty; filled with millions of happy homes; blessed with comfort and opportunity. In no nation are the institutions of progress more advanced. In no nation are the fruits of accomplishment more secure." [8] No talk of cycles here! No "invigorating rhythms" of industry! No psychological mysteries, no sunspots!

These outbursts of the "Great Engineer" were not mere Republican palaver; they were expressions of the high faith of business men and college economists generally. Those were days when the all-wise queried confidently, *Whither Mankind?* Among the many spokesmen of the New Capitalism, Julius Klein answered: "It is the sheerest folly to contemplate the return to pre-war normalcy." [9] The very thought of pre-war business levels was, according to Klein, "utterly mediæval" and "babbling, antiquated twaddle." Of course, America was utterly different from Europe. "In general, the whole environment of American industry—labor scarcity, abundant raw materials, large domestic markets—has created a combination of circumstances vastly different from those prevailing in Europe," [10] wrote Klein.

Faith in the ultimate validity of existing business institutions and civilization has scarcely suffered any impairment as a result of the passing of the Great Boom, although a new rationalization has retreated to the old cyclical faith as the Great Hope. Alfred P. Sloan, Jr., summoned seven hundred American "leaders of thought" to a banquet at the Century of Progress last year. From their counting-houses and their classrooms they came to Chicago. There they spoke, each in his unshakable tranquillity and complacency oblivious to the thought of a rotten-ripe and moribund civilization plunging headlong to its destruction. Asserting that "our progress is practically unlimited," Mr. Sloan led the chorus of seven hundred. Charles G. Dawes, Chairman of City National Bank & Trust Company, unworried apparently by the condition of his financial institutions, chimed in with this: "Industry is on the threshold of great achievements." Arthur S. Draper, editor of the *Literary Digest,* claiming no authority of a Digest ballot, said: "My personal view is that the standard of living will be raised, that social relations will steadily improve, that international relations will grow better." Irving Fisher, political economist of Yale, assured the "seven hundred" that "with proper treatment [*sic*] we can reach and surpass all former records of prosperity." F. H. Haggerson, president of the Union Carbide Company, said: "We are facing the future with confidence." William Randolph Hearst: "The Century of Progress is ahead of us and not behind us." Robert L. Lund, sales-maker of *Listerine,* prophesied: "This progress will continue." Charles M. Schwab, Chairman of Bethlehem Steel Corporation, throwing out a broad hint, said: "Given freedom of action to work out its problems, business and the nation are set for better days for a number of years to come." Walter Dill Scott, president of Northwestern University, declared that "the history of the world from the beginning of time indicates that there has been a constant acceleration in the rate of progress." In all the seven hundred tiresome "previews of industrial progress in the next century," there crept not one word of blunt realism on the present state of capitalist civilization.[11]

It would seem as though some malicious fate had immunized the spokesmen of a decadent civilization to any germ of understanding of the impending doom of their indefensible economic system. When events were leading up to the toppling of the throne of the Romanovs, Nicholas II wrote in his diary: "Went paddling in a canoe." The historian of the Russian Revolution observes of that late royal nit-wit that "between his consciousness and his epoch there stood some transparent but absolutely impenetrable medium." [12]

The economist who first described the behavior of business society as "cycles" performed a poor service for the custodians of its political and economic power. Under the fatal misapprehension that periods of "prosperity" alternate endlessly with periods of "depression," "they have given themselves over to a delusion that they may believe a lie." The delusion of "cycles" has enabled them resolutely to ignore the steady downward movement which would be far more accurately described as a vortical descent into ruin.

The economic system whose aim and methods we have *briefly* illustrated in the preceding chapters of this volume offers many *indexes of decline* by which its total life-period may be gauged. In all of the varied manifestations of the business economy touching the kind and quality of goods which it produces, we detect the phenomenon of irremediable decay, a fact which over-shadows in significance all of its temporary upturns in the quantity and *movement of goods*. The presentation [advertising] of its wares to the body of essential consumers harassed by an ever-contracting economic ability to command goods and services has grown more, not less, florid, fantastic and fatuously dishonest. The range and manner of its sales appeals have incorporated more, not less, irrelevant pressures in its frantic efforts to dispose of its products. In the variety and ephemeral and useless quality of its multiform and endlessly proliferated gadgets, the system has been characterized by more, not less, preposterous attempts to keep its factories and sales forces busy. Its idolatrous consumption, commandeering the grotesque social prestige of actors, athletes, and the socially élite for its less easily merchandisable goods, has become more, not less, pronounced. Science has been more, not less, debauched into a peculiarly meretricious form of superstition in the wheedling of half-educated masses to buy what they do not need and cannot safely use. The counterfeiters of goods have employed more, not less, adulteration, in a more, not less, organized fashion in order to lower the costs while maintaining or increasing the selling price of commodities. The fight against the introduction of consumer standards to prevent rational consumption has ever become *more,* rather than less, sharp. Distribution under trademarked names, with an enormous increase in the sale of nationally advertised brands, has made consumers more, not less, ignorant and *brand conscious.* Invention has been sabotaged, or misused through the device of *progressive obsolescence,* with more, not less, disregard for rational progress. Those who profit by the cumulative poisoning of consumers have more, not less, defiantly ignored the considerations of human toxicology. Professional services, such as medicine, have shown a disposition to cling more, not less, tenaciously to the provision of such services on the exclusive basis of private gain rather than of sound craftsmanship and social and individual need.

The index of decline in the provision of useful and honest goods and services, while not a statistical index, points clearly to increasing difficulties and tensions in balancing potential production and actual consumption. This is primarily neither a problem of under-consumption nor over-production, but a problem of the over-accumulation of capital in the hands of private enterprise whose only concern is with its profit-yielding capacities. Such a concern of the enterprisers is irreconcilable with any fundamental regard for the interests of the masses of consumers, and in the long run, with any safeguarding of the very ends of profit that are sought.

The exploitation of the profit-seekers has now centered upon the quality and the utility of their goods and services. Quality and utility are more completely subject to their control than are the mechanisms of price and wages. Prices are more responsive to governmental policies or to uncontrollable movements of the market; wages are likewise more conditioned by the effectiveness of labor organization or by the state of the labor market. There are fixed limits determined by custom and human toleration to the possible exploitation of both prices and wages. There are hardly any limits to the exploitation of goods and services through the progressive deterioration of quality and utility. This is consequently the chief area in which business seeks to maintain the disproportion of income from its vastly over-capitalized structure. In this area also the decay of business civilization is most glaring and therefore most easily and graphically depicted, provided and to the extent that the services of engineers, chemists, and toxicologists are available for the guidance of consumers. Business knows this far better than do the forces of discontent that seek fundamental social changes. It has become the common practice of business to buy up these skills, wherever possible, as soon as they are applied, or someone threatens to apply them, in the interests of those who consume. Business usually has no difficulty in obtaining these skills and turning them to the ends of sellers and against those of buyers, for there are no organized groups in society to offer full and well-remunerated opportunity for them to work in the interest of consumers.

Both the *magnitude* of production and the *magnitude* of income for the consuming and working masses are tests which stand second in importance to the *character* of production in terms of quality. A writer in the liberal *Nation* declares that "the ultimate test of national welfare is to be found in the magnitude of production which is available for the satisfaction of human wants." [13] "Magnitude" is *not* an adequate or ultimate test! Six hundred million pounds of sugar and six hundred million gallons of water that go into 13,000 million bottles of carbonated beverages *more* than satisfy the requirements of magnitude—for anyone. Tested in terms of quality and utility, this particular "magnitude" of production is altogether wanting. It is far worse for the population already consuming too much sugar and artificial flavor and color in its foods and beverages. Magnitude of income, even when stated in terms of *real* wages, is likewise not an ultimate test, apart from the considerations of quality and utility. Whether it is better to endure slow starvation in an economy of scarcity or to suffer poisoning in an economy of abundance is a choice to which a rational community will not wish to be confined.

It is not simply an economy of abundance but an economy of *abundant quality* that satisfies all the requirements of a worthy social objective. The "trial of the galoshes" in Moscow is a practical and dramatic expression of the striving toward such an economy. Capitalism is not simply an economy of scarcity; it is something far worse—an economy of *scarce inferiority,* in which the scarcity, as we have shown, is not more deliberate than the inferiority. The same technical skills which have made possible the ending of scarcity have likewise made possible the ending of inferiority. Revolutionaries have not made the most of their opportunities when they have emphasized the contrast between an economy of scarcity and an economy of abundance. Economists have talked and written as though there were no problems of kind and quality, but only of footage and tonnage, and barrels. The issue which must be joined is infinitely more important—scarce inferiority *versus* abundant quality! The inadequacy of seeking relief from scarcity alone is well illustrated in the recent food poisoning of one hundred members of a relief camp in the Malibu Mountains of California.[14]

The precise amount of a worker's wage has only a relative importance. Of transcendent importance is the question: what does the wage command in the quality and utility of goods and services? The size of the pay envelope is not enough, if it simply enlarges the worker's ability to command more fraudulent, shoddy, rickety, adulterated, sleazy, short-lived, or rancid and toxic goods. If scarcity be relieved and inferiority be accentuated simultaneously (a mere artifice of "recovery" which business *now* seeks!), who will say that the cause of human welfare has been advanced? A program of "immediate demands" cannot afford, in its absorption with relieving scarcity, to ignore inferiority. Such a program opens the way for a business subterfuge, since a business loss on the issue of scarcity may be retrieved by falling back on a still greater exploitation of inferiority. That this is true is evident from the bitter resentment which business already harbors toward those who are attacking it on the grounds of its inferior products. There appears to be a full realization in business circles, and especially in advertising circles where most of what passes for economic thinking for business is done, that if the existing economy sustains a loss at this point, its entire morale and its hope of large-scale continuation of exploitation of the masses will have been shattered. Its last line of defense for profits in a period when profits are threatened as never before in modern history will have been broken. There must, therefore, according to the best business strategists, be a forming of a solid business front against any increase of social controls over the character, kind, and quality of goods. All the hoary sanctions of freedom and democracy and cherished institutions must be invoked and distorted as necessary to make them seem applicable, against the threats of exposure of fraudulently advertised, mis-branded, adulterated, and toxic goods. Leaders of the coöperative movement and social democrats who propose to insinuate them-selves into power through instrumentalities over which the ruling class of business holds absolute control are contemptuously tolerated or even on occasion flattered by those in power who are intelligent enough to know that such measures hold no *serious* threats of interrupting their plans for continued profit and domi-nation of economic life. Business is fully cognizant that the hos-tility which may be generated against it on the limited grounds of a larger share of purchasing power and better distribution of income can never become a driving force in as *large* a group as can the hostility which is bred of demands for *both* abundance and quality of goods. The number of those who are exploited on the job may be decreased by lowering the labor item in the costs of production through the substitution of machines for men and of unskilled and transient labor for skilled artisans; the number of those who are exploited by the adulteration of the product must perforce increase. If, therefore, to the discontent of exploited labor, still largely conscious of wage levels alone, is added the discontent of the defrauded and poisoned masses of the displaced, unemployed workers,—non-wage-earners—there will be a force against which *reaction* cannot prevail in its hour of desperation. That hour may not be distant. It is the part of wisdom to prepare the broadest possible defense against the excesses of reaction.

A social system does not need to reach the bottom of its whirling descent before drastic modifications in its political habits are adopted. It needs only to experience unprecedented difficulties in achieving its normal purposes in order to arouse grave apprehension for the security of its ruling class. Such apprehension is a common phenomenon in the post-War western world. The will to survive, in a ruling class, is reinforced by the consciousness of waning powers. It is not the inherent weakness of the system which generates such fears, but it is the consciousness of that weakness. Another *index of decline* is to be found in the number and severity of persecutions by the ruling class. There is good historical reason to believe that the excesses of repression practiced in fascist Italy and Nazi Germany may appear mild in comparison with those of American reactionaries once they are fully cognizant that the theory of the inevitable cycle of regaining prosperity is a delusion and that social movement henceforth is more accurately to be described as a vortical descent. The traditions of extreme and brutal repression were never more firmly entrenched in Italy and Germany than they are in the United States.

The years of so-called prosperity themselves afford ample source material to indicate that the business system was then preparing inevitably for an acceleration of its decline. Even today there is no general disposition among the "accepted" economists to turn to this material for an understanding of their so-called cycle. Frank recognition that a profit system *inevitably* irrupts in wars, depressions, and wholesale deterioration of goods, to say nothing of gross inequalities in ability to command goods and services in times of "prosperity," is not to be found in official and respectable circles, except in rare cases.

The World War has been made a scapegoat for everything from lax morals to attenuated incomes. In pacifist circles it has been good propaganda to ascribe the current crisis in business civilization to the War. Carrie Chapman Catt has phrased that common belief in these words: "It is well to remember that the cause of the great depression which is, at present, overwhelming the world with its terrors, was a war too great for the nations to conduct or to pay for. The depression is the penalty." This is a highly convenient half-truth for bankers and politicians who do not wish to face the more fundamental causes of crisis. Bankers and brokers can well afford to subsidize "peace" organizations for the purpose of popularizing such a half-truth. Leonard Ayres, of the Cleveland Trust Company, voices it in these words: "Great wars are accompanied by prosperity, and followed by depression. This is an ancient truth that has been noted and recorded through the ages, but one which each new generation tends to forget." Therefore, Mr. Ayres concludes, "the true lesson of this depression is that we cannot afford any more great wars." [15]

Wars do indeed accelerate the process of social disintegration, but the process of disintegration is itself a cause of war, not an effect. Only the acceleration is an effect of war. Wars and depressions are inherent in the economy, and are normal phases in its long decay. Pacifists perform an eminent service for their business benefactors to the extent that they obscure this fact. The only deterrent which stays the war for which absolutely unprecedented preparations are being rushed by all the major powers is the knowledge which bankers and cabinet ministers possess that the coming war will in all probability so accelerate the normal disintegration of capitalism that social revolutions, through a rising of the masses and the soldiery in desperation, will surely be placed on the order of the day. The deterrent is not, however, a preventive, for capitalist society has unleashed forces of conflict over which it no longer has any effective control.

The causes of the current crisis, in terms of the vast over-accumulation of capital, the widening scissors between productivity and employment and between productivity and real wages, together with the resulting maldistribution of consuming power, and the relationships of all these factors, are set forth in the chart at the bottom of this page.* It will be seen that real wages and

* INDEX OF DIVIDEND AND INTEREST PAYMENTS, REAL WAGES, COST OF LIVING, EMPLOYMENT, POPULATION GROWTH, PRODUCTIVITY, AND CONSUMPTION, DURING PROSPERITY, 1923–1929

	1923	1924	1925	1926	1927	1928	1929
Dividend and Interest Payments							
Unadjusted to Cost of Living	100.0	107.1	113.9	122.5	155.3	168.1	211.8
Adjusted to Cost of Living	100.0	107.3	110.9	119.6	153.9	168.4	212.2
Real Wages	100.0	102.9	101.3	102.9	105.4	107.0	107.4
Cost of Living	100.0	99.8	102.7	102.4	100.9	99.8	99.8
Employment							
Unadjusted to Population Growth ..	100.0	92.3	95.6	97.3	94.8	93.2	97.0
Adjusted to Population Growth ..	100.0	91.0	92.9	93.1	89.5	86.7	89.0
Population Growth ..	100.0	101.4	102.9	104.4	105.9	107.4	108.9
Productivity							
Volume of Production	100.0	93.5	104.8	107.7	105.4	111.3	118.6
Output per person	100.0	101.3	109.1	110.3	109.9	117.9	120.8
Consumption	100.0	98.2	100.1	101.3	100.3	101.2	103.6

Sources: Dividend and interest payments indices are derived from the Taylor Society *Bulletin,* October, 1932, compiled by Emmet H. Welch, Research Department of the University of Pennsylvania. Dividend and interest payments indices, adjusted to the cost of living index, give the real income from property, and are therefore comparable to real wages. Cost of living index is taken from *Statistical Abstract of the United States,* 1933, page 292, as is the index for real wages. Employment figures, unadjusted to population growth, are taken from *Statistical Abstract of the United States,* 1933, page

consumption rose but slightly during the period of so-called prosperity, whereas the income from property rose out of all proportion to income from work. In relationship to population growth, employment fell 11 per cent; and even without adjusting the index of employment to population growth there was an absolute decrease of 259,896 wage earners between 1923 and 1929, according to the census of manufactures. Job-competition was therefore sharply increasing. There was no employment prospect whatever for the rising generation except through the ruthless and inhuman underbidding of one worker by another in the labor market. The scarcity market of labor, *the only condition conceivable under which labor exercises any effective control over its income in a society where labor is a competitive commodity,* had vanished. The rulers of society were riding high, under the illusion of permanence, but they were also riding inevitably for a fall. The conditions of distribution, in terms of quantity as well as quality, were subject only to their unbridled acquisitiveness. There was, in fact, a stock promoter, a ticker-tape-watcher, not an engineer, in the White House. The class in power was likewise a group of stock promoters "between whose consciousness and their epoch there stood some transparent but absolutely impenetrable medium."

In 1929 the income recipients of $5,000 a year or less, in their purchases of consumers' goods, created 78 per cent of the *effective demand*. On the other hand, the 513 persons having incomes of over $1,000,000 spent $87,000,000 and invested $1,045,-000,000, or twelve times as much as they spent. In the same year,

---

300; and with the population growth taken from the yearly estimates of the Census Bureau, we have calculated the weighted or adjusted employment figures. Productivity indices for both volume of production and output per worker are taken from *Recent Social Trends*, "Labor Groups in the Social Structure," by Leo Wolman and Gustav Peck, Vol. II, page 805. Consumption indices are taken from *The Power Age*, by Walter N. Polakov, pages 206-207. All figures have been adjusted to a 1923 base in order that percentage increases during the period may be comparable.

28,000,000 families with incomes under $3,000 spent sixteen times as much on consumers' goods as they invested.

These simple facts, ascertainable at the time, are quite enough to account for the sorry debacle into which the profit system has plunged the masses. There is no need for Mechanical Engineer Flanders to invoke the "invigorating rhythms of industry," for Wall Street editors to call upon Daniel Webster, for Mr. Price to invent the "peculiar cycle of mass psychology," for Mrs. Catt and Mr. Ayres to make the World War more hideous in its import than it really was, or for M. Moreux to study the sun spots in order to assign intelligible causes for the whirling descent of capitalism. Economic activity geared to the profit interests of a small investing minority, with scant or complete disregard for the masses whose well-being can never be served except by an economy of *abundant quality,* results in precisely the *scarce inferiority* which, through booms and depressions alike, becomes increasingly intolerable.

CHAPTER XIV

Survival of the Misfittest

BUSINESS IS A SYSTEM OF GLORIFIED IRRESPONSIBILITY in which the most shrewdly acquisitive rise to the top and the most indomitably acquisitive stay there (at least for the duration of the system). The leaders of business are not only totally lacking in any professed responsibility for the socially healthful functioning of the system, but they are even more strikingly lacking in any exceptional ability in matters of technology. Their servants, the technicians, are not to be confused with those whose power directs the operations of the system. In power derived from cash-register abilities, and in that power and its irresponsible uses alone do the rulers of business society possess any distinguishing fitness.

The essential control of business is in the hands of a few thousand men. Since the beginning of the twentieth century, financial capital has superseded industrial capital in importance. Financiers have solved the troublesome problem that was forever recurring during industrial capitalism, of how to use and control money without owning it. As financial capital superseded industrial capital, management and ownership of industry were divorced without leaving too much fraternal affection among these several recipients of property-income.

Corporations elevated business men to positions where responsibility decreased as the apex of the corporate pyramid was approached, and the misfittest were enabled to survive. With the use of other people's money, and with the divorcement of ownership and control which eliminated risks of ownership for those who played for high stakes, plus the corporate form of business enterprise which centralized power without social responsibility, investment bankers were in a position to concentrate in their hands control of wealth without moral or legal obligations to those who stood to lose by that concentration. *The Modern Corporation and Private Property,*[1] coupled with later researches by one of its authors, Gardiner C. Means, shows that while 49.2 per cent of all non-financial corporate wealth was controlled by two hundred corporations in 1930, depression, like prosperity, has seen the steady growth of concentration until by 1932, 55 per cent of all non-financial corporate wealth was held by the same number of corporations.[2]

In 1920 there were 30,139 banks in the United States, but by 1933 that number had decreased more than 50 per cent, leaving only 14,623 as the total number of banks.[3] The Chase National Bank, The National City Bank, Bankers' Trust, Central Hanover, Irving Trust Company of New York City, the Continental National Bank and Trust Company of Chicago, and the First National Bank of Chicago control $6,727,663,690.14 or about one-eighth of the total banking resources of the country.[4]

Concentration of *control* in banking is difficult or impossible to measure. It cannot be determined statistically as can banking resources. Interlocking directorates have become, only in the last decade or two, a thing of common practice. Lewis Corey, in his *House of Morgan,* estimated that 167 individuals in the Morgan-National City Bank and Chase National oligarchy held over 2,450 directorships in corporations with assets of 74,000 millions of dollars which was then, in 1930, 22 per cent of all corporate assets.[5] J. P. Morgan's anonymous and, of course, sympathetic biographer, writing in *Fortune,* indicates the subtle meaning of control. He uses the word "control," in speaking of Morgan's power, "in a very special sense." He explains that "one director or a very little stock plus the enormous prestige of a house which has placed most of the great loans of a generation may amount to a *human* control, a *personal* influence, which no single man or group of men can withstand." [6] J. P. Morgan and members of his firm have great power attached to their function of making loans or withholding loans, as they see fit, dictating the terms of those loans, whether to a private corporation, to government officials, or to foreign powers.

What manner of men hold such enormous powers over the masses that they ultimately determine whether millions shall eat plentifully or merely subsist at a dangerous level of physical inefficiency? What thoughts and pastimes crowd their abundant leisure? What course, in view of their mentality and essential culture, are they most likely to pursue in the event of still greater crises in the system over which they preside with powers that any ancient despot would have envied?

Morgan's biographer in *Fortune* remarks that "no man has ever seriously contended that he [Morgan] was a man of intellect," but he hastens to assert that "any degree of erudition among American bankers is rare." He concludes that "Mr. Morgan himself would probably be the last to pretend either to an understanding of his age or to the possession of an important mind." [7] Intellect, erudition, understanding, and an "important mind" are not necessary *survival qualities* in business society; they might even prevent survival. There is no other man in the United States who exercises the degree of control over economic life that J. P. Morgan does—the man who spends most of his time with his tulips or on his regal yacht, or in other pastimes away from his office.

In reflecting upon the abilities of America's banking rulers, it is pertinent to bear in mind that recent Yale experiments with apes show that they can be taught to earn and handle money and furthermore that "this ability is retained after loss of the frontal association area" of the brain. [8]

During the period of prosperity for the vested interests, there were countless expressions of the view that more profits for the rich meant work and a larger income for the workers. Economists from great institutions of "learning" were quick to give their academic approval to these views. Thomas Nixon Carver, noted economist of Harvard University, was so impressed with the evidence of prosperity in the twenties that he felt sure it was being dispersed to every man, woman, and child. "For the first time in history the masses themselves, in this country, are emerging into a condition of prosperity comparable to that of the aristocracies of any previous age," wrote Carver in 1928.[9] "We can predict with absolute certainty that such prosperity as the nation as a whole achieves will be diffused and *not concentrated* if we look carefully after the occupational distribution of our population. . . . There is absolutely no reason why the widely diffused prosperity which we are now witnessing should not permanently increase."[10] [Italics ours.] Yet, at the very time these statements were being made, income from property rose to the heights termed "prosperity" while the number of workers employed decreased and the real wage increase was only 7.4 per cent compared to 112.2 per cent increase in real income from dividend and interest payments.

Shifting our inquiry from Harvard to the offices of business executives we find William S. Knudsen, executive vice-president of the General Motors Corporation, expressing his idea of how the depression is to be ended, just as he started for a European trip aboard the North German Lloyd liner, *Europa,* recently. "Sooner or later some one will stand up, look around at the depression, ask 'What's this all about?' and get busy and end it," said Knudsen, who did not bother "to stand up and look around" himself.[11] He might have seen, if he had bothered to "look around," shamefully exploited stevedores and stewards, without looking an inch beyond the deck of the North German Lloyd liner.

The National City Bank Bulletins (mouthpiece of the Morgan interests) "enlighten" us as to the causes of the depression as viewed by those who have large financial interests. "The problem of the depression centers upon the cause of unemployment, and since business men are always eager to give employment when they can sell their products, they certainly have not been deliberately responsible. They have been as helpless in the situation as the wage-workers themselves. The direct cause has been a state of world-wide disorder in trade relations which has been beyond the control of any individual employer or group of employers." [12] That a system should not be tolerated in which control of industry does not carry with it responsibility for the running of that industry, in the sense of serving society, seems self-evident. Let the workers and consumers but presume to try to take control of industry and accept responsibility for its operation, and it will be quickly seen who *now* controls it. It is amazing that those who wield so much power should so carelessly admit that they take no responsibility for the working of that system. When the gods of profit are propitious and all goes well for business, it is these same barons of industry who hasten to claim credit; but let the gods become unpropitious and the barons at once look about them helplessly and assign all sorts of mysterious and usually foreign causes for the trouble. "Employers were not responsible for the spread of unemployment resulting from this loss of purchasing power among great groups of producers and from the evident derangement in trade relations," [13] the National City Bank writers would have us believe. Yet the facts of productivity, wages, decreasing employment were all evident during prosperity to show that there was an over-accumulation of capital. If trade relations keep getting out of gear periodically, it might be pertinent to inquire if those relationships are ever or ever can be in harmonious adjustment under capitalism. They were in "derangement" at the height of prosperity; the derangement of prosperity was the obvious cause of the crisis of the era immediately following.

Alleviating suffering without too great cost and of course without levying upon the accumulated wealth of the industrial and financial magnates has always been proposed by business as a solution of crises. Most of the task of alleviating want in the past has been left to kind-hearted individuals whose lowly station and commonplace tasks brought them into personal contact with the individual sufferer. In the early days of organized philanthropy those who were forced to accept relief were termed destitutes, paupers, indigents, and incorrigibles, which notion surviving in the mores is one reason why many unemployed are reticent today about receiving relief. The title of one of the oldest philanthropic organizations still in existence, the *Association for Improving the Condition of the Poor,* indicated no idea among the philanthropists of eliminating the causes of poverty; its policy and its personnel expressed the ideas then current, that poverty was a policy of Providence and not a condition for which personal social responsibility existed among those whose acts and engrossments prevented any approximation to equality of income distribution. Social work today is still trying to pick the man up after he has fallen off a cliff rather than aiming to prevent his fall; and is trying to adjust people to their environment, with no idea that perhaps the environment rather than the people needs changing. Frankwood Williams threw a bomb into the Philadelphia Social Work Conference several years ago by describing social work in "backward" Russia and concluded that Russia's system was *eliminating* the causes of mental and social maladjustments whereas business society accentuated them.[14]

Business men are too busy trying to think up new methods of getting new "suckers" for their products; and the owning population is too busy tending their tulips or dogs, or supervising the peasantry who give a note of old world beauty to their estates, to be very much concerned about the victims of depression. Manufacturers of dog food made from *horse* meat are trying to persuade owners of dogs that "the findings of chemists and scientists" prove "first, [that] horse meat is richest in proteins and nitrogen, and second, that it is the natural food for dogs." However, "many doting owners of dogs are reported to have revolted . . . against feeding their pets anything which they themselves would not consume." Chappel Brothers, chief manufacturer of dog food, has kindly made a concession and will avoid in the future the issue which has *"stirred dog lovers so deeply"* by adding to their line a new *beef* Ken-L-Ration![15] [Italics ours.] An advertisement in a recent *New Yorker* shows a woman of the upper classes feeding her insignificant and useless house dog on Borden's Golden Crest Milk because it's "richer, better-tasting Grade A. . . ."[16] Abercrombie & Fitch Company advertise in their current catalogue a "dog Xmas stocking" which contains among other things a mewing cat's head, a rubber chop, a chocolate flavored rubber bone, and, not to break puppy's heart altogether with imitations, "a tin of the finest beef for Xmas dinner."[17] The December (1934) number of *Woman's Home Companion* offers four suggestions for doggie's bed—a bed for every canine fancy: "modernistic," "Colonial," "Chippendale," and "French Provincial."[18] There are, besides dog lovers, fish lovers among the idle rich who are particular about what food they have for their fish and who provide a profitable market for the enterprising business men who are concerned only with pleasing those who have money for fish and dogs if not to provide for a more even distribution of income to the poor. Dr. George C. Supplee, director of the research laboratories of the Dry Milk Company, a Borden associated company and caterers to fish, announced that "for aquarium fish fanciers, who wish to match the color of their fish, the food will be offered in eight colors."[19]

Private property is the first consideration of those who profit by it, not only in time of a general economic crisis, but also in disasters such as shipwrecks or tragedies occurring in industry. The history of the struggle to secure adequate safeguards for workers in factories, and payment of workmen's compensation for industrial accidents has been a long and not altogether successful one. Industrialists still do not accept responsibility for many poisons and occupational diseases, nor do they accept responsibility for unemployment of their own workers through insurance of any kind. And in every state where compensation has not been provided for by law, the most determined and effective resistance is made by industrialists against any such "socialistic" provision. Accumulated corporate surpluses for providing stockholders with continuous dividends is, on the other hand, a sacred property obligation to be discharged in times of boom and of depression. Even "unemployed" machinery requires uninterrupted "wages" in the form of interest charges on capital, while no responsibility for the wages of unemployed workers is accepted. During the Morro Castle disaster hearings, the salvage laws were brought out in bold relief. The Ward Line's servants, knowing their master's mind, were far more concerned with saving salvage costs arising out of the sending of an S.O.S. call than with the lives of the passengers. The line, quite without any sense of wrongdoing and entirely in accordance with commercial folkways, appealed through counsel to the United States District Court to limit its liability to a total of $20,000, which would be less than $158 per corpse. One's heirs may not even confidently expect the passage money back in case he is drowned or burned to death at sea. If anyone doubts this, let him but read the elaborate and minutely fine print contract which forms a part of what one gets in buying an ocean steamship ticket. Business responsibility for disasters in all branches of industry is in no sense proportional to the degree of control of business over those branches. The next time a man dies from eating lead-poisoned pears, we suggest that the grower and seller refund not only the man's nickel, but pay some round sum like $10 for one visit of his child to the kind of a physician which the owner of the commercial apple orchard sends his own children to for winter pallor or "spots before the eyes."

Business men know of no way to meet the economic crisis except by slashing wages, lowering costs, and increasing the productivity of labor. They introduce labor-saving devices, close down old plants and make more efficient the old machinery; they rack their brains to think of ways and means for throwing the burden of the depression on the workers and the lower middle class. The "share-the-work" plan was a marvelous discovery with this import. More men were to be hired with the total pay-roll remaining the same—thus forcing each man's pay down to a sum too low to permit him to subsist with any degree of decency. A survey conducted by the President's Committee on Economic Security admitted that some employers were paying their employees such low wages that relief had to be supplemented. Harry L. Hopkins, Federal Relief Administrator, said, in commenting on the survey, that workers working full time had no place on relief rolls "which were not intended to carry burdens properly the responsibility of employers." [20] The worker who was asked to share his work was appealed to by many groups of patriots who told him that it was his duty to be magnanimous and that he should be glad he had *any* job to share. The Home Relief of New York City carried the idea of *made-work* to a ludicrous extreme. This useless *made-work* was supposed to preserve the morale of the men, even though many of them had to be out all day in biting cold weather with inadequate clothing, and if they got sick their pitifully low work-relief was stopped. But the "morale" of the unemployed must be preserved. It is the one thing for which business cheerfully assumes responsibility.

The history of every depression is full of efforts by the unemployed workers to prevent starvation, and of the employers meeting these efforts by force. The resulting riots when written up in the newspapers are said to be communist in origin, but everything which is in the nature of a protest or which does not flatter the crazy system of starvation-amidst-plenty, is said to be "communist." Not to be a "communist," according to those who profit by the system, would be quietly and patriotically to die of starvation without any attempt to get food. John H. VanDeventer, editor of the *Iron Age,* organ of the steel industry, referred editorially and with great disdain to "the organized labor leaders, social minds, uplifters, downpushers and communists" who testified at the steel code hearings, and added that "if the suggestions regarding maximum hours, minimum wages, compulsory insurance and soviet management were to be adopted, iron and steel, from the cost standpoint, would be put into the category of precious metals." "Steel," he continued, "will cheerfully follow the line of flight of the blue eagle, but it will determinedly fight the buzzards that follow in its train." [21]

"It is disturbing to honest, hard-working, fair-minded, middle-class citizens [the paid backbone of our country] to note the reluctance of the present government to hand out to unreasonable, rampant labor groups the same brand of treatment that has been meted out to employers this year," says Floyd W. Parsons of *Advertising & Selling*. "There is nothing more destructive of national morale," Mr. Parsons concludes, "in a time like the present than evidence of a policy of babying labor extremists engaged in anti-social [obviously meaning anti-commercial] excesses." [22]

Members of the National Wholesale Druggists' Association have also objected to the shorter hours and wage increases which the NRA proposed. One wholesaler, William J. Schieffelin, Jr., claimed "that if the NRA insisted on the shorter hours and higher wages proposed, it might even lead to the abandonment of the century-old custom of giving employees Thanksgiving turkeys." [23] Improving the condition of the poor, indeed!

At the same time that Harold Ickes stated that "a bloodless revolution has occurred, turning out from the seats of power the representatives of wealth and privilege," [24] incomes over $25,000 were increasing and incomes under $5,000 were decreasing. While incomes below $5,000 were shrinking, Mr. Ickes stated that "we are not in this world to work like galley slaves for long hours at toilsome tasks, in order to accumulate in the hands of 2 per cent of the population 80 per cent of the wealth of the country." [25] But that is precisely the situation which the "New Deal" has served to perpetuate. Certainly not even a cabinet officer could honestly affirm that the "New Deal" had done anything direct, clear cut, and forthright to transfer a part of the 80 per cent of the wealth to the 98 per cent of the population. Has it not indeed assured business men of the certainty of continuance of their profits and of the certainty that high taxes will not be applied to high incomes? "One of the most ominous signs about the New Deal," the *News and Leader* (Springfield, Mo.) stated, "is one that so far has gone almost unnoticed—a little disclosure made in compilation of the most recent income tax statistics." These statistics show "a growing concentration of wealth in the hands of the middle and upper income groups, and a decline in the position of the ordinary, middle-class citizen." [26]

When profits are picking up, an easy attitude toward the depression is one of business optimism. Lewis H. Brown, president of Johns-Manville Corporation (Morgan concern), said in an address before the New York Building Congress, in July, 1934: "Personally, I am no longer concerned about what the brain-trusters may do to us. We are on the way out of the depression. Recovery is taking place. The emergency is over. The time of desperate measures hurriedly conceived is past. . . . We are going forward into a new era. This country is still a place of opportunity. The people of this country will continue to enjoy the highest standard of living of any country in the world. And while the future is going to be quite different from the past, America is still—and will continue to be—a democracy." However, Mr. Brown's recovery, corporation style, means to make more secure the "system of individual thrift and private investment that has been the foundation upon which this country of ours has been built" and in which the "profit motive has been the activating impulse that has made this system work." [27] Concentrate on profits, and the millions who are unemployed will somehow or other, no one is quite sure how, be taken care of! That is the extent to which the owning class can think of solving the problem of recurring crises. They do not even express ideas capable, if applied, of dealing with the situation, much less proposing "to take steps."

When questions about unemployment are asked, the usual answer is let the unemployed take care of themselves. "To the thoughtful man," an article in *Food Industries* (McGraw-Hill) states, "it is a source of satisfaction that such a leader as Owen D. Young is recalling to the attention of the country that all persons can and must do much more for themselves than they are now doing in the way of providing for their own subsistence in periods of unemployment." [28] Yet when the unemployed take that advice seriously as some "hunger-crazed 'squatters' on a city dump" did when they braved blazing gasoline to get at the contents of cans of tainted prunes being destroyed by public officials, the police and Deputy United States Marshal prevented them from reaching the prunes. "Who cares? It's something to eat," one man shouted in reply to the Deputy Marshal's warning that the food was tainted.[29] When the unemployed tried to provide for themselves in the building of Hoovervilles on the margins of our big cities, they were forced, in many instances, to tear down their shacks because they were unsightly to those who must have sightliness in their own environment at all cost, and because they would bring down real estate values of nearby property owners.

Police Commissioner John F. O'Ryan (now retired) indicated that he knew the part the police were supposed to play, in keeping the unemployed from demanding food or means to get food, in a speech made before the Brooklyn Rotary Club shortly before his resignation. He said: "If law and order is not preserved, normal people tend to heed professional agitators and to regard themselves as a class that must demonstrate or perhaps riot to bring about a change in conditions." This tough and distinguished preserver of law and order and defender of democracy would not have us think there are classes, for that might presuppose a degree of partiality on the part of the police. "There is no law or other method of establishing classes or castes," Mr. O'Ryan declared. To a mind which has been immersed in legality and its physical sanctions, if classes are not created by law, *there cannot be any*. "Such things do not exist in America. That is America. Many so-called capitalists have nothing but a shoestring and many so-called laborers refuse to labor." [30] Poor buffeted capitalists; how hamstrung by worthless working men!

Fascism is the attempt of the government and business to meet crises primarily by stabilizing depression standards of living. It is pertinent, therefore, to describe briefly the fascist solution in both Italy and Germany.

Italy emerged from the World War heavily in debt to her allies. Having depended greatly upon foreign loans, the economic life of Italy was seriously affected when the loans were stopped. When industrialists could not get loans they sought aid through inflation which sent the lire down to about one-third of its wartime value. Coupled with the fall in the value of the lire went, of course, a corresponding rise in the cost of living, which prostrated the small tradesmen and caused great suffering among workers and farmers. Agrarian disorders followed. The industrialists attempted to control the situation but became, in 1919 and early 1920, completely demoralized. Workers here and there seized control of factories. However, the former employers induced the leaders of the workers to accept arbitration with promises of higher wages and representation. After regaining control of the factories, the owners organized their forces and prepared to take advantage of the demoralization which thereupon afflicted the ranks of labor. Benito Mussolini was alert to his opportunities.

Under the pretense of conciliating classes, fascism suppressed the working class, and gave full reign to the owners. "In its social aspects, Fascism endeavors to conciliate the conflicting interests of the different classes," Paul Einzig, the pro-fascist English economists, states.[31] "Strikes and lock-outs were outlawed from the very outset of the Fascist regime, and for over ten years there has been no strike or lock-out in Italy."

"The year 1927 was one of widespread economic depression ...," Augusto Turati, General Secretary of the Fascist Party, wrote in the International Yearbook of Fascist Studies, 1928.

"It was necessary for the Government of the Fascist Party to take steps with the object of bringing about a reduction of wages from 10 to 20 per cent. . . ." That reduction was never rescinded. Paul Einzig comments upon it: "In no country was it so easy as in Italy to obtain the consent of employees to a reduction of wages, in accordance with the fall of prices and with the depressed state of industries." [32] Later, he says: "Thanks to the establishment of industrial peace, wages in Italy are more elastic than in any other country." [33] That sentence might be precisely translated as follows: Thanks to the imposition of industrial peace by employers upon workers, workers will tolerate more reduction of wages in Italy than in any other country.

In Italy taxes have risen 50 per cent since the advent of Mussolini. Every worker must belong to his syndicate and all syndicates are brought together under a Ministry of Corporations. Membership to each syndicate means little except the "privilege" of being taxed. The tax amounts to 300,000,000 lire a year. Italy also has a sales tax, besides all the other forms of taxation, which is placed on the wholesale end of distribution, but which is passed on easily where no protest of consumers can be heard, and where no pressure exists for compelling the retailer to absorb it.[34]

That concentration of wealth has gone on unabated in Italy under fascism is evidenced by the number of small tradesmen who have been forced into bankruptcy as a way out of their dilemma. In the depressed post-War year, 1921, bankruptcies totaled 1,896, while in 1933 they had risen to 21,308.[35]

Italy has reduced the standard of living of those still working and has forced the worker to support more people on his wage. The average wage in 1932 was 1.75 lire an hour for industrial workers and was lowered to 1.5 or about 8 cents an hour in 1933,[36] which is about the equivalent of homework wages—the lowest wage of any working group in the United States. "Fortunately the Italian people is not yet accustomed to eat several times a day. Its standard of living is so low that it feels scarcity and suffering less," Mussolini declared in a speech to the Italian Senate on December 18, 1930.[37]

Il Duce is now planning to take all women workers out of Italy's industry for several reasons.[38] (1) Woman's primary duty is to increase the population for future wars. That takes her time and energy and interferes with her factory or office job. Therefore, her duty to the State comes first and she should give up her job. It is the fascist-capitalist way of meeting the increasing unemployment problem. (2) By taking women out of industry, men must support them wholly, thus decreasing the real wages of the men.

It is to be expected that Thomas W. Lamont—partner of J. P. Morgan, whose loans to Italy helped to entrench fascism—in his article, "Italy's Economic and Social Progress since 1922," should give as one of the high achievements of fascism the fact that "today strikes are practically non-existent." [39] The negligible loss of working days since the advent of fascism is proof to Mr. Lamont that workers are contented and industry is stabilized, the exact kind and degree of content and stability that a business man finds most gratifying.

In Germany the situation is similar to that of Italy. Nazism is the means whereby the industrialists and financiers of Germany have met the crisis—by reducing mass living standards to new low levels, and at the same time forestalling threats of riots, revolts, or even articulate disapproval in public or private conversation and of course in publication. Post-War Germany presented a picture of economic and social demoralization. Despite the generous aid of the Social Democratic leaders, German capitalists were not able to sustain the profits which they thought were rightfully theirs. Mass discontent because of inflation and growing unemployment was leading to strikes and militant demonstrations, all of which was displeasing and disquieting to the barons of big business. Hitler promised to silence all the opposition to the industrialists who in a *quid pro quo* arrangement smoothed his way to power. By the use of the mass threats of the brown shirts, concentration camps, a few fires, and many murders, Hitler could promise the industrialists that there would be no internal disturbances to worry them. With the opposition crushed or driven underground, German industrialists have prospered. Profits in the heavy industries increased 80 per cent during 1933 at the same time that wages in those industries decreased 20 per cent. The armament industries prospered most of all.[40] Profits in the Hoesch armament works increased from 12,500,000 marks in 1932 to 23,700,000 marks in 1933. Krupp earned 35,000,000 in 1933, an increase of 15,000,000 marks over 1932. Most of these profits were due to the new policies of rearming, decreasing wages, and the curtailment of public health and recreation services and social insurance.

Other methods for assuring the economic rulers that their program of raising profits will go through without disturbance from angered masses of workless and underpaid people, include the work of the Minister of Propaganda, Paul Joseph Goebbels, and his vast propaganda machine to prepare the hungry for psychological endurance of increasing deprivations. "Reich to glorify hunger as virtue," the New York *Times'* headlines read in the account of the Propaganda Minister's speech. "The greater the distress, the greater will be our defiance and our determination. . . . In spite of everything we will overcome it," said Goebbels.[41] *Italian fascism and German Nazism show their true kinship and the social and economic meaning which is at the root of every fascist regime everywhere—in the glorification of starvation standards of living.* Mr. Hjalmar Schacht, Minister of Economics, in a speech at Leipzig, emphasized the same note. The German people must be prepared "to face with great soberness" the economic emergency "which international policy has forced upon us." [42] It is the function of the Propaganda Minister to correlate all that is good, fine, and moral with intense suffering, and then envelop the whole with an aura of romance, with all the heroes of Germany's past called in to show that patriotism demands the bearing of hardship nobly. It is noteworthy that in each of these countries no provision is made by which the Thyssens and the Krupps shall share the hardships nobly or in any other way.

The chief characteristics of business men transcend all national boundary lines. When confronted with similar problems and exigencies under which their own welfare is the issue at stake, they react in Germany as they react in Italy. The principles of business conduct are so far universalized, deriving, as they do, from the motivations which underlie the machinery of money in all languages and in all countries, that the individual business man could not, if he would, behave one way in Germany and another way in the United States when faced with the problems arising out of his own ignorance and cupidity. Having risen to power through the exercise of no important or praiseworthy skills, his abilities to master a difficult situation in terms of broad social considerations have, if he ever possessed them, completely atrophied. Having no skills or integrated knowledge upon which to build any system of consistent ideas or attitudes renders him completely lacking in the integrity which could find a solution that would satisfy any considerable number of people. Successful acquisition is the key to the power of the commercial enterpriser and reveals those limited aspects of his behavior and modes of thought which determine his character. For the retention of his power he will fight, when pressed, with all the modern techniques of social organization and all the death-dealing appliances of science which his money can command. Italian, German, British, French, and American business oligarchs are blood-money brothers underneath the superficial differences of language, race and religion. No single praiseworthy human trait has anything to do with his survival qualities nor need be called upon to aid so long as his system continues after a fashion to work. His is, in short, a system whose last and highest leader and statesman must of necessity be a gangster! Which relates the end to the beginning, for long ago Mercury, the god of trade and commerce, was also the god of thieves.

PART II
OUTSIDE THE PARTNERSHIP

CHAPTER XV

Unrest in Lilliputia

WHEN JONATHAN SWIFT TOOK HIS GULLIVER first to Lilliput and then to Brobdingnag, the contrast between the pygmies and the giants was emphasized in terms of geographical location. The Lilliputians were antipodal to the denizens of Brobdingnag. Between them lay the full globular mass of the earth.

The logic of a developing profit economy has separated the giants of modern industry and finance from the Lilliputians of early capitalist enterprise by a world whose limits are defined by the full space of a century. The first manufacturing enterprise in America to assume a corporate form, the Boston Manufacturing Company had, in 1830, 76 stockholders and a paid-in capital of $300,000! [1] From that far-off beginning, inauspicious enough by comparison, there has developed a system of corporate enterprise which completely dominates the economic life of today. In 1931, there were 381,088 such corporations reporting to the Commissioner of Internal Revenue. Their total reported "assets" and "liabilities" were $296,497,029,000.[2] Among these giants of industrial and financial enterprise, 632 super-Brobdingnagians had total assets above $50,000,000 each, or together far more than one-half of the total corporate assets of the country. Against this century-long development of corporate enterprise with its ever increasing concentration into fewer and larger institutions, there have been no effective checks. It represents a process that has continued without interruption through the booms of prosperity and the pangs of depression alike.

The inevitability of merger, implicit in the rules of the system, has not discouraged the small enterpriser from attempting to apply restraints to his successful competitors, the large corporation enterprises. In these efforts he has had the support of other elements in the population that share his anachronistic attitudes, and, together with him, make up the lower middle class of modern society. Anti-trust legislation was enacted in the last decade of the nineteenth century with the effective assistance of the muckrakers and demagogic attacks upon the "malefactors of great wealth." These were so many gossamer threads used to tie down the sleeping Gulliver.

The *little men* have thought to restrain their giant competitors whose share of the national income has appeared out of all proportion to equity. The disparity in income is not open to question. For example, twelve executives in the tobacco industry receive salaries equivalent to the gross income of thirty thousand tobacco farmers and their families. The 339,407 persons having net incomes above $5,000, in 1932, 61.7 per cent of whose income was derived from ownership of property, received as much as the gross income of all farm owners and tenants in the United States and more than the total wages of all factory workers. In periods of depression, incomes from property possess a rigidity which is not characteristic of any other type of income. The rules of the system work at all times to protect unequally the various types of income-recipients. It is in the nature of things that these disparities should elicit large volumes of protest somewhat proportionate to the widening of the gap between the Brobdingnagians and the Lilliputians.

The most significant political and social phenomenon of the post-War era has been the rise of fascist movements which, in their incipiency at least, are the expressions of a Lilliputian revolt —a determination of the *little men* to place drastic checks upon highly concentrated capital. Fascism has been defined as an advanced stage of capitalism, characteristic of the system when confronted by a degree of crisis in which the political instruments of nineteenth century democracy fail to function according to prescribed purposes. This definition ignores the vital question of the initiative in the formation of the fascist movement. Is it, as some hold, simply the "movement for the preservation by violence, and at all cost, of the private ownership of the means of production"? Or is it, as others believe, "a revolt of the ruined middle class and peasantry"? This difference of viewpoint seems to concern itself primarily with the inception of fascism, and not with the ultimate support which it claims.

So far as mass support is concerned, it is clear that the ruined lower middle class and peasantry provide that. It is equally clear that this group dominates the early stages of the formal movement. Since, however, the aim of this group is to stabilize and not to overturn a decadent capitalism, it has only to demonstrate its potential political powers to gain the indispensable financial support of the profit-making class or important sections thereof. At this stage there is a conjoining of the lower middle class and big business elements in defense of interests which to the former are visionary and to the latter are substantial. The motives of these two sections of the bourgeoisie differ markedly: the lower middle class aims at the recapture of its vanished privileges, while the owning class aims at the retention of its threatened power. Thus the blood of cultural kinship is thicker than the water of economic circumstance. Without this union, which persists after the removal of its economic base, every uprising of the ruined lower middle class and peasantry would coalesce with the discontent of the property-less workers in a social revolution aiming at the expropriation of the upper bourgeoisie instead of its defense. It is also true that a larger or smaller amount of discontent of the workers, lacking class consciousness, also fuses with the fascist movement, thus further complicating the class character of its support. There is nothing novel in this situation, inasmuch as business men have always been able to claim the loyalty of the most divergent and even basically opposite interests in their hour of deepest need.

There is nothing particularly exceptional in the irony that the fascist movement which the discontent of the lower middle class initiates is finally turned to the aggravation of the very conditions which originally inspired it. Political movements are generally subject to numerous contradictions and irrationalities that defy the simpler explanations. American society is today passing through that period in which the effects of the crisis and of governmental policies upon the lower middle class are among the indexes for gauging the prospect of fascism.

Even if the status of the *little man* is a tenuous one in the logic of modern business, even if he is as doomed to extinction as the most inexorable laws of a social system can operate to eliminate a vestigial encumbrance, he may yet in his desperation have a fling at power, with consequences which the events in Nazi Germany no longer leave to the imagination for their clear understanding. For any comprehension of the basic tendencies in American society today, it is necessary to define in terms of their economic and cultural position these complaining Lilliputians, to understand approximately what the economic crisis has done to them, and to observe their reaction in deprivation.

(The Lilliputians may be defined as those persons gainfully employed in the United States who, because of income, preferred occupation, social position, ownership of stock or property, have a stake in the existence and perpetuation of a business man's economy without having any real control of it. They both own and work. The more precarious their status becomes, the more strenuously do they attempt to turn back the hands of time in order to retrieve what has been lost. Therefore, the group tends decidedly to be reactionary.)

The National Industrial Recovery Act has served to declass the *little man* (as owner) with greater rapidity than did governmental policies before the New Deal. Incomes from wages and salaries, that is, all of them which are under $5,000 a year had, by August, 1934, decreased 16 per cent since the "New Deal" went into effect. Net income of corporations increased 35 per cent over the same period of time. "The salary of the average college graduate holding an office position is lower than before the advent of the NRA," according to Lawrence W. Zimmer, in charge of the New York University Employment Bureau.

By an Executive Order of March 7, 1934, a National Recovery Review Board was created to make a survey of code authorities in the various industries. The Board was authorized to ascertain if the codes permitted monopolistic practices and the oppression of small enterprises. More significant than the Board's Report itself was the nature of its reception at the hands of government officials. Both Johnson and Richberg denounced the Report, without refuting the facts in it. "In virtually all the codes we have examined, one condition has been persistent, undeniable and apparent to any impartial observation," the report stated. The codes have offered "an opportunity for the more powerful and more profitable interests to seize control of an industry or to augment and extend a control already obtained." The Report concluded that "in industry after industry, the larger units, sometimes through the agency of what is called an 'institute,' sometimes by other means, have for their own advantage written the codes, and then, in effect and for their own advantage, assumed the administration of the code they have framed. Thus privilege has exerted itself to gather more privilege." The Federal Trade Commission's report of the facts concerning the effect of the Steel Code upon small enterprises and upon the consuming public fills out one of the gaps in the Darrow Report. The Steel Institute not only wrote the Steel Code but it also has full charge of the administration of the Code. When the first Darrow Report charged that monopoly control existed in the industry, a second code was drawn up, approved May 30, 1934. According to the third Darrow Report, this "contains most of the features of the original code which are attacked by the First Report of this Board." [3]

In case after case the survey found that those administering the Codes were men whose chief interests were to increase the monopoly control of their industry, and they were using the Codes to further it. "Profit-making power has been multiplied for the one purpose of gathering more profits that will mean still more power for still more profits," the report maintained. That thousands of small enterprisers have complained and have asked for relief shows to what extent little business is being squeezed in the interests of the recovery of profits for the large companies.

With the growing discontent caused by the economic crisis and enhanced by a governmental policy administered with strict regard for the needs of big business, it is to be expected that numerous organizations will arise which have as their purpose the restoration of the lost *status* of the small enterprisers within the framework of the existing system.

The successes of Mussolini's Black Shirts and Hitler's Brown Shirts have stimulated ambitious men in the lower middle class in many lands to reach for political power through the organization of similar unofficial militia. It is too early to say whether the many "shirt" organizations which have sprung up in the United States are rooted in basic social conditions or amount to nothing more than lifeless imitations of the foreign patterns. In their present strength they are hardly deserving of the publicity which mention of their names provides. Taken out of their social context, in which for the moment they are of slight consequence, it is possible to give a sensational review of their activities. This may be good journalism, but it is not an accurate assessment of their social significance. In wide sections of the United States they are entirely unknown, and in rare instances only have they begun the practice of bringing their military ritual to the streets. Until they appear regularly on the streets with impressive numerical strength, they are in a stage of development far removed from a position of threatening the prevailing form of government. Years before the accession of Nazism to power in Germany, millions of Brown Shirted Storm Troopers were familiar sights. *In the United States, the stuffed shirts of big business still pre-*

sent a far more serious problem than all the colored shirts of the lower middle class put together.

A sober estimate of the "shirt" organizations in the United States at the present time leads to the observation that the formally organized fascist movement is growing after the manner of mushrooms. Its numbers may be counted in the tens of thousands, but not in the millions which its leaders claim. Given a continuation of the social crisis and deepening of discontent generated by it, some one of these organizations may suddenly acquire impressive numerical strength. Even in their present weakness, however, the "shirt" organizations are an indication of the excesses and absurdities of which large sections of the American population are capable when political illiteracy, social prejudices, and economic deprivation conjoin.

Art J. Smith, erstwhile leader of the Khaki Shirts of America, has been sentenced to prison for perjury which he committed at the trial of Athos Terzani. Terzani was accused of slaying his friend Antonio Fierro at a meeting of the Khaki Shirts which they attended as anti-fascists. The only evidence against Terzani was the perjured testimony of the members of the Khaki Shirts, and he was promptly acquitted when a jury heard the case. The manner in which the prosecutor's office of Queens County, New York, proceeded was more ominous in its implications for a future fascism in this country than was anything perpetrated by the Khaki Shirts themselves, even though one of Smith's lieutenants, Frank Moffer, subsequently confessed to the murder of Fierro.[4] The story of the Khaki Shirts of America is of little value except as it is an indication that ex-servicemen commonly have the necessary qualifications for becoming the storm troopers of a future fascist movement.

It is well known that the Nazis and the Khaki Shirts engaged in abortive negotiations for cooperation. In telling how Art Smith became anti-Semitic in order to get Nazi support, William Dudley Pelley, another would-be fascist leader, disclosed that he, too, has enjoyed the confidence of the Nazi agents in this country. When the Silver Shirts held their first meeting in New York City on November 3, 1933, in Kreutzer Hall, East 86th Street, there were many members of the *Freunde des neuen Deutschland* present. The publications of both organizations, *Liberation* and *Amerikas Deutsche Post,* were sold at the meeting. The Nazi salute, "Heil Hitler!" was given by Nazis and Silver Shirts alike. Major Luther Powell, Pelley's Chief of Staff and a man with a Ku Klux Klan record, stated: "Of course we are in sympathy with the Hitler movement in Germany, and constantly in touch with his representatives in America." [5]

Four years ago Pelley started the Galahad Press and published some of the revelations from the Voice. A year later he went to Asheville, North Carolina, to start the Galahad College to promote his economic and Christian teachings. Then he formed the Foundation of Christian Economics, the Liberation Fellowship, and about three years ago, the Silver Shirts and the magazine, *Liberation,* which has, since the litigation arising out of the violation of the Blue Sky Law, become *Pelley's Weekly.* The *Silver Ranger,* the newspaper of the Silver Shirts, founded in November, 1933, in Los Angeles, has had a rather uncertain history as the editor, James H. Craig (now editor of the *Constitution Legion Herald,* organ of the Constitution Legion of America, formed in August, 1934), was forced to stop publication for lack of funds and aid from the "Field Headquarters." In starting his own movement of "shirts," Craig gives some interesting side-lights on William Dudley Pelley and his Silver Shirts. James H. Craig went through his own private adventure in eternity which, unlike Pelley's seven minutes, lasted half an hour. Craig was thus mystically equipped to lead his own movement. Having claimed that he had a much more determined "call" than did Pelley, he proceeds to give the details of his relationships with the Chief (Pelley). [6] A national newspaper, the *Silver Ranger,* was to be established, according to Pelley's plan, and Craig was asked to be the editor. Also the purchase of a large building and an entire section of land for the purpose of housing five hundred horsemen and their mounts was to be made. "The $100,000 'Field Head-quarters' project vanished into thin air. The section of land and the barracks were dropped from the conversation. Not a single 'trooper' or a lone horse ever put in an appearance," Craig states in his leaflet.[7] No money came from the Chief and for a long time no one could learn of his whereabouts. The *Silver Ranger* was suspended for lack of funds. Craig's *Constitution Legion Herald* is as anti-Semitic and red-baiting as was Hitler's first program and is full of phrases to attract the lower middle class.

In one breath Pelley talks in Biblical language of peace, love and "the Lord of Righteousness and Justice," and in another breath he exclaims: "Out of America with the whole insolent, mischief-making, lecherous lot of them . . . they and their satraps, their eunuchs and their mongrels!"[8] Alfred Rosenberg, chief anti-Semite of Hitler's Reich, has never been more vituperative in his outbursts against the Jews of Germany than is Pelley in this and many other passages of hate.

Pelley's method is not only that of enlisting individual members in his Silver Legion, but also of capturing other organizations *en masse*. Since the formation of the Silver Legion, other elements have been joining it. "The better element from the ill-fated Ku Klux Klan is moving into the ranks of the Silver Legion in heavy numbers with each week that passes," Pelley wrote in August, 1933. The national organization of the Protestant Italians in America has also seized upon the Silver Shirt work about 8,000 strong, according to Pelley. *Today* published a letter from Paul A. Toal, Foreign Adjutant of the Silver Shirts, to Royal Scott Gulden welcoming Mr. Gulden and his "Order of '76" into the ranks of the Silver Legion. Mr. Gulden denied the report of affiliation, however.

The most vicious anti-Semitic document ever published is known as the *Protocols of the Learned Elders of Zion*. Henry Ford, in his *Dearborn Independent*, precipitated an issue, from which he later retreated, by their publication. They are now being republished in this country under the sponsorship of the Silver Legion. The *Silver Ranger* reports an organization in Seattle, Washington, known as the AV's (probably the American Vigilantes), active in the printing and distribution of 10,000 copies of the *Protocols*.[9] The Leader of the AV's, alleged to have been a leader in the late Liberty Party of Seattle, informed the Chief of the Silver Shirts of the plan to bring his former organization into the Silver Legion *en masse*. While the Silver Legion is still numerically weak, even a little of this slanderous poison which it purveys is too much!

Pelley has made admissions of contact with the Nazi agents operating in the United States. The activities of these emissaries of Hitler in the United States have been generally confined, however, to the German part of the population. The formal organization of Nazis in the United States is now known as the Friends of New Germany (Bund "Freunde des neuen Deutschland"), though rapid changes in name and personnel of the group have occurred during the past two years. The activities and the organization of the Friends of New Germany are strongest in the Eastern States, but there are "locals" in four Pacific Coast cities. However, by means of local German newspaper editors, their pro-Hitler sympathies are being disseminated throughout the country. In New York City alone they claim a growth of four hundred new members a week. The Nazi uniform of Germany and the entire social program of the Hitlerites have been transplanted here as a part of the movement. The *Bund* is in close contact with the official Nazi Party in Germany, and German consuls throughout the United States have been active participants in the work of the *Bund*. The Nazi swastika is accorded equality of honor with the Stars and Stripes at all meetings. In spite of emphatic gestures in the direction of *"true Americanism,"* this movement of Nazis in the United States is still characterized by an obvious hybridity. It is an exotic growth on American soil nourished by the triumph of the Nazis in Germany, and carries little appeal as yet beyond the confines of the unassimilated German portion of the American population.

In the summer of 1934, two hundred German boys were encamped near Princeton, New Jersey, under the direction of the Friends of New Germany. With Nazi swastikas emblazoned on their brown shirt sleeves, these boys were taught military training and rigid regimentation by their leader, Hugo Haas.[10]

Under the joint auspices of Nazis and distinguished American *patriots* there is being circulated in the United States at present a book entitled *Communism in Germany*. Every school teacher in the city of Baltimore received a copy *gratis*. It contains one foreword written by Adolf Hitler and another signed by the members of the *Committee to Combat the World Menace of Communism* (American section). Among the well-known American names on this list are those of Hamilton Fish, Jr., Ralph M. Easley of the National Civic Federation, Harry Jung of the American Vigilante Intelligence Federation, and Walter S. Steele who is manager of the *National Republic*. The book purports to be a collection of the harrowing atrocities of Communism committed in Germany. The American sponsors state:

"Here is a challenging book. It should be read by every thoughtful citizen because it presents the history of the life and death struggle Germany has been waging against Communism. It reveals that the subversive methods and the destructive objectives of the Communists in Germany are the same as are employed in the United States by those enemies of civilized nations.

"The value of this German exposé as an object lesson to other countries has led our committee to place it in the hands of leaders of public opinion throughout the United States." [11]

The book identifies *fascism* with the purpose of destroying "the Communist Internationale . . . a task for the nations of the whole of the Christian and civilized world." This view of fascism is widespread throughout the patriotic societies of the United States. It was present here, however, long before the triumph of fascism in Italy and Germany. It acquires a definitely fascist character only because the Nazis of Germany have appointed themselves as the defenders of the Western world against the spread of Bolshevism, and the American patriots are inclining to accept Hitler's leadership in this task.

Down in Chattanooga, Tennessee, George W. Christians has established an organization headquarters for a group which now describes itself as the "American Fascists" in bold red letters on all the envelopes mailed from there. Mr. Christians signs himself as "Commander-in-Chief, Crusader White Shirts," and "President, Crusaders for Economic Liberty." The "General Orders" sent out by Mr. Christians, on a single printed sheet on which has been superimposed a large red cross, is explanatory of the technique of his organization. It reads, in fact, as follows:

"The first objective should be to take control of the local government in the following manner: March in military formation to and surround the governmental buildings. Then, by sheer numbers and a patriotic appeal, force the officials to accept and act under the direction of an economic adviser appointed by the President of the C. F. E. L. [i.e., Mr. Christians]. This adviser's first duty will be to repudiate the public debt and utilize the payments assigned thereto for the public welfare. . . .

"As soon as you are fully equipped and prepared to go to Washington, report to the Commander-in-Chief of the Crusader White Shirts at Chattanooga, Tennessee, stating the number of men, how equipped and the time required to reach Washington, but do not move until ordered. Nothing must fail."

Like Mr. Pelley, Mr. Christians is opposed "to all of the rotten Socialism of the Roosevelt Administration." Mr. Christians claims to be the originator of the statement that Roosevelt is only the "Kerensky of the American revolution," but Dr. Wirt denies his indebtedness to this source. Mr. Christians is at once committed to warfare against the "gold standard racket" and socialist-communist solutions of social organization—a typical fascist attitude. It is further to be noted that the appeal of Mr. Christians is distinctly to the discontent of the lower middle class and farmers of the country. But like the other "shirt" and "patriotic" leaders of aspiring fascist movements in the United States, his movement has not yet taken root in any mass discontent. He is a widely touring and energetic lecturer, having appeared on the Pacific Coast last spring with his appeal.

On March 4th of last year, headquarters were opened in Newark, New Jersey, for the "United States of America Union of Fascists." [12] The headquarters were announced as those of a national movement which claimed not less than five hundred thousand members. There is at present no national commander, but the national headquarters are in charge of Gaetano Asone. Mr. Asone served in the Italian Army during the World War and claims to have been active in the building of Italian Fascism before coming to the United States eleven years ago. He disavows any connection with Italian Fascism, however. Article 1 of his Constitution declares that the Union is an organization "of American citizens who believe in God and the American flag." A printed program calls for "winning power for fascism." The program calls for a "dictator only in the event that Communism or other troubles develop here." A uniform featuring the American flag on the shirts is worn by the members of the Union. The Union of Fascists, the Khaki Shirts, and the National Federation of Fascists marched in uniform in Newark, New Jersey, October 12, 1934, for the first time. [18] City officials reviewed the march and, with several thousand members from the Italian-American societies, held Columbus Day exercises in which Governor Moore (now United States Senator) of New Jersey participated.

Another fascist organization calls itself "The Paul Reveres." The announcement of its launching was made in the *National Republic*.[14] Its president is Colonel Edwin Marshall Hadley, who is well-known as a Red-baiter. The Pledge of the Paul Reveres reads as follows:

"For God and home and country, we, The Paul Reveres, associate ourselves together for the following purposes: To uphold and defend the Constitution of the United States of America; to maintain law and order; to foster and perpetuate real Americanism; to combat actively at all times and in all places those things that threaten the downfall of our country; to turn the white light of truth upon the loathsome doctrines of communism, socialism and anarchy; to promote the welfare of the individual by avoiding the pitfalls of paternalistic or socialistic measures that ultimately would make the state everything and the individual nothing; to promote peace upon earth by possessing a strength that will prevent invasion by foreign enemies and that will protect us from the threat of domestic traitors; to transmit to our descendants the blessings of liberty bestowed upon us by our forefathers. For these purposes, we, The Paul Reveres, pledge ourselves to the full limit of our mental and physical strength, so help us God." [15]

The American Vigilante Intelligence Federation, with headquarters in Chicago, is "dedicated to revealing the boring-from-within tactics of anti-American groups." It is headed by Harry Jung who is also president of the National Patriotic League. Branches of the Vigilante Intelligence Federation are to be found in several places throughout the United States, and their behavior is strikingly fascist in character.

Organizations of the character of the two just named have been a common phenomenon in the United States, particularly during the post-War period. They exhibit a tendency to spread in strike-troubled areas of the country at present.

Up to this point we have dealt with lower middle class organizations of a fascist character that at least make the pretense of being national in the scope of their organization. There are local organizations, too numerous to list by name, that are operating along similar lines and principles, but within the limits of cities or regions. As examples of these, mention may be made of the *Order of Cincinnatus* in Seattle and the *National American Bands of Action* in St. Louis. In eastern Ohio and western Pennsylvania, the *American Blue Corps* is appealing for recruits, specially for those who have "had military training," on the basis of a program of opposition "to the diabolical sabotage of our United States government and the rights of its Christian Gentile American citizens by the detrimental and traitorous underhanded activities of all the unscrupulous plundering worshippers of the Golden Calf—the international and un-American Jews, politicians and monopolists, breeders of Red Communism, crime and war."

In addition to all these organizations there are numerous unattached individuals who are spreading the ideas of fascism from the platform or through the medium of their publications. The most distinguished of these protagonists of fascism is Lawrence Dennis, author of the volume "Is Capitalism Doomed?" and associate editor of *Awakener*. John Spargo, ex-socialist, contributes articles.[16] Mr. Dennis, as an astute observer of social trends in the United States apparently awaits the further ripening of the crisis before attempting to launch a formal organization which *Awakener* has described in the following typically fascist language: "An inspired popular movement of the American masses which would first renovate the political machinery of our nation and eliminate government by minority, blackmail and class logrolling. Such a movement would be dominated by a strong executive power at the top, which would hold its mandate, not from shifting and vacillating rival groups, but from a great patriotic national organization of the people, which would cut across the lines of all classes, and personify the unwavering policy and weal of the nation as a whole." [17]

Mr. Dennis does not want to be anti-Semitic in his approach to the national problem, but he warns that the failure of the Jews to identify themselves with the national purpose and culture may lead to the development of an anti-Semitic policy in American fascism. According to Mr. Dennis, business men like Gerard Swope and Owen D. Young, with their "vague sort of economic fascism," will never make good dictators for "the people must have a prophet, and prophets have never come out of the world of profits." Mr. Dennis' activities have thus far been confined to his writings in *Awakener* and his books, and to public debate in which he has championed the ideas of fascism.

The Ku Klux Klan which declined about eight years ago is again being revived in many parts of the country. Circulars have been found in widely scattered parts of the country saying, "Communism will not be tolerated! The Ku Klux Klan rides again!" At Freeport, Long Island, in September, 1933, long and detailed plans were made during a three days' retreat.[18] In New York and California, the Klan has shown sympathy with the Nazi groups, and in the South many of its members have joined the Silver Legion. Harry W. Garing, Grand Dragon of the Ku Klux Klan of the State of New York, issued a scathing attack on Jews and promised the Friends of New Germany support in their activities. The Westchester Ku Klux Klan held an organization meeting on September 8, 1934, after three years of inactivity, at which praise of Hitler, criticism of the "New Deal," attacks upon the "communism" of Roosevelt, and an anti-Jewish policy were much in evidence.[19] In Atlanta, Georgia, the Klan entered the textile strike in August, 1934, to fight against the workers for the mill owners. Having only been rejuvenated some three months before the strike broke out, the Klan was not yet ready to show its strength, but it is preparing to do so when the next southern strike breaks out.[20] The Klan has retained the hoods and torches of primitive times under which to hide its work.

The Russian Fascists, located in Putnam, Connecticut, are concerned only with anti-Communist work directed against the Soviet Government.[21] They publish a magazine called the *Fascist*.

The Order of Black Shirts or, as they are sometimes called, the American Fascisti was organized in Atlanta, Georgia, in the spring of 1930.[22] Its magazine, the *Black Shirt,* was started at that time but the State of Georgia refused to grant it a charter, and it moved to Orlando, Florida, where it was successful in obtaining permission to operate. When this was later rescinded, the movement broke up. Some of its members went to High Point, North Carolina, and tried to form a company union in order to break the textile strike there during the summer of 1934.

The position of "patriotic" and veteran organizations in the emergence of a fascist movement requires some elucidation at this point. Their appearance in general has had little to do with what we have described as fascism. In American history they are easily dated. A complete list of such organizations indicates that they became a part of the social trappings of the United States in the late nineteenth century. This was the period in which profound changes occurred in the American social structure. It was then that large concentration of wealth began to be a decisive factor in the economic life of the country, and the millionaires emerged as a dominant political force. Imperialism became an American objective. Class lines were more clearly drawn, and the first important articulate class consciousness among workers was evidenced in the appearance of an American labor movement. The traditional "success" ladder was no longer so easily scaled as the legends of poor farm boys and log cabins had it. At the top of this social stratification was thrown up a class of *nouveau riche* who possessed the requisite economic power for an American bourgeois aristocracy, but the social tinsel was yet to be supplied. "Ancestry" became a badge of distinction. This was a national development which found one of its expressions in the appearance of a number of "patriotic" groups. Lower middle class people, having a revolutionary heritage, found that the "patriotic" organizations provided them with social standing.

Oddly enough these new cults were compelled to enshrine a revolutionary tradition inasmuch as the ancestors had been revolutionists, but the outlook upon contemporary society which they possessed corresponded far more closely to the toryism of the early days than it did to the revolutionary viewpoint of the ancestors. The longer the line of descendants, the greater the gap between the historical significance of the event itself and the appreciation of it by those who have ceremoniously enshrined it. The removal of tea-sipping, dilettante, chauvinistic daughters from their mothers who crouched behind improvised barricades to make wadding for muzzle-loaders is not so great in terms of years as of worlds. The decadence of "patriotism" in the United States and the evil days upon which the tradition of the American Revolution has fallen were well illustrated by former Mayor John P. O'Brien of New York, who, when reading a campaign speech obviously prepared by another, closed the address by appealing to the electorate to "go forward in the spirit of 1-7-7-6," pronounced as though calling a telephone number.

Having a social origin rooted in the emergence of an imperialistic and *grande bourgeois* development in the United States, it follows that the "patriotic" societies are consistently found on the side of militarism, the "open shop" and all other antiradical tomfoolery. While not organized in the first instance for the express purpose of aiding fascism, they naturally gear into such a movement when the conditions of the social crisis bring it forth. It is not to be thought that all "patriots" are themselves members of the highest ranks of the middle class. Many of their members have come from the ranks of the lower middle class with valid claims of ancestry, and they have joined the societies for the prestige which is thereby conferred upon them. These latter often outdo the authentic owning class in defense of the institutions that support the class claims of great wealth.

On January 9, 1931, the First Anti-Communist Mass Meeting was held in Carnegie Hall, New York City, "to combine the expressions of protest which the various patriotic, civic, church and labor organizations have voiced individually against the unlawful activities of the communists into one great public demonstration." In this Mass Meeting there were listed some seventy-six participating organizations with "more than 300 chapters, posts and branches of local organizations." [23] At the second meeting of this group in 1932, a statute to bar communist literature from the mails was urged, along with a number of other measures to check radical activity in the United States.

In some sections of the country today these organizations are definitely associated with the activities of the fascist organizations.

In San Diego, California, George N. Speer, Commandant of the Veterans of Foreign Wars, announced the following plan: "We will make a complete canvass of our 18 posts throughout the county to determine how many men and automobiles would be available in the case of an emergency. Each man will be assigned to a post so that every outlet from the city can be blocked." [24] It will be noted that it is not entrances to the city which are to be blocked to prevent radical invasions, but the outlets through which the radicals might attempt to escape from a veterans' "pogrom" against all dissidents.

The society women of California are not leaving all the shooting to the veterans. The Friday Morning Club, society women's club of Los Angeles, now hold their regular weekly meetings at the police pistol range in Elysian Park and take instruction in pistol shooting in order to "learn how to shoot in defense of [their] homes." "This is not a social organization, for we are engaged in something dangerous," Mrs. Louise Ward Watkins, president of the Club stated and went on to add that "women elected to membership must be prepared to be on the firing line" against communism.

Vigilante activities are commonplace affairs in the State of California today whenever organized labor attempts to win for itself tolerable living conditions. Terrorism is not confined to the Imperial Valley. The San Joaquin Valley is under the same kind of a regime. The general strike in San Francisco was the occasion for the unleashing of terrorism against all "radicals" in which the lower middle class joined enthusiastically to further the purposes of the reactionaries of privilege.

In 1931, eight men were given preposterously heavy sentences for trying to organize a strike of melon-pickers in Imperial Valley. The Post Commander of the American Legion explained the role of the Legion in the convictions thus:

"The way to kill the Red plague is to dynamite it out. That's what we did in Imperial County. The judge who tried the Communists was a Legionnaire; fifty per cent of the jurors were war veterans. What chance did the Communists have? That's the way we stamped it out in our county." [25]

In September, 1931, Major General James G. Harbord, addressing the New York State Convention of the American Legion, prodded the Legionnaires to a sense of their political destiny by urging them to "take political leadership into their own hands and assume the responsibility of shaping their country's policies, both foreign and domestic." [26] He predicted that within fifteen years they would "dominate both the state and federal governments, have a majority in both houses of Congress and have one of their number in the Presidential chair." It has remained for the few, like Major General Harbord, to invoke the mystic beauty of mass killing. In the same address in which he urged the Legionnaires to assume political leadership, he informed them that "there is still something in war which in the last analysis man values above social comforts, above ease and even above religion. It is the mysterious power that war gives to life, of rising above mere life."

The California, 1934, State Convention of the American Legion discussed a plan to establish a penal colony in the "practically inaccessible lands west of Point Barrow, Alaska," where undesirable aliens, reds and agitators might be sent.[27] The New York Legionnaires, in their convention in August, 1934, were told by the National Commander, Edward A. Hayes, that a return to old-fashioned patriotism was one of the vital needs of the country, and also that the Legionnaires should help "wipe out communism in the United States." [28] In his speech before the Illinois Convention of Legionnaires, he said: "In making war on the radical teachings that exist, the Legion is taking the leadership in the thing *for which it was organized*. [Italics ours.] It is a bulwark of protection to America against the communistic menace." [29] It must always be remembered in this connection that in the parlance of patriots the word "communist" includes not only the real communist but every other type of dissident, however mild, as well. A "political code" was drawn up at the 1934 convention of the Veterans of Foreign Wars, held in Louisville, Kentucky, October 4, 1934, which included the following resolution concerning the restriction of immigration: "That aliens not be employed on public works and that aliens in this country be registered and finger-printed." [30] Communists were also denounced at this meeting.

On February 28, 1934, the Utopian Society (US INCORPORATED) was formed in California. The organization is said to have a membership of 560,000, and has seemingly swept the state of California.[31] It has combined the phrases of radicalism, such as the abolition of the profit system, with staunch patriotism and anti-Communism. It was founded upon the technocratic theory of a more equitable distribution of wealth (the Society would have each family receive a salary of $4,700 annually),[32] but few in the secret order have any idea of how that can be attained. Because of this fact, the organization is very well named. The majority of its members are decidedly of lower middle class origin, housewives, clerks, salesmen, and storekeepers. "The great middle class is moving to the charity rolls," writes Aaron Allen Heist in the *Christian Century,*—"a million and a quarter of them in a relatively unindustrialized state long regarded as a retired man's paradise." [33]

Another organization—the Townsend group—started by F. E. Townsend, a physician in Long Beach, California, centers its "utopia" upon the attainment of an old-age pension which would give every one over sixty, two hundred dollars a month. The pension stipulates that the money is to be given only on condition that the recipient spend the total amount within thirty days. The money for thus relieving those over sixty is to be raised by means of a sales tax which would tax the consumers of the lower middle and working class. The present aims of the group go no further than getting signatures for the plan so that it can be presented to Congress during the 1935 session. They claim to have two million signatures already.

The Kingfish is dead! Long live the King! In August, 1934,

Huey P. Long, Senator from Louisiana, was given much more power over his own state than any other political office holder has ever had under bourgeois democratic government in this country. From 9 until 11 o'clock on the morning of November 13, 1934, forty-four bills were passed which made Long the complete dictator of his state. Committees approved of bills they had never seen and passed amendments which had never been officially printed. One bill gives the Kingfish control of thousands of jobs in the state; another bill gives him the right, through his appointee, the State Bank Examiner, to determine whether or not an applicant may be relieved of his debts under a two-year private debt moratorium. Other measures passed by the farcical Legislature give the Senator powers of imposing taxes on property, through the medium of a puppet board, which allows complete control of all business enterprises. He also has control of all registration offices and determines the qualifications of voters.

Long, like Hitler, announces that the only reason his province is not Utopia is because of outside opposition. "We've got bureaucrats, autocrats, hobocrats and fifty-seven varieties of 'crats' that are trying not only to run the United States Government but sticking their noses into the affairs of individual states," the Senator stated, and continued with the question, "how in hell do you expect Louisiana to progress under present conditions? If I was left alone and Louisiana could get out of the Union, instead of the 2,000,000 or 3,000,000 population we would have maybe 45,000,000 people right here. This State would become the Empire of Utopia." [34] However Long has hopes of controlling much more than the state of Louisiana. He has already cemented his alliances in other states. His "disciple," Theodore G. Bilbo, former Governor of Mississippi and newly elected Senator from that state, won such a complete victory in the last elections that Senator Long's influence is spread over another 46,000 square miles. Mrs. Caraway, Senator from Arkansas, also belongs to Long's school of politics, having learned the art of politics under the Kingfish's tutelage. [35] It is not too far removed from reality

to foresee the time when the Louisiana Senator will hold virtual
dictatorial powers over the states of Mississippi and Arkansas,
besides his own state, which would give him control of an area
almost as large as Germany and much larger than Italy proper.

A typical display of Long's methods of gaining political support
is seen in the purchasing of new gray uniforms for 1,500 university cadets, the "loaning" of many thousands of dollars to university students to go to the Vanderbilt-Louisiana State University
football game, and the hiring of a 125-piece band, all of which
was to set off the Kingfish in a parade which he led through
Nashville.[36] On November 17, 1934, the Louisiana dictator
went to the Louisiana State and University of Mississippi football game surrounded with bodyguards, collegiate "rooters" and
his magnificent Louisiana State University band. With collegiate
bands, smartly uniformed, playing Irving Berlin compositions,
the display of having wealth and generously giving it to the
people, coupled with his debt moratorium and his "share-the-
wealth" plan, the Senator knows how to sway the crowds.

"If I was running this country I'd guarantee a fortune of not
less than $5,000 and more if necessary, to every American family
to provide for a home, the education of their children and something to eat and something to wear," the Senator declared in an
interview with the United Press.[37] Yet at the time when the
Kingfish and the Mayor of New Orleans were battling for the
control of New Orleans' "Tammany Hall," and workers picketed
the lodgings of the Senator to ask for the elimination of the display of arms and for bread to eat, the Senator did not seem so
concerned about his "share-the-wealth" plan. The Senator is in
a better position to take the honors of Shirt Number One—despite
the fact he has not gone in for shirts—than anyone else on the
American scene today.

On November 16, 1934, the Senator announced his regime to
be "the greatest triumph for human uplift and sober government
this country has ever witnessed." [38] Centering complete control
in himself, voicing a few general radical phrases and having no

purpose of eliminating the profit-making system which is the basis for the tricking and cheating of the overworked and underpaid, the Kingfish has shown himself to be completely fascist in purpose and general method.

The social unrest which is engendered by the working of the business system is not only the soil in which an informed and workable philosophy of social change grows, it is also the condition in which demagogues flourish. The Art Smiths, the Pelleys, the Guldens, the George W. Christians, the Townsends, and the Huey Longs are the political "deformities" to which the business system of the du Ponts, the Owen D. Youngs, the Sloans, and the Morgans gives birth. From among the demagogues who are self-appointed "deliverers" of the hosts of the despoiled but still "patriotic" masses, the *de facto* rulers of America may yet be compelled to choose an American Hitler for their own purposes. A successful traffic in adulterated goods requires a corresponding contamination of the political mind. A policy of severely and deliberately limiting the supply of goods must have the support of a deliberately distorted social and political program. The "demagogues" of merchandise must ultimately rely upon the demagogues of politics for assistance in maintaining their system of plunder.

Fascism in both Germany and Italy, at its incipient stage, sought to meet the political requirements of the lower middle class by throwing the Lilliputians a psychological sop through ritual regimentation. But Fascism has only continued the process, which was begun under the democratic stage of capitalism, of the economic annihilation of the lower middle class. The Little Man gets "protection" against radicalism but at the ultimate price of complete political suppression and further economic disability.

Long ago, Gilbert and Sullivan wrote in "Iolanthe":

"Bow, bow, ye lower middle classes,
    Bow, bow, ye tradesmen, bow, ye masses."

This has ever been the command of the rulers of capitalist society. That the lower middle classes, the tradesmen, and the masses finally rise up from their low station in a capitalist society which has turned fascist, is only a *delusion* which serves their rulers in a determination to make them bow the lower—a bit later. They only rise who rise to rule without a partner, especially when that partner is an oligarchy of wealth which proposes to share neither its political nor its economic power.

CHAPTER XVI

The Capitalist Whom Prosperity Forgot

THE FARMER's quandary under capitalism, the world over, is that of being in all essential respects a business man without the business man's assured and efficient access to and control of governmental machinery. He is a support and stay for the business system without being an equal beneficiary. The farmer represents, in other words, the weaker—hence the exploited—member of a formal partnership which makes him both partner and competitor. He is *partner* in his belief that business principles and methods and institutions are eminently sound and desirable to perpetuate and defend; he is a weak *competitor* of financiers and industrialists in that he exercises no effective control over the market even for his own products. He is ignorant to an astonishing degree of the mechanism by which, in every combat with business enterprise, he comes out like the corpse at the funeral, prominent, but out of the running.

Prior to the Civil War, the farmer was the ruling member in the partnership of the enterprisers. The landed aristocracy ruled national politics until the day that Southern rebels fired on Fort Sumter. Those cannon shots were a salute to the new ruling class of financial and industrial magnates who were concentrated in the northern and eastern states. Since that time, the rule of industry and finance has often been challenged and vilified by the landed capitalists of the South and the West, but it has never been seriously threatened. The logic of all capitalist development has served further to entrench the group of business enterprisers that Lincoln served in the name of "preserving the Union" and "emancipating the chattel slaves." Stripped of their idealistic camouflage, both of these northern objectives of the Civil War were highly realistic measures which served the industrial capitalist's requirements for an unimpaired internal market for his goods and a free labor market in which a competitive *wage* embodied the principles of a new slavery.

The economic state of the farmer was deeply depressed before the present depression. Between him and "prosperity" there stood at every point some forbidding institution, or vested right, or legal buttress, or mechanism of the reigning group of capitalists. The abnormal rise in land values during the World War was the occasion for delivering the farmer, bound hand and foot as a mortgagor, to the financiers who control the credit structure of the system.

Farmers' *debts* to the ruling mortgagees rose to $8,500,000,000 by 1933, or two and a half times greater than they were in 1910. *Land values* meanwhile fell to a point 20 per cent below the level of 1913. From the 1919 level where farm property was valued at a total of 78,000 million dollars, a drop to 44,000 million dollars had taken place by 1932. Gross farm income fell from 15,000 million dollars in 1919 to 5,200 million dollars in 1932. Farm commodity prices hit a mark which was 52 per cent below the pre-War level. This decline was plain and far advanced long before the stock market crash of 1929. In the vise-like grip of finance capital with its superior control over the mechanisms and tricks of the market and of technology, the farmers' financial plight was a sad one even while "prosperity" was zooming into the stratosphere of easy money for the "dough" boys.

To all of this, the answer of the reigning capitalists is that farmers in their extravagance over-reached themselves. The abnormal land values of the war-time demand for agricultural products to feed not only the internal market but also a large part of fighting Europe were seized upon by farmers as their opportunity for excessive capitalization, but they were also recognized as properly sustained values under capitalism by the financiers who lent heavily upon them. In other words, the fault of the farmers, if there was fault, lay in their striving manfully to become bigger and better capitalists and more typical, without, in any effective degree, learning to control or taking the power to control the mechanisms of credit and of business enterprise. They were striving to emulate, to be sure in a weak and lagging and second-rate fashion, a pattern cut out by the financial and industrial "leaders" of society; surely these latter should be the last to deny that emulation is flattery.

Whenever the farmer turned from his function of producing and selling, a function which he exercised where prices were set in a "free market," subject only to *world* conditions, and sought to function as a buyer of industrial and commercial products, he was again confronted with an exploiting mechanism of the real, capable, and experienced capitalists (with government and technology on their side). Their market maintained prices, which the farmer was, like all other consumers of their goods, compelled to pay—prices which were freed from the influence of *world* factors and subject only and entirely to internal and artificial, government supported factors such as the tariff. Surely no greater farce, unless it be the measures of the AAA, has ever been perpetrated than that of Hoover's special session of Congress in the spring of 1929 which adjourned with the utterly ruinous Hawley-Smoot tariff measure, after having been called into session for the express purpose of relieving the farmer. After the Hoover-Hawley-Smoot tariff disaster wreaked upon beseeching farmers, it was inevitable that the farm belt, ignorant of the real basis of their economic plight, should bolt the Republican camp and support *any* anti-Hoover Democrat offered them.

The United States Department of Agriculture presented figures to show the price discrepancy between agricultural and industrial products, as the matter stood in November, 1933, after eight months of the "New Deal." Farm products averaged 71 per cent of the pre-War prices, whereas prices of goods the farmers must buy had risen to 117 per cent of the pre-War levels. The increase in the prices of farm products was more than wiped out by the increase in the prices of industrial goods. Averages, however, mean little in estimating the farmers' difficulties. A few specific items better illustrate the problem. Overalls, an indispensable garment, had doubled in price since the beginning of 1933. Gasoline for tractors in Oklahoma cost 9 cents a gallon as compared with 4½ cents a year before. Truck tires jumped from fifteen dollars to twenty-one dollars.[1]

Squeezed as the farmer is by the financiers who control at every essential point the credit structure in which the farmer has tried to exist as a small free enterpriser, and despoiled as he is by the enormous and fatal discrepancy of selling his products in a free world market and *buying* his consumers' goods in a monopoly home market, there is another capitalist mechanism which is even more ruinous to him and at the same time ruinous to the great mass of consumers of the foodstuffs which he produces. With a few exceptions, the agricultural producers of food supplies have completely lost control of their own markets. Into the picture of the farmers' plight has come of late the processing or manufacturing and packaging distributor who has set up a typical capitalist monopoly of distribution between the farm producer of foodstuffs and the ultimate consumer of these foodstuffs. A representative of the processors has put the matter neatly and indeed with manifest pride. "Do you know," asks Alec M. Patterson, director of the Bakers' Guild of Texas, "that a bushel of grain passes through from 10 to 14 trade arteries before it reaches your table as a pure wholesome, healthful bread? . . . Fourteen transactions. . . . Fourteen times a payment of wages!"[2] "Wages" is a convenient word which business men employ to cover up the collection of profits. Trade arteries are so many toll gates where a capitalist stands with a policeman or the U. S. Department of Justice, or the NRA by his side to exact a fee (*not* a wage) for the passage of goods from producer to consumer. "Fourteen transactions. . . . Fourteen times a payment of *profits*," would be the more accurate way of describing the mechanism.

The price-spread between what the farmer receives and what the consumer pays for his food represents the toll of the processing and packaging distributors. Dr. Frederic C. Howe explains the situation in gross figures, as follows: "Taking the five major crops comprising 78 per cent of the total value of foods consumed, a rough estimate shows that the value received by the producers in 1929 was 40 per cent of the total retail value, which was $19,021,000,000. In other words, the farmers received $7,566,-000,000 while consumers paid $19,021,000,000. It cost us nearly $12,000,000,000 to process and distribute $7,500,000,000 worth of materials [the amount] which the farmer received." [3]

The Commissioner of Markets for New York City has "estimated that New York housewives paid an annual tribute to food racketeers of $16,000,000." [4] With a poultry business in this area amounting to $90,000,000, the tribute to the racketeers is a triflingly small sum compared to the proportion of the consumer's dollar which the processors and packagers and regraders and labelers collect and retain for themselves, and in many instances the services of the processor are not more valuable than those of the poultry racketeer, while in some instances his services are infinitely more harmful to the ultimate consumer than are those of the trucking or labor racketeer. The racketeer at least does not in general pollute the commodity or add injurious chemicals or otherwise make it less edible and digestible. So much cannot be said for many of the processors. In other words the enormous price-spread between farmers' income and consumers' outgo for the same products is matched by a quality-spread that is even more injurious to both farmer and consumer. This quality-spread lessens the demand for fresh, wholesome food which the farmer is prepared to produce, and, in terms of what quality the consumer's dollar will command of any article, there is effected a serious inflation of the consumer's currency.

The slogan of National Cheese Week which said, "Serve Cheese and Serve the Nation," [5] would more accurately have said, "Serve Cheese and Pay Tribute to the processors." While the law compels the makers of process cheese to describe it as such on the box or package, the advertising of this cheese in newspapers and on the radio and on the grocer's counter avoids using the qualifying word "process." It is, in fact, imitation cheese diluted with water and skimmed milk and often it is "old, rancid, spoiled cheese (what used to be called bar-room cheese because it was more easily enjoyed by those who were not quite sober). The consumer pays for this product with its disguised and chemicalized flavor, the regular price that he would for the good genuine cheese. The advertising talks of its healthfulness and special digestibility and delicately omits to mention its origin and mode of manufacture; home economists without even understanding these things, tell housewives how to use the stuff in cooking, and the farmer sells in a market which takes less of his milk products and pays him a lower price for them. The farmer *sells* less food value; the consumer *gets* less food value at the old price." [6]

Milk has become a national scandal rivaling in its sordidness the story of the munitions makers. Many infants, as a matter of fact, will never get over the milk hurdle to become the victims in youth and manhood of the war-makers. Milk, which under a simpler economy passed directly from the farmer-dairymen to consumers, must now flow through great capitalist monopoly processors and distributors with a resulting price-spread and decreased consumption which are destructive to both farmers' and consumers' welfare. During the "Drink More Milk" month of October, 1934, in which a great advertising campaign featured the advice of the highest government officials in the land, the people of New York actually consumed 5,000,000 fewer quarts than they did in October of the preceding year when there was no high-pressure advertising campaign, and when milk was also in the price-reach of many more consumers.

During the five-year period, 1928-1933, the "earnings" of four groups of milk distributors were as follows: Philadelphia, 30.7 per cent on "net plant investments"; Boston, 22.4 per cent; Saint Louis, 14.6 per cent; Chicago 25.8 per cent. The AAA arrived at these figures by eliminating the processors' charges for idle property, and excessive depreciation and obsolescence figures. Whereupon *Food Industries* objected to this method of figuring on the ground that "a great many mergers took place in the period 1927-30" and that the costs of carrying idle plants are as legitimate as farmers' costs in carrying idle cows.[7] From the figures of "earnings" of these four groups of milk distributors, it is evident that *depression* never touched these enormous capitalist mechanisms which have been interposed between farmers and consumers. There are two giant commercial dairy companies, both of them institutions chiefly of Wall Street's high finance, and *not* of the farm and the farm worker. In 1932, the National Dairy Products Corporation reported net sales of $231,196,979.72, representing a profit of *79 per cent* on working capital. In the same year, the Borden Company reported sales of $186,301,203, which represented a profit of 18 per cent on working capital. Thomas H. McInnerney, president-director of the National Dairy Products Corporation, received, in 1932, a salary of $168,000. Ten executives of the National Dairy Products Corporation received salaries totaling $546,064. Arthur W. Milburn, director of the Borden Company, received a salary of $108,350, while eleven executives of the Borden Company were paid $467,949 in salaries.[8]

In view of these excessive profits of milk processors and distributors, it is not surprising to find Calvin Bullock, well-known investment expert, analyzing the position of the big milk distributors as extraordinarily favorable. Nor has their position, according to Mr. Bullock, become less favorable under the NRA. In describing the effect of the Agricultural Adjustment Administration on the distributors' profits, Mr. Bullock says: "It is rather surprising to note that the spread between retail prices and prices to the farmer has tended to widen recently in spite of the pressure that might have been expected to be exerted to reduce this margin." Mr. Bullock asserts that "the influence of NRA on the dairy industry has been relatively small," and in support of that conclusion he offers the testimony of the National Dairy Products Corporation's own statement that the wage increase effected by the Code will amount to only one and one-half per cent of last year's sales.[9]

In Boston, the price which farmers received for 34 per cent cream declined slightly, while the distributors' margin rose from 10.6 cents to 13.7 cents per half pint. In Detroit, the farmers' price declined sharply while the distributors' margin increased from 7.5 cents to 9.3 cents. In Minneapolis and St. Paul the farmers' price for 35 per cent cream increased somewhat, but the dealers' spread increased five times as much.[10]

The farmers' position, in sharpest contrast to that of the stockholders and high-salaried executives of the processors, is a picture of unmitigated tragedy. On the average, only one-fourth of the dollar which the consumer spends for dairy products reaches the farmers.[11] Emanuel Stein told the sub-committee of the Committee on Agriculture of the House of Representatives the story of a New York farmer who produced 7,027 pounds of milk from April 1st to April 16th for which he was paid at the rate of $1.09 per hundred pounds. "The cost of producing this milk, exclusive of his interest on his farm value and depreciation on property, was $1.06, which meant for one-half month, he got a total of $2.10 out of which he had to pay his own labor, that of his family, interest on investment, his depreciation,"[12] and with the balance he could have hired an auditor to calculate his profits! In other words, this New York farmer had a margin of 14 cents a day to distribute under the items of *labor,* interest on investment, and depreciation on property. If he followed the practice of the processors and distributors, he would capitalize his "goodwill" at 10 per cent of his total net assets; but in the market the *farmer* sells in, namely, that of the big milk distributors, "goodwill" has no value whatever. It is only the *big* business men who can make "goodwill" into a profitable asset.

Along with the farmer, the consumer suffers as a result of the market monopoly which high-finance capital has thrown between them. State Legislatures, as well as Federal agencies, are far more solicitous in their desire to accommodate themselves to the wishes of the distributors who are powerful, well organized, and energetically staffed, than they are to regard seriously the needs of farmers and consumers. Many of the laws which, on the surface, appear to reflect an interest in the public health, such as the laws requiring pasteurization, serve *primarily* to fatten the purses of bloated investors and high-salaried directors more than they safeguard the health of children and the sick. Processes such as pasteurization require large capital investment which, under a banking-business economy, becomes the financiers' opportunity for muscling-in to collect a fee which is exactly what the traffic will bear and out of all proportion to any socially useful function. Not even a farmers' coöperative is any guarantee of protection against these financial interlopers. Eighteen years ago the farmers of New York State organized themselves into the Dairymen's League and succeeded in increasing the selling price of their milk without extra cost to consumers. In 1920, Borden's *captured the League.* While the League, therefore, wears the Borden yoke, it operates under the legal exemptions of a farmers' coöperative, a subterfuge which violates everything *but* the law. "From the time the League-Borden alliance was formed, in 1920, to the early part of 1933, the farmer's share of the consumer's dollar was reduced from 36 cents to 15 cents, and the dealer's share increased from 64 cents to 85 cents." [13]

The Rural New-Yorker, while pointing out that "the Borden-League monopoly is the immediate cause of these chaotic conditions of the industry," correctly shows that "the ultimate sponsor of this combination is a bi-partisan coalition in State politics." [14] We have here, in one aspect of the workers' and the consumers' welfare, a fairly complete picture of the way in which a system driven by profit operates. At the expense of both workers and consumers, the tentacles of big business not only reach into the

pockets of those who must live by their work, but, in the act of
so doing, control and utilize for their purposes the essential
"control" and normative mechanisms of society, from the state
with its legislative and police powers down to the institutions—
newspapers, radio, and university—that serve to bias the thoughts
of the people in favor of the expert plunderers.

Bread runs milk a close second in the scandalous and pervasive
monopoly conditions which huge financial concerns have created
as a way of increasing the price-load which the traffic will bear.
Again and again it has been shown that there is no relationship
between the price of bread and the price of the wheat and the
labor which go into it. Wheat sold by farmers is exposed to the
fluctuations of the world market; flour and bread sold by big
business are sheltered by the monopolistic controls of the millers
and bakers. What the consumer pays for bread, therefore, is out
of all rational relationship to what the farmer receives for his
grain. From a government source we learn that *"the American
retailer alone often receives more for selling a loaf of bread* [i.e.,
passing it out to the customer] *than the farmer gets for producing the wheat from which the bread was made."* [15] But this is
not the whole story, for the retailer is only one of several processors and distributors that collect a toll in the passage of bread
to the consumer. The milling corporation, the wholesale baker,
and the advertiser (even the du Pont interests with their ubiquitous Cellophane) exact their substantial shares in the trans-
action, each one of these often receiving more than the farmer
who produced the wheat.

In 1931, an American farmer could take the proceeds of a
bushel of his wheat and buy with it 7.3 one-pound loaves of
bread. A Hungarian farmer could take a bushel of his wheat to
market and return with 18 one-pound loaves of bread. The
English wheat producer could exchange his bushel for 23.3 one-
pound loaves of bread. The French peasant could come home
with 42.4 one-pound loaves of bread purchased with the price of
one bushel of wheat. After stating these significant facts of

comparative bread prices, the *Consumers' Guide* hurls this challenge at the farmers and consumers: "If you gave the bakers in this country—free of charge—all the ingredients they put into your bread, you would still be paying more for your bread than people in England, France, or Hungary pay for theirs." [16] For which the business gentry have only the hackneyed reply about what you can do and where you can go if you don't like this country. (Personally we like it so well that we think it may not be long before millions of others who like it, too, may be ready to rescue it from the clutches of its business wreckers.)

Not long ago the New England Bakers' Association held a convention in Boston where it was announced that today "the biggest emphasis is on the appearance of the products." [17] This is in line with the emphases of all salesmanship in the new Age of Cellophane. Appearance is not only served through modernistic packaging, but is equally well served by chemicalized "freshness." The house organ of the National Food Bureau throws light upon the interests which business is concerned to protect. "There are good and sound commercial reasons why most people should eat white bread. . . . It is safest and most economical to transport the refined flour and to get it to the consumer in the form of bread than it is if whole wheat flour were used, since the latter tends to spoil more readily." [18] Why should it interest the National Food Bureau to ask if food that *keeps* well is healthful food? Like all other commercial concerns its chief interest is in "the good and sound commercial reasons" for the consumption of the food that they make the largest profits from, and these reasons revolve primarily around the question of durability or keeping qualities, at any cost of palatability or health or wholesomeness.

Attention has already been called to the high-pressure campaign of General Mills to increase the consumption of bread. Miss Betty Crocker is the presiding genius in this campaign. Miss Crocker's booklet on "109 smart new ways to serve bread" was the chief feature of a campaign for which General Mills appropriated $300,000 of your money and ours, to be expended in three months during the spring of 1934.[19] Later General Mills launched a "nation-wide educational campaign sponsored by the baking industry" in which schoolboys and girls were offered prizes for the best letters on "Why Bread is Good to Eat Four Times a Day." [20] The baking industry, like the public utilities, knows the value of penetrating the schools now with its propaganda to bear fruit in future years. It not only offers prizes to grade and high-school students, but it also provides grade and high-school teachers, gratis, with a booklet for classroom use, entitled, "How to Keep Well Nourished." The Nebraska Millers' Association meeting in Omaha some time ago voted unanimously to support the National Food Bureau in the efforts to "clear from school textbooks all unfair and scurrilous references to white bread and white flour." Dr. Corson of the National Food Bureau had reported to the Nebraska Millers that seventy health books used in the schools of various states "say unkind things about white flour and white bread." [21] He did not report, as a qualified scientist in a disinterested relation to the subject would, that the authors of the seventy health textbooks *should* as a professional duty "say unkind things about white flour and white bread."

The *Southwestern Miller* described the efforts of General Mills to increase bread consumption as "the most extensive campaign ever actually undertaken in the United States" for this purpose.[22] *Advertising Age* called it a "sensational effort to reverse the declining line of flour companies." [23]

Such high-pressure campaigns to increase the consumption of bread, or any other food or commodity, are organized for the exclusive purpose of buttressing the investment and earning structures of the corporations which finance capital has interposed between farmers and consumers. They are wholly indifferent to the economic situation of the farmer, for whose grain they do not expect to pay more as a result of the increased demand if they can avoid it, and to the nutritional and economic interests of the consumer whose consumption of the nutritionally *least* desirable products is *most* profitable to the processors. An expert on bread and the baking process testifies that processes are in common use today for retaining in the baked loaf "almost all the water used in mixing the dough." He further asserts that his observation during the past three years has led him to the conclusion that "the quality of the bread distributed in the metropolitan area has steadily deteriorated," and that "during the past six months this tendency has been accelerated." [24] The same man makes the following report on some of the practices which the business exploiters of the "staff of life" find highly remunerative: "The use of alum and of aluminum compounds is generally forbidden by law. Laws are not always respected. Ammonium carbonate is an excellent gas producer and leaves no residue in the bread. Dough and batter stiffened with alum and inflated with ammonium carbonate can be puffed up indefinitely. Just now I find on the market, doughnuts, crullers, rolls, biscuits and so-called English muffins, which are mere shells." [25]

M. L. Langford, of the Sanitary Grocery Company, told a Senate Committee last year about the use by bakers of a patented product known as "Arkady." The magic of "Arkady," according to Mr. Langford, "is to cause greater absorption of water by the flour, with a saving of sugar and yeast." [26] The "saving" from the consumer's standpoint is a loss, pure and simple, exactly as though a portion of his purchase had been stolen from him by a sneak-thief—but, of course, a far safer and more respectable type of larceny than that committed by common crooks.

The North Dakota Regulatory Department reports wholesale deception in loaves that are labeled "whole wheat bread." Their analysis and investigation reveal that there is little, if any, true whole wheat or graham bread being sold. "We have examined," says the Department, "a number of these breads sold throughout the state during the past several months, and analysis shows that the amount of whole wheat flour present varied all the way from 30 per cent to 100 per cent." [27]

As in the case of milk, so in the case of bread, governmental policies operate to protect the financial interests of the processors to the detriment of farmers and consumers. The Department of Agriculture might now more accurately be styled, the Department of Agricultural Processing Concerns. *Food Field Reporter* announced recently that the NRA is conducting a "secret" drive against price-cutting in bread. "Some highly secret action designed to stop price-cutting under the baking industry code," says the Washington Bureau of *Food Field Reporter,* "is being undertaken by the NRA." [28] The NRA drive against price-cutting in the baking industry, as in other industries, is just one phase of its vigorous activities to support the gouging of consumers by price-fixing in the interests of the financiers. At the same time "NRA officials appreciate the delicacy of the situation" [29] in thus serving the exploiters of the people's bread. Any lingering illusions that may be cherished by innocent liberals concerning the Consumers' Advisory Board should be finally dispelled by the information that Karl Hauck, member of the Consumers' Advisory Board, is described in *Food Field Reporter* as "a travelling ambassador whose business it is to persuade recalcitrant bakers that price-cutting is not a nice practice in which to indulge." The mysterious character of Mr. Hauck's methods is evidenced by the following statement: "Details of Mr. Hauck's activities could not be learned, nor could it be ascertained to what localities his travels have taken him. Nevertheless, it is understood that he has been kept rather busy in his efforts to keep the bakers in line." [30] *Food Industries* reports Mr. Hauck's presence in Louisville, Kentucky, where he "has been investigating the competitive situation in the bakery trade." [31] When Alec Patterson, of the Bakers' Guild of Texas, conducted a campaign to keep the price of bread *up,* he persuaded all the leading clergymen on a given Sunday to preach a sermon on the evils of price-cutting.[32] In *effect,* a revised version of the Lord's Prayer in the Texas churches that Sunday was,

"Give us this day our daily bread at prices that hallow and enrich the investments of the processors and distributors."

The fundamental course of the development of American economic life may be seen in as commonplace an article as a loaf of bread. In June, 1913, when the farm price of wheat was 82 cents a bushel, the price to consumers per pound loaf of bread was 5.6 cents, of which the processors and distributors received 4.2 cents. In May, 1933, when the farm price of wheat was 59 cents per bushel, the price to consumers per pound loaf of bread was 6.5 cents, of which the processors and distributors received 5.5 cents.[33] Furthermore, the consumer got a far better loaf of bread in 1913 than he did in 1933. Increasing price- and quality-spreads from prime producer to ultimate consumer, i.e., increasing disparities between prices paid by consumers and income received by farmers, and between quality delivered by farmers and quality which would be available through consumer-oriented processing, are an essential element in the logical working out of the present economic order.

Another method for achieving the effects of an enormous price-spread in farm products as they pass from the farmer to the consumer is through the manufacture of *specialties*. Attention has already been called to the way in which General Mills, by the introduction of *Wheaties, Bisquick,* and *Softasilk,* greatly increased the rate of profit on its investment even at the depths of the depression. In 1932, a package of *Cream of Wheat* which sold for 22 cents contained wheat which cost about $1\frac{1}{2}$ cents. Kellogg's *Corn Flakes* which sold for 10 cents a package contained corn which cost about 2/5 of a cent. *Puffed Rice* which sold at the rate of 60 cents a pound contained rice which would cost about 3 cents a pound. *Puffed Wheat* which sold at the rate of 68 cents a pound contained wheat which cost about $2\frac{1}{2}$ cents a pound. *Wheatena* which sold at 22 cents a package contained about 1 cent's worth of wheat.[34]

In no case does the specialty have any added nutritive value, and in some cases nutritive value is diminished by the destruc-

tion of the vitamins or loss of protein or minerals in the manufacturing process. *Cream of Wheat* is identical with semolina
which can be purchased from any macaroni factory at a small
fraction of the price for which the trade-branded article sells.
In two Connecticut cities where there is a large Italian population, many thrifty families have been known to buy their wheat
cereal in the form of semolina.

The meat packing industry of the United States is for all
practical purposes in the hands of four big packers. The District
of Columbia Supreme Court has held that these corporations are
in competition and that consequently there is no violation of
the anti-trust laws. This judgment is unquestionably correct
technically, as a similar judgment would be on other huge corporations dealing in the nation's foodstuffs. But the fact remains
that all legal safeguards for the producers of goods and their
ultimate consumers are all too easily circumvented, and that
effects very similar to a complete monopoly are obtained by
these corporations. During the late drought, the United States
government purchased 10,000,000 head of cattle, but it has been
reliably reported that there will be no uses made of this enormous
quantity of meat such as would effect a downward movement in
the price of meat. Such a price-decline would be detrimental to
the profits of the packers, and it is not among the purposes of
government to interfere in that area. The government makes
enemies, when enemies are to be made, among less substantial
people than the Cudahys, the Swifts, the Armours, and the Wil-
sons. Millions of the impoverished, whose enmity is not now
politically important to Mr. Wallace or Mr. Tugwell, may go
without proper food on account of the high prices of meat, but
the "New Deal" is committed to policies which have as their
effect the increase in the number of millionaires, or to be more
exact, in the increase of yearly private incomes which are in
excess of $1,000,000. Twenty-six new incomes of such proportions
were achieved in the first year of the "New Deal,"[35] while new
millions of hungry and miserable folk have been added to the

rolls of the destitute. It is not necessary to spend time in the detailed examination or rationalization of the motives which lie beneath the policies of government; it is only important that their effects be weighed and that judgment be fitted to the effects.

The following story is, admittedly, only a single example, but it is nevertheless a true story of what happens to farmers in an economy where they are stepchildren:

"A hard-working woman farmer sent twenty pigs to market from her DeKalb County, Ill., farm. Back came a check for 68 cents. Neighbors found her weeping: 'I nearly broke my back carrying slops to them.' She had had to sell just when drought compelled thousands of farmers to dump their livestock on the market. The pigs were only a quarter of the size proper for ham and bacon, good only for sausage. The Agricultural Adjustment Administration processing tax took three times the amount of the final check from the gross proceeds. Food and lodging for the pigs awaiting slaughter took four times the amount. Other expenses included 7 cents for the Meat Board's 'eat more meat' advertising campaign." [36]

There are 400,000 farm families in the United States that depend upon tobacco for their major source of income. In 1932, their average *family income* from their tobacco crops was about $250. This was gross income from which all expenses had to be met. In 1932, twelve officials of the tobacco companies received combined salaries of more than $2,500,000. In addition to these salaries, they received 20 per cent on capital investments in the tobacco manufacturing business. All other stockholders received the same rate on their investments. The profits on the tobacco manufacturing enterprise totaled $146,000,000 in 1932. These profits which were paid strictly on the basis of stock *ownership* and not upon any personal service rendered amounted to $41,000,000 *more than the gross income from the raising of the tobacco which was received by the 400,000 families engaged in its production.* Furthermore, the profits to money investors were moving along an upward grade while the income of the farmers engaged in tobacco production was plunging catastrophically downward. Between 1923 and 1932, the income of tobacco growers *declined* 66 per cent. In the same period the profits of the manufacturers *increased* nearly 100 per cent! [37] While 400,000 poverty-stricken farmers' families eke out an existence with the help of about $250 each from their major crop, tobacco, vast fortunes erected on their sweat and grime are the objects of litigation by persons who never performed a socially useful day's work in the acquisition of their titles or claims to titles to the tobacco millions. Smith Reynolds (scion of the *Camel* family) who met an untimely death under suspicious circumstances, left a widow, former Broadway actress, to contend with the courts and a former wife of the deceased for the possession of an estate of $25,000,000.[38] This is the capitalist system reduced to its primary elements that anyone can understand! The lawyers in this litigation will collect as their fees and expenses as much as the annual income of a thousand farm families.

The "big four" in cigarettes, *Camel, Chesterfield, Old Gold,* and *Lucky Strike,* spent among them approximately $40,000,000 on advertising in 1934.[39] All such excessive costs of distribution must of necessity be passed back to the farmers, and on to the ultimate consumers. Forty million dollars spent on advertising alone, almost entirely on irrelevancies, for the purpose of swelling the bank accounts of investors to the tune of something like double that sum!

It is appropriate at this point to emphasize how completely the control of the processors and distributors ramifies into every aspect of economic, political, and *cultural* life. In 1933, the American Tobacco Company's *Lucky Strike* advertising maintained the broadcasts of the Metropolitan Opera with an outlay of $375,000 for the season. This year, the American Tobacco Company abandoned its support of the broadcast because of its "limited class appeal." [40] The Lambert Pharmacal Company, makers of *Listerine,* was prepared, however, to come to the rescue of culture, and so during the season of 1934, the nation's music lovers, if Grand Opera fans may be so described, are dependent upon the great mouthwash bottlers, the meretricious advertisers de luxe of American big-time advertising.

A writer in *Advertising & Selling* is not satisfied with the present costs of distribution, and offers the following proposal: "This, then, is my contention. Let us add to the cost of distribution. Let us raise the prices of all meritorious articles that American consumers have not yet taken to their bosoms, as evidenced by low sales. Spend the extra money on distribution. Hire men and women, sales promotion and advertising." [41]

Another force which threatens to make farmers still greater and more obvious failures as capitalists and business men is now appearing on the horizon. It is the development in the field of agrobiology. By advanced chemical treatment of the soil and even of seeds before planting, it is now estimated that agricultural yields may be increased many times over with the result that a very large portion of soil now under cultivation will no longer be required to provide the food supply for the population. The already rapid liquidation of farmers from a capitalistic status to one of peasantry and peonage will be accelerated if developments in agrobiology come, as they must inevitably come, under the control of the institutions of finance capital. Individual farmers have in the past not possessed the requisite capital to compete with the large processors and distributors in the marketing of their products, with what results we have briefly indicated. Agrobiology in farming will also require large initial investment of capital and technology and employment of experts and subsidizing of colleges and university professors and scientists, which means an opportunity for finance capital to exploit on an enormous and enormously profitable scale the *productive* as well as the *distributive* side of agriculture.

As a capitalist the farmer is already doomed to extinction. As a worker on the soil, prospects for increased exploitation and displacement of his diminishing labor at the hands of the real capitalists confront him.

Up to the present time the numerous farmers' revolts in the United States have taken the form of protests by little capitalists against big ones. Farmers' simple demands for higher prices for agricultural products presuppose the continuation of the existing price-structure of a business society. Farmers' demands for higher tariffs on their products likewise presuppose the perpetuation of a national economy in which the laws of scarcity dominate the market. Yet in the very nature of capitalist economics and politics, finance capital, which today possesses its largest stake in the sale of industrial goods, will maintain at all costs the price advantages which industrial goods today hold over agricultural products. Equalization is not possible until farming has been placed entirely on a factory basis with finance capital in command there as elsewhere, *or* until farmers acting as consumer-workers in concert with other consumer-workers effectuate equalization by taking command of industrial as well as agricultural production and distribution, and proceed to operate the unified system on the basis of abundance and quality *in the interests of themselves and others as consumers.*

The farmers of the United States possess a secure tradition, albeit a largely forgotten one, of rebellion against intolerable tyrannies. The small land owners of New England swelled the ranks of the revolutionists who fought under the command of the landed aristocrats of Virginia against "taxation without representation." The tyranny of the mentally infirm George III was mildly benevolent in comparison with the ingenious, elaborate and ramifying economic tyranny of the despotic processors and distributors of finance capital that are today pushing the farm population of the United States to ever lower levels of servitude.

CHAPTER XVII

American Scapegoats

WHAT MUSSOLINI accomplished with one hatred and Hitler with two, the American counterpart, if ever called upon, should accomplish with far greater facility, having four hatreds at his disposal. Mussolini *was* a fascist *genius,* to lead a triumphant fascism with only the "reds" to crush. Only ordinary fascist ability was required by Hitler to rise to power on the prostrate forms of the "reds" and the Jews. Any nincompoop fascist should be able, in this land of the richest assortment of hatreds where they increase by the law of geometrical progression, to gain power with the help of four scapegoats—the "reds," the Jews, the Negroes, and the aliens.

Not only are there some four million Jews in the United States as compared with the six hundred thousand in Hitler's Reich, but there are more than twelve million Negroes and at least five million unnaturalized aliens. And as for the "reds," they include, in the parlance of reactionaries, not only the members of the Communist Party but the members of organizations of every shade of dissidence. (*The Red Network,*[1] a *Who's Who* of dangerous radicals, lists not only Karl Marx and William Z. Foster but Mayor LaGuardia of New York City, and Mrs. Franklin D. Roosevelt as well.) It is a well-established part of American political tradition to utilize prejudice against these groups for demagogic purposes. The Ku Klux Klan for a time actually reached a dominant position in the politics of at least six states largely through its successful exploitation of race prejudice and religious intolerance, and insinuated its corrupting influence into the federal government.

Each, or all of these groups, serves on occasion as a target for mass discontent which is thus thrown into channels that do not disturb and hold no threat to the vested interests of business and the business-state. In a complex economy where few have the faintest notion how it actually functions, any assignable cause for social distress and chaos repeatedly and graphically put before the mass of people is capable of belief. The scapegoat is a very ancient device for permitting people to enjoy the *double* pleasure of sinning realistically and atoning vicariously.

Negroes have always been the most defenseless of American scapegoats. While the total population of the Negroes in the United States is 11,891,143,[2] the group is so unorganized, except in ways that facilitate its degradation and exploitation (as in its other-worldly religion), so little aware of the nature of its own problems, and so discriminated against that it exercises no control whatever in government or industry. The group is largely agricultural, forming 30.3 per cent of all farm laborers. Negroes predominate in the domestic servant group, one of the lowest paid, least organized occupations of all. They make up 90 per cent of all porters on steam railroads, also notoriously low paid, 75.3 per cent of workers in the fertilizer industry, and 72.7 per cent of all home laundresses.

The wage scales of Negro laborers, even where the work is the same as that done by white workers, are very much lower than those of the whites. As income determines standard of living, it is readily seen that the living standard of Negroes is lower than that of whites in the same industries. In 1927 the Bureau of Labor Statistics made a study of the differences between the wages paid to Negro and white workers in cotton compresses in ten southern states and found that in every process, except one, Negroes were paid from $2 to $15 less than were the white workers. Such facts could be duplicated in any industry in which both whites and Negroes work. The complete study made by the Commissioner of Labor of Virginia, 1927, and also the study made by Ira de A. Reid on rates in Pittsburgh corroborate this thesis. The high percentage of Negroes among the most exploited groups of farm laborers and among domestic servants shows that they tend to fall into the lowest paid occupations even when they do not directly compete with white workers. Negro workers have had to take the lowest wages or stay out of work and income. Because the Negro worker has no bargaining power and no labor organization and has been forced to accept the lowest subsistence wage, he has had to live in the most run-down houses in his community and everywhere to jeopardize the health of himself and his family. The proportion of child labor among Negroes has always been about three times as great as that among native whites.

The problem of housing among Negroes is two-fold: one of income and the other of discrimination. Income dictates that only houses of the poorest type can generally be had; discrimination dictates that only houses on the outskirts or in segregated sections are available.

Since the "crash" of 1929, the Negro has been the first to be fired, or, if not fired, to be the subject of wage slashes. The federal government reports for October, 1933, show that, out of all the families in the country on relief, 18.4 per cent or 600,000 were Negroes, although the number of Negro families is only 9.4 per cent of the total number of families. As the majority of Negroes in the South are on the land, many were included among the mortgagors whom the Federal Farm Credit Corporation was designed to help. However, as loans from the Corporation were based on security assessed by *local* committees which barred Negro members as completely as do southern election boards, it is evident that there was no hope of relief from the government. That 800,000 acres of land belonging to Negroes was lost between 1930 and 1933, and that two and a half million acres had been lost in the previous decade, only shows that neither the Hoover nor the Roosevelt administration has helped the impoverished Negro farmers. The crop-reduction program of the AAA has worked added hardships for Negroes. While the white land owner was getting a higher price for his cotton, the wages of those still laboring in his fields (largely Negroes) remained the same, and tens of thousands were thrown out of work because of the 25 per cent reduction program—provisions in the contracts to the contrary notwithstanding.

Negroes have not been able to improve their working conditions by collective bargaining. The American Federation of Labor has either evaded the question or has actively discriminated against Negro labor. In twenty-two "international" labor unions, in industries where Negroes form a considerable number, Negroes are barred from membership by constitutional provision.[3] Some unions have no specific anti-Negro provisions in their constitutions, but they emphatically discourage Negroes from joining. At practically every annual convention of the American Federation of Labor, resolutions are passed to the effect that the Federation "welcomes into its ranks all labor without regard to creed, color, race, sex, or nationality and that its efforts have been and will continue to be to encourage the organization of those most needing its protection, whether in the North or South, or West, white or black."[4] Practically all of the railway unions continue to exclude Negroes. The Brotherhood of Maintenance of Way Employees and the National Rural Letter Carriers' Association admit Negroes but refuse to seat them at conventions or allow them to hold office, which makes membership little more than the privilege of paying dues for the white members' benefit.

A. Philip Randolph of the Brotherhood of Sleeping Car Porters introduced a resolution at the 54th annual convention of the American Federation of Labor, October, 1934, calling for the expulsion from the Federation of any union which drew the color line. Randolph made a stirring speech in favor of his resolution, which would have been accepted had not the well-oiled machinery of Green, Woll, Tobin, *et al.*, ignored the oral vote, and then by maneuvering succeeded in having the committee's recommendation of non-concurrence accepted.[5]

A few unions encourage Negro membership and give them full privileges after admission, such as the Longshoremen, the Hod Carriers, Common Building Laborers, Tunnel Workers, Boot and Shoe Workers, United Mine Workers, the International Ladies' Garment Workers, and the Amalgamated Clothing Workers. There are some independent unions which Negro workers have organized themselves, such as the Railroad Men's Independent and Benevolent Association, the Dining Car Men's Association, and the Pullman Porter's Organization. Negroes are included in all Communist labor organizations without discrimination.

Because of the treatment accorded Negroes in the majority of the Federation unions, they have, in many instances, been in a position to "scab" or break the strikes of the Federation. Claude McKay put the situation of the Negro strike breaker succinctly, in his "Home to Harlem." " 'But it ain't decent to scab,' said Jake. 'Decent mah black moon!' shouted Zeddy, 'I'll scab through hell to make mah living. Scab job or open shop or union am all de same jobs to me. White mens don't want niggers in them unions nohow. Ain't you a good carpenter? And ain't I a good blacksmith? But kain we get a look in on our trade heah in this white man's city? Ain't white mens done scabbed niggers outa all the jobs they useter hold down heah in this city? Waiter, bootblack, and barber shop? I got to live and I'll scab through hell to live.' "[6]

The National Association for the Advancement of Colored People, in its 1933 Report, states that under the National Industrial Recovery Act, Negro workers have in many places been displaced by white workers, or, where they were not displaced, have been allowed to stay only on condition that they would not demand the code provisions. A small pink sheet accompanied the Negroes' pay check in one industry of the South, which said: "To all colored employes: The wages you are paid now are more than this company can pay and stay in business unless each worker produces more. . . . If the 'false friends' of the colored people do not stop their propaganda about paying the same wages to colored and white this company will be forced to move the factory to a section where the minimum wage will produce the greatest production. . . . Stop your 'friends' from talking you out of your job." [7]

Some wage differentials are as high as 30 per cent.[8] Under the President's Reemployment Program, *Section 6,* there is a paragraph to the effect that employers can pay workers less than 40 cents an hour if the workers before July 15, 1929, were getting less than 30 cents. As Negroes were practically the only group getting less than 30 cents at that time, it is a direct and dishonest discriminatory provision allowing employers to hire Negro workers at rates as low as 10 cents an hour. This not only keeps the standard of living of Negroes atrociously low but encourages racial antagonisms between Negro and white workers. In many industries in which Negroes do particular processes, those processes were designedly excluded from the codes and Negroes cannot therefore benefit by the wage provisions. The differential between the textile workers' wage in the North and in the South where the majority of Negro workers are located is another form of discrimination under the NRA. In other cases in which the NRA has maintained an equality of standards, the whites who have been unemployed are supplanting the Negro workers. Under a new system of race discrimination, with not enough jobs for all, Negro or white, the dilemma of accepting unemployment or lowered standards is the only choice offered today to millions of Negroes. As Negroes comprise from one-fourth to one-half of the total population of the South, "prosperity" is a white-race-conscious prosperity there until the Negroes are permitted to share fully with the whites all the benefits of "improved" conditions for labor.

Race discrimination against Negroes is as old as the presence of this group on the American continent. It is an element in the

American social *milieu* which could be made to serve the cause of fascism with great effectiveness. On October 27, 1934, Claude Neal was abducted from the State of Alabama, carried across the state line into Florida, mutilated with a fierce sadistic frenzy by a mob of "whites" and then lynched.[9] Here was a clear case involving kidnapping, torture, and murder covered by the so-called Lindbergh Kidnapping Law. Since the mob's crime was of an interstate nature, the Department of Justice of the Roosevelt Administration had no alibi for inaction under the plea of non-interference with state authorities. The lynching was publicly announced and "invitations" sent out twelve hours in advance of its perpetration, and Attorney General Cummings was notified of the situation before Neal was tortured to death. Governor Sholtz, fully informed of the intentions of the mob, made no move to protect the victim. Neither did the Department of Justice at Washington which is always alert even to the point of sending scores of its picked agents to the scene by airplane and fast motors when a wealthy victim of kidnappers is abducted. Will Mr. Roosevelt retain his Attorney General in the face of this negligence, or will he limit his presidential anti-lynching activities to eloquently phrased speeches before the gatherings of the Federal Council of Churches of Christ in America? We have already noted Joseph B. Keenan's astonishment at the behavior of a Washington audience in applauding the picture of Dillinger at a movie house. Where is Mr. Keenan's Department of Justice when kidnappers and torturers are publicly announcing their crime long in advance of its commitment? The case of Claude Neal alone is sufficient to brand as hypocritical the whole law-enforcement structure of government. Law is and long has been essentially limited to the protection of the wealthy and their property. Mr. Roosevelt encircles the island of Cuba with warships when Wall Street's property is endangered there. He lands marines in China when the interests of the same property holders are affected there. Against the murderous attacks of lynchers, involving only Negroes, obscure and propertyless, he makes a humane-sounding but highly generalized speech which elicits much applause from the churches—and no action for the Negroes or for union labor or radicals in the South or anywhere else.

As often as not the possession of a black skin appears to be accepted by Southern "authorities" as presumptive evidence of guilt. This situation is of such long standing that the entire American people has been calloused to its barbarity, even though considerable moral indignation has been evidenced by Jews and others, who see no relationship between persecution of Jews and the murder of Negroes, against the atrocities which German Nazis have committed against the Jews of that unfortunate country. There can hardly be any questioning of the surmise that the German anti-Jewish and anti-radical atrocities, revolting as they have been, have fallen far short of the atrocities to which the Negroes of the United States have been subjected for generations. There is in this situation an example of middle class hypocrisy in which the lower middle class of the United States excels! Self-appointed custodian of the *world's* morality, it claims special indulgence for its own territory and its own inhuman excesses. The Japanese treatment of the Chinese, the Turkish treatment of the Armenians, and the German behavior toward the Jews have aroused in it an indignation which may serve all too well as a happy device of forgetting its own home-grown varieties of racial hatreds and atrocities.

One of the numerous Shirt movements, which have sprung up since the depression, has been the Order of the Black Shirts which originated in Atlanta, Georgia, in the spring of 1930. The official publication of the American Fascisti, *The Black Shirt,* gave the definite aims of the organization in their issue of August 22, 1930, among which appears: "To maintain and forever secure the white supremacy for our posterity against the amalgamation of races." This "supremacy" was to be maintained by ousting Negroes from their jobs by means of intimidation. However, the victims of the intimidations happened to include servants of many people who had considerable means, and efforts were brought to bear to eliminate the Black Shirts from Georgia. If the intimidations had not interfered with any white convenience or threatened whites with the necessity of paying a higher wage to their house-servants, the protests from the Negroes would only have led to a riot, in which Negroes would have been the only victims.

When the Silver Shirts are not talking of "Jew Communists" it is "Negro Communism" upon which they are vociferating. "The South is a hotbed of negro communism," [10] William Dudley Pelley wrote in his magazine. There are pronounced fascist elements discernible in a number of solutions for our economic ills which are floating around at present. Walter B. Pitkin, prolific author of best sellers, admits that everybody is falling back into a lower grade job. "Second grade people take third grade jobs," [11] which leaves the lowest level—or marginal laborer, which includes a large proportion of Negroes—outside the going economic system. Mr. Pitkin would solve the problem of the "outsiders" by segregating them in the American Concentration Camp—the "Subsistence Homestead Community"—set up by the Government. However, since the Negro is also by local custom and hatred barred from that form of relief and cannot accept Mr. Pitkin's advice and apply for admission in the present Community projects, he can only look forward to special Negro concentration forced-labor camps if and when fascism appears.

Three thousand seven hundred and sixty-two lynchings have not occurred since 1889 without giving evidence of a sadistic and psychopathic hatred of whites toward Negroes. Practically all of the lynchers have been white and their crimes have been committed in an orgy of blood-lust. Arthur Raper says that "many of the men lynched in 1930 were captured after extended man-hunts organized by undeputized armed men who used bloodhounds and conducted some type of mock trial before the lynching." [12] That the sheriffs and courts of the South have not bothered themselves a great deal about these murders is also proof that the hatred has, to an extent, become legalized and a folkway—characteristics of fascism. "The San Jose lynchings were unavoidable," said James Rolph, Jr., the late Governor of California, when Brooke Hart's alleged kidnappers were taken out and lynched before the eyes of thousands. "Lynchings are not pleasant," Rolph went on to say, "but crime is an infection in our national system. Medicine is never pleasant to take, but if it effects a cure it is always worth the momentary unpleasantness." [13] That attitude is indicative of a growing official sympathy with and public toleration of the actions of frenzied mobs. The growing impatience with slow trial-by-jury and the possibility of no conviction for an innocent but despised member of an "inferior" race leads to a legal temper which serves well under a fascist form of government.[14] With Madison Grant to serve as the propagator of specious Nordic superiority claims and the courts to use lynching methods of quick expiation for crime (a crime, being anything which violates law, comes by definition to be anything which violates any decree some lawless racketeer at that moment in office decides to make), a fair foundation has already been laid for an American fascism.

The most celebrated case of legal lynching in all the years of race discrimination is found in the now famous Scottsboro case. On March 26, 1931, a freight train carrying two white girls, seven white boys, and nine Negro boys, left Chattanooga, Tennessee. The white girls and boys had been seeking work in Chattanooga and were going home, presumably to Huntsville, Alabama. Soon after the train left the Tennessee City, the Negro boys made their way to the back of the car where they encountered the white boys and girls. A free-for-all fight gave victory to the Negro boys. Being ejected from the train, the white boys decided to "get even" and wired ahead to Stevenson to the effect that a group of Negroes was stealing a ride on the train. As a result, nine Negro boys were taken to the jail in Scottsboro, Alabama. The girls showed no marks of violence, no lacerations, no signs of struggle, and the girls were known to be of questionable sexual habits. One of the girls, Ruby Bates, later repudiated her testimony. The boys were incarcerated and within fourteen days Judge A. E. Hawkins of the Ninth Alabama Circuit Court had condemned eight of the Negro boys to the electric chair—the penalty for rape in Alabama—and one to a life sentence because of his extreme youthfulness. Each man was condemned separately, and each conviction led the citizens of Scottsboro to demonstrate with rousing cheers and the music of bands.

The facts of the case were gathered by social workers and investigators of some fifteen leading liberal organizations in the country. A New York lawyer, Samuel S. Leibowitz, agreed to act as trial lawyer. The International Labor Defense, with Joseph Brodsky as chief counsel, has, so far, saved the lives of the boys. On November 7, 1932, the United States Supreme Court set aside the death sentences and forced the Alabama courts to conduct new trials. One of the boys was again condemned to die. The case was appealed once more, but on June 22nd, Judge Horton set aside the verdict of guilty for Haywood Patterson, the only one of the boys to be re-tried. The case was again tried, with Judge W. W. Callahan presiding, and on November 20, 1933, three of the boys were again condemned to die. The case went to the Supreme Court of Alabama for the second time where the sentence was upheld. The appeal to the Supreme Court of the United States stayed the execution set to take place December 7, 1934.[15]

After Madison Grant, America's foremost publicist on "Nordicism," has eliminated by deportation all aliens who cannot claim Nordic blood, he realizes that there will still be left "an immense mass of Negroes and nearly as many southern and eastern Europeans intellectually below the standard of the average American." [16] However, this problem is not difficult of solution for a mind like that of the American edition of *Rosenberg* (Hitler's *Nordic* lieutenant), for "the practice of sterilization . . . can be resorted to with good result."

Four million Jews in this country—except those few prominent merchants, newspaper editors, bankers, insurance, and copper magnates, who are in a position to buy from the fascist dictator an Aryanism, legalized by "decree," for themselves and their immediate families—should be much concerned with the question, "Will America go fascist?" If it does, will there be a frenzy of anti-Semitism? Mussolini has shown impatience with the absurd *Nordicism* of the Nazis. So far as the fundamental ends sought by fascism are concerned, anti-Semitism is an incidental manifestation of a local variation of the fascist pattern. The politics and economics of fascism have need of anti-Semitism only in the sense that every deep prejudice or hatred in the situation confronting it is exploited as a powerful organizing force. There can be no condoning of the savagery with which the Nazis have treated the Jewish population in Germany. But this particular depravity is not absolutely necessary for the fundamental purposes of Nazism. Some of the distinguished protesters against the maltreatment of Jews in Germany, like Bishop Manning and the New York *Times,* have come dangerously near embracing the more fundamental and deep-rooted and dangerous purposes of fascism even on the occasion of their protestations.

Business and journalistic and liberal protest against Nazi atrocities in Germany is no guarantee that this same class in America will not embrace fascism and commit its own peculiar excesses in due time. Practically all the German liberals—religious, economic, and political—found it possible to adjust themselves to the idea of a crass dictatorship as an ideal state, when it arrived, for what were to the liberals sound and convincing and socially persuasive and businesslike reasons. Already there has been a clearly noticeable softening of middle class protest in the United States against Nazi *anti-Semitism*. It is clear that the upper brackets of this class (the part which owns the press among other things) has a huge financial stake in post-War Germany and cannot afford too many risks for its foreign investments. A successful boycott and economic isolation of Germany would imperil these investments, by leading very likely to a radical overturn of the German reactionary state. Great department stores in New York City have been publicly writhing under the lash of this dilemma. Merchant princes and other Jews in this country who are concerned more with their profits

than with the fate of their fellow (but, lower middle class, lowly
and proletarian) Jews will try to buy their way into the good
graces of the American *Duce* if he is inclined to exact the sacrifice of blood from the less "patriotic" and reliable Jews. If the
German prototype is followed closely here, this will prove easy,
as prominent Jewish families in Berlin have found they could
be made "Aryan" by decree. "That means," said James W.
Gerard, former Ambassador to Germany after a visit to Berlin
in August, 1934, "so long as they are rich they can be useful." [17]

Judging by the various Shirt movements which have been
started in America, the future American fascists seem destined
to be strongly anti-Semitic. However, as these may be only lifeless imitations of the German model, they are not a sure indication
that American fascism will be strongly anti-Semitic. A more
indicative sign is the fact that fascism in its *early* propaganda
is anti-big business, and most of the lower middle class associates
big business and big and exploitative banking ("Wall Street")
with Jews. Current discontent in the Middle West and South
has often been directed against the Jewish bankers of New York.
However, the fact that the most influential and most powerful
banker, J. P. Morgan, is not a Jew and that Wall Street's chicane
derives at least as much from Gentile schemers as from Jews is
never considered. There is also a great deal of anti-Semitism
in the United States today which is not directly tied up with hostility toward big business. There are many unwritten laws and
local codes, real estate men will admit, which prevent property in
certain districts from being sold to Jews, exactly as to Negroes.

To prove, as does the noted anthropologist, Franz Boas, that
there is nothing to the Aryan or the Nordic superiority is of
little value when no respect for facts and scientific study is to
be found. One of the eminent German anthropologists, Eugen
Fischer, was one of the first to disprove the homogeneity of any
race and went so far as to say that every individual is a racial
unit. However, upon the advent of Hitler, Herr Fischer's position
was jeopardized and he was forced to exhibit publicly that he

had been wrong in his previous discoveries and that the German people are unique and superior and that the Aryan must be perpetuated at the expense of the non-Aryan.[18] Many college professors and savants show the same traits in all countries. Science in all lands is the drab and slut of industrialism and of the military state.

That the *Protocols of the Learned Elders of Zion*,[19] translated by Victor E. Marsden, Russian correspondent to the anti-Semitic paper, the *Morning Post* (London), could have as wide circulation as they do at the present time is some proof that there is a tremendous anti-Semitic sentiment already in the country and ready to flare into a great flame of antagonism and violence. The *Protocols* were offered as proof of a "world conspiracy" of the Jews to get all lands and wealth in their hands in order to destroy all religions except that of Judaism. It was first translated into English in 1921 and was brought to notice in America by Henry Ford. Mr. Ford commented upon the Protocols in the New York *World* as follows: "The only statement I care to make about the PROTOCOLS is that they have fitted the world situation up to this time. THEY FIT IT NOW." [20] Mr. Ford's anti-Semitism was flamboyantly set forth in his articles in the *Dearborn Independent*. Some of these articles claimed that the international socialist movement was a part of the Jewish imperialistic conspiracy. Ford was compelled to retract, but the *Protocols* still go on.

According to William Dudley Pelley, Jews are communists. There are some who plead with the Jews to become anti-communist. "As a friend of the Jewish people," said James W. Gerard in a series of forums conducted by the Junior League of the Sharey Tefilo Temple, "I want to state that if the American Nation ever gets the idea that the Jewish race and communism are synonymous there is a possibility of a pogrom in the United States that will make those of the Czar's era in Russia look like a small parade. The Jewish race is noted for its ability to build up culture and nations, and the members of the race have nothing in common with communism, which seeks to tear down culture and government." [21] Mr. Gerard fails to realize that an *anti*-communist attitude is a surer way to fascism than an anti-Semitic attitude, and that the poor and uninfluential Jews will be caught by fascism even if the powerful leaders are safely converted to Christianity, Aryanism, and anti-communism as they have been in Germany.

"The Christian public sees Jews everywhere in authoritative positions in the Administration," says Mr. Pelley. "It sees Jews everywhere in authoritative positions on our Relief Committees, it sees Jews everywhere in authoritative positions in our finance and commerce. The preponderance is too menacing, says the Christian public. If Jews are everywhere in control by the attestments of our own vision, and we are suffering increasing woes, then it must follow that somehow or other these Jews are responsible." [22] But the imitator of Hitler has found a way out. "The Jews have the money but the Gentiles have the numbers. No matter what measures toward repression may be taken—in the sacred name of preserving existing institutions—it will be a very fine thing in that hour not to be a Jew." [23] He means, of course, a *poor* Jew. The Strausses, the Warburgs, the Kuhns, and the Kirsteins are in no danger, in this country or in Europe, or if there is a momentary threat to such high-placed persons, it quickly passes, for good business reasons.

Perhaps the most astonishing evidence of growing anti-Semitism is found in the *Conquest of a Continent* by Madison Grant, a book which attracted some attention when it appeared a year or so ago. Its introduction by the well-known but sociologically deficient scientist, Henry Fairfield Osborn, makes it even more dangerous. Mr. Osborn says in his introduction: "The theme of the present work is that America was made by Protestants of Nordic origin and that their ideas about what makes true greatness should be perpetuated. That this is a precious heritage which we should not impair or dilute by permitting the entrance and dominance of alien values and peoples of alien minds and hearts." [24] In showing his enthusiasm for this stupid work, he concludes: "It is with the greatest pleasure that I have written a few words endorsing this book as the first racial history of America, or, in fact, of any nation. I stand with the author not only in nailing his colors to the mast but in giving an entirely indisputable historic, patriotic, and governmental basis to the fact that in its origin and evolution our country is fundamentally Nordic." [25]

According to Grant, the birthright of Nordic culture was allegedly sold for "a mess of industrial pottage" when the Polish and German Jews along with the worst elements of southern Italy came to transform the United States. Even this situation is not, according to Madison Grant, too hopeless, if we act immediately, as the United States is at present 70 per cent Nordic and 80 per cent Protestant.[26] The most recent Census statistics show that only 54,576,346 people in the country belong to any religious bodies,[27] and of these, 18,605,003 are Roman Catholics, and 4,081,-242 are Jews, all of whom Mr. Grant would exclude from his category of the "elect." As some five million of the remaining are Negro Protestants and include, therefore, an element of "serious proportions," it is somewhat difficult, to say the least, to see how Mr. Grant figures that 80 per cent of the people in the United States are still Protestant.

It is comforting to know that the "great majority of the Senators of the United States are still of old American stock and so are the members of the House of Representatives." Also that "the Army and Navy are still overwhelmingly Nordic, so that with these elements in our favor we are still in a position to check the increase of the other elements and contend against their deleterious effects upon our institutions." [28] That sociology and anthropology should be so used even prior to the appearance of a fascist movement is some indication of the lengths to which Americans may go.

Madison Grant would begin to make a Nordic America by the "*absolute* suspension of all immigration from all countries; and the signs of the times indicate that such suspen-

sion is inevitable." [29] Also "no one should be allowed to enter
the United States, unless a visitor or traveller, except white men
of superior intellectual capacity distinctly capable of becoming
valuable American citizens." [30] Mr. Grant does not offer a method
of determining the presence of such qualities and capabilities, but
perhaps it is assumed that he will take that responsibility and
become Director of Immigrant Evaluation and Allocation. The
aliens who are not citizens "should be deported as fast as they
can be located and funds made available." [31] Walter B. Pitkin, the
most wordy sage yet developed by Columbia University, would
concur, as would "Shirt" leaders of various colors. There are six
million aliens, Mr. Pitkin estimates, and "these 6,000,000 make it
hard for several million Americans to find work. Why should we
tolerate their presence? It seems downright silly. . . . Finally, we
should begin deporting as many of the 4,000,000 not yet applying
for citizenship papers as we can pack off without too serious
trouble to them or to us." [32] Mr. Grant, like the Veterans of
Foreign Wars, the American Legion, the Order of '76 and Silver
Shirts, among others, would make registration compulsory "for
the carrying out of any proper system of deportation." The respectable upper-middle-class New York State Federation of
Women's Clubs, meeting November 12, 1934, at Buffalo, discussed a resolution calling for "universal registration, including
finger-printing if desirable." The authors of this resolution
thought such a drastic measure was necessary in view of the
alleged fact that "recent widespread disorders, including damage
to property, personal injuries and loss of life, besides numerous
individual and gangster crimes, have been traced to aliens who
have unlawfully entered the country or unlawfully remained
after entering on temporary permits." [33] That lynchings by native
born whites by the score can go on yearly without state or federal
officials lifting a hand to stop them even when forewarned, did
not concern these "select" women in their discussion of "recent
crimes of national interest."

White men have a duty to perform—"the duty of policing the

world and maintaining the prestige of the white man throughout the Seven Seas"—according to Madison Grant. Anglo-Saxons, he judges, have one chief fault and that is over-sentimentality which has been illustrated in their allowing the "lower races in Europe and elsewhere" to come to this country. But white men must wake up to their "destiny," for "sooner or later we may be called on to help protect the White race and the English language in these countries," namely, Great Britain, Canada, South Africa, Australia, New Zealand, and many of the smaller islands. The process of eliminating the "lower races" will somehow guarantee the "peace of the world and the preservation of its civilization." [34] How many warships and how many lives and how much treasure should be lost to "protect the English language"? Have Greek, Latin, and Sanskrit no claim to the blood of our soldiery?

The lack of understanding of economics among anthropologists and many sociologists is appalling, but that some one should think the peace of the world can be guaranteed by the process of being chemically pure (especially as there is no such thing in racial matters) and segregating all elements which are not in Mr. Grant's particular and unscientific brand of "pure" is the most fantastic peace measure yet proposed. Does Mr. Grant, Mr. Osborn, or Mr. Pitkin think that the lily-white Nordics remaining, who are destined to have an ever lower standard of living under capitalism, will always keep the peace of the world? If so, they have probably underestimated the high-fighting and low-thinking qualities of their factitious "Nordics."

During the San Francisco general strike, Governor Merriam of California sent a telegram to President Roosevelt and a copy to Secretary of Labor, Frances Perkins, asking that immigration officials on the West Coast be instructed to deport aliens "who shall be found guilty of participating in or in any way aiding any violent and unlawful action or riot." Secretary Perkins, that eminent, one might almost say prototype, liberal, knowing only too well the traditional position of the state in respect to militant minorities, quickly wired her reply: "Answering your telegram to me in regard to action by Federal immigration authorities, I assure you that the Department of Labor will cooperate with California officials to the full extent authorized by law. The applicable immigration statutes authorize the department to take into custody and deport, first, any alien who has entered the United States unlawfully; second, any alien who advocates disbelief in or opposition to all organized government or teaches communism or otherwise falls within the scope of the act of October 16, 1918, as amended by the act of June 5, 1920; and third, any alien who is sentenced to imprisonment for a term of one year or more because of conviction in this country of a crime involving moral turpitude committed within five years after the entry of the alien into the United States. . . . The Commissioner of Immigration and Naturalization at Washington has today again wired to the district director at San Francisco to act with promptness in any case in which there is evidence presented to or discovered by him indicating that an alien is deportable under these or other provisions of law." [35]

Sheenies, niggers, polacks, dagos, wops, hunkies, all "Scum of the earth"! We are the pure lily-white Nordics upon whose shoulders has been placed the responsibility for the continuation of all that is fine and good in our civilization. Jesus, Spinoza, Galileo, Kepler, Copernicus, Einstein, and Socrates, have no place in it. It is up to us to bring peace to the world through the ruthless suppression and elimination of all the evil nationalities in our midst! . . . This is the stuff which carries an appeal in wider circles of the economically and politically illiterate American masses than many are inclined to admit. It is poison —or dynamite—of the most dangerous sort. The state of knowledge among the lower middle class of America should be labeled with a skull and cross bones, thanks to a century of regimented and chauvinistic "free" education. It is poison which can only serve to regiment the illiterate unwittingly behind a program of mass destitution and mass goose-stepping and flag-waving which the uninterrupted rule of the profit-makers may require.

Negroes, Jews, foreigners, parliamentarianism, internationalism, liberalism, socialism, communism may, any of them or all of them, be threats, if deliberately organized as such, *against* the fascist domination of a given society. Some of them are not, and cannot be in any significant way, hindrances to a business-political dictatorship of the most extreme reactionary character, since their interests are so closely intertwined economically and socially with the state and business figures who pull the strings in the early stages of the fascist puppet show. The persecution of these minority groups will make them simply the hapless victims of a social reaction whose altar inevitably calls for a blood purge of the unfortunate and unpopular, and for burnt offerings.

CHAPTER XVIII

He Who Does Not Own Shall Not Eat

An ancient maxim found in an ethical code to which the leaders of Western society profess some sort of allegiance declared that work should be the sole claim to the right of consumption. Society, however, is not run on the basis of the authority of ancient maxims. Its principles are formulated strictly in accordance with the needs of its ruling class as that class itself sees them. Consequently, the right to consumption in modern business society is most firmly established on the basis of ownership. This in the last analysis is the significance of the prior consideration everywhere accorded to the rights of property and the rights of income derived from property ownership. He who does not own eats only on sufferance granted by those who do own. Stuart Chase speaks of "the declining importance of ownership," and observes that "it is not of cardinal importance who owns what" in the distributive age which he believes we have entered. Mr. Chase asserts that "technological abundance is breaking the stranglehold of private ownership on the means of production." [1] The facts overwhelmingly attest the counter-proposition that *private ownership is tightening its stranglehold upon technological abundance,* and in so doing is placing rigid limits upon the right to consumption involved in *work.* The owners of industry or the more powerful owners of the financial mechanisms upon which industry is dependent exercise absolute power over the jobs of the millions who work and therefore over their rights to consumption. On their own rights to consumption, the owners are answerable to no authority except that of the impersonal forces of the market. The market, in so far as it is subject to any human control, is in turn dominated by the interests of owners. Governmental relief measures are likewise subject to the will of those who own.

Individual capabilities have little or nothing to do with income, the right to amass wealth, or the choice of preferred occupations. An analysis of some 10,000 examinations which were given at the Adjustment Service for adults in New York City shows, according to the report of Paul S. Achilles given before the 1934 annual meeting of the American Psychological Association, held at Columbia University, during September, 1934, "that there was no relation between the high intelligence of these unemployed as shown by tests, and the comparatively low salaries they had been able to earn." [2]

In the summer of 1934 it was estimated that, since 4,234,000 families were on relief, there were somewhere between 15 and 17 million people—13 per cent of the entire population—who depended upon "charity" for their existence. President Roosevelt, in his speech on relief, in September, 1934, said "it is estimated that 5,000,000 [families] may be there [on relief] by February." [3]

Isador Lubin, the Commissioner of the Bureau of Labor Statistics, estimates that there are 3,000,000 workers permanently displaced. However, failing to account for the improvements since 1929 in technical equipment, his figure is extremely conservative. Miss Ollie Randall, assistant director of Emergency Relief in New York City, 1933, made the following statement to Lionel Houser of the *World-Telegram:* "We must have some program that will admit the fact that this mass of white-collar people will never be reabsorbed by commerce, and that will put them into other useful occupations at state expense doing jobs that will add to our culture and develop our educational system." [4]

The unemployed will have to be given relief or *make-work* employment which means they will have to be fed rather than work to feed those who profit from production. But the large profit-makers will use *every means* available to have unemployed fed by those who earn salaries and wages. Not only must those who still work bear the large burden of those who are unemployed, but labor is destined, under the rules of the system, to receive an ever decreasing proportion of its productivity in the form of wages.

Twenty million families, or 71 per cent of the total population, had incomes, in 1929, less than $2,500.[5] Forty-one per cent of the population had family incomes less than $1,500, allowing them only a "subsistence and poverty" standard of living.[6]

In the realm of consumption, the spendthrift days of the late twenties as they are seen today, in retrospect, were not so hilarious. As a matter of fact, the authors of *America's Capacity to Consume* state that *"the nation as a whole* was not living beyond its capacity—as measured by what we could produce."[7] Actual production of goods and services produced was valued at 81,000 million dollars in 1929. If all the plants had been working at full capacity at that time, 97,000 million dollars' worth of goods and services could have been produced. Production of consumption goods, the value of which has been estimated at 70,000 million dollars, could have been increased to 86,000 millions if full plant capacity had been utilized. This was not utilized because it was deemed unprofitable to do so. The owners of industry, and the owners alone, determine what part of the plant capacity shall be utilized and the kind and quality of goods that shall be produced.

If every family in the United States which was getting an income under $2,500—a figure which does not indicate a luxury standard of living—had had its income raised to that amount, it would have been possible in 1929 to meet its consumption needs if existing plant capacity had been fully utilized. That means that without scrapping any old machinery, hiring any more workers or shortening the hours of work, but merely using the equipment available in the last year of "prosperity," every family could then have had a standard of living with an "adequate diet at minimum cost." But the unequal distribution of wealth, which is determined by ownership and non-ownership, stood in the way of realizing this goal.

With the total population getting over $2,000 per family, and the present plant capacity utilized to meet the needs of that increased purchasing power, poverty could be eliminated. It is grimly ironical that, just as productive capacity reached the point where it could support adequately the consumption needs of the entire population, and those in official positions were saying that "the poor house is vanishing from among us," [8] purchasing power, or *the legal right to consume,* fell so low that production, to be profitable, had to be *curtailed.* But poverty and profit are integrally related and to attempt to eliminate the one and keep the other is so much wasted effort.

The Public Health Service in ten states has been gathering statistics on the length of life of people according to occupations and finds that there is a great mortality difference between the unskilled worker—or lowest paid worker—and business men. Unskilled workers die off twice as fast as the higher paid business and professional men. The table reported by the survey reduced shows:

Deaths per 1,000 population

Occupation	Tuberculosis	Pneumonia	Accident
Agricultural workers	46.5	43.4	15.1
Skilled men and foremen	72.1	59.7	34.2
White collar workers	65.8	50.5	18.7
Unskilled workers	184.9	135.9	51.7
Professional men	26.2	38.8	14.5

The report concludes that, although some occupations are especially hazardous to health, "diet, housing, amount of medical care, contact with infected persons and low income are believed to play the chief part in causing so many more deaths, especially from tuberculosis and pneumonia, among men in the low-pay classes." [9]

Contrary to prevailing opinion, child labor has not been completely abolished under the NRA. The codes in the industries which have employed the majority of child labor, with few exceptions, still permit it. Despite the fact that newspapers have played up the child labor clauses of many codes, "the provision in the code proposed for the newspaper industry [nullifies] the child labor restrictions, by permitting boys and girls of any age to sell papers at any hour of the day or night except during school hours." [10] Child labor in the beet fields, the cranberry bogs and the onion beds, has not been eliminated, and these tasks with other agricultural occupations accounted for 54 per cent of all child labor in 1930.[11]

One-fifth of the children of the United States have suffered definite injury to their health during the depression, according to a study made by the Children's Bureau of the Department of Labor in the summer of 1933 which found that "the sum of the evidence at hand points to the fact that the nutritional condition of children in many communities is showing increasingly serious effects of the long periods of unemployment and want." [12] These have been insufficient food or the wrong kind of it, poor housing conditions, lack of medical care, and in many cases the disastrous effects of anxiety and the sense of insecurity that prevails wherever there is no work. Malnutrition in New York City jumped from 16 per cent in 1930 to 21 per cent in 1932 among 300,000 school children. Malnutrition among mothers is given as one cause of the effects of malnutrition in infants. City reports corroborate the findings of the Children's Bureau. The Health Department of Detroit, in their "hunger survey" in the summer of 1933, found that 18 per cent of the children in eighteen selected schools were not getting enough to eat. Of those who were malnourished, 60 per cent were found to be anemic. In 1932, a 29 per cent increase in malnutrition over the previous year was found among school children. The Jewish Community Health Center in Philadelphia found that malnutrition among Jewish children rose 23 per cent from 1928 to 1932, while other children examined showed an increase of 42 per cent for the same period.[13] In mill towns, mining camps and other slump industry communities, the population has suffered much more. A great increase in rickets has been reported from several localities in Maryland, Pennsylvania, New York and Connecticut.

Many hospitals' reports show deaths from various diseases, while the direct and final cause of death may have been starvation. News items, once in a while, will read, "THREE MEN FOUND STARVING," or "UNCONSCIOUS FROM LACK OF FOOD." [14] But news generally is more concerned with society and its affairs. A long column was given to Miss Ella Virginia Von Echtzel Wendel's dog, Toby. Miss Wendel, being the last survivor of the Wendel line, was entitled to a prepossessing news item for her dog. "Toby was buried in Irvington, N. Y. where lie Toby I and Toby II. The third Toby lived seven years," etc., etc., etc. . . . The Wendel dogs died as they had lived in the lap of luxury, while the Wendel estate which provided their comfort included some 26 old-law tenements unfit for human habitation.[15] A news item of three human beings who were starving was very brief, saying in part: "Three cases of starvation or undernourishment were reported by the police yesterday. Doubled up on the sidewalk close to the building line at Fourth Street and the Bowery [the flop-house section of New York City], an unidentified man about sixty years old was found to be a starvation case. . . ." [16] How many others met the economic crisis by slow starvation is not known. They live, suffer, and, with no energy to fight the system which makes for their degradation, die unknown, without benefit of death notices in the *Times* or the *Transcript*.

Daniel Willard, the president of the Baltimore and Ohio Railroad, is alleged to have stated that he would rather steal than starve if he were unemployed. Luckily for those who have wealth, the unemployed have not felt the same way. Many have been so indoctrinated with the sanctity of private property that they would rather starve than fight. Others have found that since the police, law, and the courts, are all on the side of property starving is really a much easier way out than stealing.

As the decline of capitalism continues and fewer workers can be employed in productive enterprises, a solution of the unemployment problem suggested by those in the owning class is usually that women must not hold jobs which men might have. Women are not considered unemployed if they are supported by men. It is important to note that in the two countries in which the decline of capitalism has been the greatest—Italy and Germany—women have lost all economic status. A news item of September, 1934, reports that Mussolini is planning to take all women workers out of Italy's industry. Mussolini made his position clear in an editorial in his newspaper, *Popolo d'Italia* of Milan, in which he said: "The working woman creates the problem of population (decrease) as well as that of unemployment. Work, even where it is not a direct impediment interfering with propagation, foments independence and consequent physical and moral habits antagonistic to conception." [17] (Woman's duty under fascism is to rear children; the more children, the bigger will be the army to enforce fascist plans. Male children are given better care than female children for the same reason.) "The exodus of women from the field of labor doubtless would have economic repercussions in many families, but a legion of men would lift humiliated heads and a hundred times more new families would enter the national life. . . . It is necessary," Mussolini concludes, "to convince ourselves that the same work that causes in women the loss of her generative attributes brings to man the strongest physical and moral virility."

Germany has taken even more drastic measures against women. Not only have they been taken out of industry but they are being kept "in place" by numerous decrees. For example, in April, 1933, all cosmetics were barred. "The German women must *revert* to the Germanic mother. A female running around rouged and painted, has no right to call herself a German woman and cannot possibly become a National Socialist." On April 12, 1933, a year of housework was made compulsory for every German girl. On June 1, 1933, a tax on spinsters was decreed to provide loans to women who would quit their jobs and marry. A loan of 1,000 marks was granted to each newly married couple, to be paid off at one per cent a month, with twenty-five per cent to be deducted for each child of the union. Walter Darre, German Minister of Agriculture, thought of the ingenious idea of dividing women, like cattle, into four classes: those who would be the breeders of the leaders of the German race—of course all-Aryan; those who could breed satisfactory children but not leaders; those who could marry but could not have children; and those who must never marry. "The German woman should be proud to bear children for the field of honor," Von Papen is reported to have said.[18]

The editor of *Nation's Business* applauds the determination of Mussolini to eliminate women from gainful occupations and proposes the same measure as part of the solution for the economic difficulties of capitalism in the United States. He says: "More than one thoughtful man in this country has wondered if part of our economic troubles are not to be laid to the influx of women into industry. The census figures show a surprising shift. In 1890, of 11,000,000 married women in the United States, 515,000, or a little less than five per cent, were gainfully employed. In 1930, we had 26,000,000 married women and 3,000,000 of them, or between 11 and 12 per cent, were employed. Of all women, married and unmarried, 11,000,000 were employed in 1930 as against 4,000,000 in 1900. The startling figure is not that of women workers but of married women workers. One-third of the married women of the District of Columbia are employed. Have child-bearing and home-making ceased to be worth-while occupations? We used to inveigh against women and child labor. Then our women leaders pleaded for women 'recognition.' What would happen if we replaced 3,000,000 married women workers with 3,000,000 unemployed men? Would our world come to an end or would it come nearer an economic balance?" [19] American club women have also sponsored the proposal to eliminate women from industry. "Back to the Home" was the title of a symposium for the speeches read before the New York State Federation of Women's Clubs at its session in Elmira in November, 1933.[20]

The sales tax is nothing more or less than a device fostered by those who own for the purpose of passing the burden of relief for the millions of the unemployed to those whose income is derived from work. It is the first principle of a business economy that property and income from property must be protected against all inroads by the claims of humanitarian considerations. When the bankers of New York City threaten to move the Stock Exchange into the state of New Jersey if a tax is placed upon stock transfers, and then brazenly dictate a sales tax to provide funds for the maintaining of the city's unemployed at the lowest subsistence level, the liberal Fiorello LaGuardia knows his masters' voice. The New York City sales tax, announced as a measure "to relieve the hardship and suffering caused by unemployment," has been fixed to "relieve" the merchants as well. By fixing a schedule which places a tax of one cent on purchases from 13 to 62 cents, and a tax of two cents on purchases from 63 to 99 cents, and so on, merchants collect about 3 per cent on their gross sales. They must pay the city only 2 per cent "to relieve the hardship and suffering caused by unemployment." The remaining 1 per cent is a clear gain for the merchants. One large New York department store with an annual turnover of $80,000,000 thus makes a profit of $800,000 through a measure which was dictated by banking interests. The average New York family with an income of $1,500 a year will pay about $15 in sales taxes. If this were levied directly upon small incomes, there would be a volume of protest that might well strike terror into the banking dictators of the city. But by levying the tax, a few cents at a time, upon the recipients of small incomes, the bankers

in effect steal pennies from dead men's eyes and then divide the
loot with the merchants of the city.

According to that eminent economist, Professor Willford I.
King, unemployment is in no sense the responsibility of those
who own both the machinery of production and the jobs of
those who operate it, but is an unfortunate twist in human
nature. "Even in the worst of times," according to Professor
King, "the man who is willing to do any kind of work of which
he is capable for any price offered will find it difficult to avoid
getting a job." [21] There are still at least twelve million Americans
who are plagued with the difficulty of avoiding work! Unemployment, according to this spokesman of business, in the School
of Commerce of New York University, would seem to be just a
sudden mass movement of the indolent propertyless who have
become so impressed with the ways of the idle rich that they decide to emulate them by declining to work.

The New York State Economic Council, of which Merwin
K. Hart is the leader, would revert to a property qualification
for the exercise of the franchise. The Council fears that the unemployed, if permitted to vote, may some day make demands
which will remove the present exemption which property claims
from all social obligation to provide for the victims of its policies.
Deputy Attorney General Henry Epstein of New York State
would also deny relief workers the right to organize. The Deputy
Attorney General says: "There should be no matter of 'demands'
because they are not properly in a position fairly or reasonably
to make demands. It is the State they are dealing with. In matters
of this kind we have found that the workers can be made to
understand the true nature of the relationship with the Government." The reply of the editor of the New York *Post* to the
Deputy Attorney General is altogether appropriate: "The Deputy
Attorney General's attitude, at bottom, springs from a view of
the unemployed as paupers who ought to be satisfied with any
scraps given them." [22]

Those who have suffered serious malnutrition, or nervous breakdown from the anxieties of insecurity, or outright starvation and death, during the present economic crisis, have not done so because they were idle but because they have been propertyless. Successful idleness is a trait only of those who own. Which raises serious doubts about Mr. Chase's "declining importance of ownership." Or if added evidence of the fundamental importance of ownership is required, it is to be had in the latest report of the Bureau of Internal Revenues.[23] Incomes of $1,000,-000 or more increased from twenty in 1932, last of the years of *Bourbon* Republicanism, to forty-six in 1933, first of the years of "New Deal" Democracy. There are at least forty-six Americans who simply could not understand what Mr. Chase is talking about. The number of incomes in every category from $25,000 up increased. In 1932, there were 25,089 such incomes, and in 1933 there were 26,142. Chalk up the difference, 1,053 votes, for the "New Deal" and "the declining importance of ownership." Wages and salaries, incomes from work, *decreased* by $567,565,091.

CHAPTER XIX

Under the Shadow of Gompers

THE AMERICAN FEDERATION OF LABOR is the largest and most unsuccessful business institution in the United States. Its purposes and methods are essentially those of the business world into which its leaders, Gompers and Green, have with gratuitous servility tried to insinuate themselves as full and recognized partners with the *de facto* rulers of America. The results have been all that the business world could desire and all that the workers of the country should detest. Objectives which could have been justified on the grounds of immediate goals have been transformed into ultimate and sufficient ends beyond which the imagination of the business-minded councils of labor leaders has not desired or dared to venture.

With the present leadership of the Federation and the program to which it is committed, organized labor is completely estopped from functioning as a force against business reaction no matter to what lengths that reaction finds it necessary to proceed.

The Federation has never been able to organize more than about 10 per cent of the total eligible wage-earning population. At no time has it been able to influence more than 14 per cent of the workers in the mining, manufacturing, transportation, and building trades—the industries in which unionization is greatest. When organized labor was an independent and effective force on behalf of workers in Germany, it controlled about 49 per cent of the wage-earners of that country.

The policy of indifference toward the organization of the unemployed has kept the numerical strength of the Federation at a low figure. The number of unemployed trade unionists who have lost their standing in the unions just as they have lost their industrial citizenship greatly exceeds the number of present members in the Federation. In March, 1933, the number of unemployed former trade unionists was estimated to be 3,639,184 or 26.6 per cent of the total number of the unemployed in the whole population. In August, 1934, Frank Morrison, secretary of the Federation, estimated the number of paid-up members and unemployed trade unionists as five and a half million. Only 40 per cent of these were paid-up members.

The principle of the "closed shop" has, as applied by the Federation, had the net effect of subjecting the great mass of workers, both employed and unemployed, to the wage and bargaining conditions of the "open shop." By its exclusiveness in emphasizing craft unionism and its indifference to the organization of the unemployed, it has left 90 per cent of the wage-earning class to the victimization of owning-class "liberty" and "freedom of contract." This policy has tended decidedly to depress the "closed shop" conditions under which the members of the Federation work, and to strip their collective bargaining of any real power.

Press reports have estimated that over 500,000 workers have been organized since the enactment of the National Industrial Recovery Act. This gain, however, does not offset the membership losses which occurred in 1931 and 1932. Nor does it compare at all favorably with the gain in the membership of "company unions" during the same period. The Brooklyn Chamber of Commerce is correct when it states that an increase in the membership of the American Federation of Labor "to 20,000,000 or 30,000,000 is very real and most alarming" to business interests in the event that such an increase occurs. Progress of the Federation in that direction to date should leave the Chamber of Commerce in a state of comfortable mental security.

At the Federation's 1934 Convention, after a heated debate over the archaic form of craft unionism, the "industrial" or "vertical" unionists scored a nominal and partial victory. While old craft unions are to remain intact, according to the resolution which was adopted, new industries are to be organized along industrial lines. Matthew Woll in supporting this innovation did so with a reference to the workers in these new industries as "the now unorganized and *perhaps unorganizable workers*." [1] [Italics ours.] It is easy to imagine how much enthusiasm Mr. Woll will put into the organization of the "unorganizable workers."

The Preamble to the Constitution of the American Federation of Labor reads like a fighting document, but no one unfamiliar with the language of the Constitution would ever guess it from the Federation's record or from the attitudes of the Federation's leaders. "Whereas, a struggle is going on in all the nations of the civilized world between the oppressors and oppressed of all countries, a struggle between the capitalist and the laborer, which grows in intensity from year to year, and will work disastrous results to the toiling millions if they are not combined for mutual protection and benefit," etc., etc. These words are themselves a sufficient indictment of the leaders of the organization which was thus historically and theoretically pitted in opposition to the "oppressors." From this theoretical opposition, organized labor has been led step by step into a servile collaboration with its oppressors.

Coöperation, peace, and unity between capital and labor and the government, all that any fascist despot could wish, was always the emphasis of the business-minded Samuel Gompers. President Roosevelt stressed this characteristic of Gompers in his speech at the dedication of the Gompers' Memorial. "He [Gompers] understood well the fact that those who serve the Government serve the people as a whole. . . . Mr. Gompers understood and went along with that thought during the years of the war, and we have many evidences of his acceptance of the fact that the horses pulling in harness were the horses of the employees and of the employers as well." [2]

William Green, early in his career as president of the Federation, pleaded for a stronger coöperation between employers and employees. He gave business every assurance that he expected to follow in the footsteps of his predecessor, Gompers. "There seems to be an understanding of peace and unity between labor and capital in Miami," he said soon after taking office. "Labor and capital cannot hate each other if they understand each other. Misunderstanding is the cause of strife. Understanding means concord." [3] Concord of the "oppressors" and the "oppressed." While the Federation Convention was in session in October, 1933, Green delivered an address in the National Cathedral in Washington in which he referred to the Biblical story of Ruth as an illustration of the ideal relationship between employer and employee. "Today, if we could have that same feeling of brotherhood, that same spirit of loving kindness in industry, that the reapers had with their employer, we would have much more happiness in this world and much less unrest, distrust, and woe," [4] declared the leader of the oppressed. These are not mere words for William Green; they are the principles which he strives to promote.

At the 1934 Convention of the United Mine Workers of America, the NRA was proclaimed the "greatest charter of freedom since Lincoln's emancipation proclamation." John L. Lewis and other officers of the union declared, in their report to the Convention, that the adoption of the Bituminous Coal Code under the NRA marked a turning of the road toward rational operation of the coal industry. "We are happy to be privileged to cooperate with the operators in the industry and the representatives of our government in effectuating stability and a more rational existence for the coal industry and those who depend upon it, whether they be operators or mine workers." [5] When leaders of organized labor collaborate so happily with employers to stabilize industry and thus voluntarily give up their reasons for organization, namely, the enforcement of labor's demands through the pressure of the strike, then the outlawry of strikes—a typical fascist measure—will be accomplished with ease.

The recent growth of company unions and the collaboration policy of the officials of the American Federation of Labor, nullify labor's force as a defense against business reaction. There is no evidence that the American trade union movement will recognize, in time, its real class interests. The Cigar Makers' International Union offered last year to turn over $50,000 to the cigar industry to help the employers eliminate competition. Such collaboration is purchased at the price of $50,000 plus the sacrifice of any legitimate purpose of unionization.[6]

In political as well as economic organization, the leaders of the Federation have pursued a consistent course of class collaboration. Their refusal to parallel trade union organization with an independent political organization of labor has not been due to any failure to understand the importance of political action but has grown naturally out of the general policy of collaboration. This policy has been described as "non-partisan" but the non-partisanship has applied only to choices between the various political parties of capitalism. The policy has been aggressively and bitterly partisan in choices between capitalist and anti-capitalist parties, demanding close collaboration with the former and war-to-the-death on the latter. Gompers was proud of the "non-partisan" declaration of the Minneapolis Convention of the Federation which read:

"We must have with us in our economic movement men of all parties as well as of all creeds, and the minority right of the humblest man to vote where he pleases and to worship where his conscience dictates must be sacredly guarded."

In 1917 Gompers assailed the radical element which was growing in the Federation and which demanded a labor party. His reasons for opposing a labor party were stated in the *American Federationist,* March, 1917, as follows:

"Political conditions are such in the United States that the wage-earners have been united to one or the other of the two strong political parties and that they are bound to these parties by ties of fealty and of tradition. It would take years ever to separate any considerable number of workers from their fealty to the old party. In addition to these, economic interests such as tariff policies are a strong factor in determining the party allegiance of wage-earners. The formation of a new party would seem the formulation of a complete political program for the wage-earners. In drawing up such a policy, it would be impossible to avoid controversial questions and hence it would be impossible to secure the united action of the wage-earners upon all questions." [7]

With this piece of chicane, the bankruptcy of labor's leadership was complete, and the masses of workmen were led straight into the shambles of the war.

The post-war situation, with its changed economic and social problems, did not alter the Federation's policies. In the 1929 Convention, the organization still believed that "the non-partisan political policy of the Federation [had] proved its worth more and more each year" and offered as proof the fact that 135 members of the House of Representatives had "voted right" on measures of interest to labor and 110 members had records which were "exceedingly fair" to labor! [8]

"The American Federation of Labor is not on the political treadmill of either of the major political parties and never has been," says Green. "As an organization, our members are not Republicans, Democrats, Socialists nor Farmer-Laborites. *But the American Federation of Labor does not hesitate to say that, as an organization, we are strongly opposed to communism and the Communist Party.*" [9] [Italics ours.] The members of the Federation are free to vote for any party standing for "American ideals," which means any capitalist party or any anti-Communist party.

The Executive Council of the American Federation of Labor issued a press release which quoted William Green as saying: "I think we have made it plain many times recently that the

American Federation of Labor is seeking to curb hasty judgment in the matter of strikes and that the strike should be used
as the last resort. . . . It is our desire that the American Federation of Labor shall be in every respect above any kind of reproach. We shall have traducers always, or at least as long as
there is greed in the world, but we have built dignity and integrity and thorough Americanism into our movement." [10] Concerning the Labor Truce which President Roosevelt proposed
for industry, William Green, President of the Federation, said:
"We want to settle our differences in the conference room. . . ." [11]
Other labor leaders such as John P. Frey, president of the Metal
Trades Department of the Federation, Frank Morrison, secretary
of the Federation, and Charles P. Howard, president of the
International Typographical Union, enthusiastically endorsed
what may prove to be the first real step toward arbitration of a
compulsory nature.

If capital and labor should engage in forthright class struggle,
"then religion and ethics have failed," Mr. Green told the members of the First Congregational Church of San Francisco on
October 7, 1934. "The American Federation of Labor refuses
to embrace such a philosophy or accept such a pessimistic theory,"
he went on to say. The struggle in the industrial field is not
between classes but rather between "the forces of self-righteous-
ness and those of righteousness," said Green. [12]

In the report of the Executive Council of the American Federation of Labor to the 1934 Convention, held in San Francisco,
there is no single word which indicates that labor leaders sense
the gravity of labor's situation or understand the reactionary
drift of business and industry. One finds only a pleading with
employers to "join hands" and bring about prosperity. That
prosperity for the mass of workers is by definition precluded
in such a society as this one, is not considered.

"Labor's efforts must be directed to keeping it [NRA] and
strengthening it as an instrument for the future, in the interests
not only of labor but of industry as well," William Green said

at the United Mine Workers' Convention, held in Indianapolis, January 29, 1934.[13] [Italics ours.]

The Bituminous Coal Code, accepted by the leaders of the United Mine Workers, contains an out-and-out compulsory arbitration feature. If any controversy "threatens to interrupt," says the Code, "or has interrupted, or is impairing the efficient operation of any mine or mines to such an extent as to restrain interstate commerce in the products thereof," it shall be settled by one of the six regional coal labor boards, and during that settlement, "neither party to the controversy shall change the conditions out of which the controversy arose, *or utilize any coercive or retaliatory measures to compel the other party to accede to its demands.*"[14] [Italics ours.] This is out-and-out fascism. Arbitration assumes equality between the two parties in controversy, and that equal representation will assure fair settlement. That labor and industry are not equal participants but that industry has the overwhelming power on its side is evidenced by the outcome of the settlements by all previous boards of arbitration and by the increased anti-labor tendencies of all such boards in recent years.

John L. Lewis, president of the United Mine Workers of America, stated in his speech before the members of the Commonwealth Club of San Francisco, on October 10, 1934, that the present economic system is being reconstructed on the theory that capital and labor are partners.[15] "To oppose such a movement," Mr. Lewis emphasized, "is not only a crime against labor, it is a social blunder which may lead to the toppling over of our whole economic edifice"—which would indeed be a tragedy to Mr. Lewis. Having enunciated pure fascist doctrine, he bemoaned the fact that in "fascist or dictator-ruled" countries, "labor was a pawn in the hands of a completely centralized governing group," yet in stating that labor would not be content until its partnership becomes a real one, he constructs in his imagination a picture of society which all experience should have taught him is fanciful in the extreme.

One of the most important theorists of the American Federation of Labor, Louis Lorwin, prophesies the role of labor in the coming years. He says: "Inevitably, if the government lends its aid to unionism, it will demand in exchange that the unions surrender some of their traditional liberties and adhere more closely to strictly constructive functions in industry. The trend toward a *semi-legal, quasi-public unionism* [labor's position under fascism] in the United States is a phase of a movement which seems world-wide in character. In all industrial countries, the voluntary or so-called 'free' type of unionism is having difficulties in maintaining itself, if it has not been entirely destroyed." [Italics ours.] "Here in Italy," Mussolini said to a newspaper reporter, "we have done away with strikes and lockouts, we do not waste our time in brawls." [16]

Gompers gained a high degree of respectability for himself as a reward for his repudiation of the real interests of labor in support of the World War. He was appointed by President Wilson as the representative of Labor to the Council of National Defense, October, 1916. Before this the Labor movement had been viewed with indifference or hostility and Gompers felt pride in this recognition. Labor representatives were sent on important war missions: to rally the French and British trade unionists to Wilson's aims, to prevail upon Kerensky to keep Russia from making a separate peace, to carry out the dictates of the war-making state.[17] Labor's "excellent" war record, however, did not alter the reactionary attitude of the courts. Injunctions were upheld and boycotts declared illegal. It is ironical that when most of the employers had abandoned their war-time cooperation with labor and had accepted the inevitable struggle, Green should still say:

"We believe that the conference room is a better method than the strike field. We believe that peace and goodwill will make more money for the mill owner than passion or hate." [18]

Henry H. Heimann, executive manager of the National Association of Credit Men, discusses current labor problems in his review of business conditions sent to the 20,000 members of the Association in which he says: "Most industrialists will state that the men at the top of Union Labor take a *broad outlook*. True, they are vigilant in their protection of labor rights, but they do not seek their objective over the dead body of industry. They are too intelligent for that. The difficulty in the A. F. of L. and other national labor organizations is the lack of control and impotency of the leaders to command or direct the local leaders. It is the bottom of the organization rather than the top that causes the trouble." [19] [Italics ours.]

The reactionary *Business Week,* while criticizing severely many of the labor leaders, has only friendly words for Sidney Hillman, head of the Amalgamated Clothing Workers' Union. The comment editorially is that he "is regarded as friendly to industries which cooperate with labor organizations." [20]

The present officers of the Federation use every opportunity to fight radical activity. If as much energy were expended to fight the growing menace of fascism, perhaps it would not be so inevitable. President William Green, because of his collaboration policy, is concerned only with fighting radicals, and not with fighting capitalism. He seizes every opportunity to point out that the "destructive, unethical and impractical" radicals— "those misguided groups"—are not in any way connected with the Federation. At a meeting of the American Society of Newspaper Editors, held April 18, 1931, he appealed to the press to aid in discriminating between the true leaders of labor and the radical leaders. He warned the press that "there is an eternal conflict constantly going on between organized labor, and these destructive, unethical and impracticable groups, many of which receive organization inspiration and financial support from abroad. . . . They represent a philosophy that is in constant opposition to the philosophy espoused and advocated by the American Federation of Labor. There can be no compromise on the part of the bona fide labor movement with these groups which use the name of labor as a password to legislative assemblies, public meetings and religious organizations." [21]

Matthew Woll, vice-president of the Federation, urges even stronger measures than does Green. He not only repudiates socialism, but he would aid the government in checking its spread. Business men can well be grateful to the leaders of the American labor movement who confine their attacks to radicalism and thereby keep labor occupied in an internal contest, while the captains of industry are engrossed with the problem of maintaining the existence of capitalism.

The Federation officials have not condemned Fascist Italy nor Nazi Germany with the intense hatred shown in the denunciation of Soviet Russia. Samuel Gompers denounced the Soviet Union soon after it came into being.[22] The Federation has not become any more reconciled to Soviet Russia than Gompers was in 1919. When the Soviet Ambassador, Alexander Troyanovsky, took up his duties in this country, the Federation immediately became the self-appointed watch dog for the vested interests and issued a long document to President Roosevelt showing the alleged network of Soviet propaganda in this country.[23] President Green has referred to Russia as "the menace to Labor" on a number of occasions. It is ironical that the workers of the Soviet Union have received recognition by the United States not because of, but in spite of, the efforts of the leaders of organized workers in this country.

After the general strike of San Francisco had collapsed, Silas B. Axtell, general counsel for the International Seamen's Union of America, urged the striking marine workers' union to purge their ranks of all communist elements. "Communist" has become the epithet which anybody who doesn't like something—particularly in labor—can use. It is supposed to cover all opposition to the officials of the unions, or to the employers. Mr. Axtell also had to point out that "freedom" (whatever that means to Mr. Axtell) was being denied in Russia. "My experience . . . in the United

States, on the waterfront in New York and on the East coast,"
Mr. Axtell affirms, "convinces me that none except riff-raff, un-
stable mentalities, are susceptible to these [communist] doctrines.
. . . Nevertheless, their ceaseless chatter has interfered with the
organization of seamen in strong unions which could accomplish relief." [24]

Because many rank and filers are becoming disgusted with
the Federation leadership, the latter has retaliated by announcing
the growing danger of communism in the unions. John L.
Lewis and Matthew Woll presented a resolution to the 1934
Convention which took a firm stand against "extremism." At
the Executive Council meeting in August, 1934, William Green
announced that communists had penetrated the unions with
the purpose of gaining control of the Federation. "Let the communists and their advocates know," he said, "that the American
Federation of Labor will not remain complaisant when such
a destructive and subversive force is attempting to capture our
organization. There can be no harmony and no coöperation
between communism and trade unionism. Their philosophies
are in direct conflict." All leaders were urged to "ferret out the
communists within our ranks and to expel them from membership when it is clearly established that they are members of
the communist organization and engaged in communist propaganda." [25] It is unmistakably clear that while official labor "co-
öperates" with the plunderbund on the right, it sees its sole duty
toward the left as that of ruthless and unending warfare—surely
a state of affairs and an outlook ideally adapted for easy transi-
tion to a fascist labor configuration.

Matthew Woll cannot make a speech—particularly an important one such as his 1934 Labor Day speech—without saying
something about the "common foe," communism.[26] By "common foe" he means *in common* with Ralph M. Easley, representative of manufacturers. Mr. Easley, in a speech made the
same day, said, "to meet this situation [of increasing unrest and
communism] and remove this disturbing factor, it is essential

that the investigating machinery should be restored to our Department of Justice and power and adequate funds given to it, so that our government may officially know of the activities of the communists and be prepared to deal with them." [27]

As a business institution, the American Federation of Labor is increasingly in a hopeless position. The displacement of Labor by machines in one important industry after another renders it increasingly ineffective as a fighting force on behalf of better living standards. Finance capital shows a marked tendency to concentrate in those industries where labor costs in production are lowest or where they are being progressively lowered. In twelve of the major industries of the United States, labor costs have already been decreased to a point where they are less than 10 per cent of the total costs, in some of these the labor item constituting not more than 3 per cent of the total outlay involved in production. Eight of these twelve low labor-cost industries [Petroleum, Automobiles, Sugar Refining, Flour Milling, Meat Packing, Paints, Corn Products, Chemicals] are among the industries that have experienced the least depreciation of stocks on the Exchange. Finance capital is clearly seeking out those industries where disturbances from labor sources are least likely to occur. This fact gives a powerful impetus to the general movement for the installation of labor-saving devices. In turn, it effectively destroys the scarcity-market of labor, and therefore makes increasingly impossible any successful functioning by organized labor as a business institution. Labor, therefore, to be effective against business reaction must not only find strong allies outside its own ranks, but must forthwith abandon the controlling policies of its leadership which inhibit new alliances. Specifically, these new alliances must be found (1) among the masses of the unskilled workers who are not, as Matthew Woll says, organizable under the present policies of the American Federation of Labor, (2) among the sinking lower middle class, (3) among the special racial and social groups that are victimized as the scapegoats of *reaction*, and (4) among that still larger element commonly called "consumers" who may be aroused to fighting indignation against the exploiters and adulterators of goods.

Race prejudice, anti-radicalism and collaboration of normally antagonistic social and economic classes are three of the character-istic features of extreme business reaction when it has reached the fascist stage. The leadership of the American Federation of Labor is deeply involved in all three. Until that leadership is displaced, there is no reasonable prospect that organized labor in the United States will effectively oppose the powerful tendencies toward a crasser business dictatorship any more than it opposed the very businesslike and bankerlike participation of the United States in the World War.

PART III
GOVERNMENT

The Business-State

THE NATURE OF THE STATE IN BUSINESS SOCIETY is a question second to no other in importance. Upon a correct understanding of the character and purposes of government depend all questions of social strategy for remaking society in the interests of consumer-workers. As long as there is any lingering illusion about the existence of a government of the people, by the people, and for the people, the strategy for establishing an economy of abundance and quality will contain a wide margin of error.

The tradition of free democracy in American society persists in spite of overwhelming evidence against it. "Majorities determine governmental attitudes because they elect the personnel of government,"[1] says a writer in the *Ice Cream Trade Journal.* The most firmly entrenched traditions in social thought are often the most baseless in historical facts, since the force of a tradition is conferred upon it by the current necessities of the established order rather than by history. There was, for example, never present in American social and political life anything that corresponds to the prevailing tradition of democracy upon which millions rely for protection against dictatorship. Those who hark back to the days of Jefferson and Jackson for the democratic tradition in American life are forgetful of the real social relations which obtained in those days. Never was a "democracy" more completely restricted to the ruling class of society than in the days when the fundamental labor force of the country was in the thraldom of chattel slavery and when even the free labor of the commercial and rising industrial states was wholly unorganized and generally outside even the provisions of the franchise. There was not even in that heyday of alleged American democracy a free public school system which for many connotes the existence of a political democracy. In addition to all these restrictions upon the democracy of those far-off days, half the adult population— the women—had scarcely entertained the idea of participating in political life; and Thomas Jefferson himself declared it unthinkable that women should ever descend to the obviously masculine sphere of politics. Whence then, the force which sustains the tradition of the democratic principle in American life? Since it obviously lacks a historical basis, it must have been preserved and perpetuated for reasons which lie deep in the political necessities of American civilization.

There have been only two instances in American history when a real transfer of political and social power from one group to another has occurred, and both of those instances were the occasions of wars. The Revolution of 1776 resulted in a transfer of power from an imperialist crown and its ruling class to a colonial bourgeoisie; and the Civil War resulted in a transfer of power from a landed aristocracy to a commercial plutocracy, and in neither case was a democracy — as popularly conceived — built upon the ruins of its war-destroyed predecessor. Nothing could be further from the facts than to assess a political "overturn" such as that which occurred in 1932 or the even more impressive shift of 1934 as a transfer of power from one basic social class to another. On the contrary, a single class simply changed the personnel of its political executives, and it is a fundamental necessity for realistic political thought to grasp this fact—which we propose to demonstrate.

The illusion of democracy persists for the sole reason that it is a convenient cover for the rule of a minority—the type of rule that has characterized American politics from the inception of organized western society upon this continent, and must perforce obtain wherever there is a class-divided social system. The rule of a minority, or of a majority for that matter, so long as it is expressive of the will of a single homogeneous class, is none the less a dictatorship when it is not required to utilize its police powers to the full extent. The powers of ideological considerations may be sufficient to maintain a dictatorship unimpaired, with the necessity for the direct application of police force arising only occasionally. The dictatorship of business is, in fact, maintained in the United States today by the force of ideas, and resembles in all its essential purposes and features the dictatorship of more *insecure* capitalist groups in countries like Italy and Germany. The measure of insecurity is the measure of the police powers of repression which are adopted by the ruling class of a capitalist economy.

Our immediate concern, however, is not so much with the question of what government has been like in America's past, but how it functions today with reference to the conflicting groups that make up American society.

At the Conference of Pharmaceutical Law Enforcement Officials, held in Washington, D. C., May 10, 1934, Frank C. Purdum, pharmacist and member of the Maryland State Legislature, discussed the relationships of pharmacists to politics. Mr. Purdum throws the following light upon American democracy and the way in which pharmacists function in its political processes: "In conclusion, let me digress briefly into a discussion of practical politics. Legislative experience and the ability to fraternize with other members of the legislature are really great helps. . . . Most representatives are partly or wholly controlled by district leaders or bosses as they are generally called. These bosses are not always bad and their friendship is worth cultivating. *It may only cost a cigar, highball or lunch*." [2] [Italics ours.]

Perhaps no better picture of the network of government, business, and their subsidiary agencies could be given than is presented in the elaborate chart of the National Live Stock and Meat Board reproduced on the following pages. Every major industry or business has a similar working chart which guides it

PUBLIC RELATIONS
NATIONAL LIVE STOCK AND MEAT BOARD

REPRESENTING ALL BRANCHES OF THE LIVE STOCK AND MEAT INDUSTRY

1933-34

Working With Many Different Interests In Behalf of MEAT

EDUCATIONAL INSTITUTIONS

- Elementary Schools
- High Schools
- Normal Schools
- 4H Clubs
- Libraries
- County Agents
- Board of Education
- State Supervisers
- Domestic Science Schools
- Vocational Training Schools
- Colleges and Universities
- Am. Library Asso
- Home Demonstration Ag'ts

BUSINESS INTERESTS

- Public Utilities Co's
- Electric Companies
- Gas Companies
- Bakers Ass'ns
- Department Stores
- Telephone Companies
- Chain Stores
- Railroads
- Farm Equip't Co's
- Food Foundations
- Stove Companies
- Advertising Agencies
- Refrigerator Co's
- Outdoor Ad Interests
- Food Manufacturers
- Hardware Stores
- Life Insurance Co's
- Furniture Stores
- Glass Manufacturers

UNITED STATES GOVERNMENT

DEPARTMENT of AGRICULTURE
- Bureau of Home Economics
- Bureau of Agricultural Economics
- Bureau of Animal Industry
- Office of Experiment Stations

- Dep't of Interior
- Dep't of Labor
- Post Office
- Navy
- Army
- Federal Board of Vocational Education
- Veterans Administration
- Civil Works Administration
- Civilian Conservation Corps

RESEARCH AGENCIES

- Nat'l Research Council
- Scientific Research Workers
- Clinical Research Workers
- College Experiment Stations

NEWS AND PUBLICATION INTERESTS

- Daily Newspapers
- Breed Journals
- Weekly Newspapers
- Meat Trade Journals
- Hotel and Restaurant Magazines
- Market Dailies
- Agricultural Journals
- National Women's Mag
- Medical Journals
- Dietetic Journals
- Hospital Journals
- Home Economics Journals
- Western Newspaper Union
- Associated Press
- International News Serv.
- United Press
- National Editorial Ass'n
- House Organs
- State Editorial Ass'ns
- College Publicity Dept

Research

Education

Medical / Physicians

- INDIVIDUAL PHYSICIANS
- STATE HEALTH COMMR'S
- CITY BOARDS of HEALTH
- MEDICAL SCHOOLS
- HOSPITALS
- COUNTY MEDICAL ASS'NS
- INFIRMARIES
- CHILD HEALTH ASS'NS
- INSTITUTES of HOMEOPATHY
- SANITORIUMS
- FOOD AND MILK INSPECTORS
- SUMMER HEALTH CAMPS
- STATE MEDICAL ASS'NS

Dental / Oral Hygiene

- INDIVIDUAL DENTISTS
- AMERICAN DENTAL ASS'N
- STATE DENTAL ASS'NS
- CITY DENTAL SOCIETIES
- DENTAL ASSISTANTS
- ORAL HYGIENE
- DENTAL SCHOOLS
- DENTAL HYGIENISTS
- JOURNAL of AM. DENTAL ASS'N
- DENTAL STUDENTS MAGAZINE

DIETETIC PROFESSION

- AMERICAN DIETETIC ASS'N
- STATE DIETETIC ASS'NS
- STUDENT DIETITIANS
- FOOD CLINICS
- CITY DIETETIC ASS'NS
- HOSPITAL DIETITIANS
- NUTRITION SPECIALISTS
- COMMERCIAL DIETITIANS

ORGANIZATIONS

- WOMEN'S CLUBS
- CHAMBERS of COMMERCE
- FEDERATION of CHURCHES
- BUSINESS AND PROFESSIONAL CLUBS
- Y.W.C.A
- ROTARY CLUBS
- KIWANIS CLUBS
- LIONS CLUBS
- PASTOR'S ASSOCIATION
- AMERICAN LEGION
- BOY SCOUTS of AMERICA
- PARENT-TEACHER ASS'N
- ADVERTISING CLUBS
- FARM BUREAUS
- NATIONAL CANNERS ASS'O

Welfare / Charities

- EMERGENCY RELIEF COM'S
- VISITING NURSES ASS'NS
- AMERICAN RED CROSS
- ASSOCIATED CHARITIES
- CATHOLIC CHARITIES
- JEWISH CHARITIES
- SALVATION ARMY
- VOLUNTEERS of AMERICA
- PUBLIC WELFARE SOC'S
- COMMUNITY CHESTS
- JEWISH WELFARE SOC'S
- DISPENSARIES
- UNEMPLOYMENT RELIEF ORGANIZATIONS
- ASSOCIATION OF HOUSEKEEPING CENTERS
- FAMILY SERVICE ASS'NS
- WELFARE COUNCILS
- MEMORIAL FUNDS
- INDIVIDUAL WELFARE WORKERS
- MASONIC HOME

NURSING PROFESSION

- NURSING ASSOCIATIONS
- AMERICAN HOSPITAL ASS'N
- VISITING NURSE ASS'NS
- HOSPITAL NURSES
- REGISTERED NURSES
- PUBLIC HEALTH NURSES
- PUBLIC SCHOOL NURSES

CATERING INTERESTS

- HOTEL ASSOCIATIONS
- RESTAURANT ASS'NS
- CATERING ASS'NS
- HOTEL STEWARDS
- HOTEL CHEFS
- HOTEL AND RESTAURANT MAGAZINES
- TEA ROOM MANAGERS
- COLLEGE INSTITUTION MANAGEMENT DEPART'M'TS
- LUNCH ROOM MGR'S
- SODA FOUNTAIN MAGAZINES
- SUMMER CAMP STEWARDS
- DELICATESSEN MANAGERS

RADIO INTERESTS

- NATIONAL CHAIN
- INDIVIDUAL STATIONS
- WOMEN'S PROGRAM DIR'TORS
- HOME ECONOMICS SPEAKERS

in its public relations and business policies. Special attention should be called to some of the subsidiary social agencies and governmental adjuncts of the Meat Board. Not only is the United States Government with its various departments such as the Bureau of Home Economics pictured as an effective arm of the Meat Board, but other agencies, such as Colleges and Universities, Libraries, Daily Newspapers, Authors of Textbooks, Federation of Churches, Y.W.C.A., Pastors' Association, American Legion, National Women's Magazines, and Radio Interests, are claimed by the Meat Board as departments which further its interests. There are, on the other hand, some most significant omissions from this chart. Labor is not among the partners of the meat industry. The gratuitous manner in which labor leaders are accustomed to think of themselves as partners in collaboration with business and government is apparently not shared by business itself. Neither is there pictured in the chart any organization which, by any stretch of the imagination, could be considered an independent agency working in the interests of consumers. In the great tie-up between business and government, with more than a hundred subsidiary institutions, there is no place for organizations which represent the opposed interests of the essential consumers in American economic society.

The Roosevelt Administration has outdone all of its predecessors in creating the illusion of serving not only the interests of business, but also those of consumers and workers. The illusion that the NRA inaugurated a revolutionary epoch by its recognition of the consumer is widespread and persistent. Large numbers of consumers are coming to understand the tricks of salesmanship where it concerns the goods they buy over the counter from private distributors; but many of these same enlightened consumers, when they enter the area of political matters, retain a childlike faith in government-sponsored illusions. At least the Administration will look after us, they say, because it declares its deep solicitude for consumers; and especially must this be true of an Administration which is the first in American history to give such prominent and official recognition to the interests of consumers. Has not the NRA a full-fledged Consumers' Advisory Board? Is it not adequately staffed with outstanding liberals who are above suspicion of being "influenced" by anti-consumer motives?

The alert consumer could have answered, and a few who no longer believe in Santa Claus did answer, these questions a year ago. Now the record is open to all, and no good reason for illusion remains—except the powerful propaganda which sustains it. The Consumers' Advisory Board is not a bold *blue eaglet* but a retiring *white dove*. The Blue Eagle of the NRA is, appropriately, a bird of prey, symbolizing the way in which business plunders consumers.

The status of consumers under the NRA is allegedly *advisory*. Actually it is not even that, for there is no record, after more than a year of existence, that the Consumers' Advisory Board has either offered any appreciable, sound, forthright and uncompromising advice on behalf of consumers or that anybody has paid the slightest attention to whatever advice it has proffered. It might be more appropriately styled the Consumers' Ornamental Board. As such it fulfills the highly important function (from the standpoint of business interests) of deluding the millions of consumers into a belief that at last there is an Administration that cares for their interests.

When it came to setting up the code authorities for the administration of NRA principles in industry, it was General "Crackdown" Johnson himself who declared: "Industry is going to regulate itself." This declaration was in response to a proposal that consumers be represented on the code authorities. The statement explains, without his vivid language, the General's attitude toward the Consumers' Advisory Board, to say nothing of his attitude toward consumers, which is even more unprintable in character.

When the Consumers' Advisory Board received more than 1,000 protests against prices under the Cleaning and Dyeing

Trade Code, the publicity bureau of the NRA issued a release stating that "telegrams and letters pouring into the offices of the Cleaning and Dyeing Trade Code Authority indicate the enthusiasm and approval with which the trade and consuming public generally are accepting the minimum prices fixed for the industry under the Code Provisions."[3] Either there was poor messenger service between these government departments, or there was deliberate suppression of news in the publicity bureau of the NRA. Whichever it was, it amounts to the same thing. Consumers do not have any important advisory relationship to the NRA, as Consumers' Research has frequently pointed out. Even if they were to have such a relationship, advice, particularly when not vigorously proffered, is as easily ignored as given. In government circles, advisory committees are customarily appointed so that the advice can be (a) delayed or diluted, and (b) ignored when it is given. Consumers must have power, not simply an advisory capacity, that springs from organized pressure, before their interests are served in any important degree in a system that operates on the basis of pressure politics.

It requires no considerable amount of space to show that the members of the Consumers' Advisory Board are not themselves *consumers* in any effective political sense. Their social traditions and viewpoints are not such as to fit them for decisive struggle against predatory business in the interests of consumers. A consumer, to be politically effective, must be more than a well intentioned liberal who views issues with a calm dispassionateness from some lofty height above the battle, with a town house and a country estate (with hot and cold running water) far from the commoner of the teeming Ghetto or of the crossroad hamlet of Missouri or Alabama.

The hand of the Administration was revealed by its course of action in the matter of consumer-protection, as seen in the history of the Copeland-Tugwell bill. This type of legislation was not one of the major concerns of Washington officialdom. Administration forces could have been marshalled behind a measure emodying the protection for consumers that is now so sadly lacking n the provisions and enforcement of the existing Food and Drugs Act. Instead, the pressure of powerfully organized busiaess interests prevented even the *consideration* of effective conumer legislation. The Administration acquiesced in this situaion and diverted its attention to a program of industrial recovery. t turned the matter over to the well-known patent medicine estimonializer, Senator-Doctor Copeland. The consequences are hat even the emasculated Copeland bill died as unfinished legisation; and the old fraud in advertising and the old methods of heating the consumer at every turn are continued.

A series of County Consumers' Councils, now under the guidnce of the Consumers' Division of the National Emergency Council, was authorized more than a year ago as a gesture of the Administration's solicitude for consumers. A few indefatigable iberals over the country have done their best to make these County Consumers' Councils function in the protection of conumers, but their efforts have been nullified completely by Washngton's half-heartedness and red tape. Instructions sent out by he Consumers' Division of the National Emergency Council how plainly that the County Councils were never intended to unction as anything more than useful illusions of an industrialsts' and bankers' government for diverting the complaints of onsumers from effective expression. "Bulletin No. 1" insists hat "the Councils are to be guided absolutely by the fact that hey have no inquisitorial or enforcement powers whatsoever, nd are to proceed in a spirit of friendly co-operation in getting t the facts." After this generous douche of cold water, if any County Consumers' Council should persist in getting really inlignant about conditions, its complaints are to be routed through uch a network of directors, councils, authorities, administrations, oards, divisions, and commissions that no possible effects of a seful character could be registered. It is not surprising to hear hat one chairman of a County Consumers' Council reports: "It s rather a shame that my Council, which started work so hope-

fully, should go so completely to pieces as it has." [4] That many
of these farcical consumers' councils have gone completely to
pieces is a tribute to the intelligence of their members. At least
some of them have learned the valuable lesson that they have
been hoodwinked by an utterly worthless and incoherent rigma-
role.

The "New Deal's" solicitude for labor has been equally illusory. It has, however, consisted not only of the kind of flapdoodle
which has been used with the County Consumers' Councils, but
has gone further and functioned effectively as a strike-breaking
and labor-exploiting mechanism.

The evidence is now complete to show that the National Industrial Recovery Act was conceived as an answer to the growing
demand for legislation that would aid labor. The United States
Senate was on the verge of passing the bill calling for a 30-hour
week for labor, when the Chamber of Commerce intervened and
succeeded in substituting the N.I.R.A. The ability of big business to sidetrack threatening legislation and convert popular protests into measures that serve its interests and its interests alone
is amazing to contemplate. The outstanding result of the social
ferment of the early days of the Roosevelt Administration was
the enactment of a measure which vested substantial power in
the trade associations of industry by the suspension of anti-trust
curbs. "In other words," said Hugh S. Johnson, "NRA is
exactly what industry organized in trade associations makes it.
What was a trade association before this Act? Under the Anti-
trust laws it was a barely tolerated organization with about as
much legal sanction and sustained effectiveness as an Old Ladies
Knitting Society." [5] Johnson went on to describe the trade associations under the N.I.R.A. as fully implemented arms of
government with powers to police industry by self-created law.
Labor and consumers were to have a place in the new scheme,
but the place of observers! "The NRA, instead of agreeing to
appoint labor members to authorities administering codes, is
working on a plan for the creation of governmental boards, in

cluding labor and consumer representatives, to observe industrial operation." [6] Labor and consumers may observe industrial operations to their hearts' content and to their impoverishment without sitting powerlessly upon the boards which have the authority and use it to entrench still further the control of industrialists over the whole social mechanism.

Section 7a of the N.I.R.A. has been hailed by labor leaders as their charter of emancipation. But collective bargaining, so far as law is concerned, was guaranteed by the Clayton Act, the Bankruptcy Act, the Railway Labor Act, and the Norris-La-Guardia Act, long before the enactment of the N.I.R.A. When the N.I.R.A. was being written both General Johnson and Donald Richberg approved the incorporation of a clause to the effect that "nothing in this title shall be construed to compel a change in the existing satisfactory relations between employees and employers of any particular plant, firm or corporation, except that the employees of any particular plant, firm or corporation shall have the right to organize for collective bargaining with their employers as to wages, hours of labor and other conditions of employment." [7] This provision was not finally included in the N.I.R.A. but the fact that Johnson and Richberg favored it is important evidence of the position of the administrators of the NRA on company unionism. It is also sufficient explanation of the way in which the NRA has in fact functioned as a strike-breaking agency. There has been no "cracking down" on recalcitrant employers in big business. One after the other they have successfully challenged the right of labor to impose "closed shop" conditions in their industries. When labor has been on the point of winning the right to organize and bargain effectively the Administration has stepped in with the assistance of high labor leaders and nullified its efforts. No single strike of any large significance has been won by labor under the NRA.

When General Johnson started on his swing through the West in the summer of 1934, he stopped at Waterloo, Iowa, where he declared that recent events in Nazi Germany made him sick.

He proceeded westward to California where the San Francisco general strike was in progress. At Berkeley he made a speech which was a clear incitation to violence, and unmistakable fascist fruits were produced immediately. He shouted to his audience in the Johnsonian manner that the "subversive element" which had precipitated "civil war" in California would be wiped out "as you clean off a chalk mark on a blackboard with a wet sponge." "It would be safer," he thundered blusteringly, "for a cotton-tail rabbit to slap a wildcat in the face than for this half of 1 per cent of our population to try to strangle the rest of us into submission by any such means as this. Let's settle this thing and do it now." [8] Immediately the lawless mobs of business gangsters went into action. Meantime, the American Federation of Labor, through William Green, was busy disavowing the efforts of San Francisco workers to win a small victory against the powerful forces of reaction. In his Chicago speech, Green declared the strike *unauthorized,* which had the moral effect, at least, of approving the actions of General Johnson and the San Francisco mobs.

Johnson is out of the NRA but the policies of opposition to labor's organization go on. The shrewder and less outspoken Richberg has made it plain that such words as "closed shop" and "open shop" should be eliminated from the NRA dictionary.

Frances Perkins, first woman member of a President's cabinet, has been repeatedly outspoken in favor of restoring profits but far less energetic and enthusiastic on behalf of labor. "The savings of many people are invested in industry, and they are entitled to expect the maintenance of profits," says Miss Perkins. This explains the work of the Secretary of Labor in setting up the numerous arbitration boards which have had the uniform effect of maintaining profits at the expense of labor. "The close relation between good wages and steady profits is very clear in our American economy," [9] Miss Perkins declared in her Labor Day Speech on September 3, 1934. Even then the report of the Commissioner of Internal Revenue was in preparation to prove precisely the opposite, namely that profits under the "New Deal" were soaring in such a way as to double the number of incomes in excess of $1,000,000, while good wages were farther than ever from realization. There was a "close relation" between wages and rising profits only in the sense that as one went down the other went up.

Business tories hope to gain still more complete mastery over the situation than the Roosevelt Administration has so generously granted it by the removal of the restrictions of the anti-trust laws. "There is still plenty of possibility," says the Washington correspondent of *Business Week,* "that a powerful over-riding industrial board may take over the whole NRA and FTC [Federal Trade Commission] as well." [10] Business is indeed insatiable for power. What is desired, of course, is that the anomalous Section 7a of the N.I.R.A. shall be removed as a source of any embarrassment whatever, and further that strikes shall be declared illegal altogether.

Having scored what it considers the most significant victories in the history of capitalism in the United States, there is going to be no hesitation on the part of the business world to seek ever greater conquests of power. As a writer in the *Glass Packer* sees it, "the entire business world, in all its ramifications; manufacturers, processors, packers, brokers, wholesale and retail distributors speak through its official mouthpiece, the trade association." [11] Having been thus brought together as a unified force, the wishes of business men will, it is expected, command ever greater respect in the councils of government. "In bringing together the various factors in industry in closely knit relationship to combat tyrannical laws, NRA has unconsciously and unintentionally served a most useful purpose. Never before in the country's history have the various lines of trade been welded into such compact units, nor have they ever before functioned so successfully and harmoniously in a common cause. In this fact perhaps," says the writer in the *Glass Packer,* "is the greatest hope for the year to come." [12] Any effective legislation on behalf of the interests of consumers and workers may as well be classed among the impossibilities under the business-state. The business oligarchy declares its intention of maintaining "constant vigilance" in the years to come, and whenever necessary to work, as the writer in *Glass Packer* puts it, with "lightning action to produce the facts, figures and arguments that will serve to sway the legislative mind." [13]

When, therefore, during the future sessions of Congress, attempts are made to write legislation covering the rights of labor to organize and bargain collectively or otherwise to increase the purchasing power of the masses of those who live by income from work, the entire business world will be on hand, represented in the form of its officially established trade associations, to defeat all such efforts and to go still further in curbing labor. When consumers seek the kind of protection that was contemplated in the Tugwell bill, business unified and all-powerful in its persuasiveness over the legislative mind will be even more effective than hitherto in forestalling the enactment of any protective legislation that would circumvent on behalf of consumers the multiform frauds of advertising.

If there has been any doubt in the minds of the uninformed about who owns the government and all its various agencies, it should be dispelled by the forthright statement of the Secretary of the Treasury. "The last thing I want," says Mr. Morgenthau, "is that any business man should be afraid of his Treasury Department." [14] Any *business man! His* Treasury Department! The Secretary had become a bit worried lest business men fear the taxation powers of the Treasury.

The business men, i.e., the big ones, not only *own* the Treasury in the sense that they are the tax-payers whose views *count* with the government, but also in the sense that they are in these times of economic disarrangement dependent upon its bounty for carrying on their industrial and financial enterprises. The providing of huge doles to industry has become one of the most important "chores" that government performs. "When it has been made plain," says the editor of *Oil, Paint and Drug Reporter,* "that the pump is in good working order and is drawing from the well good, clean water, free from pollywogs, snails, waterspiders, algæ, and other contamination, confidence will be right there in all its smiling beneficence, and *government can give up the priming and go about its more appropriate chores.*" [15] [Italics ours.] "Business must govern," says the same editor, for "government (in the political sense) is inseparable from business." [16]

A recent development in the intimate relations of business and government is seen in the increasing disposition of government to underwrite the investments of business. The Roosevelt Administration has undertaken what has been widely publicized as a great housing program. This ostensibly is infused with a broad social consciousness. Closer examination, however, reveals that it is only one more way of helping stricken building industries to regain a position of handsome profits. Speaking of the National Housing Act, a writer in the *Executive Purchaser,* says: "Through a very simple system of financing this Act provides the means whereby private finance and enterprise can resume their normal functioning in every community with complete assurance as to safety, liquidity, and reasonable profit. . . . The government simply stands back of the note of each borrower, insuring the lending institution against loss on the loan." [17] Speaking over the radio, James A. Moffett, chairman of the Federal Housing Administration, said: "The program assigned to us is a straight business proposition. . . . In order to accomplish even a small part of the task, the active help and support of property owners, business men and bankers throughout the United States will be required." Of course, the support of property owners, business men and bankers is required for the successful functioning of government in any of its undertakings, and *vice versa* the enterprises of property owners, business men and bankers require the support of government for their success. In its housing program, which would be more appropriately named a profit program for the building trade, the Federal Housing Administration is resorting to all the conventional business methods of advertising. It has published a "manual for breaking down the customer's resistance and selling him the idea of fixing up the place." [18] There is absolutely no program of general social welfare upon which the business-state could embark that would not first have to be subjected to the limitations of business welfare.

Throughout our discussion, we have shown numerous ways in which government is always found on the side of business against workers and consumers. The canners' Code will serve to illustrate the proposition once more. Canners are permitted to ignore the provision for workers' hours when dealing with "perishables." Perishables have been defined in the Code as products required in a fresh condition for packing and which would deteriorate within 48 hours. Bulletin No. 12 of the Code Authority lists the following as a few among the "perishables": Apples, Pineapples, Potatoes (sweet), Pumpkin, and Quinces.[19] A kindergarten pupil could see through the sham of this listing. Workers may be employed in excess of 60 hours a week when working on these "perishables."

A most serious hazard for consumers has recently been discovered in six Middle Western States where 50,000 acres have been found to contain concentrations of a rare and poisonous metal, *selenium*. This poisonous metal is absorbed from the soil by many plants which are eaten by livestock and humans. Henry G. Knight, of the United States Department of Agriculture, announced recently that the Department is attempting to remove these 50,000 acres from cultivation "as unostentatiously as possible." [20] The announcement was not made generally public, however, but at the session of the Association of Official Agricultural Chemists. "Unostentatiously" would not be the way to go about protecting the lives of consumers, if there were any great seriousness of purpose in the protection.

The leaders of American industry and finance, in close coöperation with the various departments of government, are laying detailed plans for the complete abrogation of the ostensibly democratic forms of government. "To wage a successful war you need an absolute monarch. I have yet to hear of a democracy or a republic waging a successful war," said Irénée du Pont in his recent testimony before the Senate munitions investigating committee. Colonel Charles T. Harris, director of the War Planning Division of the War Department, has assured the committee that the War Department does not contemplate during war the existence of any such labor status as that implied in Section 7a of the National Industrial Recovery Act. "It is my information that Section 7a would be abrogated in the event of war, that is so far as these war plans are concerned," said Senator Bennett Champ Clark. To which Colonel Harris replied: "You can't have two bosses in time of war." Colonel Harris is reported as agreeing with the members of the Senate committee that it "wasn't ethical" to pay a soldier in the trenches a dollar a day and at the same time to pay workers $10 or $15 a day for working in industry. Obviously Section 7a or any independent status of labor would not be consistent with any military mobilization of labor at pay equivalent to that received by the men in the trenches.

Documentary evidence may be lacking to prove that men in Wall Street attempted to persuade Smedley D. Butler to lead a veterans' march on Washington, but a letter from John J. Raskob to R. R. M. Carpenter proves beyond dispute that Raskob wanted Carpenter to "take the lead in trying to induce the du Pont and General Motors groups, followed by other big industries, to definitely organize to protect society from the suffering which it is bound to endure if we allow communistic elements to lead the people to believe that all business men are crooks, not to be trusted, and that no one should be allowed to get rich."

No better illustration could be given of the circuitous but purposeful manner in which government comes to the defense of threatened business interests than is contained in the recent proposal of the President of the United States to *take the profit out of war*. Considerable opinion has been roused against the munitions makers through the exposures of the Senate Investigating Committee. This, therefore, is a most opportune moment, from the standpoint of government and the traffickers in death, to throw a sop to public opinion. The utter impossibility of taking the profit out of war before it has been taken out of peace will be generally missed by the sentimental pacifist. Much light is thrown upon the intentions of the Administration by the statement that "the boys in the trenches got $1 a day and the boys in the munitions factories got $8 to $10 a day." No program is offered, but the plain implication of the President's policy cannot be missed, that in the next war labor is to be militarized by paying labor a soldier's wage. But it may be asserted without fear of later contradiction by history that equalization of income in time of war will not be extended to property owners and big business. Only the wage-workers in the trenches and the wage-workers in the factories are to be placed on an equal footing under the ruthless domination of the greatest combination of exploiters history has ever seen, business and government. There will in all probability be a government guarantee, through the kind of investment underwriting that the "New Deal" has specialized in, of returns on the investments of those who will constitute the great army of $1-a-year men, men who are in fact $100,000 to $1,000,000-a-year men with government jobs to assure their economic domination.

Finally, the character of the state is evident in the principles which govern the courts in their decisions relating to the respective rights of manufacturers and consumers. These principles have been established by legislation and evolved through judicial interpretations. In cases involving false advertising, the controlling principle is the protection of competing manufacturers, not consumers, from the dangers and disadvantages of the falsehoods. The courts claim that this is the intent of Congressional legislation or the lack of legislation. At one period in its work, the Federal Trade Commission conducted extensive inquiries into medical advertising with a view to eliminating some of the obvious falsehoods which involve serious hazards to consumers. *Marmola Prescription Tablets,* an "obesity cure" manufactured by the

Raladam Company, was declared by the Commission to be falsely advertised and injurious.[21] The Circuit Court of Appeals for the Sixth Circuit held: "Nothing is always safe, not even water to drink; nothing is so scientific today that it may not be discarded tomorrow; little is so chimerical today that it may not be scientifically accepted tomorrow. It was long a 'scientific' fact that the world was flat; travel under the sea or in the air was long a scientific impossibility; Darius Green was the archetype of credulous ignorance." [22] The layman will find it a little difficult, no doubt, to follow the connection between an "obesity cure" of thyroid tablets and a flat earth, airplanes and submarines; but of such erudition is much of legal lore concocted. Justice is indeed blind; and, in addition, deaf to the most audible claims of human welfare against the plainest quackery. When the case of *Marmola Prescription Tablets* eventually reached the United States Supreme Court, the justices held that it was "impossible to say whether, as a result of respondent's advertisements, any business was diverted, or was likely to be diverted, from others engaged in like trade." There is no ground of action within the legal structure of American jurisprudence on which to proceed against a consumer's menace of this sort except the ground that the *unique* guilt of one manufacturer operates against the interests of other manufacturers. As a ground of action, "unfairness and injury to the purchaser is insufficient unless at the same time competitors are injured." [23] Which is very much like saying that common thieves must filch from each other before a ground of action exists against them.

Whenever business men find that there are gaps in the law through which they lose legal protection for their interests, they proceed instantly to close up such gaps by whatever pressure is necessary. If the Federal Trade Commission were similarly concerned and alert in the protection of consumers against the menace of such products as *Marmola Prescription Tablets,* it would proceed at once, upon learning from the courts that legal protection is not provided by existing statutes, to seek the enactment of protective legislation.

Manufacturers have grown brazenly audacious in their claims for "the institutional rights of merchandise"—a phrase invented, so far as we know, by one of the journals of the motion picture industry in its call to battle against the boycott of films. Although the libel law was originally intended to protect high officials from defamation and to prevent political disturbances, this law has latterly been invoked as a protection for merchandise. This is understandable in a society which is largely organized around the *rights* of merchandise. "With the development of industry," observes Oscar Cox, "the protection of property and the right to profits in trade against decrease or interference forced themselves under the protective covering of the libel law." [24] Any successful establishment of the "right" of merchandise to exemption from all criticism that might benefit consumers will be the complete enthronement of manufacturers' property.

In the San Francisco *News* of May 18, 1934, there appeared headlines which read, "Packers Win Court Battle Over 'Stale' Canned Salmon." The caption might have been more accurately descriptive if it had said, "Spoiled Canned Salmon Wins Court Battle Over Consumers." A federal judge in San Francisco dismissed a prosecution against a San Francisco packing company with a fine of $25. A thousand cans, representative of a lot of 350,000, had been opened by food and drug experts for examination and from 4 to 35 per cent of the samples were found to be decomposed. The judge, who does not appear from the record to be an expert in the packing of fish or in the effects of decomposed salmon on human health, declared that it was almost impossible to pack fish wholly free from taint and furthermore that it was a " 'shock' to his 'sense of justice' " to prosecute a packer under the conditions applying to this shipment. It is noteworthy that the newspaper report of this legal episode does not carry the name of the offending packer. Inasmuch as there is the gravest doubt regarding the possibility of reconditioning putrid fish with any safety for consumers, and inasmuch as newspapers consistently suppress the names of the guilty packers, it will be well for those who wish to avoid the use of brands that are involved in these cases to request the Food and Drug Administration (United States Department of Agriculture, Washington, D. C.) to send them regularly the *Notices of Judgment* which announce all cases where the Food and Drug Administration proceeds against the manufacturers and processors of harmful products. These *Notices of Judgment* are, under the regulations of the Food and Drug Administration, *free* on application. Recent experiences indicate, however, that requests for *Notices of Judgment* are often ignored by the Food and Drug Administration. Repeated insistence and unwavering persistence in the requests may be necessary, therefore, to obtain this invaluable information from a government agency.

CHAPTER XXI

Defense of the Business-State by Idea-Control

Wᴴᴇʀᴇ ᴛʜᴇ ɪɴsᴛɪᴛᴜᴛɪᴏɴs ᴏꜰ ᴛʜᴏᴜɢʜᴛ-ᴄᴏɴᴛʀᴏʟ are in the secure possession of business, balloting by the electorate is simply going through the motions of democracy in order to anoint the predetermined outcome with the holy oils of tradition. Education, by which the minds of the masses are sympathetically conditioned to the acceptance of the established order, is a far better and cheaper measure of defense for the business system than is the use of the armed forces.

The control of educational agencies by business is not necessarily obtained by outright ownership or bribery. The compulsions of obedience to the interests of the business system are often more refined than is presupposed in any sordid conveyance of money to the "molders of social thought." Money is plentifully employed for these purposes, but many are the labels which may be attached to financial transactions. *Loans* have often been advanced on a strictly friendly basis as, for example, when Doheny received the note of a Secretary of the Interior for $100,000, and in reciprocation was awarded large oil concessions also on a friendly basis. Gifts to charity, when they reach impressive proportions, carry with them the spirit of the giver, and in such cases the "spirit" is generated by the essential motives of the business enterprise. Cathedrals cost money; and the architectural beautification of religion is a well-known concomitant of the concentration of wealth in a society. Universities require endowments for research; and promising young scholars must be subsidized during their training. Newspapers *depend* upon income from advertising; and the big advertisers, as well as most of the little ones, lead the business enterprise.

It is not the "right" but the will to criticize that is usually weakened by receiving the benefactions of great wealth. The social effects, however, are not different from what they would be if the transactions were forthrightly described as bribery. It is enough to say that all of the major institutions of a business society which have to do with the molding of opinion exist by reason of the financial support of those who alone are in a position to provide assured income. Churches, schools, newspapers and radio-broadcasting would find it impossible to survive in a system of private enterprise if the money of the private enterprisers were withdrawn from them.

The church is the most ancient of the institutions which mold the thought of millions. Its importance in a business society is of the first rank. It is peculiarly the custodian of the moral codes by which social relationships are governed. Dominant virtues are defined by the economic necessities of the prevailing system of making and distributing goods. In other words, it is not the least of the functions of religion to confer moral sanctions upon whatever is deemed urgent for the controlling economic forces of society. Historically, this is plain to all; the danger of missing the point today lies in the common belief that contemporary society has reached a degree of refinement in which such definitions of virtue no longer are dominant.

But how else are we to understand the perennial flux of religious ideals or the constant shift in religious emphases? Today, it would be impossible to stir Christendom in support of a crusade to recapture the Holy Sepulchre, but once it was necessary in the interests of a rising European commercialism to keep open the trade routes to the East—routes which the Saracens had closed—and the church sprang forward with great and sacrificial fervor to rescue the Holy Sepulchre from the hands of the infidel Saracens. Once Mother Church herself held a monopoly in God's favors and in his lands as well—a land monopoly which interfered with the conquest of the world market by an emerging capitalism—and a new religious form, Protestantism, which exalted *individualism* in the approach to the deity was required to give moral sanction to the *laissez-faire* of the new system of production and to break, by one and the same stroke, the monopoly in God's favors *and* lands. Once the new imperialism required the spread of Western material culture to stimulate the demand for consumers' goods in a world market and access to the raw materials which the "heathen" were indifferently exploiting or neglecting. God's love of the "heathen" was discovered simultaneously with the "heathen's" importance as a consumer of goods and a holder of riches in raw materials. When chattel slavery supported the ruling agrarian aristocracy, religion argued that dark pigmentation was a proof of the fact that its possessor was not made in the image of God and that the Negro, having no "soul," was a proper creature for exploitation as a chattel slave. When, however, a rising group of industrial barons required an open market in labor as a commodity, the Negro was assigned a "soul" and his emancipation became a holy crusade. When war, involving unprecedented destructiveness and mass murder, was believed to be the only way of protecting an American business stake of $4,000,000,000 in Allied victory, there was not the slightest difficulty in enlisting the full force of the churches in the murderous business. Patriotism, visibly expressed by placing the flag in Christian pulpits, became the highest virtue of the moment. Out of 200,000 clergymen in the United States, only ninety were in any way articulately opposed to the participation of the United States in the World War.[1]

All of the prominent leaders of the Federal Council of Churches of Christ in America were strong in their support of the War, some of them being among the super-jingoists of the time. The attitude of the church and church leaders toward the War is of sufficiently recent date to be a part of the pertinent material evidence by which the relationship of the church to the economic order must be judged. There are some who see in the War record of the church simply a wholesale defection of clergymen from the Gospel of Peace. This is to miss the deeper significance of the socio-economic connections of the church. Support of peace in times of peace and of war in times of war is no notable inconsistency when both positions are seen to represent the church's moral approval of the behavior of the dominant economic controls of society. In all places and ages it has been the function of institutionalized religion to construct moral sanctions for the economic necessities of the surrounding and sustaining community. The sources of social morality lie deep in these necessities and not in any abstract good. The church is both *in* the world and *of* it. Churchmen who today react sentimentally against the horrors of war will react similarly tomorrow against the horrors of peace when the economic order with which the church has become intimately identified is, or may be plausibly argued to be, at stake.

It is something of a fad today for church conferences to pass ringing resolutions which denounce war. This has its value for peace unquestionably, but the more important and guiding considerations are to be found in the church's attitude toward the Roosevelt Administration and not toward the "unknown" war of the future. A more fundamental struggle is *now* going on which involves the basic structure of business society. On which side of that struggle do we find the church? On Labor Sunday, September 2, 1934, the executive committee of the Federal Council of Churches of Christ in America issued a message with the request that it be read in all the churches. "The purposes sought [by the Roosevelt Administration]," said the document, *"are divine in their character,* if, as we steadfastly believe, the heart of Jesus Christ is a revelation of the divine." [2] To the majority of literate people this statement will be something of a theological cryptogram, but to its authors it was obviously intended to be the highest possible ecclesiastical sanction within their power to confer. Concretely, the purposes sought by the Roosevelt Administration are the stabilization of the profit-economy, "recovery" in terms of widening the gross disparity in income (in which aim there was significant progress in the first year of the "New Deal"), and *the prevention at whatever necessary costs of the establishment of an economy of abundance and quality*. The North Carolina "holiness" preacher who handled the rattlesnake was safer, by far, than the church which has embraced the "divine" purposes of the "New Deal" or, to put the matter in more general terms, has embraced the standards and hallowed the enterprises of an economic system whose chief characteristic is highly organized predation. It is estimated that the chances of the "holiness" crank were four out of five for a recovery from the venom which the serpent's fangs discharged into his bloodstream. The historical evidence is *all* against the chances of survival for any institution, ecclesiastical or secular, that has received into its bloodstream the toxicity of a system whose working code makes virtue of fraud and plunder.

The range of opinion in the church is admittedly vast, reaching all the way from the prevailing fundamentalist, race-discriminating ecclesiastical bodies of the southern states which produced not *one* war-time dissenter among their clergymen, to the few individuals like the Reverend William B. Spofford who took the Federal Council of Churches to task for its endorsement of the "divine" purposes of the "New Deal." In his own Labor Day sermon, Mr. Spofford spoke concerning the message of the Federal Council, as follows: "I do not believe that they [the purposes of the Roosevelt Administration] are divine in their character. No more so than the Nazi government of Germany, or the Fascist government of Italy, and for pretty much the same reasons. The purpose of the administration, stated repeatedly and frankly, is to preserve the profit system, which, in my previous talks, I have attempted to show is outworn." [3] The social significance of the church in a business society cannot be gauged, however, by the brave utterances of a few individual clergymen or by reference to the most reactionary sections of the country, geographically and ecclesiastically. It must be evaluated on the basis of the prevailing attitudes of its liberal or advanced leadership in high places, such as the leadership of the Federal Council of Churches. This is not only fair but it is also the sociologically right method.

The munitions inquiry of the Senate Investigating Committee revealed some amazing doctrines among missionaries. The Reverend Paul Young, missionary of the Christian Missionary Alliance in Ecuador, wrote a letter to his brother, John W. Young, president of Federal Laboratories, Inc., makers of tear gas, in which he said: "Six or eight Indians showed a desire to follow the Lord and we prayed with them. Yesterday I saw the Minister of War again and made arrangements to demonstrate today. . . . The War Minister asked me to quote prices on 100 'billies' and 200 grenades. . . . Some of the Indians had made previous beginnings, but had been pulled down by sin. Indian workers need a great deal of prayer." [4] If Mr. Young, missionary, is dismissed as a member of a small fundamentalist sect, Bishop Francis J. McConnell, foremost liberal of the Methodist Episcopal Church and four years president of the Federal Council of Churches, may not be so treated. When Bishop McConnell speaks, his words carry the authority of a long and distinguished leadership in American Protestantism. Bishop McConnell joins the company of those Christians who say "that war is a dirty, filthy business, but that we now and again have to go through it . . . in the hope that war will somehow work in the end to destroy itself." "This position," he hastens to admit, "is far from ideal; but taking the world as it is, I think we can make a good argument for its being at least measurably Christian in this world of ours where nothing is fully Christian." This qualified acceptance of war in the international field makes all the more striking his belief that in the social conflict "it is entirely possible for all the greater changes necessary to a co-operative social order to come without any violence." Both positions, however, are markedly weighted in favor of the ruling business class which asks only that Christians fight its wars "now and again," calling them "dirty, filthy," or what they will. It also asks nothing more than that the great body of Christians disavow the overt or covert coercions of those who attack the business system, and support, by the illusion of democratic social change through the use of the ballot, all the covert violence of the defenders of the business system. Bishop McConnell obligingly accommodates on both points. The confusion of ecclesiastical thought on the nature of capitalist society is nowhere better illustrated than in Bishop McConnell's words regarding the question of a business dictatorship. On one page we read: "There is, however, much more danger in n hour like the present of the dictatorship of moneyed groups than of socialist groups." Later on we encounter this assertion: "One difficulty has been that *we have had* [italics ours] industrial dictatorship in the United States whose first concern . . . has been with dividends and investors." *Have* we had a "dictatorship" as Bishop McConnell asserts in one instance, or *have* we had only the "danger" of a dictatorship of moneyed groups as he states in the other instance? It cannot be both ways. Again, with apparent rejection of the notion that there is or has been a dictatorship of moneyed groups, the Bishop affirms that "the popular will can do what it will by law." But this assertion is laid open to grave question by his reference to a field in which he has had intimate dealings with bankers. Bishop McConnell is and has been for many years the head of the Board of Foreign Missions of the Methodist Episcopal Church. In this field his testimony has a cogency that is devastating when he says that "the banks have more to say about the policy of the missionary society than all the contributors of missionary funds, and missionaries and missionary officials put together." [5] This is a startling statement and, coming from so eminent an authority, it ought to make the front page headlines in China, even if it does not broaden the scope of the Senate inquiry into banking practices. How, we must ask, is society going to rid itself of the dictatorship of the bankers in areas where the bankers have a really vital stake—the billions of

dollars that are tied up in the control and ownership of industry—
if missionary officials are bound and gagged (however subtly)
by a dictatorship where only a few paltry millions are involved.
It does not in the least surprise us, but it ought certainly to interest the simple-hearted giver of a missionary dollar for the
purpose of evangelizing the "heathen" to know that in the formation of the policy of the missionary society "the banks have
more to say than all the contributors of missionary funds, and
missionaries and missionary officials put together." Perhaps the
fundamentalist missionary brother of the president of Federal
Laboratories, Inc., is not so unusual a phenomenon after all.

Summing up the rôle of the churches in the matter of social
change, Bishop McConnell states frankly that "the verdict of
historical research would . . . have to be that the Church, or the
churches, have never yet reached the understanding of themselves or of Christianity which would make it safe to entrust
powers of physical coercion to them." The State does not ask
the church to exercise the powers of physical coercion; it asks
only that the church exercise the necessary control over the
minds of men so that the State's own use of the powers of physical coercion will find no obstacle in the moral judgments of
ecclesiasticism. That is the rôle which the State confidently ex-
pects the church to fulfill. Bishop McConnell well says, "the
corporate forces of the church are so often on the side of social
repression."

The outstanding leaders of the American business dictatorship
are almost all prominent members of the religious communions.
The sympathetic biographer of J. P. Morgan may have been off
his guard when he stated that "he [Morgan] dominates the
American Episcopal Church, having financed the limited edition
of the third revision of the American Book of Common Prayer
and served long as a vestryman of his father's old church, St.
George's." [6] Andrew W. Mellon not only contributed munifi-
cently to Pittsburgh's new Presbyterian "cathedral," but under-
wrote, financially, the campaign for an old-age clergymen's fund

in that denomination—a campaign which was headed by Will Hays, now of moviedom. In October, 1934, the Methodists of the nation held a sesquicentennial convention in Baltimore at which Daniel C. Roper, Secretary of Commerce and a prominent Methodist layman, presided! [7] The late William S. Vare, Republican boss of Philadelphia whom the United States Senate several times declined to seat, never found the doors of the Methodist Church closed to him. The Vare Memorial Methodist Church of Philadelphia perpetuates, by reason of his financial contributions, the family name. Rockefeller money made possible the noble edifice on Riverside Drive, New York City, where the Reverend Harry Emerson Fosdick comforts the Rockefeller dynasty with this declaration: "Personally, I dread the thought of collectivism which Russia represents as I would dread the devil." [8] So does John D. Rockefeller, Jr., dread it!

Bishop Francis J. McConnell was chosen "spiritual adviser" of the newly formed National Laymen's Back to the Church Movement. New York members of the Advisory Council of the Movement included John F. Curry, late leader of Tammany Hall, John H. McCooey, late Brooklyn henchman of the Curry machine, patent-medicine Senator Royal S. Copeland, prominent Methodist layman, Will H. Hays, and Charles D. Hilles, Republican boss of New York. [9]

The churches are gradually but surely being enlisted in the struggle on the side of business to combat the social forces that are demanding a new world. The Reverend Clarence W. Kemper informed 3000 Baptist delegates to the Northern Baptist Convention last year that "the teaching of two Jews, Jesus and Karl Marx, is struggling for supremacy today, dramatically in the great populous countries of the Orient and more seriously than we like to confess in the Western world." [10] The Reverend Henry Sloane Coffin, president of Union Theological Seminary, threw down the gage of battle to the radical neophytes of the institution at the close of the 1934 session of that most radical of theological seminaries. "They can't make this seminary the guinea pig for some future Soviet," Dr. Coffin announced. The students who don't like "Union's ideals" can go back where they came from or "choose a seminary closer to their hearts' desire," said this wealthy mentor of the country's future theologians.[11] It is increasingly difficult for divines to omit reference to the present Soviets of Russia or to the dangers to business in future Soviets in this country. "I hope I always shall be horrified at the conditions in Russia," says the Reverend J. V. Moldenhawer, of the First Presbyterian Church, New York City, and he probably will be.[12] Speaking in the First Baptist Church of New York City, the Reverend Earle G. Griffith, of Erie, Pennsylvania, declared that socialists and communists "are spending more than $2,000,000 a month in this country alone to fasten this hideous philosophy on the American people." Of the Soviet regime, Dr. Griffith said: "The present Russian government are destroyers of chastity, exploiters of children, and destroyers of personality through a history of anarchy and assassination." Dr. Griffith apparently feels strongly enough about the matter to do a little fighting in the flesh when the time comes. "If I had ever voted for a candidate from the Socialist party," he said, "I would go at once and buy up all the Ivory soap in New York City, and also purchase two large wire brushes. Then I would go down to Atlantic City, and spend the rest of my life trying to scrub out my ingrained pollution."[13] Procter & Gamble should not alter their production plans on the basis of this statement, for Dr. Griffith is not likely ever to cast a vote for a socialist candidate. The Reverend James J. Henry told a congregation of the Park Avenue Methodist Episcopal Church, New York City, that radicals "are simply suffering from industrial insanity and that they are seeking to destroy our industrial system."[14] The insanities of industrialism, entailing the slow starvation or the slow poisoning of millions, seem to be hidden from these clergymen whose wealthy parishioners and benefactors are made more comfortable in their plundering by such fervent denunciations of those who seek to build a new economic order of sanity.

The moral codes of the church are pervaded with emphases that are wholly congenial to the defense of business practices and interests. Today, the customary plea against regimentation and in favor of freedom is a rationalization of the desire of business to escape any and all restraints upon its predatory activities. Frightening phrases are a specialty of the pulpit, phrases which, in the interests of an economy of scarcity, serve to frighten the impressionable away from collectivism. "Enslaved abundance" is the characterization which one of the outstanding religious liberals, Professor Hornell Hart, formerly of Bryn Mawr, now of Hartford Theological Seminary, has applied to a system which achieves the end of poverty through collectivism. "If enslaved abundance were possible," writes Professor Hart, "most Americans would prefer freedom, even at the cost of want." [15] This is a polite way of saying that sheer starvation is to be glorified in the name of a wholly factitious freedom. It is not greatly different from Herr Goebbels' determination to "glorify hunger" in the Third Reich by appealing to an equally factitious nationalism. If it is true that most Americans prefer the spurious freedom of a business dictatorship in which their rights are limited to starvation and to the choice of which one of their "rights" they will go to jail in defending, it is largely because of the successful educational work of men like Professor Hart. When Herbert Hoover appeals for "liberty," all but the incurably naïve understand that it is the liberty of private economic enterprise for which he asks. Religious leaders, like Professor Hart, making the same plea are more generally, though improperly, above question. Religious appeals for freedom, at the price of want if necessary, are not less tainted with a covert defense of the established order because they employ an archaic and tricky language of idealism that has the odor of the crypt of an old cathedral.

The leadership of the present-day church, at least in Protestant communions, is definitely committed to a philosophy of liberalism. In the stage of economic development through which we are passing, the liberal approach to social questions is eminently suited to the purposes of business reaction. Mr. Roosevelt consistently employs the language of liberalism, *the appearance of not taking sides,* while invariably following a course which has a single eye for the defense of property and profits. It is the distinct service of liberalism that it takes out of its disciples the courage to make "unscientific" judgments or to speak out plainly against the inequities and iniquities of the business system. Liberals profess a revolting abhorrence of all *propaganda,* except of course their own subtle and serviceable propaganda to the effect that social forces are not arrayed in mortal combat in which the very life of the masses is the point at stake. The liberal always speaks of his own propaganda, which is as false as it is serviceable, as "education." Foremost among the religious liberals of today is F. E. Johnson, of the Federal Council of Churches. In reviewing a book by Benson Y. Landis on "Must the Nation Plan?" Mr. Johnson says that "readers who want to be educated about the new trends and policies that have appeared in our economic and industrial life without being subjected to propaganda could scarcely turn to a better source." [16] A liberal is, of course, when he is honest, simply an unconscious partisan. When the fact of the brutal struggle that pervades modern class-divided society finally forces recognition from him, he must then take sides, just as the Tories and the revolutionaries before him have done, but his belated partisanship is then almost certain to be enlisted on the side which he has always served unconsciously.

Much of the moral energy of the modern liberal church goes to the service of transcendental ideals which are neither here nor there in the world of reality. These transcendental ideals are termed "spiritual values"—which is a way of taking them out of the workaday world of social struggle. Thus Professor Hornell Hart says that "Jesus himself repeatedly discouraged demands for justice." Jesus required only love, and, according to Professor Hart, "even if that program [of Love] could not succeed in abolishing war, in rectifying our present grossly inequitable distribution of income and power, or in reorganizing the social order in other ways, it would still be the essential and exclusively Christian procedure, for to adopt it is to enter into the Kingdom which Christ came to establish." [17] At the Presbyterian General Assembly last year, when one of the members attempted to get a hearing in behalf of the Scottsboro boys, Mary Amelia Steer, Secretary of the Board of Christian Education, replied that "we want the hearts of these women so filled with the love of Jesus that we have no time for such things." [18] *This* is the perfect expression and summing up of the traditional and present-day function of the church on *all* socially vital and crucial matters. Such otherworldly freedom from partisanship, any alert religious leader could see, is the most effective form of partisanship and work for the *status quo* that can possibly be devised.

The tie-up of the churches with the business system is not always so indirect as merely conditioning the minds of Christians to an acceptance of all the injustices and inequities of the established order and its rulers. The church is an institution with vast property holdings and investments which are part and parcel of the property system of capitalism. The Archbishop of Chicago, Cardinal Mundelein, appeared in the recent trial of the Insull defendants and gave "character" testimony on behalf of Harold L. Stuart. "On my petition and recommendation," said the Archbishop, in reply to a question of one of the defense attorneys, "Mr. Stuart received one of the highest orders the Catholic Church can confer. . . . Without Mr. Stuart's services we could not have built the International College of the Propaganda Fide in Rome." [19] What pertinence this has to the scheme which swindled investors out of a hundred million dollars is probably clear in the Church's definition of "character," but from the standpoint of any high-grade ethical code divorced from the service of business ends it is entirely irrelevant. Ancient custom has, of course, made it the part of wisdom to divide all the larger takings with the moral censors of society. When Mr. Stuart makes a gift to the College of the Propaganda Fide in Rome, when Mr. Morgan finances the third revision of the American Book of Common Prayer, and when Mr. Mellon brightens the old age of retired Presbyterian clergymen, all these great magnates of God are but storing up treasure where moth and rust do not corrupt!

The *Christian Herald* advertising in *Food Field Reporter* declares that it "gives every one of its food advertisers double value for every advertising dollar they spend, for this influential magazine reaches two mighty food markets for the cost of one." The first market is described as that of "well-to-do housewives, who daily buy foods for their families." The second market consists in the fact that "these same housewives are regular church goers, and periodically buy food in tremendous quantities for church suppers, festivals and luncheons." [20] The *Christian Herald* announces that one of its surveys shows that its readers annually bake 500,000 cakes for their church affairs. The attendance at "these affairs exceeds 400,000,000 annually." If we were statistically minded we would emphasize the awful scarcity of cake at these affairs, for on the basis of the *Christian Herald's* figures the average is only 1/800 of a cake per person. Pretty thin slicing, and very poor advertising for the church paper to put in a food trade journal. However, that is beside our point, for what interests us is the frank admission of the *Christian Herald* that its constituency is among the "well-to-do," and that the churches (or their women) are absorbed in the task of preparing 400,000,000 meals (with or without cake) annually. Naturally, with the burden of such onerous spiritual tasks and such regular and adequate eating, the women have no time to think of the Scottsboro boys.

We are glad to learn that there is to be an improvement in the ethical standards of the purveyors of Holy Writ, thanks to the NRA publishers' code. The code explicitly "cracks down" on the chiselers among the publishers of the Bible. "No member shall publish advertising which is misleading or inaccurate" in its efforts to circulate the Word of God. "No member shall use advertising or other representation which refers inaccurately to any competitor. No member shall wilfully induce breach of existing contracts by false or deceptive means." Furthermore, discriminatory price-cutting is banned. The "children of light" had apparently been learning much from the ways of Mammon. Now God's children have got NRA Blue Eagle wings.

After the churches come the schools in the historical development of agencies for the molding of opinion. The secularization of the schools, which was accomplished under the formula of the separation of church and state, did not establish the independence of the schools. On the contrary it ushered them into a new bondage of the mind, one that better served the purposes of the new nationalist capitalist state.

It is often asserted that the present economic system, so obviously piratical in nature, is tolerated only because the "people" live intellectually on the plane of a seven-year-old's mentality. The assertion overlooks the all-important fact that the educational agencies of society must perforce yield to the will of the controlling interests and that the human educational output corresponds pretty closely to the needs of those controlling interests. If there is a prevailing level of mentality that suggests the intellectual processes and equipment of a seven-year-old, it is only because it is to the interest of the ruling business class that social mentality generally be kept at such a level.

Even higher education must not be *too* high, or it interferes with the stability of socially organized predation. It is common practice for educators who are under the dominance of the ruling social motives to defend a deliberate deterioration of the intellectual quality of students by pleading, in the educators' defense, the youthful immaturity of students. Nicholas Murray Butler, in his latest annual report as president of Columbia University, holds that there is no excuse in the phrase "academic freedom" for "permitting immature students to undertake comparative studies 'of despotism, of democracy, of republicanism, of Communism, of Nazism or of Fascism.' " [21]

While it is considered unsafe for "immature" minds to pursue free inquiry into comparative studies of politics, there are no dangers involved for colleges or organized predation in developing high skills in ping-pong. The president of Oklahoma City University recently announced that the university "would soon give academic credit for ping-pong, archery, skating, fraternity and sorority membership." [22] It is, of course, highly proper that students should receive academic credit for their major activities while in residence at the Oklahoma seat of learning.

Into an educational scheme which includes ping-pong and football, there fit naturally, when occasion requires it, hilarious student festivals organized around bonfires of dangerous books, such as those which make comparative political analyses. Goose-stepping with firearms under the direction of the nationalist state is likewise not offensive to the immaturity of students, particularly if care is taken to curb any intellectual disposition which students might acquire in the direction of turning their knowledge upon the plunderers of business society. Nicholas Murray Butler will handle the intellectual problems of immaturity, and the full machinery of the nationalist state will see to it that goose-stepping is not omitted from the curriculum of the colleges and universities.

It would be an unfortunate circumstance if the intellectual average of students rose much above the requirements of operating cash registers, and, as the studies at Yale University have shown, the frontal area of the brain of apes may be lost without any serious impairment of the ability to assess cash values. If the intellectual average does rise to a plane where fundamental social, political and economic questions can be handled by students, it must rise under the impulse of extra-curricular and extra-mural forces.

Inadvertently and altogether without conscious intent, the heads of great universities often impart a basic wisdom in regard to the nature of society and the rôle which educational institutions play within it. The president of Yale, Dr. James Rowland Angell, has recently given utterance to a proposition which is as important for inquiring and immature minds as anything that could be learned by four years' academic residence at New Haven, Connecticut. The trend toward the equalization of wealth, if there is one, is viewed as having sinister consequences for the great universities. In his latest report to the trustees of Yale, Dr. Angell points out that "if the present tendency to excessive taxation of personal income persists, or increases, as it may, and if this be coupled with further assault by inheritance taxes upon testamentary estates, the two largest sources of income for these institutions will almost inevitably dry up or, in any case, be gravely impaired." The feeding hand is ungraciously bitten, and it is altogether appropriate that educators rally to the defense of untaxed wealth. "Current social and political trends, accentuated, if not directly provoked, by the economic depression," says Dr. Angell, "contain a menace for the great endowed institutions which should not be overlooked." Universities, contrary to uninformed popular opinion, do not owe their existence to any absorbing intellectual curiosity in the body politic, but, according to Dr. Angell, they "have owed their power to assemble great bodies of scholars, to create great libraries and laboratories and museums, very largely to the gifts of generous benefactors, often in the form of legacies." [23]

But Dr. Angell has given only half of the lesson. After the universities have received the generous gifts of business men, they must in the nature of things become investors of finance in the industrial enterprises of the country. The investments of private institutions of higher learning amount to $1,225,558,000, divided as follows: 24 per cent in public utilities, 18 per cent in railroads, 17 per cent in industrials, 27 per cent in real estate and 7 per cent in government bonds. "America's capital investment in higher education," according to William E. Berchtold, "is greater than its capital investment in the telephone and telegraph industry, and three-quarters as large as its investments in the textile industry, or the iron and steel industry." [24] The business of assembling great bodies of scholars is, therefore, as closely bound up with the perpetuation of the existing economy as is any other business of large proportions. The college and university presidents and the heads of their laboratories whom Alfred P. Sloan, Jr., invited to his dinner at the Century of Progress grounds in Chicago were men whose stake in the system ranked as high as their industrial colleagues'. Revenues from the universities' investments are entirely dependent upon the maintenance, at any cost, of the present economy. An endowment is of no use to a university if that institution cannot invest it profitably. Friendly relations with financiers and industrialists has, therefore, an economic basis which does not exist for any such abstract principle as that of academic freedom.

The picture is still incomplete. We have yet to consider that education has become one of the most important and effective arms of the business enterprise through the establishment of research fellowships and scholarships. Through this system of grants from industry, the ablest young scholars are placed in the indebtedness of business, and the running expenditures of laboratory research are met. The way in which a leading university, a large corporation, and a prominent magazine and its editor become intimately associated is shown in the case of W. H. Eddy, food editor of *Good Housekeeping,* who was recently awarded a research fellowship by Standard Brands, Inc., for "working on the chemistry of the vitamin B complex" [25] at Columbia University. The University of California recently received a grant of $5,000 for a study of the effects of chewing gum on dental health. Among the thousands of such grants and fellowships which business makes available to colleges and universities, we cite the following with the names of the business donors and the educational recipients: [26]

Standard Brands, Inc.:
    Cornell University—Department of Hotel Administration.
    Oregon State Agricultural College—Fleischmann Fellowship.
    Johns Hopkins University—Fleischmann Fellowship.
    University of Minnesota—Fleischmann Fellowship.

Du Pont de Nemours and Company:
University of Chicago.
University of Michigan.
Princeton University.
Stanford University.
Virginia Polytechnic Institute—*37 fellowships*.
Coca Cola Company:
Johns Hopkins University.
R. J. Reynolds Tobacco Company:
Johns Hopkins University.
National Milling Company:
Michigan State College of Agriculture and Applied Science.
Dairy and Ice Cream Machinery and Supplies Association, Inc.:
Iowa State College of Agriculture.
University of Minnesota.
University of Wisconsin.
American Cyanamid Company:
University of Wisconsin, Agricultural Experiment Station.
Corn Industries:
University of Chicago—two fellowships.
State University of Iowa.
University of Rochester.
University of Wisconsin—two fellowships.

Merlin H. Aylesworth, director of public relations of the National Electric Light Association, has given an excellent summary of the business man's idea of how to utilize college professors, especially those poverty-ridden academicians who are poorer than Job's turkey and who do not mind doing a little grubbing for the private utilities in order that the children may have shoes. Addressing the managers of the utilities, Mr. Aylesworth said:

"I would advise any manager who lives in a community where there is a college to get the professor of economics interested in your problems. Have him lecture on your subject to his classes. Once in a while it would pay you to take such men getting

$500 or $600 a year or a thousand, perhaps, and give them a retainer of $100 to $200 a year for the privilege of letting you study and consult with them, *for how in heaven's name can we do anything in the schools of the country with the young people growing up if we have not first sold the idea of education to the college professors?*" [27] [Italics ours.] The profound contempt of business for a college professor's academic soul is measured with precision by the suggestion of $100 as an annual retainer, financially suitable to sell him the idea of "education."

The "Old Counsellor" worked for $50 a week at a job that would have commanded ten to a hundred times as much if performed by a real business man. It may be necessary to refresh our minds by recalling that the "Old Counsellor" broadcast financial and investment advice in the days of the glory that was the Insull utilities' empire. The "Old Counsellor" was hired to give the impression of being a disinterested and impartial adviser in matters pertaining to investments. Thousands heeded the words of the unidentified expert that came in soft and well-modulated tones over the air. The Senate Banking and Currency Committee, looking into the Insull affair, disclosed that the "Old Counsellor" was Professor Nelson, of the English Department of the University of Chicago, and that he read his radio advice from a manuscript prepared in the offices of the investment firm of Halsey, Stuart & Company.[28]

In a system where prices are governed by the load-carrying possibilities of the traffic, the services of college professors evidently rate a low potential.

Now and then, of course, a really munificent gift—even from the standpoint of business standards—goes to an institution. In the late years of prosperity, the American Telephone and Telegraph Company gave $3,000,000 to the California Institute of Technology. This far-famed educational institution has also been the recipient of large benefactions from Westinghouse and General Electric in the form of equipment. In April, 1928, Dr. Robert A. Millikan, head of the California Institute of Technology, wrote an article in the *Atlantic Monthly* in which he spoke with high praise of the nationalization of British radio. "The program that is on the air in England is incomparably superior to anything to be heard here," wrote Dr. Millikan, "for the English government has taken over completely the control of the radio." There came a grant of $3,000,000 from the American Telephone and Telegraph Company. After that Dr. Millikan's attitude toward nationalized radio underwent important modifications. Having been at the beginning one of the most enthusiastic sponsors of the proposed non-profit Pacific-Western Broadcasting Federation, Dr. Millikan became convinced that the privately and commercially owned broadcasting corporations supplied all that was necessary for "the disinterestedness and integrity of education" in broadcasting.[29]

Elsewhere we have discussed the alliance between Borden's and the Dairymen's League of New York. This alliance, which has been so useful to the distributor, Borden, in plundering farmers and consumers, was brought about with the aid of Professor Leland Spencer, of New York State College of Agriculture at Cornell. "Dr. Spencer not only fostered this combination personally," says the *Rural New-Yorker,* "but he helped a small group of his associates in the State College to devote the influence, the prestige and the resources of that great public institution to this perfidious and sinister monopoly."[30] In Nazi Germany, they have a word for such effective combinations; it is "coördination." Many an American educator has already shown himself to be a willing agent in achieving the "coördination" of business, government, and education.

Dean Roswell C. McCrea, of the Columbia University School of Business, reported to the president of the University last fall that "our modern urban industrialism carries with it an unconscious regimentation of thought and feeling, of work routine and consumption habits more dominating in control and regrettably more destructive of genuine personal freedom than all of the governmental or conscious personal regimentation we are likely to face in our generation." [31] The Professor is of the opinion, however, that "the masses revel in these unconscious compulsions and resent emancipating propaganda." There is no doubt that Columbia University in the person of its president resents "emancipating propaganda." But Dean McCrea comes much closer to significant truth about our times when he says that we are in an "era in which the study of business is more closely welded to the study of economics than ever before." This being true, we are not likely to find much "emancipating propaganda" emanating from the schools of business administration, for "the collegiate school of business occupies the most strategic post on the economic front." [32] It was perhaps giving away a secret when *Food Field Reporter,* trade journal of the food industries, disclosed the fact that leading universities, including Columbia, sometimes have their business courses and instructional material prepared for them by interested industries. In a recent announcement of the appointment of E. L. Rhoades as traveling editor of *Food Field Reporter,* it was stated that he had "organized educational courses and developed instructional materials *for the packing industry* for use in courses given in co-operation with Columbia University, University of Cincinnati and Maryland State College." [33] [Italics ours.]

One favor calls for another, and the universities generously reciprocate, not only with many substantial forms of service to the business enterprise, but also with academic decorations for the financial and industrial potentates. Samuel Insull[34] holds the following honorary degrees: Sc.D. from Union College; LL.D. from Northwestern University; LL.D. from Notre Dame; and LL.D. from Queens University. Martin Insull[35] was elected a trustee of Cornell University in October, 1931, and was not asked to resign his trusteeship even after the stockholders of Midwest Utilities had forced his resignation as president, or even after he had escaped into Canada under the cloud of an indictment for theft.

New York University made J. P. Morgan[36] a Doctor of Commerce and delivered the diploma to him in his own study. John T.

Flynn observes that ordinary millionaires are required to come and get their diplomas, but Morgan is not ordinary in anything except, as his biographer in *Fortune* remarks, his "mind." Walter Gifford is a Doctor of Williams and of Colgate. W. W. Atterbury is a Doctor of the University of Pennsylvania, Yale, Villanova and Temple. Julius Barnes, high potentate of the United States Chamber of Commerce, has fulfilled the requirements for honorary doctorates from Harvard, Dartmouth, Pittsburgh and Syracuse.

This brief sketch of the relationship between the business world and educational institutions goes far to explain the abrogation of ordinary civil liberties on the campuses of educational institutions.

In October, 1934, a group of two hundred fascist students from Italy made a propaganda pilgrimage to the universities of the United States. The fascist press of Italy leaves no doubt about the nature of their mission. When the loyal sons of Mussolini arrived at City College in New York, they were greeted with a demonstration of anti-fascist students. Incidentally, it has been discovered that the freshmen at City College rank higher in intelligence than the lower classmen of any other eastern university. The president of City College, Dr. Frederick B. Robinson, is on the other hand a contributor to Bernarr MacFadden's notorious *True Story* magazine, second to none as a vehicle of vicarious sex thrills.[37] Twenty-one City College students who participated in the anti-fascist demonstration were expelled. The expulsion could easily be justified on the ground that the demonstrating students already knew more than they could learn from Dr. Robinson and his faculty, and if perchance they still needed any of the sober wisdom of the president they could have it for 15 cents in a copy of *True Story*. Needless to say, this was not the ground of the faculty's decision to terminate abruptly the matriculation of the students. Professor Harry A. Overstreet, of the philosophy department and lecturer at the New School for Social Research, gave a statement to the *Campus* (student publication) in which he deplored the fact that the Italian visitors could not have been courteously received and courteously informed "of our own fundamental belief in free speech and the liberties of men." [38] Perhaps the Italian students already knew enough of the record of "free speech" at City College not to take too seriously any exorbitant claims of that character.

California and Louisiana have been running neck and neck in the race for the honor of being the keystone state in American reaction. In both states there has been striking evidence of the way in which educational institutions mirror the current political attitudes of the class in power. Robert Gordon Sproul, president of the University of California, addressed 3,300 freshmen in August at the opening of the 1934 session with emphatic warnings against student radicalism. "I have grown infinitely weary with the deprecation of America and American institutions by pseudo-intellectuals hanging on the fringe of a student body or faculty," [39] said Dr. Sproul. The remarks of the president were vigorously applauded by the students. But the matter did not end, as is often the case with much applauded speeches, with hearty clapping of hands. Student vigilantes in both units of California's University, at Berkeley and at Los Angeles, went into action. Sturdy athletes, ping-pong players and half-backs, vowed to rid the campuses of the "red menace." Committees were appointed to patrol the university grounds and to lay hands on all and sundry who were suspected of entertaining doubts regarding the sacred character of American institutions in general and California institutions in particular. Four students[40] were suspended in the red-baiting hysteria which President Sproul had so successfully fostered on the opening day of school. The provost of the Los Angeles unit issued a nation-wide appeal to fraternities to become active "helpers of the United States in its day of difficulty." An editorial in the university paper, the *Californian,* provided the following new California version of Voltaire: "The university will defend to the death the rights of its students and faculty . . . freely to discuss and study all subjects, yet it most firmly opposes any student action, or the encouragement of any student action, to overthrow our government. And there are methods of prevention.

... Just as there are vigilantes in the East Bay community there will be vigilantes in the university community, designed to blot out student Communists. . . . That action and force will be generated by student vigilantes and will meet with the approval of the university community." [41]

In Louisiana, Huey P. Long has annexed the state university as an appendage to his show. President James M. Smith being installed in the university as his personal representative, Senator Long's conduct and career may not be criticized by students. The editor of the *Reveille,* college publication, printed a student letter criticizing Mr. Long's burlesque, and Dr. Smith immediately suspended the publication with the warning that "these are abnormal times" and Senator Long is "virtually dictator of the university." The dismissal from the university of the editor led to student protests which resulted in the dismissal of twenty-six other students. Long himself is reputed to have thundered in the Louisiana State Senate: "I'll fire any student that dares to say a word against me. I'll fire a thousand. We've got ten thousand to take their places. That's my university. I built it, and I'm not going to stand for any students criticizing Huey Long." [42]

In the summer of 1934, the New York State legislature passed the Ives Bill which makes it compulsory for all teachers in public and private tax-exempt educational institutions throughout the state to take an oath, on penalty of losing his position, pledging allegiance to the Constitutions of New York and the United States. The protests of teachers have been feeble indeed. A Columbia University professor made the typical comment that the taking of the oath "is a direct order, so there is no question about signing it." [43] Few of the professions surpass the academic in the supineness of their members. The trends are obvious. Still blinder loyalties will be sworn to by what some one has called the "order of scared rabbits" if and when the business-state requires it. Ping-pong minds have left no powers of healthy indignation and resentment against the contumelious incursions of swaggering business men upon the domain of the intellectual life.

Students graduating from high schools in the City of New York are required to make the following pledge adopted by the Committee of Superintendents: "I hereby declare my absolute and unconditional loyalty to the Government of the United States of America and to the State of New York and promise to support with all my power the government at all times in its measures for carrying out the law." No alterations whatever will be required in this pledge to adapt it to the uses of an outright fascist regime, unless it be the insertion of the name of *der Fuehrer*.

Harvard University is the largest business institution among the universities, having, in addition to its $40,000,000 plant, investments of $128,520,000. Its record is decidedly spotty. The blot of A. Lawrence Lowell, one of the trio of Back Bay plutocrats who pronounced the final verdict of death upon Sacco and Vanzetti, will never out. Although his successor, James B. Conant, rejected the gift of Hanfstaengl for a traveling scholarship in Germany, the liberal Dean of the Harvard Law School, Roscoe Pound, proceeded forthwith to accept an honorary degree from the University of Berlin.[44]

Nicholas Murray Butler has become the self-appointed custodian of liberalism in this country. In an address at the Parrish Art Museum at Southampton, Long Island, he declared that all talk of the maldistribution of wealth in the United States is the "sheer invention" of radicals.[45] Dr. Butler's liberalism is further clarified by the maintenance at Columbia University of an active agency of Italian fascist propaganda, the *Casa Italiana*. The *Casa Italiana* conducts propaganda through a paper and regular speeches. The consul-general of the Italian government in New York contributed $3,000 toward the maintenance of the institution last year.[46]

Professor W. P. Montague, of Columbia University, created something of a sensation at the International Philosophical Congress in Prague last year when he advocated the creation of fascist communes within the capitalist democracy.[47] The unemployed are to be enrolled in Professor Montague's fascist communes for periods of one to three years. Professor Montague had probably not been informed of Dr. Butler's view that immature student minds should not be exposed to a study of comparative political systems, or else his idea was intended only for the international philosophers, and not for repetition or discussion on Columbia's campus.

Education other than the adaptation of immature minds to the intellectual levels required by the moronic culture of business is an idea which is inconsistent with a capitalist society. Mass moronism is not a characteristic of man in his natural state. It is a product deliberately fostered in keeping with the requirements of low-grade intellectual regimentation. To the end of producing this uncritical regimentation, the business men of America have built what is by far the largest educational plant to be found in the western world. A better instrument for producing a fascist mentality never existed in either Italy or Germany prior to the triumph of black reaction than exists today in the schools, colleges and universities of the United States. In the very nature of things, they must one and all serve the cause of social retrogression so well exemplified in the fight which Duke University[48] has undertaken to combat lower electric power rates for the simple business reason that it holds enormous investments in power companies.

The power of the press is second to no other educational force in modern society. Its evolution from the early days of the industrial revolution marks the course of a century's economic development. Coincidental with America's coming of age in the early nineties, newspapers ceased to be primarily media for the dissemination of news and became primarily organs of salesmen. Until 1890, subscriptions and sales accounted for more than half the total revenues of all newspapers. After that date, the proportion of income from advertising rose steadily beyond the half-way mark. Today, about 75 per cent of all newspaper income is derived from advertising and only about 25 per cent from sales and subscriptions.[49] Professor Willard Grosvenor Bleyer, Director of the School of Journalism at the University of Wisconsin, estimates that from two-thirds to five-sixths of the revenues of newspapers come from advertising.[50]

"Because the business of newspaper publishing has grown tremendously in the last half century, newspaper publishers, rather than newspaper editors, are the dominant element in American journalism today," says Professor Bleyer. The days of Greeley, Dana, Watterson, Reid, Nelson, and Murat Halstead have gone forever, but newspapers still attempt to maintain the show of quasi-public institutions. "Every business operated for a profit finds it difficult to render disinterested service to the public," [51] observes Professor Bleyer. The service of salesmanship is, as we have shown in the early chapters of this volume, inconsistent with any disinterested service to the public, and it is into the service of salesmanship that the newspapers have been drawn by the irresistible economic forces of the times. This is not a "trick of fate" as Arthur E. Morgan, president of Antioch College, would have the public believe in the case of films and the radio, but is in strict keeping with the laws of growth and survival in a system of private business enterprise.

Democracy and a profit-economy—any profit-economy—are mutually contradictory conceptions; and the "freedom of the press" and private ownership of newspapers are similarly contradictory. Newspapers are the best examples of non-violent coercion—pacifists please note!—in an anti-democratic business dictatorship. On this point the record is clear and should be beyond debate.

The absolute "coördination" of the press which characterizes the regimes of Italy and Germany has not been enforced in the United States, but the difference is chiefly one of degree. On the question of maintaining the profit-system there is no compulsion because none is necessary so far as the newspapers are concerned, inasmuch as the owners of newspapers are committed to that proposition without compulsion. Newspaper publishing is as much a business as is pawnbroking, and as such is an integral part of the system.

Now that it can be told, Louis Wiley, business manager of the New York *Times,* states that in the first great drive of the NRA the newspapers "knew what was expected of them and they carried out their duty in a democracy." Something smacking of "coördination" was believed to be necessary, for "those were days when common action of a united people was essential," writes Mr. Wiley. But essential for whom and for what? The issues were so delicately balanced, and the whole economic system was so stricken that "an ill-timed jest by one of our national humorists would have caused the whole recovery structure to break down in the building." [52] A tottering or jeopardized social structure requires humorless days as well as sugarless ones. Can it be that our national humorists were instructed to look away from Washington when they laughed, or to make Angora and Peiping the butt of their jests? Laughing at Hitler in the columns of the *Frankfurter Zeitung* or the *Deutsche Beobachter* in 1934 would be as venial as for a medieval saint to laugh at God, we know. But are we to believe on the authority of the business manager of the New York *Times* that laughing at Roosevelt in the summer of 1933 would have been considered equally reprehensible? If so, the revolution was nearer than we thought, or else the rulers of America were in the grip of a veritable psychosis. A dictatorship is far advanced and overt, when the suppression of humor becomes an instrument of national policy.

The press has been one of the most effective strike-breaking agencies in the current labor disputes of the country. Edgar Kobak, vice-president of the National Broadcasting Company and chairman of the Advertising Federation of America, declares that "advertisers, through their support of the means of communication, are directly contributing to the maintenance of the most effective single agency for keeping the industrial life of the country on an even keel." [53] Labor strikes rock the industrial boat; advertisers assume the social responsibility for keeping it on an even keel. Whoever sees in advertising only a gigantic scheme for ballyhooing commercial products to consumers misses the larger social significance of this billion dollar adjunct of the business enterprise. In the San Francisco general strike, Mr. Kobak declares that "the educational efforts of the newspapers and radio stations, promptly and intelligently applied, *crystallized public sentiment against the general strike* [italics ours] . . . thus quickly ending the entire unpleasantness." [54]

The editor of *Editor & Publisher* discloses the secret of a new journalistic method for crystallizing public opinion against strikes. "Three responsible reporters working on the New England mill strike," says Marlen Pew, "have reported to me that certain photographers from Boston and New York newspapers have not only faked pictures to indicate violence in the Saylesville, R. I., labor disturbance, but have actually encouraged young hoodlums to assault guards and thus start action for pictorial purposes." [55]

In the longshoremen's strike in Seattle, business leaders used large paid-advertising space in the newspapers for the purpose of supporting the editorial policies of the press in crystallizing public opinion against the strike. Vigorous cartoons were used in these advertisements which declared "When 185 won't work, 3200 can't work," "Stand up and be counted for Seattle," "Vanishing ships—a closed shop is a closed port." [56] Does any one suppose that under the free, democratic institutions of the press, the strikers could have advertised right back at them? Describing the effects of this business advertising against the strike, Christy Thomas, general manager of the Chamber of Commerce, declared that it "completely changed public sentiment." Furthermore, "this advertising laid the foundation in the public mind for *forceful measures.*" [Italics ours.]

In the Scripps-Howard paper of San Francisco, the *News,* Heywood Broun's column was supporting the general strike. But on Tuesday, July 17, Broun said: "I still think that the lawless employers should be restrained and if they don't like it here I see no possible objection to sending them back where they came from." This was too much. The second edition appeared minus Broun. Doing duty in his place was an innocuous little chat about children in the home, from the pen of Mrs. Franklin D. Roosevelt.[57]

Liberty was screaming loudly against the "reds" who, it alleged, were the sole fomenters of the general strike. According to its own claim, newspapers, manufacturers, and civic authorities reprinted its blatant fascist outbursts.[58] Perhaps no better symbol of the state of liberty under business democracy could be had than the fact that it has been taken over as the name of Bernarr Mac-Fadden's weekly.

Newspapers are generously provided with anti-Communist publicity. According to a story in *Editor & Publisher*, this publicity is paid for by a "patriotic organization," admittedly sponsored by certain big industries which are not named.[59]

Albert D. Lasker told his Harvard audience that "no more vicious calumny has ever been put forth than the suspicion that the press, in any major or important way can be influenced editorially by its advertising patrons." Yet it was Mr. Lasker's own advertising agency, Lord & Thomas, which entered energetically into the political campaign of California for the purpose of defeating Upton Sinclair, by providing radio "entertainment" that was nothing more than thinly concealed business propaganda. Is Mr. Lasker, after many years of association with advertising, wholly innocent of its purposes and methods? "Through the *multiplicity* of advertising," declared Mr. Lasker at Boston, "the press in our generation has become increasingly independent." Against Mr. Lasker, Marlen Pew testifies to the effect that "interference with newspaper freedom by local public utility concerns seems to be an almost *universal editorial complaint in the United States.*" [Italics ours.] "Everywhere I travel, North, East, South or West," says Mr. Pew, "editors are found telling how some gas, electric, transportation or telephone magnate, or his press agent, has swung the advertising club over their heads or, perhaps, given them a swift ride on a mortgage plaster or bank loan." [60] Both Mr. Lasker and Mr. Pew cannot be telling the truth. The discerning will decide for themselves which is lying.

The chairman of the Association of National Advertisers' Government Relations Committee reveals that at one time the "public was tremendously swayed emotionally in favor of the Tugwell bill," and that letters which poured into the White House were 1,000 to 1 in favor of the bill. "Then business got busy," says Mr. Lichtenberg, "and placed the facts before the public, and the letters shifted to 1,000 to 1 against the bill." [61] It would be highly informing to know just how this representative of the Association of National Advertisers has access to the facts about the White House mail, and by what right in a "democracy."

Not only is the press, under the domination of advertisers, organized to keep industry on an even keel by crystallizing public opinion against labor, but it is equally alert in its organization to keep industry on an even keel by crystallizing public opinion against those who are fighting the battles of consumers. *Time* and *News-Week* have recently refused to carry advertisements of Consumers' Research. At the present time, there is a concerted drive being made by advertisers and newspapers to rehabilitate advertising in the confidence of readers. The Mergenthaler Linotype Company is sponsoring a campaign through the press of the entire country, using a cartoon which depicts such books as "Your Money's Worth" and "100,000,000 Guinea Pigs" as dogs barking and biting at the heels of "newspaper advertising" which is represented as pushing all by itself the "recovery" cart. The Mergenthaler Linotype Company has proposed that newspapers throughout the United States carry advertisements using cartoons which are designed to recover the reader-confidence of the country in advertising. By the middle of November, 1068 newspapers had given their answers on the proposed campaign. Of this number, 933 or 87 per cent approved the plan as submitted. Only 16 newspapers were definitely opposed, leaving 98.5 per cent to support the campaign with or without modification. "Great idea; will do all we can to cooperate," was the typical reply received from the *Reminder* of Cudahy, Wisconsin. "Yes!" chorused hundreds of editors from the centers and the crossroads of 48 states.

The birth of the Radio Corporation of America gave to the vested interests another method of dictatorial control over the thoughts of the people. The R.C.A. was originally formed to keep patents, vital to wireless communications, in America; and, while succeeding in carrying out the purpose of the founders, the people of the United States are no better off than if the patents belonged to some company in Great Britain. Owen D. Young and his associates in General Electric have succeeded in controlling 60 per cent of all goods sold through the Radio Corporation. Westinghouse through an agreement with R.C.A. is granted the right to manufacture the other 40 per cent.[62] The Radio Corporation of America owns the patents and equipment necessary for broadcasting stations as well as the complete control over all air traffic to and from foreign countries, and with such a monopoly, of course, goes the right to fix rates which guarantee high profits. The Corporation maintains that a monopoly is needed (and allowed under the Webb Act) to keep these patent rights within the United States.

An informing account of what happens to any group desirous of setting up a broadcasting station for educational purposes only was given by Gross W. Alexander, minister of the Rosewood Methodist Church in Los Angeles, at the First National Conference on the Use of Radio as a Cultural Agency in a Democracy. Mr. Alexander was made manager of the Pacific-Western Broadcasting Federation, Ltd., set up in 1928. The Federation was a non-profit corporation sponsored by the California Congress of Parents and Teachers, the California Federation of Women's Clubs, several colleges and universities, nine different religious bodies (including Catholic, Protestant and Jewish) and various other civic, social, educational and professional groups. The Federal Radio Commission granted a permit to the Broadcasting Federation for a fifty-thousand watt station with unlimited time. At the time no other station had such a powerful watt permit.

The Los Angeles Chamber of Commerce sent representatives to Washington to protest. Depositors were told that if they contributed to the enterprise their credit in the banks would be jeopardized. The Radio Corporation of America submitted affidavits to discredit the non-profit organization. In the beginning, the Broadcasting Federation had the support of Dr. Robert A. Millikan, head of the California Institute of Technology. But after the American Telephone and Telegraph Company gave $3,000,000 to the Institute, Dr. Millikan lost interest. Later as head of the National Advisory Council on Radio in Education Dr. Millikan stated that "any talk about the danger of monopolistic control on the ether . . . is not well considered." [63]

The Pacific-Western Broadcasting Federation sought the aid of the Carnegie Corporation of New York, John D. Rockefeller, Jr., the J. C. Penney Foundation, the Julius Rosenwald Fund, the Twentieth Century Fund, the Commonwealth Fund, and other philanthropic foundations but found them "to be as cold as steel." Finally, in January, 1930, Dr. Millikan wrote Mr. Alexander stating that at a meeting of the National Advisory Council Owen D. Young presented some "concrete and important facts," to the effect "that it was possible for any educational group which the Council might set up to obtain all the facilities for nation-wide broadcasting that it could possibly use, without any expense whatever, the sole conditions being that the audience must be large and the commercial companies which furnish the facilities are to have nothing to do in any way, shape, or manner with the broadcasting program." "You see how clever was the part played by the master hand in industry," said Mr. Alexander. "Obviously, to the undiscriminating, it would be illogical to duplicate facilities at considerable cost when the national chains are available gratis to the educators themselves." [64] When the Senate Interstate Commerce Committee asked Mr. Aylesworth about the educational programs his organization was permitting, he replied that they were "good advertising." The Senators could hardly believe Mr. Aylesworth and repeated the question in another form, asking, "and those public service programs are a part of the business game of popularizing your own company?" Mr. Aylesworth answered "yes." [65] The Pacific-Western Broadcasting Federation could not be financed and had to abandon its efforts to broadcast purely educational programs. Broadcasting remains a *business* monopoly.

The Radio Corporation of America not only controls the radio patent pool but has interested itself "in the motion picture production, distribution, and exhibition, and the phonograph industry, in vaudeville, in music production, in television, in manufacturing and selling vacuum tubes, in producing and marketing equipment for broadcasting and receiving, and in various other allied arts and industries." [66] The Corporation owns or controls over 3,800 patents in the radio field. After negotiations with the Pantages circuit, a Radio Corporation agent was quoted as saying: "We are going ahead with our competitive program more competitively than ever; we are going to buy and build theatres, and *what competition we can't swallow into our organization we will dynamite out of the field.*" [67] [Italics ours.] When Merlin H. Aylesworth was made president of the National Broadcasting Company by the Radio Corporation of America, he also held another important position, that of director of public relations (polite term for propagandizing through newspapers, magazines, and educational institutions) of the National Electric Light Association.

The case of the Reverend Robert P. Shuler is of first-rate importance in the question of the freedom of the air. Whether or not Mr. Shuler is a charlatan has nothing to do with the significance of the decision handed down by the District of Columbia Court of Appeals. The Court ruled that the Radio Commission was "in all respects right" in ruling Mr. Shuler's station off the air. "If it be considered," the Court's decision stated, "that one may, without let or hindrance from any source, use these facilities, reaching out, as they do, from one corner of the country to the other, to obstruct the administration of justice, offend the religious susceptibilities of thousands, *inspire political distrust* and civic discord or offend youth and innocence by the free use of words suggestive of sexual immorality, and be answerable for slander only at the instance of the one offended, then this great science, instead of a boon, will become a scourge and the nation a theatre for the display of individual passions and the collisions of personal interests." [68] [Italics ours.] The highly important phrase in this decision is that in which the Court forbids the use of the air to "inspire political distrust." Such a phrase is open to the broadest interpretation, laying a ban upon political criticism as strict as any in Nazi Germany. This is an abrogation of an ancient distinction which courts have made between agitation which has been permitted to the fullest extent (in legal definitions at least) and overt acts of violence or incitation to acts of violence. *Inspiring political distrust* does not come under the definition of overt violence or incitation to violence, and the District of Columbia Court of Appeals has therefore placed new restrictions upon freedom of speech at least as far as the air is concerned.

The Court apparently entertained some concern that broadcasting should not "offend youth and innocence." If this concern were applied to much of present-day ribald advertising, there would be almost universal suspension of permits to commercial station owners.

Arthur E. Morgan, chairman of the Tennessee Valley Authority and head of Antioch College, is the author of the most naïve explanation yet brought forward purporting to throw light on why commercial interests gained control of the motion picture industry. Dr. Morgan was discussing the use of radio as a cultural agency, and, even though his direct reference was to the films, he apparently intended to include radio in his explanation of the commercialization of educational implements. "It was by a *peculiar twist of fate* [italics ours] that a tremendous educational implement was put into the hands of people who had almost no sense of social responsibility, whose sole concern was commercial, and through that peculiar circumstance the whole color of American life, of American standards of values, has been profoundly revolutionized and debased. The fate of our nation culturally seems to have rested, to some extent, upon that accident of invention combined with an accident of immigration and an accident in the distribution of commercial opportunity." [69] Dr. Morgan proceeded to identify as the commercial interests, into whose hands the "twist of fate" committed motion picture development, "vigorous men of European descent"—men who were "exceptional in energy and in business keenness." Elsewhere Dr. Morgan describes them as coming latterly out of "the wholesale districts of New York." It might have been embarrassing to the Roosevelt Administration if Dr. Morgan had come out plainly with the charge that immigrant Jews had commercialized and debased motion pictures. Others have said it; and Dr. Morgan skirted all around the charge without coming directly to grips with it. Apparently at Antioch College, students are told that economic developments in business society are the result of "a peculiar twist of fate," an "accident of invention," an "accident in the distribution of commercial opportunity," and an *"accident of immigration."* Dr. Morgan varied the phrase once by calling it "a trick of fate." There should be no wonder that the political illiteracy of college graduates is abysmal and furthermore that it is political illiteracy infused with anti-Semitism. Dr. Morgan is a victim of what Michael Gold has termed "the Fascist Unconscious." Tricks and twists of fate and historical accidents are convenient sophistries for liberals who, for one reason or another, are unwilling or unable to recognize the nature of business society and the basis of control within it. They are possessed of a determined refusal to understand with what thoroughness all of the cultural institutions of business society are conditioned by its economic forces. Owen D. Young, Major-General James G. Harbord and Walter S. Gifford may be surprised to find themselves associated in this fashion, by Dr. Morgan, with the Russian-Jewish immigrants in the garment trade of New York's "wholesale districts."

Gandhi is a mere piker in the technique of non-violent coercion compared with the American ruling class in its use of educational agencies to prevent the frustration of its will to rule, or for that matter to prevent even the discovery of its unfitness to rule. The police power of the class-owned state is only the second line of defense for entrenched privilege which may in times of social turbulence be driven back from its educational outposts by a desperate enemy class of consumer-workers that has become educated, really educated, by the deprivations to which exploitation subjects it. In the last analysis the business-state must either *educate* or *shoot* its despoiled subject masses. In either case its purpose is only to achieve stability for its rule.

CHAPTER XXII

Defense of the Business-State by Guns

Rᴵᴄʜᴀʀᴅ B. Mᴇʟʟᴏɴ is reported to have said that "you could not run a coal company without machine guns." When Oliver K. Eaton, counsel for the United Mine Workers, asked Mr. Mellon, in the hearings of the Senate Committee on Interstate Commerce, in March, 1928, if his coal and iron police used machine guns, the brother of the next-to-the-greatest Secretary of the Treasury was evasive. "I never heard of that. They may have," was Richard's answer. Pressed if he would approve of his private army having machine guns, he said: "It is necessary. You could not run without them." [1] In a steadier moment of afterthought he said he meant he could not run a company without his private police. Anyone familiar with the notorious Pennsylvania coal and iron police, the history of the Pinkerton "gunmen," and the rôle of regular police and state troopers in strikes, knows that labor disturbances uniformly elicit a show or the use of force. After the steel strike of 1892, when the Homestead workers' union was crushed, Andrew Mellon, the greatest corporation tax-refunder, and his partner, Henry Clay Frick, declared they would employ only non-union labor henceforth. To protect themselves against labor agitators and discontent among the workers, the building of a private army was considered necessary. They also were instrumental in getting passed a state law—the coal and iron police law—which gave the privately paid guards the same power that regular police held. Besides a private army and the regular state guard used to

protect their property, the Mellon-Frick Company hired spies
to mingle with the workers, in their homes, and in the shops, to
see that labor organizers were immediately spotted and dismissed. Despite these precautions against collective bargaining,
rebellions did break out sporadically and the private police were
kept busy. State troopers were also familiar sights on such occasions.

Since the inauguration of the "New Deal" fifty strikers have
been slain and at least two hundred have been seriously wounded.
Sales of tear gas have greatly increased in the Middle West,
center of motor, steel, and mine disturbances, according to an
agent of the Federal Laboratories, Inc., of Pittsburgh. The Lake
Erie Chemical Company, chief competitor of the Federal Laboratories and now absorbed by the United States Ordnance Engineers, Inc., has a complete tear gas outfit including a 37 mm.,
1½ inch single-action shoulder gas gun, six long-range tear gas
shells, six short-range tear gas shells, four illumination parachute
flares, and one leatherette case. During recent strikes, a new gas
has been discovered called *diphenylaminechloroarsine* which will
make strikers vomit and keep them sick at least twenty-four
hours.[2] This is now preferred to tear gas as strikers in many
places have learned to carry moth balls which make them somewhat immune to the effects of tear gas.

During the San Francisco general strike, the Industrial Association, organization of manufacturers, brought 200 strike-
breakers in to move goods despite the strike. During the strike
there were many police raids on radical and labor meeting places
in which, from the meagre evidence which can be gathered, it
seems that the Industrial Association was entirely involved.
When the American Civil Liberties Union proposed to Albert
E. Boynton, managing director of the Industrial Association of
San Francisco, that it open "its complete files dealing with the
general strike to examination by an impartial national inquiry
commission of outstanding persons," the Association did not
take up the offer, but did permit the *Nation's* representatives

to scrutinize some of its files, including the "Strike Violence Memos." The complete files of the strike-breaking agency are still secret documents. While Mr. Boynton declared that the Association was "as innocent as a new-born babe," he has never explained why the Association should spend time and money gathering "news reports" if they did not intend to use them as a blacklist for employers. The Association's bulletins dealing with radical movements show that they have more than "news" interest in gathering the names of all radicals and persons involved in the strike. The *Nation* report shows that the officials of the Association had confidential information as to the time and places of the raids *before they were conducted*.[3] "An office was secured, . . . telephones and a short-wave radio receiver installed. Three outside employees were engaged . . . to visit the various police stations, emergency hospitals, and other locations where news might be obtained. . . . In addition there were employed two rewrite men and the necessary stenographic service."

Those who have any doubts about the results of the class struggle should follow closely reports of the elaborate and costly paraphernalia installed in plants to prevent the workers from protesting against their extremely low wages and intolerable working conditions. On September 15, 1934, Harry H. Bennett, personnel director of the Ford Motor Company in Detroit, authorized the employment of 5,000 war veterans, the selection to be made on the basis of "war records" primarily. While it was stated that the veterans were to be hired because of "production expansion," it is also known that Ford has been against any union in his plants, and thinks, in view of the veterans' anti-radical position, that they will make ideal workers.

"Strike-breaking is my profession," declared P. L. Bergoff in an article in the New York *Post*.[5] "I've been at this business a long time. I'm no chicken. I've made millions breaking strikes in this country. . . . The boys down in Wall Street have come to me a lot of times for advice. I've never steered them wrong." Mr. Bergoff, with an air of pride, related how he has aided in the protection of private property. "I have mobilized small armies on a few hours' notice, answering the call of railroads, traction and steamship companies in scores of American cities," the strike-breaker stated. When asked how he obtained information as to where strikes might materialize, he said: "We have men in almost every union. They advise us when agitators or Communists try to intrench themselves and create trouble. . . . Some . . . are on our payroll. Others receive a bonus for furnishing us with information." Mr. Bergoff admitted that his job is to create a private army for industry whose sole purpose is to keep labor in its place. His storm troops are organized with lieutenants, captains, and other ranks, in fact "conditions are similar to those in the United States Army . . . preparations for breaking a strike resemble the mobilization of a miniature army for actual warfare," he stated. Since the NRA, strike-breaking has consisted chiefly of "special attention to the abortion of threatened strikes." [6]

During the 1934 textile strike in Honea Path, South Carolina, six striking workers were killed by deputy sheriffs.[7] In Charlotte, North Carolina, national guardsmen used their bayonets in driving back a crowd around the Knit Products Mill. In Atlanta, Georgia, martial law was declared and national guards came to the defense of the mill owners. One report states: "Antistrike forces, backed by an unprecedented display of armament and mobile troops, and by martial law in Georgia, pressed their offensive for reopening of the mills." [8] Following Hitler's example, strikers were taken to concentration camps, and guardsmen strung barbed wire around them in open lots. Adjutant General Lindley, camp commander of the National Guard of Georgia, stated that 110 men and sixteen women would be held in the camps for the duration of the strike. Strike leaders declared that Governor Talmadge's action in declaring martial law was unjustified as there was no violence until the guards made their appearance. Mothers were among those imprisoned in the Georgia concentration camps for the "offense" of striking against starvation wages. A statement made by the woolen manufacturers admitted that the public had to pay for protection of the mill owners' property. "The strike becomes a matter of increasing importance to the public . . . the public must pay for the troops now mobilized." [9]

The Nazis in Germany were highly pleased with the authorities' show of fascism in the textile strike. Nazi headlines featured their satisfaction over the news that *concentration camps* were being established near Atlanta. Germany is more and more convinced, a dispatch to the New York *Times* stated, that "the social unrest in America, as manifested in numerous and bloody fights which are attracting increasing attention here, will force the United States more and more into a fascist direction." [10]

Not only were the guardsmen used against strikers in Georgia, but Governor Talmadge explained that "military courts" were being provided for prisoners arrested by the guards.[11] Four thousand guardsmen were called out in Georgia to break the textile strike there; nearly six thousand troops patrolled Carolina mills; and two thousand militiamen protected mill property in Rhode Island.[12] Fourteen strikers were killed during the first two weeks of the strike. Theodore Francis Green, Governor of Rhode Island, who has heavy interests in the textile mills, sent a message full of anti-communist hysteria to the Legislature asking for an extraordinary session for the purpose of ousting every "red" from the state. Just how pink a man could be before considered "red" was not specified. After five hours of heated debate the Legislature concluded that the Governor had exaggerated the "red" menace.[13] However, the Legislature voted $100,000 to hire more police. Government under business is a dictatorship of the owning class and that dictatorship is expressed more and more openly and violently as property interests require it.

In a 104-page pamphlet, issued in December, 1931, by the 33rd Division of the Illinois National Guard, entitled, "Emergency Plans for Domestic Disturbances," the following orders were given: (b) Never fire over the heads of rioters. The aim should be low, with full-charge ammunition . . . (e) Officers and men should not fear reprisal in case one or more people are killed."

"In the obvious state of unrest now prevailing throughout the world," said Chief of Staff Douglas MacArthur in the 1933 report of the Secretary of War, "evidences of which are plainly visible even in our own country, an efficient and dependable military establishment, constantly responsive to the will of its Government, constitutes a rock of stability and one of a nation's priceless possessions." General MacArthur went on to add that "as much as at any other time in our history, the Army's efficiency should engage the earnest attention of every loyal citizen." [14] The Assistant Secretary of War, Harry H. Woodring, is even more outspoken than the General in showing that the purpose of the Army is to protect the business-state against demands from the workers for better wages and working conditions. In his article entitled, "The American Army Stands Ready," which appeared in *Liberty* magazine in the winter of 1934, Mr. Woodring wrote: "Let me speak frankly! If this country should be threatened with foreign war, economic chaos, or social revolution, the Army has the training, the experience, the organization, and the men to support the government and direct the country in the national interest." [15] The caption under a picture showing national guardsmen dispersing a mob with tear gas, read: "The guard is an element of the army." When we read that guards have been called out to quell hunger riots or defeat the demands of striking workers, it is the Army which is being used for property interests against workers. Never have the guards been called out to defend the interests of the workers. Why? *Because the Army is an appendage of the business-state and functions only to protect business interests.* "The Army has sometimes been called upon to suppress disorderly activities in defiance of government by large groups of individuals," Mr. Woodring asserted. *"It has always been successful in this work,"* he is frank to admit. [Italics ours.] Mr. Woodring continued: "It is scarcely too much to state that the Army's existence for this purpose alone would justify the investment we have mad in it. Economic breakdown, unless promptly corrected, induce social breakdown. In such a crisis the Army is the only organiza tion in the country which is able and ready to maintain th government." [16]

Mr. Woodring is also prepared to state, what many in th government deny, that the Civilian Conservation Camps are part of an extensive militarization plan. "This achievement—th organization of over 300,000 men in more than 1,500 Civilia Conservation Corps camps—was the first real test of the Army' plans for war mobilization under the National Defense Act a amended in 1920," he said. "It proved both the efficiency of ou plan of defense and the equally important success of the Militar Procurement Plan—the Army's economic war plan—which i intrusted to the Assistant Secretary of War," Mr. Woodrin stated. [17] The secretary would not have us misunderstand hin "The CCC mobilization is thus more than a great militar achievement; it is a dress rehearsal of the Army's ability t intervene, under Constitutional authority, in combating the de pression," [18] and "its action in mobilizing, conditioning, feedin clothing, transporting, housing, paying, and caring for the phys cal welfare, recreation, and general morale of 300,000 member of the Civilian Conservation Corps was performed with a speec orderliness, calmness, general efficiency, and complete satisfactio of all concerned. . . . If the Army were so directed, it coul organize the veterans of the World War, the CCC men, an through them the administration of the emergency relief, into system of economic *storm troops* that could support the go ernment's efforts to smash the depression. If the Army is not s directed, it will, as always, stand by and await orders." [19] [Itali ours.] The Army is ready at all times to fight the battles of th business-state, whether it be against labor at home or again the deluded fighters of some foreign country, whenever busine interests are threatened.

Mr. Woodring might have explained that only men betwee

he ages of eighteen and twenty-five—military age—are accepted
n the CCC camps. By August, 1934, another 100,000 had been
added to the camps, making a total of 400,000. The CCC scheme
not only "conditions" the men for war purposes, but it also tries
o instill into them a loyalty to the business-state and to keep
hem from demanding a larger share in the nation's wealth.

If the Civilian Conservation Corps is merely a relief measure,
as the Administration claims, it would seem that it is a highly
costly one, and for that reason alone we are skeptical as to why
he Roosevelt Administration decided upon this particular
method for relieving the unemployed. ". . . Relief via the CCC
costs over four times as much as relief through other channels,"
he October issue of *Fortune* states editorially, and goes on to
add that the CCC cannot for a moment be considered a serious
contribution toward solving the great total problem of U. S.
unemployment." [20] That the present Administration intends to
keep the CCC camps in its program for "relief" shows that the
camps are intended to serve purposes other than relief, and those
purposes can only be military in character. It *never* fights a battle
or workers or consumers, or against the exploiting employers
like Pullman, Carnegie, the United States Steel Corporation, or
he Cuban sugar magnates. It has one sure principle only: the
defense of the "haves" against the "have-nots."

In spite of official assertions to the contrary, the military purpose
f the camps is revealed by Army men eager to impress business
nterests with their worth. The Secretary of War, George H.
Dern, in his 1933 Annual Report, said: "It is true that certain
benefits have accrued to the Army through the administration
f the Civilian Conservation Corps project. Junior officers in
articular have obtained valuable training in mobilization proc-
ss and in leadership. Staffs have been enabled to test in a
ractical way certain phases of theoretical plans. The procurement services have been afforded opportunity to meet and solve
many problems incident to emergency expansion." [21] The public,
hen, is to hear that the War Department was entirely dis-

interested in the training of unemployed men between the ages
of eighteen and twenty-five. Why were only young men chosen?
Are not older men as needful of the physical training and
the compensation as the young men? Secretary Dern makes
it clear, in his report, that the purpose of the project was to
impress Congress and the President with the usefulness of the
War Department. "The success of the Civilian Conservation
Corps *mobilization,*" he said, "has attracted attention to the
American Army's readiness to perform important tasks incident
to emergencies of peace. . . . Its latest accomplishment has demon
strated its value as an agency splendidly trained and organized
to meet and solve, upon a moment's notice, administrative and
organizational problems of nation-wide scope and magnitude." [2]
Thus the army staff is trained for war; the young men of mili
tary age are trained in the life of army camps, and become ac
customed to obey the orders of military officers; and the unrest
and resentment, caused by continuous unemployment, is allayed
all under the guise of following out a policy that work—even
made work—is better than relief. (It should be noted that over
half a billion dollars of the Public Works Administration fund
has been allotted to the War and Navy Departments.) The ad
ministrative policy has been, on the one hand, to dismiss from
the CCC camps any who might disseminate radical propaganda
even as mildly liberal an exposition as Professor Ogburn's pam
phlet which was barred from the CCC by the labor leader, Rober
Fechner, and, on the other hand, to imbue the men with the ide
of obeying military discipline.

The officers in charge of the training at the CCC camps know
what is expected of them. A letter from Major General Frank
Parker to the officers on duty at the camps reads: "There ar
two distinct duties which are incumbent upon officers on dut
with the CCC organization. First is the work of rendering
as large a percentage as possible of CCC men available an
fit for the task assigned to them by technical authorities. But
in addition to this first duty, is the second which is, likewise

of paramount importance. When these young men return to their homes upon the expiration of their service, they should bear with them not only the remembrance of work faithfully performed, but, likewise, a clear, lasting memory of the following lessons for *constituted authority;* the ability to live collectively so as to be a useful member of the unit; the habit of orderly and sanitary living; the courtesy and the coöperative spirit necessary to a proper community and, *above all, the idea that a man's highest usefulness depends upon his desire to serve at all times the interest of his unit,* whether that unit be a squad, a family or a community." [23] [Italics ours.] Business men need serve profits alone; others are to serve the community—meaning the business-state.

Pacifist pleas for disarmament sometimes frighten the Army and impel it to strive harder to impress the interests it serves. "The fact that some 5,000 officers are to be employed on this work [CCC] may prove to be a lifesaver for the Army," the *Army and Navy Register* stated editorially on May 27, 1933, "and eliminate the reduction in officer personnel which has been impending for some time." [24] Approximately 5,400 officers and 8,000 enlisted men of the regular Army are now on duty in connection with the CCC. These figures do not include reserves. In this new work with the unemployed and the emergency duty to protect factories against their workers, the Army has "saved itself" and is now not in danger of having its force reduced. Officers of the National Guard Bureau, the regular Army's link with the State militia, estimate that the guards have been called out on duty more in the last eighteen months than in any equivalent period since the World War. Major General George E. Leach, Chief of the National Guard Bureau, recently told Secretary Dern that the National Guard, with a total strength of 185,000 men, "has become a force upon which both state and nation realize they may safely rely in any emergency." [25]

The public attention has been called, in the last few years, to the "traffic in death" which has been going on for some time.

The public cannot be expected to recognize that selling materials of death for profits is no worse than selling lead-poisoned apples or a hair dye which poisons one's whole system. Because the business-state needs ammunition to fight its battles, both against the workers at home and against some foreign power, there has grown up a perfectly legal and respectable armament industry. The voluminous literature on the munitions business will be read with faulty comprehension if it does not clearly appear that the armaments industry is thoroughly at home in a capitalist civilization. It is, in fact, impossible to conceive of capitalist society giving up its deadly weapons and the traffic in them. An acquisitive society built on centuries of international looting must go armed to the teeth or else consent to a complete remaking of the map of the world. In which latter case it would no longer be an acquisitive society. The early-comers in international loot have for the past fifteen years made a few feeble efforts to change the rules of the imperialist guns, but emphatically without giving up any of the loot which was grabbed under the old rules. Late-comers in imperialism, like Japan, have been piously lectured by the League of Nations for engaging in international brigandage or "expansion" while its principal members cling shamelessly to their own colonies and mandates conquered by identical methods.

The arms traffic can no more be lifted out of its capitalistic framework than the profit motive can be deleted from its set of principles unless the capitalist framework itself is demolished. An attack upon the arms traffic if effective must be an attack upon the war-system which produced it. An attack upon the war-system is a frontal assault upon capitalism. Mr. Hugh Dalton, speaking on the Naval Estimates in the House of Commons on March 11, 1926, put the case against capitalism and its armaments enterprise as follows: "Vickers had been supplying the Turkish artillery with shells which were fired into the Australian, New Zealand and British troops as they were scrambling up Anzac Cove and Cape Helles. Did it matter to the directors of these armament firms, so long as they did business and expanded the defense expenditure of Turkey, that their weapons mashed up into bloody pulp all the morning glory that was the flower of Anzac, the youth of Australia and New Zealand, yes and of the youth of our own country? These men, these directors of armament firms, are the highest and completest embodiment of capitalist morality."

It is a grave mistake to look upon war as a relic of primitive society. The most primitive of human social organizations was not in any commensurate sense of the phrase organized to conduct mass slaughter against whole populations. War, à la du Pont, Vickers, Creusot, and Krupp, is a modern institution intricately connected with the institutions of business society as a whole; and its supporters have been among the greatest profiteers of a system which rests upon the profit motive. On May 5, 1718, James Tuckle received Letters Patent for an arms invention, the record of which is still to be found in the Patent Office Library in London. The inventor claimed great merit for a new type of "gun or machine called a 'Defense.'" The principal merit of Tuckle's gun, however, lay in the fact that it was constructed with two sets of magazines: one for round bullets to be used in killing Christians, and the other for square bullets with sharp edges to be used in killing Turks!

Since Tuckle's day there have been two centuries of technological progress, and in no other department of production has there been such a thoroughgoing application of science and technology as in the manufacture of appliances for the wholesale and indiscriminate slaughter of human beings. The "advance" of civilization has brought with it the development of industries, unrivalled in magnitude and influence, which specialize in efficient methods of destroying human life. In the name of *national defense* the governments of the world spend annually more than $4,500,000,000. At least 50 per cent of this amount goes to the industries that manufacture death-dealing appliances. Never before in the history of humanity has there been such coldly scientific and systematic preparation to murder millions.

In 1913, the United States spent 244.6 millions of dollars for *national defense* and in 1930, 727.7 millions—three times as much. Every country of Europe, except Russia, is more heavily armed to-day than in 1913, even after adjusting the increases to the wholesale price indexes of various countries. Since 1913 the world's expend-itures for national defense have risen from $2,531,000,000 to $4,500,000,000. The United States accounts for one-fourth of the whole world's madness by increasing the expenditures for national defense by almost $500,000,000 since 1913.[26] A profitable market for arms peddlers!

The outspoken Smedley D. Butler knows exactly why a busi-ness-state goes armed, and, unlike most other military or business leaders, speaks his mind on occasion. "For thirty-three years and four months," says Butler, "I was an active agent in the greatest debt collecting agency in the world—the United States Marine Corps. . . . Every year the Marines used to be off to South or Central America to collect a debt." [27]

Probably no more influential economic interests exist in capi-talist society than those which are involved in the manufacture and sale of war materials. Their lobbies are second to none. In addition to their economic strength, they have the backing of the whole war-system of modern times with all that this means in terms of the patriotic pressure of tradition.

Some remarkable facts have been disclosed by the Congres-sional investigating committee's looking into the armaments busi-ness. Du Ponts made tremendous profits from the World War. Their total dividends paid in the years 1913 to 1918, inclusive, amounted to 458 per cent of the par value of the original stock which was $100. The highest dividends paid on common stock were 100 per cent in 1916, 51 per cent in 1917, 26 per cent in 1918 and 18 per cent in 1919.[28]

Testimony from the Pratt, Whitney Aircraft Company indi-cated that the company had made a total return of $11,437,25(

n 1932 on an original $1,000 investment made in 1925.[29] The World's master salesman for armaments firms and "mystery man of Europe," Sir Basil Zaharoff, received more than $2,000,000 n commissions from the Electric Boat Company of Connecticut ver a period of years.[30] The investigation disclosed also that Germany was buying American ammunitions through camou-aged munition companies. Captain Paul Koster, a former officer f the Dutch Navy and now European representative of the Electric Boat Company, testified that "all the German firms who uild parts or machinery for submarine boats have established amouflaged concerns" in Sweden, Holland, Switzerland, and ther small countries within easy distance of Germany.[31] E. I. u Pont de Nemours Company entered into a contract on ebruary 1, 1933, with one Jungo Geira, described as "an inter-ational spy," to act as its "exclusive agent" to rearm Germany ith military propellants and explosives. Colonel Taylor, the rench representative of the du Pont Company, wrote a letter Mr. Casey on June 17, 1932, in which he said that "the German olitical associations, like the Nazis and others, are nearly all med with American revolvers and Thompson machine guns, d that there is a regular business of bootlegging of small eapons from America to Germany, the centre of which being ologne and most of the bootlegging being done by Dutch." gain on January 18, 1933, Colonel Taylor wrote that "the ntraband [this was just prior to the beginning of the Nazi gime] in arms is increasing tremendously." [32]

Armaments firms like all other profit-making institutions go any extremes to make their gains. When the chief armaments tions were discussing placing an embargo on all exports of maments going to South America, du Ponts carried on in-nsive lobbying, not in the Congressional office buildings, but the War and Navy Departments. The United States Govern-ent has declared that an embargo on arms shipments exported these warring countries of South America would be useless *other countries still continued to engage in arms traffic with*

the belligerents. In other words, if there is going to be a w
anyhow, it is not the business of the United States Governm
to interfere with profits which are to be reaped out of this w
by the arms industry of the United States. Arms manufactur
everywhere have a way of inducing a tender governmer
solicitude for their interests. Besides lobbying activities, t
du Ponts had entered into an agreement with the Impe
Chemical Industries, Ltd., of London, whose position in Gr
Britain is comparable to that of du Ponts in America, and
gether they control the world sale of explosives.[33]

Munitions salesmen have gone to the absurd extremes that
salesmen of other profit-making companies, described earlier
this volume, have gone. The Senate Investigating Commit
disclosed that American munitions salesmen have offered
train an entire South American Army in chemical warf
tactics.[34] Not only will the companies make weapons to kill,
they will spend their money training armies to use their produ
This is what the prophets of the modern business economy te
"creative salesmanship."

When relations between Chile and Peru were extremely te
some seven years ago, and the Tacna-Arica controversy was
its height, the Electric Boat Company was working night a
day for contracts to arm Peru for undersea operations. It see
from the munitions investigating committee hearings, that rej
sentatives of Vickers, Ltd., ally of the American boat compa
were just as busy on the other side attempting to persuade
Chileans that the time had come for them to spend some mo
in a submarine flotilla for *their* undersea operations.[35]

Few men in the United States Senate have equalled Cla
A. Swanson of Virginia as protagonist of a big navy. Fo
quarter of a century he was the mouthpiece of a cause dea
the Admirals and, it may be remarked, to the economic inter
of an influential corporation in his home state—the New
News Shipbuilding and Drydock Company. During the j
twenty years this latter corporation has averaged two battles

a year for the United States Navy. The warship builders are the most powerful of the armaments makers in the United States. When a Republican President of the United States came to appoint a delegation to sit at the World Disarmament Conference, the first choice fell upon this doughty friend of the shipbuilders, the man who was later to ask for a navy "Second to None," Senator Claude A. Swanson. When a Democratic President of the United States came to appoint a Secretary of the Navy, he chose the same man for the post. It is reported that the Admirals were never happier over an appointment than they were over this one, but their joy could hardly have equalled that of the battleship makers.

Hardly had Mr. Swanson assumed his new office when he demanded and received a special appropriation from the Public Works Administration of $238,000,000 for the construction of new war vessels. The Newport News Shipbuilding and Drydock Company in his home state was awarded contracts for two airplane carriers from this fund. The New York Shipbuilding Company of Camden, New Jersey, which has built thirty-two war vessels for the United States Navy since the war with Spain, and the Bethlehem Shipbuilding Corporation also share in the "recovery" profits of the Public Works Administration. As a climax to his long career of service to the shipbuilders, Mr. Swanson witnessed the passage, late in January, 1934, of the Vinson Bill. Appropriations have not yet been made for carrying out construction in full under this measure, but a program calling for more than a hundred war vessels and an eventual outlay of more than a half billion dollars is contained in the bill. A new naval race is already under way. The Japanese, British, and French Governments responded immediately to the challenge of the bill by adding to their naval appropriations. The prospects for huge profits for all the battleship makers are therefore excellent.

The armaments business is not less defensible than any other enterprise of a business character, the power companies, or the milk processors, or the patent medicine racketeers! It is operated on the same broad principles that give driving force to the whole of the business economy. Its ruling purposes are profit-making. Its methods are scrupulously businesslike. Its indifference to human welfare is complete. What more can be said about any other respectable business?

On every front where the interests of business are in any way endangered, the United States Government under the leadership of Franklin D. Roosevelt is making unprecedented military preparations. Liberal sentiment of pre-War vintage in the United States would have decried the measures of the present Administration as the height of Prussian chauvinism. But liberalism was smothered to death in the embrace of Woodrow Wilson and his "New Freedom." Without serious opposition, except from a small group of radicals who are themselves divided many ways, the forces of business reaction busily prepare to defend their interests by arms against aroused and hungry masses at home or against rivals for their markets abroad. When education and diplomacy cease to function as adequate protective arms of the business-state, the army and the navy stand ready for duty.

CHAPTER XXIII

Does American Business Need Fascism?

"I FORECAST FASCISM TODAY FOR THE UNITED STATES," said Roger Babson, business counsellor extraordinary, in an address delivered at the annual National Business Conference at Babson Park in the fall of 1933. "As the political, material or scientific advance gets too far ahead of the spiritual advance, then civilization temporarily gets out of balance. The inevitable result has been dictatorship. . . . This dictatorship will take the form of Fascism. Who the dictator will be no one knows. . . . The important thing for all is that the dictator shall be spiritually-minded and absolutely unselfish with good judgment and indomitable courage. In short I do not worry about Communism, Socialism, Capitalism or Labor Unionism. The American people will stand these selfish class conflicts for only a short time longer. Then they will rise in their wrath, clean out all selfish groups and substitute an impartial dictator who will give each group its proper place in the development of the nation. This dictator will continue in power until people again come to their senses and catch up spiritually and intellectually with the progress which they had heretofore made along other lines. Yes, statistics clearly indicate that we now are in an economic revolution of which the Blue Eagle will become the symbol of the New Era under Fascism." [1] These words come from America's most successful statistical crystal-gazer. They are a strange mixture of forthright business reaction and high-flown sentiments about spirituality—the very *potpourri* out of which the fascist mind is made.

Mr. Babson does not limit himself to prediction on the subject of fascism. In his recent volume, the *New Dilemma,* Mr. Babson places himself personally on record as favoring fascism as a kind of last resort, describing it as "a drug to relieve the pain temporarily and help the patient from committing suicide while he is out of his head."

Behind any reactionary business development there must be the economic driving force of business necessity, the same force which has, beneath all of its variegated camouflage, dictated the course of Western society and its component national units during the past 150 years. This *necessity* of business has itself been the dictating principle which has at one time called for freedom (so-named), and at another time for forcible regimentation. The dictatorship of business in the early days of the industrial revolution found "freedom" a useful social and ideological instrument with which to tear down the obstructions left in its path by the landed monopoly of feudalism. The dictatorship of business necessity in these latter times finds this "freedom" itself an impediment to the facility of its rule, and turns to regimentation under its ægis as the more useful social and ideological instrument with which to carry out its abiding purposes. Business possesses an almost divine astuteness which makes the wrath of man to praise it. Discontent generated by the inequities of business itself may for an indeterminate period be turned to the service of the pervasive business purpose. In the matter of governing, 150 years of experience have left modern business rulers with a large residue of knowledge concerning the retention and exercise of power, as well as with an exaggerated conception of their abilities and importance.

The words of H. N. Brailsford, written of Great Britain, are applicable to the United States. "I take it," writes Brailsford, "that in the present phase of capitalist development, property must control the state for positive purposes, *indisputably and without a break.* From that minimum that is necessary to secure this end the British propertied class will not shrink." [2] [Italics ours.] From that minimum necessity of regimentation and repression, the propertied class of any capitalist country will not shrink.

The liberal, of whatever stripe, holds that the propertied class under the pressure of persuasion and sweet reasonableness *will* shrink from the necessary minimum of forcible regimentation and repression, or at least the American liberal, pleading special traditions of Anglo-Saxon democracy and freedom, holds this to be true of the *American* propertied class. Liberalism as a philosophy is thus vacuum-packed and dated. Its historical and economic basis was a capitalist necessity which no longer exists. The liberal in consequence is one of those ideological survivals now entirely unattached to any contemporary economic necessity.

Remembering those who scoff at the possibility of fascism in the United States on the ground of *our* sound political and democratic instincts, it is pertinent to recall that, on the very eve of the Nazi dictatorship in Germany, liberal aversion to extreme reaction betrayed many a liberal observer into a groundless optimism concerning the disposition of the political question in the Reich. In October, 1932, the distinguished political analyst, H. V. Kaltenborn, wrote:

"Fundamentally the German's political instinct is sound. Give the German people such a choice as that between Hitler and Hindenburg and the great majority makes the right decision even at a time when passion might displace reason. Hot-headed youth, unemployed, discouraged, disgusted, has gone Fascist or Communist, but not the middle-aged burgher or his frau.... From time to time, although less often than this year, there will be an election which will justify itself by proving that the sober German majority is unwilling to accept the panaceas offered by Communism and Hitlerism." [3]

History required less than six months to reveal the fundamental error in Mr. Kaltenborn's observation—an error rooted in the typically liberal disposition to ignore the real nature and power of social forces that are at work in a crisis-ridden business society.

In less than twelve months, Mr. Kaltenborn had the extremely unpleasant experience of personally witnessing a wanton attack upon his own son by Nazi Storm Troopers on the streets of Berlin.[4]

The liberal suffers in judgment from lack of historical perspective and social realism. His rational propensities betray him into a somewhat mystical faith in "democracy." Men *ought* to be well balanced, good-natured, and endowed with common sense, reasons the liberal; therefore, they *will* be and, when faced with any kind of attack upon their group interests, they *will* reject the irrational alternative. That such rationalism is without foundation in experience escapes the liberal's notice. Affectionately embracing eighteenth-century rationalism and nineteenth-century evolution, the liberal is self-assured of the principle of evolutionary social progress and refuses to entertain the thought of stark and brutal retrogression, until the accomplished fact provides him with plenty of disillusionment but with no remedy within the limits of his liberal philosophy. Germany itself was full of liberal observers who, like Mr. Kaltenborn, underestimated the power and meaning of the Nazi movement. Their incredulity concerning the imminence of fascist rule persisted to the very day of the Nazi triumph. Incredulity is no bulwark against the development of a fascist movement either in Germany or in the United States. On the contrary, it lends at least a negative assistance to such a movement by treating too lightly the menace of extreme reaction. Between 1930 and 1933, when the threat of Nazism had become definite, it was one of the boasts of German anti-fascist leaders that *Germans were not Italians.* The fact has now been recorded that German opposition to Nazism collapsed with less resistance than did Italian opposition to the Black Shirts of Mussolini. Liberals today are in the habit of asserting that *Americans are not Germans;* the class war may be waged among Europeans, but not among Americans. Most of the liberals, however, were found prepared to applaud the establishment of Roosevelt's Reich.

The liberal also objects that the owning class lacks the necessary homogeneity to act in concert for the defense of its interests. "One fails to see how such a sprawling mass, riddled with conflicting interests, can solidify into a purposeful dictatorship," says Stuart Chase.[5] There are emphatically some matters, however, in whicn owners are quick to sympathize with and support one another. The class consciousness and solidarity of capitalists is far more pronounced than is the class consciousness or solidarity of workers. The *exposure* of a "culprit" in the business world is almost always castigated by his fellow business men as scandalmongering or muckraking. Thus, for example, *Business Week,* a McGraw-Hill publication, speaks through its Washington correspondent concerning the congressional investigation which has laid bare some of the dealings and methods of the traffickers in death-appliances: "Congressional scandalmongering with munitions makers as subjects of attack continues to embarrass the State Department. Secretary Roper thinks lurid headlines resulting may hurt our foreign trade. But Congressional committees love this sort of development so well that experienced Washington does not expect departmental protests to interrupt. Cancelled contracts resulting from the Senate's investigation already have separated several thousand American workmen from payrolls. The number promises to grow greater, as the munitions manufacturers in self-defense are preparing to show the extent to which palm-greasing enters into business with foreign countries."[6] Note the touching manner in which reference is made to the unfortunate removal of "several thousand American workmen from payrolls!" This feeling of solidarity among business men including the exposed munitions makers is well-founded, for the difference in business methods and purposes between the munitions makers and other departments of the business enterprise is negligible.

Another McGraw-Hill publication, *Electrical Merchandising,* having indulged in a few uncomplimentary remarks concerning Samuel Insull, proceeds to negate its adverse comments with the following fulsome eulogy of the man whose activities wheedled thousands of the gullible out of a hundred million dollars: "He did a very great deal for this industry and for the public. He gave opportunity to thousands, lightened the labor of millions. He rendered a dollar's worth of human service for a kopec of personal profit. Then he made mistakes—his house of cards fell down. But the constructive, the creative work he did still stands, and I say we should stick up for him." [7]

Even the comic strips in the daily newspapers are utilized as a medium of propaganda on behalf of the wealthy who fall into the custody of government charged with financial irregularities. At the very time that Samuel Insull was being brought back from his exile in the Ægean Sea to stand trial, "Little Orphan Annie" who appears in 135 daily newspapers was set to maligning blustering and brutal prosecutors who frame big-time bankers on baseless charges of defrauding the public.[8]

Class consciousness is deep-rooted in the owning-rulers of America and expresses itself in countless ways. These rulers and their satellites of the press and the professions consistently refer to themselves as a class set apart from workers and others who are outside the inner circle of privilege.

Editor & Publisher, speaking of an injustice which a manufacturer had done to an upper executive in his concern, remarked that the victim of the injustice was treated with "no more consideration than a common laborer." [9] It is common practice to dismiss common, *i.e.,* déclassé, laborers summarily and without cause. High executives belong to another class, the class of privilege, and deserve a different sort of justice at the hands of that class.

The *Journal* of the American Dental Association, spiritedly maintaining that the value of dental services is measured by the public appreciation of the size of the dentists' fees, insists that fees shall be such as to set dentists apart from common day laborers "minus any brains." [10] *Class* differentials in income are among the most fixed assumptions of business philosophy. They are among the things taken for granted, often without any consciousness of their social significance. Imagine, for example, a tobacco farmer or a Negro stevedore reading in *Editor & Publisher* that the salary of the editor and founder of the *Manchester Guardian* was a "nominal" one of $12,500.[11]

The Cunard-White Star Line, advertising in the New York *Times,* pictures the maid of some well-to-do gadabout calling up a friend, probably the maid next door, and saying excitedly, "They're going first class again." The great Atlantic steamship company assures the readers of the advertisement that "news like that does get around." [12] Presumably the verification of *class status,* through neighborhood chat, is an important consideration in booking an oceanic passage, more important than the service made available by any particular category of accommodations.

Professor John S. Gambs, of Columbia University, expresses the typical business view that "modern industrialism and modern society are almost identical." [13] Business is not only class conscious, but in its own thinking it is *the* class, which entitles it to assume all governmental functions and to identify itself with "modern society." All others are outcasts. "Business must govern," exclaims the editor of *Oil, Paint and Drug Reporter.*[14]

The case for the existence of a strong sense of class solidarity among business men does not rest, however, upon isolated examples of the kind we have instanced. In the state of California, a short while ago, one of America's foremost writers obtained a following on the basis of a program which frightened the rulers of that state into apoplectic anxiety. With apologies to the famous exposer of the meat-packers of a generation ago, it must be stated in all frankness that the EPIC program of Upton Sinclair was something in the nature of proposing to give putrefied meat a treatment with sodium sulphite. The rotten scheme of things in California, or elsewhere, may be deodorized and brightened up a bit by such treatments, but the state of putrefaction is only masked, not remedied, thereby. Granting the mildness or the futility of the EPIC program, the attitude of business California toward it should be an object lesson to all those who believe that business men are incapable of cohesion and collective defense.

They swept into action with a solidarity and a determination that left no doubts about their capacities for a united counter-attack against even the mildest of threats. Every business in the state was arrayed on the side opposing Sinclair. Something like $1,000,000 was set aside as a campaign fund to defeat the EPIC candidate. Every newspaper in the state, with one small exception, joined the anti-Sinclair forces. Differences between the Democratic and the Republican labels in journalism were shown to be, what many have always known them to be, devoid of all rational meaning. Sinclair's own Democratic label was a fluke, and the Democratic bosses of California knew it. After all, what's a little thing like an overwhelming popular mandate at the polls? Democrats are not made that way. A true Democratic candidate for the governorship in California must be anointed in the name of Farley, Roosevelt and Creel. A half million "sovereign" voters who went through the motions of "choosing" a candidate at the primaries should know now that unless they vote *right,* business and business politicians will veto their decision—either by profound silence or by forthright opposition. The business opposition to Sinclair inside the state of California was not expressed in the dignified silence of Hyde Park but in the most shrieking accents of enraged despots unaccustomed to any challenge to their will. Twenty-one thousand billboards up and down the state of California warned of the shocking perils that would descend upon the citizenry with Sinclair in the governor's chair. Business owns the billboards! Anti-Sinclair radio programs, disguised as entertainment, were broadcast under the direction of Lord & Thomas, that great advertising firm of Albert D. Lasker.[15] Fake bills, "Red Currency," marked as good only in California and Russia, were distributed everywhere. News reels, hundreds of them, showed simple-minded old men and women declaring their love of God and fear of Upton Sinclair, or depicted throngs of hoboes flooding across the state's borders in anticipation of the election of Sinclair. Business set research workers at the task of proving from Sinclair's own writings that he was an enemy of God. Aimee Semple

McPherson thundered her implications, imprecations and inspirations from the pulpit of Angelus Temple that Sinclair was Anti-Christ and that Merriam was the vicegerent of God on earth. Nothing was left undone that needed to be done to save the state of California for business, righteousness and sunkist justice. Here was no "sprawling mass, riddled with conflicting interests," but a complete solidification of business interests into a purposeful drive. If anything more had been required, California would not have lagged behind Louisiana or Prussia in the use of the multiform pressures which are in the possession of business men to enforce their sovereign will.

There is no denying that business is, in some of its aspects and stages, a competitive enterprise, and that business men fall upon one another with carnivorous intent in the pursuance of some of their ends. Big business strangles little business; and business giants grapple together in mortal combat; but in the presence of a real or fancied danger from the discontent of the despoiled and impoverished masses there is a concert of business action which suspends all hostilities in the common purpose of self-preservation. The "red network" of revolution in the United States is purely mythical, as anyone acquainted with the squabbles of the "revolutionary" groups well knows; but the black network of reaction is the prime force in a threatened business society. Ignorance of the existence of this force is the nullifying factor in the philosophy of liberalism. In the presence of any formidable opposition to the reign of property and profits, General Motors and Henry Ford could easily discover their transcendent mutuality; *Super-Suds* and *Rinso* (now pitted against each other in litigation) could dissolve amicably in the same dishwater; William Green and Owen D. Young could fraternize with brotherly deference; Franklin Delano Roosevelt and Herbert Clark Hoover could find their identity of interests greatly outweighing the tweedledee-tweedledum of their political parties' slogans.

If and when the exigencies of business seem to require the use of extreme coercion and repression, both upon the minds and bodies of men, there is an easily discoverable class interest around which business men will organize. There are no deterring factors in American traditions or in the social viewpoint of business men which may be counted on to preserve even the already highly attenuated freedom of "democratic" capitalism. Certain it is that liberalism, having lost its eighteenth-century economic basis, is neither an intellectual nor an economic force of any consequence in the coming struggle for power.

We have no desire to indulge in a repeated thwacking of liberalism in a manner which is disproportionate to its importance. The frequency of reference to liberalism and liberals in our discussion is necessitated by the all-important fact that this archaic philosophy seriously deflects much potentially useful criticism and fighting energy of informed intellectuals into channels of futility or outright reaction. Business, in its most desperate hour of need, will be deeply indebted to all varieties of liberalism and to such leaders of liberal thought as Tugwell, Berle, Bliven, Warbasse, Villard, Keezer and Douglas for their having softened or misdirected the attack upon it.

Among the most eminent American exponents of liberalism in economics and government today is the Under-Secretary of Agriculture, Professor Rexford Guy Tugwell, whose *Industrial Discipline*[16] was published shortly after the inauguration of Mr. Roosevelt. Mr. Tugwell, like most liberals, posits an ideally indivisible social interest. "Government," he writes, "may or may not be a thing which represents this social interest; it is clear, however, that it ought to be." Why "ought"? Whose imperative is this? Certainly it is not an accepted imperative of business men who, from the beginning of organized government in their behalf, have taken a quite opposite view of the function of the state. The most that can be made out of Mr. Tugwell's statement is that it would be nice if government did represent the paramount social interest in which he believes. Closer association with the mechanism of government and with business men, after he wrote *Industrial Discipline,* may or may not have led Mr. Tugwell to abandon this view of the possibilities of government; it is clear, however, that it ought to have done so.

The mistakes of liberals in their analysis of business society are not so many petty deviations which may be benevolently ignored. For, in some of their most important aspects, they lead straight into the worst forms of reactionary repression. Mr. Tugwell speaks of a possible emergency in which government may properly find it necessary to "compel or persuade a higher cooperation for a national purpose." Mussolini and Hitler would be hard pressed to give a better definition of their fundamental philosophies. What if the "national purpose" turns out to be, in *all* emergencies, what it was in the World War, simply the collective interest of the financial and industrial racketeers? If the indivisible social interest is a myth, and in its stead we have the reality of irreconcilably conflicting social classes, it follows that any "national purpose" will be defined with reference to the exclusive interests of the national plunderers. Mr. Tugwell's formula, therefore, becomes a measure for compelling all to serve the interests of the few who hold the power in his government as in all previous ones.

The liberal differs somewhat from the rousing patriot in his nationalism, though not as fundamentally as might appear on the surface. In times of emergency, he joins hands with the blind patriot in demanding the unqualified loyalty of all to interests that are vital only to the Rockefellers, the Morgans, and the du Ponts. During the World War many liberals appeared to be doing penance for their pre-War criticism of social institutions by outpatrioteering the regular patriots.

Slightly to the "left" of the liberals stand the social democrats who play a rôle similar to that of the liberals in preparing the way for fascist reaction. The social democrat accepts the principle of collaboration with business which implies an underlying acceptance of the idea of the paramount social interest. He is at one with the liberal in his belief that the "democratic" form of capitalism permits of the profound change of social institutions from a profit economy to a non-profit economy. His analysis of the state corresponds exactly to the liberal's analysis, namely, that the existing state machinery may be captured by an anti-capitalist electorate and used for purposes that are diametrically opposite to those for which the "democratic" instruments of capitalist government were evolved. In one important respect, however, the social democrat differs markedly from the liberal. He cherishes a bitterness and vindictiveness toward the Soviet Government of Russia, such as the liberal rarely finds congenial to his temper. The hatred of the social democrats for the Soviet Union and for all communist parties adhering to the Third International may have an historical basis in which all the issues were not perfectly clear, but, in effect, it fits them to be in the vanguard of the counter-revolutionary attack upon the Soviet Union. It is not surprising to find Algernon Lee speaking at an anti-Soviet rally along with Isaac Don Levine, America's foremost anti-Soviet publicist.[17] Lee is the head of the Rand School, educational center of the Socialist Party of New York, and also among the most prominent leaders of the Socialist Party in the state of New York. When better counter-revolutionaries are made, the Rand School and the Socialist Party of New York will make them.

Whether or not American business needs fascism depends entirely upon whether or not the present forms of governmental control continue to serve measurably well the fundamental interests of America's propertied class. At present, little more could be desired by the plunderers of society than that which they have in the policies of the Roosevelt Administration. As long as this is true, there is not likely to be any sharp break in the traditional governmental forms of exploitation. *Peaceful* appropriation of the common wealth is infinitely to be desired over the thoroughly violent method. Large incomes are now rising; and a million new families have been added to the relief rolls since the inauguration of Mr. Roosevelt. The new trade associations, relieved of most of the restrictions of the anti-trust laws, have full freedom of action; and the masses of the electorate have expressed their decisive preference for the "New Deal." Why, therefore, bother with fascism, asks the business man, when the American way is better—at least for the present infinitely better for the defense of his institutions than any European plan of which he has heard?

But the conditions of the present moment are not of assured permanence. "Emergency is over—crisis is here," says Kenneth M. Goode, experienced spokesman of business.[18] With all the enormous expenditures of government in its efforts to "prime the business pump," millions are still unemployed; twenty million are still on relief; the productive plant of industry is still far from normal functioning; the lower middle class is still being squeezed; farmers have not yet had a taste of equalization of their prices with those of. industrial goods; and goods are not being moved either with satisfaction to the profit-seekers or to the advantages of increased and healthful consumption by the masses.

All the elements necessary for a first-rate regime of fascist reaction are present in American tradition or in American social forces of the day. That they have not yet coalesced into a nation-wide movement of overt business dictatorship is due solely to a few minor mitigating circumstances in the American crisis. One by one these mitigating circumstances are being liquidated, with a resulting drift of the most pronounced tendencies toward fascism. Mr. Roosevelt continues to speak of a richer, more abundant life for all, while his policies and those of the business world which he serves effectuate a poorer one for all but the small group of property owners at the top.

From a wide variety of sources we have shown that business and government aim chiefly at the restoration of large profits. Remington Rand announces that it "takes pride in the fact that one of its chief functions is to help business make a profit," and that "business has more than a *right* to make profit—it has an *obligation* to make profit." [19] Raymond Moley declares, rightly, that "this Administration is as far from socialism or communism as any group ever assembled in a national government." Mr. Moley also makes it clear to business men (others never had occasion to doubt it) that the President "directly and indirectly has asserted his belief in the profit system." [20] A very wide circle of those who are outside the benefits of the profit system, as well as those who are its largest beneficiaries, inquire naïvely how a system could be run without the motivation of profit. If the functioning of American economic society depended upon the motivation of profit, it would long ago have stopped altogether inasmuch as the overwhelming majority of the population have never had any occasion to view profit as a personal concern. . . . Some years ago the head-hunting tribes of Borneo were visited by outsiders who entreated them to give up the practice of collecting human skulls. The visitors were met with the astonished inquiry of how a society could be motivated by any other endeavor sufficiently powerful to keep its social organization functioning. Profit would be a poor and inhuman substitute to offer the denizens of the Borneo jungles, but profit and head-hunting alike possess any powers of motivation solely because success in the acquisition of money here and skulls there confers the highest social prestige in these respective communities. . . . Profit is still pirate king in the Western world, and it is the underlying generative force of fascism or any other form of business dictatorship.

The rococo front of business becomes increasingly garish, bedizened and fraudulent. "Everything today from mouth washes to organized charity," says a writer in *The Executive Purchaser,* "is put over by advertising and ballyhoo." [21] The degree and character of development in modern advertising make it an indispensable technique for supporting the extremes of business reaction. The present occupant of the White House is incomparably the most superior advertiser among the presidents of the United States, and he has repeatedly utilized his advertising talents to obtain popular support for reactionary policies. Allyn B. McIntire, president of the Association of National Advertising, rightly discerns that modern advertising is integrally related to the whole of the capitalistic system. "Before I shall countenance on the part of anyone a full sweeping and complete condemnation of all advertising you must answer for me what seems a much more important question," says Mr. McIntire. "Is the capitalistic system to go? Is the profit motive to be removed from all business?" [22] Mr. McIntire is perfectly correct; any effective assault upon the wholesale mendacity of advertising is an attack upon the capitalist system and the profit motive.

High pressure sales tactics? A new one is found in the cradle of business every minute. The birth rate in sales tactics must keep pace with the population growth in suckerdom. *The number of customer-suckers in business society is exactly equal to the potential numerical support upon which business may call when it needs to put over fascism.*

Every sucker is, among other things, an actual or a potential gadgeteer. Since we wrote the chapter on gadgets, we have found a new gadget or gadget appeal daily. Goods are not moved in a business society in response to need and utility. Increasing difficulty in moving goods keeps the gadget makers and button-pusher engineers busily occupied devising new toys for the impressionable. "Four fans for every home is G-E objective," says a trade announcement. Current campaigns for air-conditioning are said to have made the public "comfort conscious." But air-conditioning is still "skimming the cream of the class market," and so the "skimmed milk" of business society must for the time being at least humor its "comfort consciousness" with four electric fans in every home.[23] We have not the slightest complaint to make concerning engineering skill *per se* or the comfort it is capable of providing for all, but we do perceive that all modern technical skills are misdirected for sales purposes with the result that gadgetry has brought a deluge of useless articles whose novelty alone sells them; and we do know that, in any such scheme, utility and comfort for the vast majority are accidental by-products of technology.

Idolatrous consumption, through the testimonializing of the

great and the near-great, is still profitable, as the weekly additions to the list of testimonializers indicate. A Fifth Avenue store is currently advertising that it has a supply of the Christmas card that their Majesties, the King and Queen of England, are sending out this yuletide. Is it possible that the suckers get a taste of royalty in such idolatry? If so, what possible rational consideration could prevent them from embracing fascism when business men need it?

The superstitions of science in Germany and the United States are running a close race. From Germany comes the announcement of a "biological discovery" to the effect that "the blood corpuscles of Jews are quite different in form from those of Nordics." The author of this announcement states that "the establishment of this fact by microscopic investigation has been deliberately prevented" hitherto.[24] Or is it only that plenty of Jewish *and* Nordic blood has been available for scientific investigation since the advent of the Hitler rule? The Nazi discovery of difference in the blood corpuscles of Jews and Nordics may well be in the same scientific class as the hormone-like substances lately discovered in yeast and the wonderful energy-giving qualities of cigarettes about which we are now reading in practically every magazine published. Science, long inured to the whoredom of business, is ready, like any economic parasite, to be the loyal slut of fascism. American science has been a faithful hussy to business, and could, if occasion arises, "find" that no communist corpuscles came over in the *Mayflower*.

The counterfeiters of what our money buys are still at large, and the Department of Justice has not even thought of apprehending them. One of the latest reports which has come to hand shows that some of the "all-wool" commodities on the market contain as much as 80 per cent cotton, and that "all-wool" generally is so adulterated that the situation constitutes the grossest fraud.

Against a system of intelligible and honest grading, the whole business oligarchy has set itself with a grim determination to prevent consumers from buying on specifications or in the light of stated qualities. The canners have recently announced that they occupy "the first line of defense for the whole of business" against any such encroachments of consumers.

It is the core of American business to accelerate the flow of goods by speeding up the rate of obsolescence on the one hand or to check the flow by the sabotage of invention and productivity on the other hand—both in the interests of anti-consumer profits. Sir Josiah Stamp, director of the Bank of England and head of the largest railway in that country, recently warned science "to put a brake on the rush of new inventions before it wrecked the whole economic order." [25] To permit the masses to consume in abundance and quality will certainly wreck the system of those who live to gather in the spondulics. But as a matter of fact, Sir Josiah's warning is hardly necessary, as business has one foot on the brake for use when needed and the other foot on the accelerator when more speed in the turnover of goods is required.

Every day brings reports of new fatalities among the users of the poisonous goods which business finds it profitable to foist upon the unknowing. Three-year-old Edward Phillip Moore died on December 3, 1934, in Richmond, California, from a dose of his mother's reducing medicine which he slipped into his glass of milk. Little Edward was given the milk by his mother and when she returned a few minutes later he announced with childish pride, "I've taken some of your medicine." The child died in convulsions in a few hours.[26] The pulp magazines which circulate by the million among the credulous multitudes carry more advertisements of these reducing nostrums than of any other single commodity. The slayers of Edward Phillip Moore had not been taken into custody "when we went to press." As a matter of fact the laws against murder do not cover this and many other varieties of profitable homicide. It will be remembered that the administrator of the Food and Drugs Act reported that he was powerless in such cases as Edward's and could only *warn* against numerous deadly potions which are being vended.

Business is a highly complex and well integrated series of frauds, utilizing methods, both in its production and distribution, which are indistinguishable in spirit and effects from the practices of gangsterism, except that the effects of business are far more socially devastating than are those of the racketeers outside the pale of law. Business mechanisms are not without their internal difficulties, and its course, viewed in the long perspective, resembles the downward spiral motion of a whirlpool. The author of the book entitled "We Have Recovered Before," would, if he had taken the longer view, have written under the title "Civilizations Have Sunk Before." Business men and college economists forget that history has its epochs as well as its episodes. But most rulers have been immured to long historical perspective. Some day, if not in the immediate future, the confident assertion, "We Have Recovered Before," on the lips of business men, will sound like the optimism of a drowning man who, having come up twice, accepts his repeated good fortune as scientific demonstration that he cannot sink.

The real tragedy of a system in its last crisis lies in the fact that it throws great blind and uncontrollable social forces into motion. The miseducated and misled masses become, in their politically illiterate groping, the terrible instrument of sinister forces that use them and then turn and despoil them further. It is an awful thing to bestir the lower middle class from its customary doltish political placidity. Out of its psychiatric depths arises an ashen terror with strong overtones of homosexual sadism suggestive of appetites and powers too long in leash. Italy and Germany have both witnessed, in the first flush of fascist power, this social phenomenon in forms to which the lower middle class in America has long been accustomed at its lynching bees. Advertising has done nothing if it has not played with criminal emphasis upon both the sex-motif and the power-motif of multitudes that ordinarily have no adequate or socially useful outlet for these deep-lying human drives. The full truth of the fascist terror in unleashing these drives upon the scapegoat of middle class civilization has not been adequately publicized. Nor has the truth of America's lynchings gone far beyond the knowledge of the ghoulish mob itself. It is well-known that the mob's victims are usually stripped bare before the final torture to death, but it is not so well-known that the torture often begins with the sex organs. A member of the lynching mob which did Claude Neal to death in Florida on October 26, 1934, has given the following description of the killing:

"After taking the nigger to the woods about four miles from Greenwood, they cut off his penis. He was made to eat it. Then they cut off his testicles and made him eat them and say he liked it. Then they sliced his sides and stomach with knives and every now and then somebody would cut off a finger or toe. Red hot irons were used on the nigger to burn him from top to bottom." [27]

An "enterprising" local photographer made pictures of the nude and mutilated body of the Negro and sold them in large quantities at fifty cents each. The mob into whose hands the authorities of Alabama and Florida "conspired" to deliver Claude Neal numbered between five and seven thousand white Americans who assembled from eleven Southern states on the invitation of the local Florida citizenry. All of this occurred in the United States in the year 1934.

Farmers and labor, while consistently and persistently despoiled by the rulers of business society, are not in revolt against the system itself. Where mass organization exists among them, it is largely misled by careerists and bureaucrats who are themselves staunch allies and collaborators with business. With William Green and Matthew Woll busying themselves requesting Congress to curb the "reds," [28] and asking the President to refuse the Soviet Government recognition, business men are relieved to a degree of the need to carry on one of their normal activities.

Civil liberties have always been unequally available to the groups that constitute American society. A Special Commission of the National Labor Board recently issued a report on conditions in the Imperial Valley in California which reveals how lightly some sections of the population regard the civil liberties which are supposed to be a part of the fundamental law of the land. "We uncovered," said the commission, "sufficient evidence to convince us that in more than one instance the law was trampled under foot by representative citizens of Imperial County and by public officials under oath to support the law." There is little that is unique in regard to suppression of civil liberties in the reign of terror against the workers of California. It is a substantial part of American tradition for the ruling class to practice terror against dissidents and minorities.

The call to fascism is being repeatedly sounded by prematurely uneasy business men. "The zero hour has arrived," writes Floyd W. Parsons, editor of *Advertising & Selling,* "when all our people, irrespective of party affiliations, who reverence this country's traditions and achievements, must unite under some strong leadership that has a definite plan, a deep sense of patriotism, methods that are practical and direct, and a proper understanding of the urgent necessity for dispelling fear instead of meeting it with ridicule." [29] The call of the first lieutenant is not heeded because it is unauthorized from the generals higher up. When the Morgans, the Rockefellers, the du Ponts, the Sloans and the Youngs decide that severer measures of repression and regimentation are required to maintain the system of legalized spoliation of workers and consumers, then the bogus democracy of business' covert dictatorship will be discarded for the iron rule of the overt dictatorship of steel, oil, Cellophane, motors and electricity. The order from above waits only upon the arrival of general economic conditions which are conducive to the complete coalescence of reactionary elements now present in the American social *milieu.* In the matrix of every capitalist democracy, fascism and an economy of abundant quality are struggling

for primogeniture. In the light of present social forces and align-
ments in America, there can scarcely be any doubt that fascism
will be the first-born of the crisis, unless unforeseen realignments
suddenly occur through a rapid acceleration of the processes of
economic and political enlightenment.

The recovery which is now being sought under the policies of
the "New Deal" is one which aims at the restoration of the very
defects which are responsible for the present plight of capitalist
society. For that reason it is accurately named "recovery." Though
often described as "revolution" it is not even "reformation." The
essential property relationships of the profit-system have not in
any important respect been disturbed. The effect of the policies
of the "New Deal," waiving the question of their purposes, has
been to tighten the grip of big business upon the system. Profits
have, in consequence, begun to increase at substantial rates, while
wages in terms of purchasing power have actually decreased,
the statistics of Mr. Richberg to the contrary notwithstanding.
"Recovery" is therefore taking place rapidly. During the two
years of the "New Deal" there have been major increases in the
following things: dividends, deterioration of goods, social insecurity, emergency relief, criminal illogic, pettifoggery and
chicane by responsible officials of state and nation, militarism, and
war perils. Under the unprecedentedly able leadership of a great
salesman, the "New Deal," like the "New Capitalism" before it,
is steadily accentuating every crisis-characteristic of the economy
of scarce inferiority. Capitalism cannot survive under the conditions of any other economy, and it is to the survival of capitalism
that the forces of the "New Deal" have been solemnly dedicated
on the altar of salesmanship. New and unparalleled crises are in
preparation as the vacuum center of the whirlpool sucks its witless
victims downwards.

NOTES AND REFERENCES

CHAPTER I. *Profit Is Pirate King*

1 Adam Smith, *The Wealth of Nations* (Fourth Edition of Edwin Cannan; London: Methuen & Co., 1925), II, p. 159.
2 New York *Times,* September 22, 1932.
3 New York *Times,* January 7, 1932.
4 Carleton Beals, *The Crime of Cuba* (Philadelphia: Lippincott, 1933), p. 364.
5 New York *Times,* August 23, 1934.
6 New York *Times,* April 24, 1934.
7 New York *Times,* October 6, 1934.
8 New York *Herald Tribune,* October 6, 1934.
9 C. F. Hughes, New York *Times,* September 9, 1934.
10 Floyd W. Parsons, "Everybody's Business," *Advertising & Selling,* August 16, 1934, p. 56.
11 Parsons, *op. cit.,* p. 56.
12 *Nation's Business,* August, 1934, p. 70.
13 New York *Herald Tribune,* October 1, 1934.
14 *Editor & Publisher,* August 4, 1934, p. 38.
15 *News-Week,* September 1, 1934.
16 *Business Week,* August 4, 1934, p. 12.
17 *Nation's Business,* October, 1934, p. 21.
18 Statement by W. H. Baker, *Electric Refrigeration News,* August 8, 1934, p. 5.
19 Editorial, *Electric Refrigeration News,* August 8, 1934, p. 8.
20 *Electric Refrigeration News,* August 8, 1934, p. 7.
21 Editorial, *Electric Refrigeration News,* August 8, 1934, p. 8.
22 *Electric Refrigeration News,* August 8, 1934, p. 8.
23 *Advertising Age,* March 31, 1934, p. 6.
24 *Confectioners' Journal,* February, 1933.
25 Claude C. Hopkins, *My Life in Advertising* (New York: Harper & Brothers, 1927), p. 101.
26 *Ibid.,* p. 156.
27 Walter Lippmann, "Recovery by Trial and Error," *Yale Review,* Autumn 1934.
28 Willford I. King, New York *Herald Tribune,* August 26, 1934.

29 *Journal of Economic Entomology,* February, 1934, p. 37.

30 F. C. Bishopp, "Insect Rogues Gallery Records Tick's Crime," United States Department of Agriculture, *Press Release,* August 26, 1934.

31 "Mister Morgan," *Fortune,* August, 1933, p. 84.

32 New York *Post,* October 3, 1934.

33 Editorial, "Through the Editor's Specs," *Nation's Business,* September, 1934, p. 11.

34 "Today's Challenge to Sales Executives," *Sales Management,* July 1, 1934.

35 *Manufacturing Chemist,* August, 1934, p. 278.

36 *News-Week,* September 8, 1934, p. 37.

37 *The Open Forum* (Los Angeles), September 15, 1934.

38 New York *Times,* July 4, 1933.

CHAPTER II. *The Rococo Front of Business*

1 Monthly Bulletins, mailed in envelopes from the *Pacific Coast Electric Bureau.*

2 *Pacific Coast Electric Bureau,* August, 1934.

3 New York *Post,* September 5, 1934, p. 8.

4 Hopkins, *My Life in Advertising,* p. 177.

5 *Ibid.,* p. 116.

6 *Ibid.,* p. 7.

7 *Ibid.,* p. 22.

8 *National Printer Journalist,* June, 1934, p. 74.

9 *National Printer Journalist,* June, 1934, p. 74.

10 *National Printer Journalist,* June, 1934, p. 80.

11 Earnest Elmo Calkins, *Editor & Publisher,* July 21, 1934, p. 53.

12 J. P. Derum, "Must Advertising Wear a Halo?" *Advertising & Selling,* September 15, 1932, p. 14.

13 *Advertising & Selling,* August 16, 1934, p. 24.

14 Edgar Kobak, Report of Annual Address, *Ice Cream Trade Journal,* July, 1934, p. 27.

15 *Advertising & Selling,* July 5, 1934, p. 3.

16 *Advertising & Selling,* July 5, 1934, p. 3.

17 Editorial, "Truth in Advertising," *Western Clothier, Hatter and Haberdasher,* July, 1934.

18 *Printers' Ink,* June 21, 1934, p. 116.

19 *Advertising & Selling,* August 2, 1934, p. 23.

20 *Electric Light and Power,* April, 1934.

21 *Printers' Ink,* June 21, 1934, p. 118.

22 James Rorty, "The Consumer vs the NRA," *The Nation*, March 14, 1934.

23 *The Drug and Cosmetic Industry*, July, 1934, p. 13.

24 J. D. Adams, in a letter, *Advertising & Selling*, February 1, 1934, p. 42.

25 *Advertising Age*, March 31, 1934, p. 4.

26 *Advertising Age*, March 31, 1934, p. 1.

27 *Advertising Age*, March 31, 1934, p. 1.

28 Frank E. Fehlman, "Does Advertising Pay During a Depression?" *Advertising & Selling*, May 24, 1934, p. 44.

29 Hopkins, *My Life in Advertising*, p. 103.

30 Albert D. Lasker, *Press Release*, Lord & Thomas, September 25, 1934.

31 Hopkins, *op. cit.*, p. 102.

32 Hopkins, *op. cit.*, p. 101.

33 Hopkins, *op. cit.*, p. 118.

34 *Advertising Age*, August 12, 1933.

35 *Advertising Age*, August 12, 1933.

36 Hopkins, *op. cit.*, p. 143.

37 James L. Palmer, *The Business Education World*, October, 1934, p. 89.

38 Palmer, *op. cit.*, p. 93.

39 *Advertising & Selling*, May 24, 1934, p. 18.

40 Anson Earl Sawyer, in a letter, *Tide*, February, 1934, p. 86.

41 James Mangan, *Advertising Age*, March 31, 1934, p. 4.

42 Mangan, *op. cit.*, p. 4.

43 A *Gimbels* advertisement, New York *Post*, October 9, 1934.

44 A *Conklin Pen* advertisement, *Business Week*, September 15, 1934, p. 34.

45 A *Parker Vacumatic* advertisement, *The New Yorker*, October 20, 1934, p. 64.

46 T. Harry Thompson, "Sampling with Words," *Ice Cream Trade Journal*, July, 1934, p. 19.

47 *Canadian Chemistry and Metallurgy*, June, 1934, p. 137.

48 Indiana Division of Public Health, *Monthly Bulletin*, September, 1934, p. 142.

49 *Manufacturing Chemist*, August, 1934, p. 279.

50 *Advertising Age*, May 26, 1934, p. 22.

51 A *Maggi's Seasoning* advertisement, New York *Times Magazine*, October 14, 1934, p. 14.

52 A *Campbell Soup Company* advertisement, *Time,* June 25, 1934, p. 18.

53 *Time—Letters Supplement,* July 23, 1934, p. 4.

54 *Advertising & Selling,* August 16, 1934, p. 46.

55 J. P. Derum, "Must Advertising Wear a Halo?" *Advertising & Selling,* September 15, 1932, p. 13.

56 A *Northern Tissue* advertisement, *Good Housekeeping,* April, 1934.

57 *New England Journal of Medicine,* August 2, 1934, p. 233.

58 *Tide,* June, 1934, p. 5.

59 "The Diet Racket," *Journal* of the American Dental Association, June, 1934.

60 J. F. Montague, *I Know Just the Thing for That!* (New York: John Day Co., 1934), p. 46.

61 *Ibid.,* p. 47.

62 Mary S. Rose, *Journal* of the American Dietetic Association, July, 1932, p. 133.

63 Agnes Fay Morgan, University of California *Clip Sheet,* October 2, 1934.

64 *The Northwestern Miller,* February 28, 1934, p. 515.

65 *Advertising Age,* July 21, 1934, p. 14.

66 A *Rogers Peet* advertisement, *The New Yorker,* September 1, 1934, p. 35.

67 A *College Inn* advertisement, *The New Yorker,* September 8, 1934, p. 70.

68 K. N. Richardson, *Manufacturing Chemist,* April, 1934, p. 116.

69 Adolf Hitler, *Mein Kampf* (München: 1930), p. 203.

CHAPTER III. *High Pressure—Low Resistance*

1 Walton H. Hamilton, "The Ancient Maxim of Caveat Emptor," *Yale Law Journal,* June, 1931, p. 1136.

2 James L. Palmer, *The Business Education World,* October, 1934, p. 95.

3 New York *Times,* August 12, 1934.

4 New York *Times,* August 12, 1934.

5 "Dollar a Week Payments," *Electrical Merchandising,* June, 1934, p. 54.

6 *National Grocers' Bulletin,* September, 1934, p. 44.

7 *Electric Refrigeration News,* August 1, 1934, pp. 1, 6.

8 Frank B. Rae, Jr., "Get a Load of This!" *Electrical Merchandising,* June, 1934, p. 46.

9 Rae, *op. cit.,* p. 46.

10 *Electrical Merchandising,* July, 1934, p. 24.

11 *Electrical Merchandising,* September, 1934, 58f.

12 *Light,* March-April, 1928, pp. 30-32.

13 Consumers' Research *General Bulletin,* January, 1933, p. 12.

14 Consumers' Research *General Bulletin,* January, 1933, p. 12.

15 *Packaging Record,* February, 1934, p. 14.

16 *The American Druggist,* June, 1934, p. 132.

17 Gerald E. Stedman, "The Surest Closing Method is Demonstration," *Electrical Merchandising,* July, 1934, p. 36.

18 M. T. Bogert, "Your Nose Knows," *The Scientific Monthly,* October, 1934, p. 349.

19 Bogert, *op. cit.,* p. 349.

20 Bogert, *op. cit.,* p. 350.

21 *Advertising Age,* April 28, 1934, p. 12.

22 Walton H. Hamilton, "The Ancient Maxim of Caveat Emptor," *Yale Law Journal,* June, 1931, p. 1135.

23 Edmund P. Learned, "Recent Books on Marketing," *Harvard Business Review,* July, 1934, p. 454.

24 Ray Giles, *Turn Your Imagination into Money* (New York: Harper & Brothers, 1934), condensed in *Reader's Digest,* April, 1934, p. 71.

25 *The American Weekly,* July 29, 1934, p. 5; and *The Practical Druggist and Spatula Consolidated,* August, 1934, p. 18.

26 *The News-Week in Business,* August 11, 1934, p. 30.

27 *A. Stein & Co.,* advertisement in *The Saturday Evening Post,* September 8, 1934, p. 55.

28 Editorial, "Preparedness Against the Strike Hazard," *Electric Refrigeration News,* July 25, 1934, p. 10.

29 *Domestic Commerce,* August 20, 1934, p. 51.

30 *Soap,* August, 1934, p. 16.

31 *Advertising Age,* June 2, 1934, p. 14.

32 Lionel Houser, "Whispers for Sale Here," New York *World-Telegram,* October 18, 1934, p. 7.

33 "Add July," *Tide,* July, 1934, p. 74.

34 Victor Sadd and Robert T. Williams, *Causes of Bankruptcies Among Consumers* (Washington: U. S. Government Printing Office, 1933).

35 Gerald E. Stedman, "Salesmen Are Only 20% Effective," *Electrical Merchandising,* June, 1934, p. 74.

36 *Electrical Merchandising,* July, 1934, p. 39.

37 *Electrical Merchandising,* June, 1934, p. 74.
38 "Sociable Selling," *Business Week,* March 10, 1934, p. 22.

CHAPTER IV. *Gadgetry: A Century of Mechanical Comedy*

1 Editorial, *Electrical Merchandising,* July, 1934, p. 24.
2 A *Lovell Pressure Cleanser* advertisement, *Electrical Merchandising,* June, 1934, p. 21.
3 A *Thor Electric Servant* advertisement, *Electrical Merchandising,* July, 1934, p. 4.
4 *Electrical Merchandising,* September, 1934, p. 23.
5 *The Hotel Monthly,* September, 1934, p. 23.
6 *Electrical Merchandising,* September, 1934, p. 59.
7 *Nation's Business,* September, 1934, p. 50.
8 *Nation's Business,* September, 1934, p. 50.
9 *The Food Field Reporter,* September 10, 1934, p. 38.
10 A *Saks* advertisement, New York *Times,* October 9, 1934.
11 *Pacific Coast Electric Bureau,* September, 1934.
12 C. M. Ripley, *Modernization Promotes Beauty and Order,* marked "GEA-2000."
13 E. S. Lincoln, *The Electric Home* (New York: The Electric Home Publishing Company, 1934), p. 310f.
14 *Review of Reviews and World's Work,* September, 1934, p. 22.
15 *Electric Refrigeration News,* July 18, 1934, p. 12.
16 Editorial, *Electric Refrigeration News,* April 4, 1934, p. 8.
17 *Electric Refrigeration News,* April 4, 1934, p. 8.
18 *Electric Refrigeration News,* August 22, 1934, p. 1.
19 Alfred P. Sloan, Jr., "The Forward View," *Atlantic Monthly,* September, 1934, p. 261.
20 *The Hotel Monthly,* September, 1934, p. 22.
21 *The United States News,* September 24, 1934, p. 9.
22 New York *Post,* September 22, 1934.
23 *Business Week,* September 8, 1934, p. 39.
24 *Public Utilities Fortnightly,* September 13, 1934, p. 320.
25 *Public Utilities Fortnightly,* September 13, 1934, p. 319.
26 *Recent Social Trends* (New York: McGraw-Hill, 1933), II, p. 862.

CHAPTER V. *Confederates of Screen, Stadium, and Salon*

1 *Ladies' Home Journal,* November, 1934, p. 48; and *Advertising & Selling,* October 11, 1934, p. 10.
2 *McCall's Magazine,* November, 1934, p. 148.
3 *The Glass Packer,* June, 1934, pp. 372-373.

4 "109 Smart New Ways to Serve Bread," a booklet published by General Mills, Inc., 1934, p. 47.

5 *McCall's Magazine*, November, 1934, p. 27.

6 *McCall's Magazine*, November, 1934, p. 143.

7 *Ladies' Home Journal*, November, 1934, p. 43.

8 Federal Trade Commission Decisions, No. 843.

9 *Business Week*, October 28, 1933, p. 22.

10 New York *Times*, September 29, 1933.

11 *Time*, August 13, 1934.

12 F. J. Schlink, "Bear Oil," *New Republic*, July 31, 1929, p. 279.

13 *Electric Refrigeration News*, August 1, 1934, p. 10.

14 *McCall's Magazine*, November, 1934, p. 148.

15 *Advertising & Selling*, October 11, 1934, p. 10.

16 *Advertising & Selling*, October 11, 1934, p. 10.

17 Alva Johnston, "Testimonials, C. O. D.," *Outlook and Independent*, reprinted by Consumers' Research.

18 F. J. Schlink, "Bear Oil," *New Republic*, July 31, 1929, p. 279.

19 *Advertising & Selling*, August 16, 1934, p. 31.

20 Alva Johnston, "Testimonials, Wholesale," *Outlook and Independent*, reprinted by Consumers' Research.

21 *Soap*, August, 1934, p. 37.

22 *Ladies' Home Journal*, November, 1934, p. 48.

23 New York *Times*, September 29, 1933.

24 Federal Trade Commission Decisions, No. 843.

25 *Time*, June 19, 1933.

26 *Food Field Reporter*, June 5, 1933.

27 George Sylvester Viereck, *Liberty*, June 24, 1933.

28 *News-Week*, July 7, 1934, p. 24.

29 "109 Smart New Ways to Serve Bread," pp. 40, 55.

30 NRA Release No. 493, August 25, 1933.

31 *Tide*, July, 1934, p. 9.

CHAPTER VI. *Science Lends a Hand*

1 *The New Yorker*, November 3, 1934.

2 *The New Yorker*, June 30, 1934, p. 60.

3 *United States Dispensatory*, p. 10.

4 *Advertising Age*, August 4, 1934, p. 24.

5 *Ledger Dispatch*, April 29, 1932.

6 *Delineator*, November, 1934, p. 77.

7 *Radio Stars*, September, 1934, p. 80.

8 *Time*, July 2, 1934, p. 38.

9 Otis Allen Kenyon, *Theory and Facts of Cigarette Smoking* (Louisville: Axton-Fisher Tobacco Company, 1934), p. 9.

10 New York *World-Telegram,* November 8, 1934, p. 16.

11 *National and American Miller,* April, 1934.

12 *Advertising Age,* May 5, 1934, p. 3.

13 *Western Advertising,* February, 1934.

14 *Western Advertising,* August, 1934.

15 *Western Advertising,* July, 1934.

16 *Food Field Reporter,* October 22, 1934, p. 34.

17 *Business Week,* July 21, 1934, p. 18.

18 New York *Post,* May 2, 1934.

19 *Restaurant Management,* June, 1934, p. 374.

20 *Restaurant Management,* October, 1934.

21 *Ladies' Home Journal,* November, 1934, p. 74.

22 *Ladies' Home Journal,* November, 1934, p. 71.

23 *Ladies' Home Journal,* November, 1934, p. 61.

24 *McCall's,* November, 1934, p. 29.

25 *National Carbonator and Bottler,* June 15, 1934, pp. 13, 14, 36.

26 *National Carbonator and Bottler,* October 15, 1934, p. 12.

27 *Food Industries,* January, 1933, p. 36.

28 Calculated from the advertisement of Howdy Company (St. Louis) in *The Crown of Baltimore,* February, 1934, p. 10.

29 *Woman's Home Companion,* May, 1932, p. 79.

30 *Ladies' Home Journal,* February, 1932, p. 110.

31 *The Saturday Evening Post,* January 16, 1932, p. 83.

32 *Journal* of the American Medical Association, July 16, 1932, p. 241f.

33 *Sphere,* August, 1934, p. 21.

34 Julian Huxley, "If I Were Dictator," *Harper's* Magazine, October, 1934, p. 529.

35 NRA Release No. 493.

36 *New Republic,* August 29, 1934, pp. 76-77.

CHAPTER VII. *Counterfeiters of What Our Money Buys*

1 New York *Times,* September 25, 1934; and October 16, 1934.

2 *Homestead News,* September, 1934, p. 5.

3 F. W. Atack, "The Canadian Food Colour Regulations," *Canadian Chemistry and Metallurgy,* June, 1934, p. 137.

4 "What Future for Glycerin?" *Soap,* August, 1933, p. 23.

5 *Food Manufacture,* September, 1934, p. 313.

6 *Siebel Technical Review,* April, 1934, p. 6.

7 *Siebel Technical Review,* April, 1934, p. 5.

8 "The Consumer and the Farmer—Both Get Gypped," Consumers' Research, February, 1934.

9 *Food Field Reporter,* September 24, 1934, p. 38.

10 *Food Field Reporter,* July 16, 1934, p. 36.

11 *American Druggist,* October, 1934, p. 149.

12 *Journal* of the American Medical Association, October 7, 1933, pp. 1163-1164.

13 G. H. Wray, "The Production of Stable Emulsions," *The Manufacturing Chemist,* June, 1934, p. 198.

14 United States Department of Agriculture, Press Service, Release of July 16, 1934, signed by H. A. Wallace, Secretary.

15 *Industrial and Engineering Chemistry,* July, 1934, pp. 762-764.

16 *Food Field Reporter,* August 13, 1934, p. 10.

17 *Soap,* August, 1934, p. 25.

18 *The Manufacturing Confectioner,* September, 1934, pp. 40-44.

19 *The Analyst,* July, 1934, p. 484.

20 Payson Mackaye, "What Grind for Coffee in Glass?" *The Glass Packer,* October, 1934, p. 646.

21 The Toronto *Daily Star,* May 17, 1934.

22 *The Saturday Evening Post,* October 27, 1934, p. 41.

23 *The Canning Trade,* September 3, 1934, p. 5.

24 *The Canning Trade,* September 24, 1934, p. 21; and November 12, 1934, p. 5.

25 *Food Field Reporter,* October 8, 1934, p. 42.

26 *Industrial and Engineering Chemistry,* September 20, 1934, p. 348.

27 *Food Field Reporter,* August 27, 1934, p. 28.

28 *Food Field Reporter,* September 24, 1934, p. 38.

29 *Food Field Reporter,* October 8, 1934, p. 42.

30 *Drug Trade News,* September 3, 1934, p. 32.

31 *Food Industries,* September, 1934, p. 389.

32 *New Yorker,* April 14, 1934, p. 29.

33 Fred C. Kelly, "How Long Can Hitler Last?" *Today,* October 6, 1934, p. 10.

34 "Notes and Opinions," *The Dyer and Textile Printer,* October 12, 1934, p. 372.

CHAPTER VIII.   *AAA-I Extra Fancy*

1 *Standardization of Consumers' Goods,* a pamphlet of the Chamber of Commerce of the United States; Washington, D. C., 1934.

2 *Advertising Age,* August 18, 1934, p. 22.

3 *Bulletin* of the United States Department of Commerce, August 10, 1934, p. 44.

4 Statement before Group 111 of the Code Authority Conference, March 7, 1934.

5 *A Survey of the Terms Used in Designating Qualities of Goods,* Consumers' Advisory Board, NRA.

6 *Western Advertising,* August, 1934.

7 *Technical News Bulletin,* National Bureau of Standards, September, 1934, p. 82.

8 United States Department of Agriculture, August, 1934.

9 *Tide,* April, 1934, p. 18.

10 *Journal of Commerce,* April 3, 1934, p. 1.

11 *Advertising & Selling,* June 8, 1933.

12 *Society of Automotive Engineers Journal,* October, 1933, p. 18.

13 *American Management Association News Letter,* June 12, 1934.

14 *Food Field Reporter,* September 10, 1934, p. 22.

15 Albert D. Lasker, in a speech in Boston, September 25, 1934.

16 *Food Industries,* September, 1934, p. 392.

17 *Electrical World,* October 15, 1932, p. 522.

18 Walton H. Hamilton, "The Ancient Maxim of Caveat Emptor," *Yale Law Journal,* June, 1931, p. 1135.

CHAPTER IX. *What's in a Name?*

1 *The Manufacturing Confectioner,* September, 1934, p. 55.

2 *Journal* of the American Medical Association, March 31, 1934, p. 1102.

3 *Printers' Ink,* March 29, 1934, p. 66.

4 *The Manufacturing Chemist,* July, 1934, p. 236.

5 *Journal* of the American Dental Association, November, 1933, p. 2079.

6 *Journal* of the American Dental Association, October, 1934, p. 1863.

7 Report (to accompany S. 2800) submitted by Mr. Stephens for Mr. Copeland from the Committee on Commerce, on Foods, Drugs and Cosmetics, Calendar No. 520, Report No. 493, March 15, 1934, p. 14.

8 *Advertising Age,* May 19, 1934, p. 19.

CHAPTER X. *The Junk Heap's the Thing*

1 New York *Times,* March 14, 1934.

2 *High Low Washington* (Philadelphia: Lippincott, 1932), pp. 176-177.

3 *Tide,* July, 1934, pp. 18-19.

4 C. F. Hughes, "The Merchant's Point of View," New York *Times,* July 29, 1934.

5 *Radio News,* September, 1933, p. 161.

6 *Advertising Age,* May 5, 1934, p. 8.

7 *S. A. E. Journal,* October, 1934, p. 16.

8 *S. A. E. Journal,* July, 1934, p. 14.

9 *Kansas State College Bulletin,* June 1, 1934, p. 9.

10 *Advertising & Selling,* September 5, 1928, pp. 19-20.

11 New York *Times,* October 24, 1934.

12 *Electronics,* March, 1934.

13 Sears-Roebuck Catalogue No. 165—Fall and Winter 1932-1933.

14 *Electrical Merchandising,* September, 1934, p. 44.

15 *Advertising Age,* June 23, 1934, p. 28.

16 *Editor & Publisher,* August 11, 1934, p. 6.

17 New York *Times,* November 9, 1934.

CHAPTER XI.   *A Brisk Trade in Poisons*

1 Chicago *Daily News,* October 24, 1934.

2 Springfield (Mo.) *Daily News,* September 22, 1934; and Tulsa (Okla.) *Daily World,* September 20 and 22, 1934.

3 Sixteenth Annual Report of the Illinois Department of Agriculture.

4 Troy (N. Y.) *Times,* November 5, 1934.

5 *British Medical Journal,* February 3, 1934, pp. 233-234.

6 New York *Herald Tribune,* October 22, 1934.

7 C. L. Williams, "Fumigation Deaths as Compared with Deaths from Other Poisonous Gases," United States Public Health Report, June 15, 1934; reviewed in the *Journal of Industrial Hygiene,* September, 1934, p. 98.

8 *Chicago's Health,* June 17, 1930, pp. 133-136.

9 *Synthetic Organic Chemicals,* A Summary of the Products of the Carbide and Carbon Chemicals Corporation, Sixth Edition, August 15, 1934.

10 *Textile World,* August, 1934, pp. 114-115.

11 *Bulletin of Hygiene,* August, 1934, p. 514.

12 *Hygeia,* July, 1934, p. 591.

13 From information issued to subscribers of Consumers' Research.

14 *Journal of Economic Entomology,* February, 1934, p. 129.

15 *New Jersey Farm & Garden,* November, 1934.

16 *Journal of Economic Entomology,* February, 1934, p. 129.

17 R. L. Webster, "The Status of Codling Moth Control with Insecticides," *Journal of Economic Entomology,* February, 1934, p. 138.

18 *Journal of Economic Entomology,* February, 1934, p. 140.

19 J. M. Lutz and G. A. Runner, "Studies on the Removal of Arsenical Spray Residue from Grapes," United States Department of Agriculture, p. 345; Reprinted from Proceedings of the American Society for Horticultural Science, Vol. 29, 1932.

20 W. B. White, "The Current Season's Experience in Enforcing Spray Residue Tolerance," *Journal of Economic Entomology,* February, 1934, p. 131.

21 White, *op. cit.,* p. 131.

22 White, *op. cit.,* p. 125.

23 White, *op. cit.,* p. 126.

24 White, *op. cit.,* p. 133.

25 W. C. Hueper, "Aniline Cancer of the Bladder," *Journal of Industrial Hygiene,* September, 1934, p. 262.

26 Hueper, *op. cit.,* p. 265.

27 Hueper, *op. cit.,* p. 268.

28 Dr. Eric C. Kunz, "Insecticide Odors to Fit Uses," *Soap,* September, 1934, p. 99.

29 *Journal of Industrial Hygiene,* September, 1934, p. 259.

30 District Court, W. D. Washington, N. D. May 23, 1934.

31 Consumers' Research *General Bulletin,* October, 1934, p. 17.

32 *Chemical Abstracts;* from Proceedings of Society for Experimental Biology and Medicine, Vol. 30, 1933, pp. 434-8.

33 New York *World-Telegram,* November 6, 1934.

34 *Rocky Mountain Druggist,* August, 1934.

35 Leonard B. Loeb, "Radium Poisoning in Water," *Journal* of the American Water Works Association, April, 1934, p. 475.

36 *Mechanical Engineering,* September, 1934, pp. 517, 519.

CHAPTER XII. *Druggéd Individualism*

1 Wingate M. Johnson, "Want to Be a Doctor?" *Hygeia,* October, 1934, p. 900.

2 *Journal* of the American Medical Association, Vol. 98, No. 17, April 23, 1932; Proceedings of the American Medical Association Congress on Medical Education, Medical Licensure and Hospitals.

3 *Journal* of the Michigan State Medical Society, November, 1933.

4 *Journal* of the American Medical Association, August 25, 1934, p. 609.

5 "Soviet Medicine Again," American Medical Association *Bulletin*, June, 1934, p. 105.

6 *Practical Druggist and Spatula Consolidated,* July, 1934, p. 9.

7 *Ibid.*, July, 1934, p. 18.

8 *Ibid.*, July, 1934, p. 18.

9 *Ibid.*, August, 1934, p. 36.

10 *Ibid.*, September, 1934, p. 24.

11 *Ibid.*, August, 1934, p. 34.

12 *Monthly Bulletin* of the Indiana Division of Public Health, August, 1934, p. 126.

13 *American Druggist,* September, 1934, p. 120.

14 *Practical Druggist and Spatula Consolidated,* August, 1934, p. 34.

CHAPTER XIII.   *Cycle or Whirlpool?*

1 Ralph E. Flanders, "An End to Unemployment," *Mechanical Engineering,* September, 1934, p. 515.

2 Notice of 55th Annual Meeting of American Society of Mechanical Engineers, December 3-7, 1934.

3 *The Magazine of Wall Street,* September 15, 1934, p. 531.

4 Joseph A. Schumpeter, *Economics of the Recovery Program* (New York: Whittlesey House, 1934), p. 20.

5 Walter W. Price, *We Have Recovered Before!* (New York: Harpers, 1933), p. 101.

6 *Ibid.*, p. 102.

7 New York *Times,* August 12, 1928.

8 New York *Times,* March 5, 1929.

9 Charles A. Beard, *Whither Mankind* (New York: Longmans, 1928), p. 98.

10 *Ibid.*, p. 99.

11 A Dinner Conference at the Hall of Progress, General Motors Building, Century of Progress Exposition Grounds, Chicago, May 25, 1934.

12 Leon Trotsky, *The History of the Russian Revolution* (New York: Simon and Schuster, 1932), Vol. 1, p. 52.

13 *The Nation,* October 24, 1934, p. 483.

14 Boston *Transcript,* November 16, 1934.

15 Leonard P. Ayres, *The Economics of Recovery* (New York: Macmillan, 1933), pp. 15, 24.

CHAPTER XIV. *Survival of the Misfittest*

1 Berle and Means, *The Modern Corporation and Private Property* (New York: Macmillan, 1933), p. 28.

2 Gardiner C. Means, Speech delivered before the American Political Science Association, December 27, 1933.

3 *Report* of the Comptroller of the Currency, 1933, p. 98.

4 *Polk's Bankers' Encyclopedia*, 1933.

5 Lewis Corey, *House of Morgan* (New York: Covici, Friede, 1930), pp. 390-394.

6 *Fortune*, August, 1933, p. 85.

7 *Fortune*, August, 1933, p. 86.

8 *Science News Letter*, October 6, 1934, p. 221.

9 Thomas Nixon Carver and Hugh W. Lester, *This Economic World* (Chicago: A. W. Shaw Co., 1928), p. 413.

10 *Ibid.*, p. 396.

11 New York *Post*, September 19, 1934.

12 National City Bank *Bulletin*, April, 1934, p. 66.

13 National City Bank *Bulletin*, August, 1934, p. 127.

14 New York *Times*, May 21, 1932.

15 *Advertising Age*, May 26, 1934, p. 14.

16 *New Yorker*, December 1, 1934, p. 52.

17 Abercrombie & Fitch, Christmas Catalog, 1934, p. 23.

18 *Woman's Home Companion*, December, 1934, p. 93.

19 *Advertising Age*, August 18, 1934, p. 12.

20 New York *Times*, September 18, 1934.

21 *Advertising Age*, September 2, 1933, p. 7.

22 *Advertising & Selling*, August 2, 1934, p. 3.

23 *The Drug and Cosmetic Industry*, July, 1934, p. 18.

24 New York *Times*, February 9, 1934.

25 New York *Times*, February 9, 1934.

26 *Press Intelligence Bulletin*, No. 201, May 25, 1934, p. 108.

27 *The Hotel Monthly*, July, 1934.

28 *Food Industries*, August, 1934, 341.

29 New York *Post*, August 16, 1934.

30 New York *Times*, August 24, 1934.

31 Paul Einzig, *Economic Foundations of Fascism* (London: Macmillan and Co., 1933), p. 11.

32 *Ibid.*, p. 31.

33 *Ibid.*, p. 73.

34 Alfred D. Buehler, *General Sales Taxation* (New York: The Business Bourse, 1932), p. 133.

35 Hugh Quigley, "Fascism Fails Italy," *Current History*, June, 1934, p. 260.

36 *Ibid.*, p. 261.

37 *Corriere Della Sera*, December 19, 1930.

38 New York *Times*, September 6, 1934

39 *Survey Graphic*, March 1, 1927.

40 Robert L. Baker, "Is Germany Facing Bankruptcy," *Current History*, July, 1934, p. 428.

41 New York *Times*, August 28, 1934.

42 New York *Times*, August 28, 1934.

CHAPTER XV. *Unrest in Lilliputia*

1 Berle and Means, *The Modern Corporation and Private Property* (New York: Macmillan, 1933), p. 10f.

2 *Report* of the Commissioner of International Revenue, 1932.

3 Third Report of the National Recovery Review Board.

4 New York *Times*, April 12, 1934.

5 *Liberation*, July 22, 1933.

6 James H. Craig, "The Cause Must Go On!"

7 *Ibid.*, p. 1.

8 *Liberation*, June 3, 1933.

9 *The Silver Ranger*, February 7, 1934.

10 New York *Post*, August 8, 1934.

11 *Communism in Germany* (Berlin: General League of German Anti-Communist Associations, 1933), p. 3.

12 New York *Times*, March 14, 1934.

13 New York *Times*, October 13, 1934.

14 *National Republic*, June, 1933, p. 23.

15 *National Republic*, June, 1933, p. 23.

16 *Awakener*, October 1, 1934.

17 *Awakener*, December 1, 1933.

18 New York *Times*, September 5, 1933.

19 New York *Times*, September 9, 1934.

20 New York *Post*, September 14, 1934.

21 From a letter from Norman B. Watson, October 19, 1933.

22 Paul E. Baker, *Negro-White Adjustment* (New York: Association Press, 1934), p. 170f.

23 Souvenir Booklet, Issued by the Committee to Combat Communism, p. 3.

24 San Diego *Sun,* March 31, 1934.
25 Marcus Duffield, *King Legion* (New York: Jonathan Cape & Harrison Smith, 1931), p. 313.
26 New York *Times,* September 5, 1931.
27 New York *Times,* July 22, 1934.
28 New York *Times,* September 1, 1934.
29 Chicago *Daily Tribune,* September 4, 1934.
30 New York *Herald Tribune,* October 5, 1934.
31 New York *Times,* October 2, 1934.
32 New York *Herald Tribune,* November 17, 1934.
33 *Christian Century,* October 24, 1934.
34 New York *Times,* November 18, 1934.
35 Webster Smith, *The Kingfish—A Biography of Huey P. Long* (New York: Putnam's, 1933), pp. 267ff.
36 New York *Times,* October 26, 1934.
37 New York *World-Telegram,* November 13, 1934.
38 New York *Herald Tribune,* November 17, 1934.

CHAPTER XVI. *The Capitalist Whom Prosperity Forgot*

1 *Social Questions Bulletin,* January, 1934, p. 4.
2 *Northwestern Miller,* March 7, 1934.
3 "To Provide for the Purchase and Sale of Farm Products," Hearing before a Subcommittee on Agriculture, on H. R. 8981, May 7, 1934, p. 11.
4 New York *Times,* September 9, 1934.
5 *Food Field Reporter,* November 5, 1934, p. 8.
6 "The Consumer and Farmer—Both Get Gypped," Consumers' Research, p. 2.
7 *Food Industries,* March, 1934, p. 98.
8 "Annual Reports National Dairy Products Corporation and Borden Company," *The Rural New-Yorker,* April 7, 1934, p. 285.
9 "Milk as Big Business Sees It," New York *Post,* May 25, 1934, p. 8.
10 Brief of the Chief of the Dairy Section of the Agricultural Adjustment Administration, filed with the Chairman of the House Committee on Agriculture, May 17, 1934, p. 4.
11 Boston *Globe,* December 7, 1933.
12 Hearing on H. R. 8981, May 7, 1934, p. 17.
13 William P. Helm, "U. S. Probes Milk Monopoly Laid to Few Big Companies," New York *Post,* August 21, 1934.
14 *The Rural New-Yorker,* August 4, 1934, p. 519.

15 *Consumers' Guide,* June 11, 1934, p. 10.
16 *Consumers' Guide,* June 11, 1934, p. 9.
17 Boston *Evening Transcript,* November 20, 1934.
18 *Food Facts,* September-October, 1934, p. 2.
19 *Advertising Age,* March 17, 1934.
20 *Journal* of the American Medical Association, November 3, 1934, p. 19.
21 *Journal of Commerce,* January 31, 1931.
22 *Southwestern Miller,* April 10, 1934.
23 *Advertising Age,* March 17, 1934.
24 Private correspondence in the files of Consumers' Research.
25 Private correspondence in the files of Consumers' Research.
26 New York *Herald Tribune,* February 14, 1934.
27 North Dakota Regulatory Department, May 31, 1934.
28 *Food Field Reporter,* September 10, 1934.
29 *Food Field Reporter,* September 24, 1934.
30 *Food Field Reporter,* September 10, 1934.
31 *Food Industries,* August, 1934, p. 371.
32 *The Northwestern Miller,* March 7, 1934.
33 New York *Times,* July 9, 1933.
34 From information issued to subscribers of Consumers' Research.
35 New York *Times,* December 10, 1934.
36 *News-Week,* July 21, 1934.
37 J. B. Hutson, Chief of Tobacco Section of the AAA, in an address delivered June 14, 1934, p. 3.
38 New York *Herald Tribune,* December 11, 1934.
39 *Advertising & Selling,* March 29, 1934, p. 18.
40 *News-Week,* October 20, 1934, p. 30.
41 *Advertising & Selling,* March 29, 1934, p. 17.

CHAPTER XVII. *American Scapegoats*

1 Elizabeth Dilling, *The Red Network* (Chicago, 1934).
2 Statistical Abstract of the United States, 1933, p. 15.
3 Charles S. Johnson, *The Negro in American Civilization* (New York, Henry Holt, 1930), p. 108.
4 Resolution of the 1897 Convention of the American Federation of Labor.
5 *The Nation,* October 24, 1934, p. 481.
6 Ira de A. Reid, *Negro Membership in American Labor Unions,* title page, a booklet of the National Urban League.
7 New York *Times,* September 10, 1933.

8 New York *Times,* January 9, 1934.

9 New York *Times,* October 28, 1934; New York *Herald Tribune,* October 28, 1934.

10 *Liberation,* June 10, 1933.

11 Walter B. Pitkin, *The Chance of a Lifetime* (New York: Simon and Schuster, 1934), p. 168.

12 Arthur F. Raper, *The Tragedy of Lynching* (University of North Carolina Press, 1933), p. 1.

13 New York *Times,* November 30, 1933.

14 Carey McWilliams, "Fascism in American Law," *American Mercury,* June, 1934, p. 182.

15 Baker, *op. cit.,* pp. 65-72.

16 Madison Grant, *The Conquest of a Continent* (New York, Scribners, 1933), p. 351.

17 New York *Times,* August 30, 1934.

18 Franz Boas, *Aryans and Non-Aryans* (New York: Information and Service Associates, 1933), p. 4.

19 *Protocols of the Learned Elders of Zion* (Seattle: 1934).

20 New York *World,* February 17, 1921.

21 New York *Times,* October 8, 1934.

22 *Pelley's Weekly,* September 12, 1934, p. 4.

23 *Pelley's Weekly,* September 12, 1934, p. 4.

24 Madison Grant, *The Conquest of a Continent,* p. ix.

25 *Ibid.,* p. x.

26 *Ibid.,* p. 347.

27 Statistical Abstract of the United States, 1933, p. 68.

28 Grant, *The Conquest of a Continent,* p. 347.

29 *Ibid.,* p. 348.

30 *Ibid.,* p. 349.

31 *Ibid.,* p. 350.

32 Walter B. Pitkin, *The Chance of a Lifetime* (New York: Simon and Schuster, 1934), p. 171.

33 New York *Times,* October 28, 1934, announcing agenda for meeting of New York State Federation of Women's Clubs on November 12, 1934.

34 Grant, *The Conquest of a Continent,* p. 355.

35 New York *Times,* July 19, 1934.

CHAPTER XVIII. *He Who Does Not Own Shall Not Eat*

1 *The Nation,* July 25, 1934, p. 94.

2 New York *Times,* September 7, 1934.

3 New York *Times*, September 18, 1934.

4 New York *World-Telegram*, October 11, 1933.

5 *America's Capacity to Consume* (Washington: Brookings Institute, 1934), p. 55.

6 *Ibid.*, p. 88.

7 *Ibid.*, p. 126.

8 Frederick Lewis Allen, *Only Yesterday*, quoting from Herbert Hoover's acceptance speech in 1928, p. 303.

9 New York *Times*, October 4, 1934.

10 *The American Child*, October, 1933, p. 2.

11 Statistical Abstract of the United States, 1933, p. 54.

12 New York *Herald Tribune*, July 28, 1933.

13 New York *Herald Tribune*, July 28, 1933.

14 New York *Times*, January 2, 1934.

15 New York *Post*, March 15, 1934.

16 New York *Times*, January 2, 1934.

17 New York *Times*, September 6, 1934.

18 New York *World-Telegram*, March 6, 1934.

19 *Nation's Business*, November, 1934, p. 58.

20 New York *Times*, November 15, 1933.

21 *Nation's Business*, November, 1934, p. 15.

22 New York *Post*, September 4, 1934, p. 10.

23 New York *Times*, December 10, 1934.

CHAPTER XIX. *Under the Shadow of Gompers*

1 New York *Times*, October 3, 1934; *Nation*, October 24, 1934, p. 48.

2 Proceedings of the American Federation of Labor, 1933, p. 307.

3 Anthony Bimba, *The History of the American Working Class* (New York: International Publishers, 1927), p. 343.

4 Proceedings of the American Federation of Labor, 1933, pp. 291-292.

5 New York *Times*, January 24, 1934.

6 New York *Times*, January 15, 1934.

7 *American Federationist*, March, 1917.

8 Proceedings of the American Federation of Labor, 1929, p. 88.

9 New York *Times*, September 4, 1932.

10 New York *Times*, October 15, 1933.

11 New York *Times*, October 2, 1934.

12 New York *Times*, October 8, 1934.

13 New York *Times*, January 30, 1934.

14 Joel L. Seidman, "Settlement of Labor Disputes," Editorial Research Reports, February 7, 1934.

15 New York *Times,* October 11, 1934.

16 Scranton (Pa.) *Times,* September 15, 1934.

17 Samuel Gompers, *Seventy Years of Life and Labor* (New York: E. P. Dutton, 1925).

18 Speech of William Green in Danville, Virginia, June 3, 1930.

19 *Confectioners' Journal,* September, 1934.

20 *Business Week,* October 3, 1934, p. 24.

21 New York *Times,* April 18, 1931.

22 *McClure's Magazine,* May, 1919.

23 New York *Times,* January 10, 1934.

24 New York *Times,* July 22, 1934.

25 New York *Herald Tribune,* August 19, 1934.

26 Matthew Woll, Labor Day speech, 1934, New York *Times,* September 3, 1934.

27 New York *Times,* September 3, 1934.

28 *Credit Executive,* September, 1934, pp. 8-10.

CHAPTER XX. *The Business-State*

1 *The Ice Cream Trade Journal,* October, 1934, p. 35.

2 *Journal* of the American Pharmaceutical Association, October, 1934, p. 1038.

3 *The New Republic,* December 20, 1933, p. 152.

4 From information issued to subscribers of Consumers' Research.

5 NRA Release, No. 2126, p. 7.

6 New York *World-Telegram,* December 8, 1933.

7 John T. Flynn, "Whose Child is the NRA?" *Harpers,* September, 1934, p. 393.

8 *News-Week,* July 28, 1934, p. 4.

9 New York *Times,* September 4, 1934.

10 *Business Week,* September 15, 1934, p. 5.

11 John S. Hall, "Assault—by Battery and Legislation," *Glass Packer,* November, 1934, p. 697.

12 Hall, *op. cit.,* p. 697.

13 Hall, *op. cit.,* p. 697.

14 New York *World-Telegram,* December 14, 1934.

15 *Oil, Paint and Drug Reporter,* August 13, 1934, p. 19.

16 *Oil, Paint and Drug Reporter,* December 3, 1934, p. 25.

17 *The Executive Purchaser,* September, 1934, p. 10.

18 *The Executive Purchaser,* September, 1934, p. 11.

19 *Canning Age,* October, 1934, p. 486.

20 *Oil, Paint and Drug Reporter,* November 5, 1934, p. 31.

21 Annual Report of the Federal Trade Commission, pp. 102f.

22 Carl McFarland, *Judicial Control of the Federal Trade Commission* (Harvard University Press, 1933), p. 88.

23 *Ibid.,* p. 89.

24 Oscar Cox, "Consumer v. Producer," Consumers' Research *General Bulletin,* October 1934, p. 9.

CHAPTER XXI.   *Defense of the Business-State by Idea-Control*

1 Ray H. Abrams, *Preachers Present Arms* (New York: Round Table Press, 1933).

2 Labor Sunday Message, September 2, 1934, Federal Council of Churches.

3 New York *Times,* September 3, 1934.

4 New York *Post,* September 22, 1934.

5 F. J. McConnell, *Christianity and Coercion* (Nashville: Cokesbury Press, 1933), pp. 19, 26, 43, 44, 52, 109, 121.

6 *Fortune,* August, 1933.

7 New York *Times,* October 13, 1934.

8 New York *Times,* January 8, 1934.

9 New York *Times,* September 29, 1933.

10 New York *Times,* May 24, 1934.

11 New York *Times,* May 23, 1934.

12 New York *Times,* September 17, 1934.

13 New York *Herald Tribune,* October 1, 1934.

14 New York *Times,* July 23, 1934.

15 *Journal of Home Economics,* October, 1934, p. 481.

16 *Information Service,* Federal Council of Churches, October 6, 1934.

17 *The World Tomorrow,* January 18, 1934.

18 *The World Tomorrow,* July 12, 1934.

19 New York *Times,* November 10, 1934.

20 *Food Field Reporter,* October 22, 1934, p. 35.

21 New York *World-Telegram,* December 17, 1934.

22 *Time,* October 15, 1934, p. 30.

23 New York *Times,* December 14, 1934.

24 William E. Berchtold, People's Lobby *Bulletin,* September, 1934.

25 *Bakers' Weekly,* January 20, 1934.

26 *Bulletin* of the National Research Council, Washington, D. C., 1934, National Academy of Sciences.

27 *Radio as a Cultural Agency,* The National Committee on Education by Radio (Washington, D. C.: 1934), pp. 112f.

28 New York *Times,* February 18, 1933.

29 Gross W. Alexander, Statement in *Radio as a Cultural Agency,* pp. 109ff.

30 *Rural New-Yorker,* July 7, 1934, p. 479.

31 New York *Times,* September 9, 1934.

32 New York *Times,* September 9, 1934.

33 *Food Field Reporter,* July 16, 1934, p. 37.

34 *Today,* March 10, 1934.

35 *Student Outlook,* May, 1934, p. 10.

36 *The New Republic,* July 5, 1933.

37 New York *World-Telegram,* October 15, 1934.

38 New York *Times,* October 11, 1934.

39 Pasadena *Star News,* August 18, 1934.

40 *The Open Forum,* November 3, 1934.

41 *The Nation,* August 22, 1934.

42 New York *Times,* December 5, 1934.

43 *Columbia Spectator,* September 28, 1934.

44 *New Republic,* September 26, 1934, p. 170.

45 New York *Times,* September 3, 1934.

46 *The Nation,* November 7, 1934.

47 New York *Times,* September 7, 1934.

48 New York *Times,* July 2, 1934.

49 *Editor & Publisher,* July 21, 1934, p. 294.

50 *Editor & Publisher,* July 21, 1934, p. 294.

51 *Editor & Publisher,* July 21, 1934, p. 294.

52 *Editor & Publisher,* October 13, 1934, p. 20.

53 *Advertising Age,* August 4, 1934, p. 14.

54 *Advertising Age,* August 4, 1934, p. 14.

55 *Editor & Publisher,* September 22, 1934, p. 48.

56 *Advertising Age,* July 7, 1934, p. 17.

57 *New Republic,* August 1, 1934, p. 312.

58 *Advertising Age,* July 28, 1934, p. 13.

59 *Editor & Publisher,* November 24, 1934, p. 34.

60 *Editor & Publisher,* November 17, 1934, p. 48.

61 *Editor & Publisher,* November 24, 1934, p. 4.

62 Jerome G. Kerwin, *The Control of Radio* (Chicago: University of Chicago Press, 1934), p. 3.

63 *Radio as a Cultural Agency,* The National Committee on Education by Radio (Washington, D. C.: 1934), p. 110.

64 *Ibid.,* p. 112.
65 *Ibid.,* p. 118.
66 *Ibid.,* p. 116.
67 *Ibid.,* p. 117.
68 New York *Times,* November 29, 1932.
69 *Education by Radio,* July 18, 1934.

CHAPTER XXII. *Defense of the Business-State by Guns*

1 Harvey O'Connor, *Mellon's Millions* (New York: John Day, 1933), pp. 207-208.
2 New York *World-Telegram,* May 28, 1934.
3 *The Nation,* October 10, 1934, p. 411.
4 *The Nation,* October 10, 1934, p. 412.
5 New York *Post,* October 24, 1934.
6 New York *Post,* October 24, 1934.
7 New York *Times,* September 7, 1934.
8 New York *Times,* September 19, 1934.
9 New York *Times,* September 20, 1934.
10 New York *Times,* September 20, 1934.
11 New York *Times,* September 18, 1934.
12 New York *World-Telegram,* September 17, 1934.
13 New York *Post,* September 14, 1934.
14 Report of the Secretary of War, 1933, p. 49.
15 Harry H. Woodring, "The Army Stands Ready," *Liberty,* January 4, 1934, p. 7.
16 Woodring, *op. cit.,* p. 10.
17 Woodring, *op. cit.,* p. 7.
18 Woodring, *op. cit.,* p. 10.
19 Woodring, *op. cit.,* p. 11.
20 *Fortune,* October, 1934, p. 60.
21 Report of the Secretary of War, 1933, p. 8.
22 *Ibid.,* p. 11.
23 *Army and Navy Register,* September 2, 1933.
24 *Army and Navy Register,* May 27, 1933.
25 New York *Times,* August 5, 1934.
26 Statistics compiled by William T. Stone, Foreign Policy Association.
27 New York *World-Telegram,* November 13, 1934.
28 New York *Times,* September 13, 1934.
29 New York *Sun,* September 17, 1934.
30 New York *Times,* September 5, 1934.

31 New York *Times,* September 7, 1934.
32 New York *Times,* September 15, 1934.
33 New York *Times,* September 14, 1934.
34 New York *World-Telegram,* September 20, 1934.
35 New York *Times,* September 6, 1934.

CHAPTER XXIII. *Does American Business Need Fascism?*

1 *The Awakener,* December 1, 1933, p. 2.
2 *New Republic,* August 22, 1934.
3 *New Outlook,* October, 1932.
4 New York *Times,* September 5, 1933.
5 Stuart Chase, *A New Deal* (New York: Macmillan, 1932), p. 171.
6 *Business Week,* September 22, 1934, p. 1.
7 *Electrical Merchandising,* July, 1934, p. 24.
8 *New Republic,* July 11, 1934, p. 234.
9 *Editor & Publisher,* November 10, 1934, p. 18.
10 *Journal* of the American Dental Association, July, 1934, p. 1262.
11 *Editor & Publisher,* November 17, 1934, p. 36.
12 New York *Times,* November 9, 1934.
13 *American Economic Review,* December, 1933, p. 771.
14 *Oil, Paint and Drug Reporter,* December 3, 1934, p. 25.
15 *Tide,* November, 1934, pp. 9-10.
16 Rexford Guy Tugwell, *Industrial Discipline* (New York: Columbia University Press, 1933), pp. 33, 18.
17 New York *Times,* December 17, 1934.
18 *Advertising & Selling,* October 11, 1934, p. 25.
19 *Collier's,* October 27, 1934, p. 31.
20 *Today,* September 8, 1934, pp. 12f.
21 *The Executive Purchaser,* September, 1934, p. 10.
22 *Newsdom,* October 13, 1934.
23 *Advertising Age,* June 23, 1934, p. 10.
24 New York *Times,* December 15, 1934.
25 Boston *Herald,* September 7, 1934.
26 Spokane *Chronicle,* December 4, 1934.
27 *The Lynching of Claude Neal* (November 30, 1934), The National Association for the Advancement of Colored People.
28 New York *Times,* December 18, 1934.
29 *Advertising & Selling,* September 13, 1934.